Jacques Delors and European Integration

Europe and the International Order

Series Editor: Joel Krieger

Published

R. J. Dalton and M. Kuechler (eds), *Challenging the Political Order*
A. de Swaan, *In Care of the State*
P. Hall, *Governing the Economy*
J. A. Hellman, *Journeys among Women*
L. Holmes, *The End of Communist Power*
J. Jenson, E. Hagen and C. Reddy (eds), *Feminization of the Labour Force*
J. Krieger, *Reagan, Thatcher and the Politics of Decline*
A. Lipietz, *Towards a New Economic Order*
A. S. Markovits and P. S. Gorski, *The German Left*
C. N. Murphy, *International Organization and Industrial Change*
F. Fox Piven (ed.), *Labor Parties in Postindustrial Societies*
G. Ross, *Jacques Delors and European Integration*
G. Ross, S. Hoffmann and S. Malzacher, *The Mitterrand Experiment*

Forthcoming

J. Keeler, *The Scope and Limits of Democratic Reform*

Jacques Delors and European Integration

George Ross

Polity Press

Copyright © George Ross 1995

The right of George Ross to be identified as author of this work has
been asserted in accordance with the Copyright, Designs and Patents Act
1988.

First published in 1995 by Polity Press
in association with Blackwell Publishers.

Editorial office:
Polity Press
65 Bridge Street
Cambridge CB2 1UR, UK

Marketing and production:
Blackwell Publishers, the publishing imprint of
Basil Blackwell Ltd
108 Cowley Road
Oxford OX4 1JF, UK

ISBN 0 7456 1246 6
ISBN 0 7456 1247 4 (pbk)

A CIP catalogue record for this book is available from the British Library.

Typeset in 10 on 11 pt Baskerville
by Best-set Typesetter Ltd., Hong Kong
Printed in Great Britain by Hartnolls Ltd, Bodmin, Cornwall

This book is printed on acid-free paper.

Contents

For Three Moores
– In memory of Betty
– With great admiration for Barry
– And much love for Jane

Preface

Jacques Delors and European Integration is a study organized around participant observation of the cabinet of European Commission President Jacques Delors during the critical year of 1991. As I explain later, the Delors cabinet has been a major instrument for Delors to mobilize the resources of the European Commission for his strategy of reconfiguring Europe. I was in residence at the Berlaymont, then the Commission's headquarters, for slightly more than the first half of 1991, for three periods of several weeks thereafter in the same year, and have kept in regular contact with the most important of my Commission informants, through several return visits each year, since. In the book the results of the field work per se are framed by chapters contextualizing the period immediately prior to, and since, the moment of research.

Participant observation is always challenging, but working with the Delors cabinet was particularly so. The cabinet is quite small but its charge includes oversight, analysis, and intervention in virtually everything going on in the European Commission and Community. Size and scope plus the principles governing the cabinet's organization mean that its members are most often carrying out a collective mission in decentralized individual ways. To avoid total dispersion I therefore had to choose from among the huge number of things that I might have observed. My method was to focus primarily upon a relatively limited number of "hot dossiers," those policy areas that I thought would turn out to be most important. This choice looks sound in retrospect and is reflected in the text that follows.

Following these dossiers meant, first of all, trying to understand what the individual cabinet members involved were doing and how their actions connected with those of others. I did this from interviewing them very often, observing them physically in various settings, usually meetings, and digesting the huge amount of paper that structured their missions (the European Commission *is* meetings and documents). I also kept in as close touch as I could with the members of the Delors staff whose concerns fell outside these dossiers. Beyond this I carried out approximately 150 extended interviews with Commission figures outside the Delors cabinet, chosen on pragmatic grounds. I needed to check my own perceptions of the Delors team against those who knew it best "in house." The people who stood to be the best observers were those in other Commission cabinets, those who had earlier served on the Delors staff, and higher officials in the Commission's Directorates General most directly involved with the cabinet in the production of analyses and materials in "hot dossier" areas. Beyond this sample I followed a "snowball" approach in generating other names. The interviews were open-ended and usually initiated by questions derived from my own curiosity and uncertainty. I also have had access to a very wide range of internal Commission and Delors cabinet documents. Commission rules forbid actually citing such materials, however. Part of the game of this kind of participant observation is working within such rules, of course. I have used such documents in the construction of my story but I have not followed usual scholarly conventions in citing them.

The way the material is presented calls for explanation. My approach is narrative, to recount the various stories of the Delors cabinet interacting with policy problems, "hot dossiers," and others, as they happened. In the Introduction I briefly consider why I believe it important to do things in this way, from a theoretical point of view. Beyond such concerns, the evident centrality of Delors and his team to the broader course of events, the understudied uniqueness of the Delors cabinet, and my own opportunity to observe them enjoined refusal to collapse the case study material into any too-rigid analytical framework. There are additional reasons for my choice of expository strategy. The European Community/Union as a political system is enormously complex, so much so, in fact, that many scholars are tempted to premature theorizing that truncates reality or to baffling journeys through multiple institutions and procedures further obscured by acronyms. My thought was that the narrative flow might help readers to see through the complexity more clearly. I hope that I am right.

From past misunderstandings I have learned how important it is to explain directly how someone like myself could have gained such privileged access to important people and processes. What turned out to be my good fortune came about almost by accident. It all began when Jacques Delors was invited to inaugurate the new Minda de Gunzburg Center for European Studies at Harvard University, with which I have been associated for over two decades. Partly because a young friend, Philippe Blanc (who had taught French at Brandeis University, where I ordinarily teach) was at that time a member of the Delors cabinet and had been one source of the invitation, I was charged with some of the details of the Delors trip. The visit was a great success. There was a huge turnout for Delors's speech and

Delors, as usual, was gracious with his time and eager to meet with my colleagues. It so happened that in addition to Mme Delors, the Commission President came to Boston with Joly Dixon, his advisor on Economic and Monetary Union, and Bruno Dethomas, his press secretary. In the course of Delors's visit I observed Joly and Bruno at work and this was what initially stimulated my curiosity about the Delors cabinet. Later that fall, over lunch in Paris with my friend Jean-Louis Moynot, then President of Clisthène, a Delorist brains trust that included many of Delors's trusted colleagues and friends, I averred in passing that "someone should study the Delors cabinet." This someone slowly became me. The process began in Moynot's dealings with Pascal Lamy, Delors's *Chef de Cabinet*, who seemed interested in talking about the project. In summer 1990 Pascal and I met and I explained my purposes, at that point quite vague. Pascal, who knew that the role of the Delors cabinet might be overlooked unless something like what I was proposing were undertaken, then offered to let me come for a brief trial period. If this worked out, he added, I might be able to stay longer. After some self-examination, for at the time I had neither leave nor financing and was reluctant to leave family on short notice, I decided to take the plunge. I came in January 1991 and survived my trial period to stay on – much longer than anyone myself included originally intended.

My debt to Jacques Delors and Pascal Lamy is obvious. The "President," who once forbade me to use this title ("France is filled up with Presidents"), thus leaving me without any way of addressing him, has made an enormous impression. It is hard not to be marked by proximity to a great project. Pascal's intelligence, help, loyalty, and confidence have been extraordinary. François Lamoureux's trenchant insights, political fervor, gruff warmth, and kindness have also been great gifts. Pascal's team put up with me with grace and openness, even when – much of the time – they had more pressing things to do. Admiration, thanks, and good memories thus go to Joly Dixon, Jean-Charles Leygues, Patrick Venturini, Jerome Vignon, Jean-Luc Demarty, Lodewijk Briet, Geneviève Pons, Bruno Dethomas, Pierre Nicolas, Fabrice Fries, Christine Verger, and Bernhard Zepter. Some of them may like what I've done, others will almost certainly not, while a few will still wonder what the point of it has been. My hope is to have avoided too many mistakes and misrepresentations. I owe apologies to some of them because, upon the suggestion of one of my editors, I simplified the story, for literary reasons, to minimize some of their roles. This should not be taken as any underestimation of the great help I received from them. The cabinet's own administrative staff, a paragon of unfailing effectiveness in extremely demanding circumstances, was consistently kind and helpful. To the scores of people in and around the Commission who also helped, much gratitude. To Philippe Blanc and Jean-Louis Moynot, who got me into this, special thanks.

On the material side, the then Provost Bob Sekuler of Brandeis responded kindly and favorably to a last-minute and unusual request for time off. The bulk of support for the project came from a Fellowship from the

German Marshall Fund of the United States. The Fund has almost single-handedly sustained scholarly interest in contemporary Europe in the United States. I am only one among hundreds who have benefited. The Mazer Fund at Brandeis and the Program for the Study of Germany and Europe at the Minda de Gunzburg Center for European Studies at Harvard have also helped. The Harvard Center, in particular Stanley Hoffmann, Guido Goldman, and Abby Collins, deserves broader thanks for being what it always has been, open-minded, generous, and welcoming. We all need to make sure that it continues, but with colleagues like Andy Moravscik, who labored carefully through an earlier version of the text, it almost certainly will. Marcia Hood-Brown was an invaluable editor. Jane Jenson gets ever better as colleague and incisive critic as the years go on.

I have enjoyed doing this work, even though it turned out to be more difficult and larger than I had originally anticipated. I started out to do a small study of a neglected but important dimension in the renewal of European integration. The research experience and the extraordinary nature of the moment when it was undertaken prompted me to confront larger questions. From the moment I arrived in the Berlaymont, on the morning of the first day of the Gulf War, Europe's business ceased being "as usual." Indeed, the meaning of everything seemed to change from day to day. I hope that I've managed to record some useful part of it. To the degree to which I have not, with all the opportunities and help I've had, it must be my own fault.

Introduction

I understood that it was often vain to try to resolve problems which do not exist on their own but which are the product of circumstances. It is only in changing the circumstances that we can change the situation of which they are the causes. Rather than using up my energy on the things which offered the most resistance, I had gotten into the habit of looking for what it was in the environment which created this resistance in the first place and then changing it: it was sometimes a secondary matter, and often a psychological climate . . . Matters being interlinked, it was necessary to pull on the thread which would untangle some knots and, step by step, the rest would fall into place.

Jean Monnet, Mémoires

Jean Monnet was the most important single architect of the European Community (EC). His method of identifying obstacles, confronting problems, and making change has provided sound practical advice to his EC successors. In addition, it also provides a way of understanding the project of extending the Community that began in the mid-1980s, culminated in the "1992" program and the Treaty of Maastricht and, more recently, has stalled.

Jacques Delors, President of the Commission of the European Communities for a decade after 1985, proceeded in many of the ways Jean Monnet prescribed. He and his Commissions were practiced in scanning their environment, seeking things that were malleable, avoiding those which were implacable, and moving step by step towards the goal of a sustainable "European model of society." These Commissions understood that most matters were interlinked. One needed to keep one's sights clearly trained on the ways specific issues fitted into larger circumstances. Delors and his teams acted strategically and consequentially. In doing so they made a great deal happen which would have been unimaginable in the circumstances of the late 1970s.

At that time, the EC was deep in the doldrums. It had enjoyed two decades of relative success which had consisted for the most part in helping to promote trade and growth among its member states. The momentous changes in economic circumstances both in Europe and in the broader international economy announced by the two oil shocks of 1973 and 1979 fundamentally challenged the social and economic strategies member states had been pursuing, including for a time their relationships with one another in the Community. They all turned, in one way or another, to national responses to the rapid internationalization of trade and finance and the restructuring of capital and employment. International competitiveness to be achieved largely through national strategies became their watchword. The Community found itself out of place in these new circumstances, with few innovative or viable solutions to suggest. Further integration of the Community ceased to be seen as the future of Europe.

By the end of the 1980s the EC had once again become a central actor. It had experienced a phoenix-like revival, and a huge new push towards European integration was underway. Moreover, with the 1985 announcement of the "1992" program to complete the Single Market, the European Commission had become a leading force in making the new Europe happen. This momentum forward, strategized and overseen in large part by the Commission, took the Community from renewed market-building towards what might be called "state-building." Talk of a federal Europe was heard again, at the same time as the Commission president, European diplomats and civil servants were leading the Community towards new status as an international actor.

Had this book been written in 1990, it would have announced the success of this project for a new Europe. It would also have narrated the astute and adroit thought and action of the Commission under Delors in carefully maneuvering through a difficult situation, "untangling the knots" so that "step by step the rest would fall into place." But the story this book tells is different for two reasons. The first is most obviously that with the aftermath of the 1991 Maastricht Treaty and the debate about its ratification the project began to stall. Behind this were a number of changes which key actors, the Commission in the first instance, had not anticipated. The EC's international setting became ever more unpredictable in the wake of the Cold War's end in 1989. The general economic situation took a decisive turn for the worse. Major parts of the European monetary system broke apart. And in this context, just as in the 1970s, member states began to lose enthusiasm for "European" solutions and retreat towards national remedies. The EC's forward momentum slowed dramatically and the European Commission, but a brief moment earlier perceived as Europe's proto-government, was becoming Europe's scapegoat.

It is not only the lessons of history which make this story different from one which might have been written earlier, however. It is also because this book takes seriously that which Jean Monnet did *not* say in his quite voluntarist fashion of describing the way the foundations of European unification had been constructed. No history is simply the results of the goals, the strategic thinking, and the careful action of those involved in making it happen. These are important to be sure, but they are not enough. The historical circumstances and conditions of the times set limits on what is possible, just as the consequential actions themselves alter these circumstances, shaping them into something which they were not before – and perhaps creating the very limits to what can be done.

Thus the stalling of the forward motion of Europe in the 1990s is not simply the result of the bad luck of having to cope with the fall of "existing socialism" to the East, the new burdens of unification for Germany, the Gulf War, and a severe economic recession – none of which was primarily the Europeans' doing – at the same time as the Maastricht Treaty negotiations and ratification were taking place. All that was unfortunate timing, perhaps. But in addition, as this book will argue, the very logic of the renewal of European integration sought by the Commission and its allies was one of the encounter between a determination to move forward and a set of circumstances which constrained further movement, in part because of the very action of moving forward. The EC after Maastricht is not the EC of 1985, even if it is not the definitive reconsecration of the European model of society which Jacques Delors, using the powers of his Commission, set out to construct.

Jacques Delors and European Integration uses a particular research method. It is based primarily upon participant observation of the staff of Commission President Jacques Delors during 1991, the moment when the Maastricht Treaty was under negotiation, which, with the benefit of hindsight, we can now identify as the turning point of his Commission's fortunes. Mobilizing the European Commission behind a clear strategy is not easy. The Commission, institutionally, is a college. Its president has few statutory powers beyond the right to preside. Generating consensus and coherence out of the college and a complicated Commission bureaucracy divided into all sorts of interest groups, clans, and cliques is a formidable task. It is here that the Delors cabinet – the primary object of my participant observation – enters in, translating presidential strategic ideas into meetings, coalitions and, ultimately, solid proposals. The ways in which it did so are essential, and completely unanalyzed, elements in the recent regeneration of European integration.

The research design and form of *Jacques Delors and European Integration* clearly indicate my belief that the European Commission, its strategies, and capacities have been important for understanding what has happened in Europe over the eventful last decade. More precisely, the book's premise is that the political lucidity of the Commission's proposals and the shrewdness with which they have been presented have been central variables in Europe's forward movement. President Delors and his team together jump-started what was a largely moribund institution and energized it to an unprecedented level of activity and creativity. The purpose of *Jacques Delors and European Integration* goes far beyond providing "thick description" of daily life inside the Delors team, interesting though this might be. It also seeks to provide a readable key to understanding the most important immediate causes for the renaissance of European integration, the particular courses which this renaissance has taken and the contradictory outcomes to which it has led. The book thus examines how the European Commission was used as a key element in Delors's broader strategy for rebuilding Europe.

Delors often called for an "organized European space" to allow the survival of a particular "European model" of mixed economy and society. He recognized that Europe had to take dramatic steps to become more competitive. In order to do so, however, it ought not to open itself up to the full floodtides of the international market, as the advocates of Europe as a complete free trade zone proposed. For Delors, it was possible instead to make the Community into a regional economic bloc whose synergies and economies of scale would stimulate European innovation. The fruits of new economic successes could then be directed towards perpetuating the "European model of society." Europe would then stand – practically – as a humane combination of institutions and ideas which could stimulate market success while simultaneously promoting social solidarities designed to ameliorate the harshness of market relations.

One aim of the strategy was to build out from the EC's economic mandate towards broader, federalizing, state-building goals. The strategy was eminently successful for a number of years. The 1992 program to complete the Single Market was energetically implemented. The Community expanded its social policy reach and made a major commitment to regional economic redistribution. It charted a clear course towards Economic and Monetary Union (EMU) and a single European currency. It began to play an increasingly important role on the international political stage. The period during which the research for this book was done was the turning point between strategic success and downturn, however. It was at this moment that the Community began to run out of steam, just as the Delors presidency itself moved towards its end.

Stories about Europe

The claim of *Jacques Delors and European Integration* is that the decisive action of the European Commission, along with the work of other actors, played a central role in pointing Europe towards a renaissance of ambition. There are good formal reasons for taking this hypothesis seriously. The European Community is a constitutionally structured political system, within which it is the European Commission's official job to propose new programs. In contrast to ordinary international organizations, the EC was set up to contain a supranational "motor" which would constantly press forward towards *more* integration – the Commission was not designed to be simply a "delegated agent" of EC member states, as some versions of regime theory in international relations would put it. The project which relaunched the EC in the mid-1980s was thus devised and proposed by the Commission. And it was this project which fell upon hard times in the 1990s. *A priori*, then, any discussion of the nature, success or failure of European Community programs should look carefully at the Commission's actions.

It is clear that the European Commission had lost a good deal of its "motor" capacity in the first quarter-century of EC history. When General de Gaulle and the French blocked Commission activism and insisted upon the interstatist Luxembourg compromise in the mid-1960s they spoke for other member states. De Gaulle's aim was to make the EC a clear confederation and to minimize supranationalist and federalist pretensions. Prospects for changing this situation of strict interstatism appeared in the early 1970s and the Commission, encouraged by certain member states, accelerated its "proposition force" energies. The painful consequences of Community enlargement to include the United Kingdom, Ireland, and Denmark (the EC has always had difficulty digesting new members) plus divergent member state responses to new economic conditions restimulated confederal propensities, however. By the early 1980s, the deepest moment of Europessimism, the Commission had reached a historic low point. That observers and theorists might be skeptical about the Commission's role after 1985 is not surprising, therefore.

What happened beginning in 1985? It is essential to underline that two separate processes intersected. It is, of course, correct to argue that the setting around the Community, the economic environment and the predispositions of key EC member states, had been slowly changing. Most explanations of the post-1985 renaissance of European integration are really about these changes around the Community. However, as the context changed, key political figures within the EC, the new leaders of the Commission among them, capitalized upon these changes to reassert the Commission's motor role and relaunch European integration. Political entrepreneurs in key institutional positions, in other words, had to be prepared to take strategic action in response to their changing environment.

Let me rephrase this. A multiplicity of changing contextual circumstances changed the political opportunity structures faced by the EC and its Commission in particular. Forces which had earlier been loath to seek solutions through the Community or allow it to propose such solutions lowered their guards. Next, agents of change, the Commission and key member states in the first instance, began more energetically to scan institutional and political environments, seek out different kinds of useful resources, and calculate strategically how to achieve "more Europe." In new circumstances the Commission could again become a central strategic actor.[1]

"Political opportunity structure" is a notion which attempts to systematize the fluctuation of avenues available to agents of change.[2] Its expositors have specified a number of its dimensions: openness/closure of formal institutions, stability/instability of political alignments, availability of alliance partners, and intra-elite consensus or conflict.[3] The underlying thesis is that the workings of institutions and the proclivities of elite social groups vary over time to facilitate or block movements for change even as they also partly shape them. Often, note political opportunity structure theorists, these fluctuations are in response to threats from the growing success of change agents. "Cycles of protest" are thus likely, which will eventually end when elites close ranks and institutions to shut down access to change agents.[4]

The concept of political opportunity structure, whose origins lie in discussions of the biographies of social movements, is adaptable to the EC. The EC's institutional architects (Spaak, Monnet, and others), after all, consciously designed the Community to be "evolutive," open to re-configuration and endowed with the reflexive institutional capacities to reorder itself over time. The Community was thus explicitly constructed to have a more open opportunity setting than nation states, along a number of different dimensions. The European Commission itself was meant con-stitutionally to be an institution whose explicit task it was to work for change – generating greater Europeanization.[5] Moreover, the very fact that the Community's "citizens" were states rather than populations in all of their representational complexities created much greater potentialities for change via the changing interplay of member state coalitions. Indeed, the Luxembourg compromise was a recognition of these potentialities and the need, at a specific juncture, to contain them. The evolutive capacities of the EC were "cyclically" limited, however. The rapidly changing circum-stances created by movement to greater Europeanization, along with other factors, were bound to reconfigure member state attitudes in ways which would eventually slow down and block further progress. This was what happened to Delors and his Commissions' strategic hopes in the early 1990s.

The European Community is a complex thing, and it will not surprise readers to learn that social science perspectives on it disagree strongly with the premises we have just stated. The EC has historically and consti-tutionally been essentially an "economic community." That many see it as completely dependent upon the economic structures and flows in its envi-ronment is not surprising. The EC is also an international organization constituted and constrained by its member states. But it is a most unusual one because its Commission has also been endowed with institutional capacities for supranational initiative (even though these capacities have been underused for much of the Community's history). This renders the use of international relations perspectives difficult, even though this has rarely deterred their practitioners. The founders of the Community them-selves were "functionalists" who believed that sharing or pooling sover-eignty in certain important areas would slowly initiate a snowball effect of "spillover" to render integration ultimately irreversible. Functionalism persists as another plausible interpretation of what has happened to the Community. Let me briefly review these approaches.

For several "structuralist" or "political economy" theories, the relaunch of European integration and the period discussed in *Jacques Delors and*

European Integration are a clear response to the "needs of capital." In the early 1980s profitability and investment in the EC were down relative to other, more dynamic zones of the world. Changing patterns of international trade and production as well as economic interdependence placed demands for convergence and policy conformity on Europe. It fell to the EC, given its long-standing trade–economy mandate, to respond. The new EC initiatives which began in the mid-1980s were, according to such analyses, taken to confront this new situation and ward off Europe's permanent decline. Presumably the organizations of capital then decided, or perhaps the logic of capitalism dictated, that these new initiatives had outlived their usefulness by the early 1990s.

If strongly Marxist versions of structuralism are rather notably absent from established debates on the EC (indicating, no doubt, the hard times upon which intellectual Marxism has fallen),[6] more elite-analytical perspectives have been prominent in discussions of the EC's recent course.[7] In this variant, if European economic problems are at the root of everything, business interest groups acted to translate underlying structural problems into specific courses of action. Business, or at least its organized parts, thus insisted on the specific political remedies which led to renewed European integration and its more recent difficulties. Structuralists are convinced that politicians are beholden to economic constraints and have few options but to respond directly to them.

No one could, or should, exclude such structural factors from a broader explanation of the extraordinary recent history of the EC. European capital obviously needed new solutions as a consequence of "the" crisis which began in the 1970s and which turned out to be *its* crisis. Nonetheless, strong structuralist arguments fail because underlying structures do not explain specific political initiatives and the choices which lie behind them. Structuralist analyses tend to instrumentalize politicians and, quite as importantly, overlook the role of institutions and ideas in the construction of political options. To be sure, the politicians who ultimately devised the options were the targets of a wide spectrum of interest pressures. But one can find influential business groups advocating virtually all conceivable scenarios of EC action in the 1980s. Some had their sights on a full globalization of corporate operations to leap over national and EC restrictions and, by dint of "regime shopping," break down European particularisms. Others demanded Thatcherite deregulation on a European scale. Still others sought to harden national boundaries and policy autonomy. A range of possible responses to capital's problems and an almost equally wide range of possible institutional locations for them thus existed.

Restoring European capitalism to some semblance of health had to be a central preoccupation of EC and other decision-makers during the period of *Jacques Delors and European Integration*. I do not want to claim otherwise. The problems lie in explanations which reduce strategies and policies exclusively to such matters. States, European Commissions and other such bodies have a range of autonomy to seek different answers to similar economic questions. The needs of capital, whether systematically or organizationally constructed, do not automatically or obviously translate into political strategies. Beyond this, government bodies must simultaneously seek answers to other kinds of questions. The answers which are ultimately found usually transcend and feed back on economic matters in crucial ways. The success or failure of capital may be as contingent upon the problem-solving skills of politicians as the decisional autonomy of politicians is constrained by economics. Moreover, if the term "crisis" when applied to the EC in the early 1980s has any meaning at all, it is that old habits – including old routines for exercising elite influence – no longer worked and that confusion existed over new ones. In crisis there are usually openings for political leaders to play a central role in setting new agendas from among the wide range of existing possibilities. Furthermore, while it is undoubtedly the case that underlying economic difficulties played an important role in the unravelling of EC strategies in the 1990s, they do not account for either the political form or the outcomes of this unravelling.

"Power resources" theorizing is a more subtle variety of political economy, blended with a good measure of historical institutionalism. It begins by positing that underlying economic processes determine the structuring of broad interests in modern democratic politics. The balance of social and political forces and the nature of policy outcomes are in turn the product of the coalitional expressions of these broad interests. Since these underlying interests and their coalitional responses tend to have relatively long lives, recent history can be periodized with reference to their moments of stability and change. In this perspective EC policy can be explained by fluctuating structures of conflictual interaction among large coalitions of social groups. The background to this story is the hypothesis of policy regularity based upon the persistence of solid coalitional arrangements. This regularity ends when these coalitions lose their mobilizational credibility, when either the nature of underlying interests changes or the policy glue of the coalition dissolves (or both). New coalitions will then arise, based upon a different balance of power resources, leading to new types of policy regularity.[8]

The most interesting variant of this story has to do with the declining economic and political power of labor.[9] Labor had been an essential interest – albeit not alone – in establishing the national economic structures and strategies of the postwar years and had been central in insisting upon continuing them in the new economic settings of the 1970s. Various attempts at, and proposals for, neo-corporatist arrangements were then evident all across Europe, often promoted by trade unions and left-wing parties. Labor strength then declined, due primarily to rising unemployment, changing composition of the labor force, and corporate restructuring. Eventually labor became too feeble to make national neo-corporatist arrangements stick. The changes in various national political equations across Europe then became essential in opening new options for governments and firms to promote more liberal, "flexibilizing," and deregulatory policy packages.[10]

In understanding the recent history of the EC, and especially the initial takeoff of the "1992" project, the power resources approach may help by providing a map of the new setting which opened up the space to try more integration. Short of lapsing into structuralism, however, it does little to account for what happened after 1985. Critics of power resources views have often tellingly argued that policy initiatives may be as important in structuring new coalitions as the converse, and they are probably correct.[11] Try as one might, it is virtually impossible to find anything which looks like a large socio-political coalition pushing in decisive ways towards "1992" and after. It is simply not possible to reduce new European options and the complex up and down cycle of the Community in recent years to a changing power resources balance.

An "interstatist" approach has become the preferred perspective of international relations scholars dealing with the EC. Its premise comes from classical international relations theories which assume that sovereign nation states are the only significant actors in an anarchic international system. Outcomes can be most parsimoniously analyzed as the product of the interactions of such states whose power is deployed in pursuit of national interests. This perspective too can find considerable support in the EC's own history. For two decades after the Luxembourg compromise in 1966 – which occurred after President de Gaulle rejected supranationalism – the Community was, by general agreement, an explicitly interstate system.

An interstatist story might go as follows. The various trials and tribulations of "economic crisis" led initially to policy divergences which threatened the very integrity of Europe. By 1982–3, however, there was a shift of nation-state preferences and interests. Here the most important event was the French drama. The failure of the Mitterrand experiment at reasserting a voluntaristic national-centered policy model symbolized the general unfeasibility of this approach once and for all. The French Left's subsequent turn towards austerity after 1983 moved French policies closer to Germany's and brought renewed French commitment to the Community. Policy convergence renewed the conditions for successful intergovernmental collaboration at European level between France and Germany, the famous "couple" upon whose happy cohabitation so much of Europe's success in the past had been based. France's turn as rotating president of the Community in 1984 becomes the key moment in this story,[12] the post-1985 renewal of European integration being the product. This shift was embodied in Mitterrand's nomination of his ex-Finance Minister Jacques Delors as the new President of the European Commission.[13] Later, in the 1990s, new definitions of member state interests led the EC into a new period of crisis.

The interstatist narrative has a great deal of explanatory power, especially when one introduces additional considerations to link evolving national interests to the roles assumed by European states.[14] Nonetheless the story is not immune from severe criticism on the grounds of its inadequate confrontation with the data. The European Community had been designed from the outset to have an important supranational dimension, symbolized best by the powers granted to the Commission in the Rome Treaty and the jurisdictional scope of the European Court of Justice. The Luxembourg compromise cut the Commission's power of supranational initiative down to nearly nothing. But the situation changed again after 1985, for reasons which I will later explore, allowing EC institutions to work more as they had been designed to work. The Community's new movement forward did begin in earnest after the French turn and the 1984 Fontainebleau European Council. But there is strong prima facie evidence that the entrepreneurial, agenda-setting, and more generally political role of the Commission after 1985 was central to what followed. The Commission wrote the White Paper on completing the Single Market, the most important act in relaunching the Community. It was the Single European Act which then changed Community treaty arrangements to allow the White Paper's full implementation. Indeed extensive supranational action plays a central role in the entire EC story after 1985. And a good case can be made, as I will later do in *Jacques Delors and European Integration*, that Commission strategizing also played some role in the emergence of Community crisis in the 1990s.

One might also consider another "international political economy" narrative, about Europe's response to a declining American "hegemon."[15] The international monetary tactics of the Reagan administration, coming after a decade of confusion caused by the collapse of the US-run Bretton Woods system, placed member states of the Community, along with others, in a very difficult situation. Subsequent American manipulation of the value of the dollar – first up, then down – in the first half of the 1980s, cumulated into another set of exogenous policy shocks. From this perspective US pursuit of its own interests in the world economy in the early 1980s largely deprived Europe of "voice," closed off options which Europe might have preferred, and had a strongly negative effect on Europe's relative economic position. In this story such US actions were symbolic of a genuine decline in relative power, as American interests in a stable general economic order slowly gave way to efforts to manipulate this order to protect US domestic positions. This change created incentives for Europe to reassert its own interests. The renaissance of European integration, in this light, was the product of growing European awareness both of possibilities for new European shock absorbers and of new European power.

It is hard to quarrel with the story itself. Europe in the 1970s and early 1980s was a "taker" of US policy which was itself designed more to prop up a faltering Amercian domestic economy than to assume responsibilities for the welfare of anyone else. Relaunching EC integration was only one option among a great many available, however. Individual European countries could have gone their separate ways to strike favorable deals with the US, as British Prime Minister Thatcher tried to do, for example. Alternatively, greater European monetary cooperation and self-assertion might have been pointed towards much larger multilateral dealing than the EC, perhaps on a G7 level.[16] In addition, a great deal more was involved in EC reinvigoration and subsequent decline than efforts to rebalance European and American international economic power. The difficulty with this explanation should thus be clear. Even though the issues upon which it focuses are very real, they point to no specific policy path. The actual path chosen calls for further explanation.

Neo-functionalists had their heyday as *the* intellectual interpreters of European integration in the EC's earlier years. Encoding the strategic insights of Jean Monnet into social science, neo-functionalists hypothesized about issue linkages that would allow the European activists in Brussels to seduce essential interest groups towards Europeanism and promote "spillover."[17] The events of the 1970s, when spillover abruptly ceased to occur, made neo-functionalism look rather naive, however. Nonetheless, after 1985 might it not be argued that the neo-functionalists had been prescient, if overoptimistic about timetables?[18] A lot of evidence can be adduced in favor of this. European activists, in particular old-timers in the European Parliament like Altiero Spinelli and Commission militants like Viscount Davignon, carried out steady agitation for "European" solutions even during the EC's dark age. In consequence there was no shortage of new proposals for relaunching the EC to elaborate and supplement those proposed in the early 1970s but never carried out. Moreover, despite the Community's moribund appearance, the wheels continued turning quietly inside EC institutions. The European Court in 1978 thus paved the way towards a resolution of the Community's persistent imbroglio about harmonization through the *Cassis de Dijon* ruling, which promoted "mutual recognition" of regulations and standards.[19] Davignon's organization of the Esprit research program for information technologies in the early 1980s was a similar advance, while movement towards agricultural policy reform and EMU crept slowly forward.

The problems with neo-functionalism are serious, however. The first is logical. Neo-functionalism can hardly be held to explain European integration both when progress is made and when no progress exists. What is most interesting about the building of the EC, that it started, stalled for a very long time, then started up again much later in the 1980s and then fell upon hard times in the 1990s, is not particularly well explained by neo-functionalism. Bureaucratic activism, policy linkages, and pious determination to promote spillover persisted throughout all of Europe's different moments, including those when nothing much happened. Moreover, if a "system" has "needs" which one can specify with any useful degree of precision (which is questionable) and, historically, one finds that these needs are ignored rather more often than addressed, there is good reason to think that their existence does not explain the dynamics of the system.

The history of the Community suggests an even sharper critique of neo-functionalism than this, however. Great moments in European integration cannot be adequately understood as the products of some kind of paroxysm produced by underlying issue-linkages. They look rather more like high-political junctures, moments when new high-level deals made it possible for specific linkages and interdependencies to become important. This was true in the 1950s, in the various movements culminating in the Rome Treaty, in the actions of de Gaulle and others in the early to mid-1960s, and, as we will show, in the 1980s and 1990s. The fatal flaw of neo-functionalism revisited is that it argues backwards from outcomes to underlying processes which, upon closer scrutiny, usually turn out to be the products of political action more than its causes.

The Limits of European Renewal

My introductory claim is that two processes interacted to get the EC up and moving after 1985. The first was a changing political opportunity structure, itself connected to broader contextual changes as impinging on EC institutions and policy legacies. The second was successful strategizing and resource mobilization by agents for change, the Commission in the first instance, along with its key member state allies, to capitalize upon these prospects. As of the mid-1980s new space existed for the Community to do new things. It was the Commission's official job to find ways to use this space. The Commission had the power and institutional right to pick and choose among possible courses of action, to set agendas. The right choices, those which made the most of the new political opportunity structures, could set the Community in motion again. Bad political work by the Commission would have wasted the opportunity.

The new, more open, setting was manipulated with astounding success between 1985 and the later 1980s. The Commission and its allies systematically confronted the Community with a full agenda of changes: the "1992" program, the Single European Act, the Delors package for budgetary reform, a renewed "Social Dimension," and EMU. The Single Market program, the *paquet Delors* to a large extent, and much in the EMU proposals fell within the general trade and market areas of the Rome Treaty. Pushing the macroeconomic policy dimensions of EMU, "Social Europe," an increased EC international policy role, and measures to address issues of "democratic deficit" all involved expanding the boundaries of Europe beyond such traditional areas. If one chooses to define the post-1985 EC's renaissance as premised upon a "market strategy," the Commission (under Delors) and its allies attempted to graft an ambitious "state-building strategy" on to it in order to make important changes in the very definition of the European game. Significantly, these state-building programs all encountered much more serious opposition than the market-building programs.

Delors and his team had gotten quite far when, in the early 1990s, serious problems arose. Two separate dynamics had come together to begin closing down the EC's post-1985 expansion. Changes in the external context were important, first of all. The end of the Cold War brought fundamental changes for everyone, the EC and European nation states included. In the process it modified the political opportunity structure for European actors, the Commission in the first instance. Basic decisions then had to be made about which new issues to face and how to face them, more often than not without a sufficiently clear idea of what the new context actually looked like and how it was developing. Moreover, in most instances the Commission had limited choices about whether or not to act, both because the issues themselves were pressing and because key member states were determined to act. In response there was a new rush to add items to the EC's priority list. Too many new proposals led to too many different efforts to pool national sovereignty. Thus as the general situation evolved the Commission became more constrained as an actor, less able to make the type of strategic calculations which would have maximized future prospects.

At the same time considerable evidence emerged that the type of "evolutive" institutional setting which had allowed the EC's relaunch after 1985 was inherently self-limiting. The eagerness with which the Commission ratcheted the Community's agenda upwards after 1989 had its own logic. In an ever more dangerously overloaded setting Commission leaders were determined to push European momentum as far and as fast as possible. If the risks of so doing had grown so had the stakes. If things could be done skillfully, the Commission's leaders reasoned, the moment might allow major Community breakthroughs. This reasoning proved misleading. The more crowded the agenda, the more likely it was that member states would find something at which to balk. Finally, and most importantly, the return to recession after the miniboom after 1985 darkened skies even more by changing the economic payoff matrix for EC expansion.

Falling on top of this was the evolution of the Community's chronic "democratic deficit." Desirous of promoting rapid integration after 1985, the advocates of the EC's great leap forward theoretically had a choice between using EC institutions as they were or trying to make them function more democratically. The risk of the latter course, that forward policy movement would become ensnared in complicated and paralyzing member state discussions about institutions, was great. Under Delors the Commission did its level best to mobilize and Europeanize key interests and thus to create some semblance of the democratic debate about EC matters that was sorely lacking. But to cope with the institutional matters it chose, with its allies, a weak compromise that involved granting new powers of "co-decision" to the European Parliament. The choice was inadequate to the problem. The rush of proposals for pooling sovereignty after 1989 thus renewed the salience of democratic deficit issues.

The fact that Commission and Community proposals had implications for the futures of ordinary people already at a loss in the face of the globalization of economic life made it possible for nationalist and populist forces to mobilize anti-Community sentiment – particularly in the glaring absence of European political culture within which the Community had moved forward. The various dimensions of democratic deficit were in themselves enough to make this possible. The weakness and incoherence of the European Parliament, the opacity of the Council of Ministers' deliberations, the alleged technocratic imperialism of the appointed Commission, and the widespread failings of member state domestic social and political forces at taking up a European political agenda worked to make important European publics feel unconsulted.

The consequences are evident. The 1992 referenda in Denmark and France on ratifying the Maastricht Treaty provided accurate snapshots of public opinion in most of the Community. The new Community has turned out to be misunderstood and unloved. The return of difficult economic times made all this worse – the promises of Delors and others that renewed European integration would foster renewed prosperity could be held against the Community. The costs of German unification fed back negatively in political and monetary realms. As the likelihood that the Maastricht Treaty would ever mean much receded, even after the agonizing season of its ratification, the ceiling began to fall in on a Commission held responsible for the real and imagined excesses of the Community.

The Commission's situation is highly complicated. Its destiny and prestige are connected to the promotion of advances in European integration. On those rare occasions when it becomes possible for the Commission to assume the leadership roles that the EC's founding fathers envisaged, it must devise successful strategies to get the Community moving. And, once new momentum has been created, wisdom based on past experience dictates that it must push forward as far and as fast as it can, in the knowledge that sooner or later the moment of open opportunities must end. Yet the very act of moving far and fast is likely to ensure that the open period *will* end. This knowledge then almost certainly plays a feedback role. A Commission which goes too far too fast is courting disaster, therefore great caution is in order. But too much caution will bring on the result that caution is designed to prevent: the end of forward momentum, this time caused by the Commission's own strategic timidity.

The Commission faces a Sisyphean task. It is encouraged to push European integration as far and as fast as is feasible while simultaneously monitoring political opportunity structures and available resources so that the Community's ambitions do not exceed its capacities. It makes sense simultaneously, however, for Commissions and their allies to push openings for movement to their limits, since given EC history it is certain that such openings will eventually close. Moreover, the further one can push integration the better positioned the Community will be, at least in theory, for the next episode. The Commission and its allies thus exist in an asymmetrical incentive setting in which taking the risk of pushing integration rapidly forward can override prudent management of political opportunities and resources.

Jacques Delors is the most successful Commission leader in the history of the Community. His aim has been to consolidate integration in order to save the European model of society, a political economy in which competitive firms in a mixed economy thrive in a broader social setting characterized by negotiation and a willingness to assume the burdens of solidarity through a humane system of social services. In order to achieve these goals he pursued a strategy in which market building – deepening economic integration – was meant to simultaneously introduce the liberalization needed to initiate the reconstruction of European competitiveness in a very harsh international market and be a stepping stone for later state building. Successful state building required regenerating European economic activity; it was necessary to "bring capital on board" before taking on the job of consolidating the European model of society.[20] The temporal dimension of this basic strategic option was such, however, that market building was likely to go further much faster than state building. This result could, in turn, imperil rather than consolidate Europe's uniquely humane version of capitalism. Avoiding this was Delors's great task. How well he was able to do so is an important dimension of the story to which I now turn.

1

Prologue: Europe Comes Alive

Jacques Delors was born in Paris in 1925. His father was a middle-level employee of the Banque de France. Ménilmontant, his neighborhood, was "popular," as the French say, and Delors grew up in the urban Catholic mold of the time which included involvement with the progressive Catholic youth movements designed to counteract declining interest in the Church.[1] After secondary education the gifted Delors, tempted towards academic work in film studies, was pressured by his demanding father to start work at the Banque. Delors thus never participated in the intense socialization processes of "Sciences Po" or a *grande école* where modern French elites were trained and learned to network; nor did he experience university life.[2] He thus began as an outsider in a country whose recent politics have been dominated by castes of technocrats.

In time, Delors developed a Jansenist form of Catholic internal discipline, becoming someone for whom victory over disorder and evil demanded extraordinary personal commitment.[3] Salvation had to be earned! By working harder, longer, and more intensively than others, Delors discovered that he could succeed better. These outlooks also made him a demanding taskmaster and severe judge of others. There is much more to Jacques Delors than austerity, however. He is capable of great charm and an enchanting smile. He refined a love of sports. He played basketball well into his twenties, became an aficionado of cycling, and closely followed soccer. He is also a jazz buff and cinephile. Recently, when Dexter Gordon, the jazz saxophonist, died, who should write his eulogy in *Libération* but the President of the European Commission!

Delors is a man of action for whom ideas are terribly important: present and future must be connected by lucid theory and analysis, both then to be confronted with what is morally desirable. Delors will seek out intellectuals for help, an unusual thing for a politician. He also delights in presenting himself as an autodidact among elites from the world's best universities. He began a life of political activism as he climbed the career ladder of the foreign exchange department of the Bank of France. At the intellectual center of this was the thought of Emmanuel Mounier and personalism, a progressive form of Catholic anti-individualism.[4] Society, according to Mounier, could not be reduced to a market writ large or a utilitarian agglutination of isolated individuals. Collectivist transformation was no solution either. Society grew from delicate interdependence in which different social groups owed one another active solidarity. Establishing a meaningful, moralized place for individuals meant making them responsible in the engagement of their social group in the active promotion of solidarity. The statist interventionism advocated by socialists provided no real answer to this problem of solidarity. The state and politics had a role, but in facilitating, rather than substituting for, the active agency of groups and moralized individuals working together. Delors was thus not immersed in, and did not emerge from, France's secular Left tradition, whether socialist or communist.

In many European countries someone with these ideas would have found a comfortable political home in an established Christian Democratic Party. In France they made Delors an odd person out. Delors did join the Christian Democratic Mouvement Républicain Populaire (MRP) for a brief moment in the 1940s. But French Christian Democracy, after flourishing briefly, was mangled by the turbulent coalitional politics of the Fourth Republic and rapidly turned conservative, losing appeal for Left Catholics. Delors then turned to trade unionism, where he came into contact with the Reconstruction group inside the Confédération Française des Travailleurs Chrétiens (CFTC).

Reconstruction, one of the central poles for French Left Catholicism, was dedicated to modernizing and energizing France's stodgy Catholic trade unionism.[5] Delors, who refused promotion at the Bank to be an active unionist, used his expertise in economics to teach in union schools and write articles – under a pseudonym – for Reconstruction's journal. Eventually, in the 1950s, he took charge of the CFTC's research department. In following this path Delors took his particular place among a generation of Christian activists who would later play major roles in French life and, in particular the renovation of the French Left.[6]

It was in the 1960s as well that Delors took his first important steps in public life, from 17 years at the Bank of France directly into the upper reaches of the Planning Commission – the first of Jean Monnet's creations in which Delors would play a central role. Encouraged by Pierre Massé, one of France's great technocrats, Delors introduced redistributive dimensions into French planning, in particular by developing incomes policies for the public sector.[7] His objectives were multiple. Planned income growth could help control France's chronic inflation. Its parameters would be negotiated generally and sectorally to help the "social partners" understand one another and create greater solidarity, common purposes, and more predictable growth. Finally, Delors hoped to begin an opening towards the system of real collective bargaining which France sadly lacked.

The innovative character of these ideas was widely recognized, but the results were small. Delors own branch of the union movement – which after the success of Reconstruction became the Confédération Française et Démocratique du Travail (CFDT) – was enthusiastic, acclaiming the new approach as a first cut at "democratic planning," its central programmatic demand. But employers and most of the rest of labor rejected the approach. France moved obdurately towards the crisis of May–June 1968.

In 1969, in the aftermath of the "May events" and General de Gaulle's departure, Delors became the social affairs advisor to Gaullist Prime Minister Jacques Chaban-Delmas. The "New Society" reforms of which he was principal architect were a refined version of his earlier ideas involving a *politique contractuelle*, a planned and negotiated program of public sector income development which doubled as an incomes policy. This time the ideas took hold. Delors was also responsible for an innovative program of job training. Chaban's experiment of "social democratizing from the Right" ended quickly, however, in the face of opposition from business and right-wing circles.

The mature Jacques Delors was forged in these two 1960s episodes. The "Delorist" vision saw the market as indispensable allocator of resources, decision-maker and source of economic dynamism. The market by itself could not, however, guarantee equity, a moralized social order, or full economic success. These things depended upon "dialogue" among different groups – employers and labor in particular – to reach clearer understandings of mutual needs about what had to be done and what could be shared. Labor had a stake in economic success and thus good reasons to accept certain responsibilities. Employers had an interest in the predictability which labor's acceptance of responsibilities would bring. "Dynamic compromise" based on persistent discussion between different groups would be the secret of success. Finally, it was not the state's job to decide for others, but to facilitate negotiations among social partners.

Working with de Gaulle, and later Chaban Delmas, both on the Right, was politically risky. Delors, at heart a moderate, shared none of the "rupture with capitalism" passion which was the French Left's stock in trade until the early 1980s. Moreover, he was impatient to be effective. To him, everything was not of a partisan piece. Important reforms could be promoted, even under the Right, by a well-prepared and determined individual like Delors himself.[8] Jacques Delors was thus out of place in 1970s, *Union de la Gauche* France when schematic Left–Right ideological confrontation dominated the scene.

Many on "the second Left," who, like Delors, had tried to work outside of classical Left–Right divisions in the 1960s, began to wend their ways into the various *courants* of the new Socialist Party in the 1970s. When Delors started his own journey, he was obliged to do penance for his past.[9] His support of a beleaguered François Mitterrand in intra-party struggles later won him the very last electable place on the 1979 socialist list to the European Parliament. In Strasbourg Delors mastered Europe's important dossiers, became chair of the monetary affairs committee, and befriended legendary Community activists like Altiero Spinelli.

When François Mitterrand won the French presidency in 1981 Jacques Delors, who had been recruited as an economics "expert" for Mitterrand's campaign, was named Minister of the Economy and Finances. Mitterrand had come to trust Delors's competence, to be sure, but there were other motives: Delors was meant to be a counterweight to some of Mitterrand's more fervently leftist comrades in other ministries. Delors quickly found himself hostage to a wide range of policies which he found unwise: nationalizations, inflationary Keynesianism, expensive new social programs. His job trying to manage the franc's stability was thus particularly difficult. He felt compelled to conciliate French employers, and this did not endear him to some of his colleagues. Finally, as Mitterrand had undoubtedly guessed, Delors personally had to prove himself and quickly became notorious in government circles for overworking his staff, for his mood swings and threats to resign.

France's deteriorating economic situation pushed Delors to the fore. He was the first to demand a "pause" in reforms, and was later the architect of the Left's first austerity program, in 1982.[10] He was central in the realignment of the European Monetary System (EMS) with the Germans in 1983, which became a turning point in contemporary French politics.[11] Austerity, which ended post-1981 reformism, was followed by industrial restructuring, attacks on the budget deficit, and a concerted and successful effort to bring the level of inflation down and stabilize the franc. Quite as important, the great turn marked the end of French economic policy divergence from the Germans and announced France's option for solutions within the context of the EC.[12] The end of his tenure as Finance Minister in early summer 1984 made him available for his new duties in Brussels.

Jacques Delors and European Integration is about the turning point of the Delorist strategy for regenerating European integration in the 1990s. It is important to situate this turning point in the life of the European Community and its institutions. This prologue will thus begin with a brief introduction to the Delors period. It will then turn to the triumphant first period of Delors's presidency of the Commission, that of the creation of the "1992" program to complete the Single Market and the development of "1992's" initial successes of Delors's "Russian Doll" strategy.

Contexts and Institutions

The first steps towards European integration were taken in the wake of World War II, in a setting characterized by talk about "nevermore war amongst us," Marshall Plan urging toward new European economic co-operation, and, above all, Cold War manichaeanism. Europe's strategists – Jean Monnet, Robert Schuman, Konrad Adenauer, Paul-Henri Spaak – were astute in their modesty. Transnational unity of purpose, they reasoned, could best be created by concentrating on specific areas. Once Europe had begun to cooperate in these areas, interdependence of policy logics would promote "spillover" into others.[13] Great proclamations of federalist principles were to be avoided.

The 1951 Schuman Plan for the European Coal and Steel Community (ECSC) proposed integrating two sectors of great economic and military importance. The six members of the ECSC (France, Germany, Italy and the three Benelux countries), who were to form the heart of the later European Economic Community, established a supranational High Authority empowered to levy taxes, shape investment, and intervene in the market. The ECSC, like so much which came later, was essentially a Franco-German deal.[14] The British were notably absent.[15] Europe then stalled momentarily when a plan for a European Defence Community (EDC) – an attempt to find a palatable way to rearm the Germans for Cold War purposes – was rejected by the French Parliament in 1954.[16] The EDC experience drove home the lesson that economics was the most fertile ground for Europe, from which came proposals for integrating agriculture and the very quick conversion of the six to a European Economic Community (EC)[17] in the Treaty of Rome of 1957.[18]

The "Common Market," as the EC was long called, became the backbone of European integration.[19] Although the Treaty talked about the "four freedoms" (free movement of goods, services, persons, and capital) the new Common Market zeroed in on three central matters: a customs-free zone, a common external tariff, and a Common Agricultural Policy (CAP). In addition, there were a number of smaller concerns, including an anti-trust policy and vague development programs for the Italian South. But the core focus was trade and the ethos strongly liberal.

The EC's executive institution, granted an exclusive power of policy proposition by the Treaty, was a Commission in Brussels composed of members appointed by EC member states.[20] Its "legislature," the body which voted Commission proposals up or down, was a Council of Ministers representing each national government. The Council was coordinated by a presidency which rotated among member states every six months.[21] Legitimacy for EC decisions derived from the democratically elected national parliaments, which appointed Council ministers. A European Court of Justice, located in Luxembourg, entertained litigation and eventually created a body of jurisprudence for those areas – mainly trade-related – where the Rome Treaty had granted EC laws precedence over national ones. A European Parliament (initially an "Assembly") was composed of members appointed by national parliaments with little power except that of being "consulted."[22]

The real glue of the new EC was the Commission. Its administration was always small, belying the imperial machinery of tabloid lore. Implementation of EC programs was almost always left to national administrations.[23] The Commission *was* appointed and *did* have the power to propose far-reaching changes. Moreover, the founding fathers wanted to establish it as an activist motor at the center of the Community whose most important job would be to expand the EC's mandate over time, but they did not want people to become aware of this too soon. The "Monnet method" – *engrenage*[24] – was a way of being federalist without making too many people frightened about it. The Commission was an easy target for anyone who wanted to perceive and/or denounce "creeping federalism." The fact that the Commission was nonetheless quickly painted as a formidable "Brussels bureaucracy" was very significant. Such labelling was a ploy in member state games to limit encroachments on national sovereignty.

The derivation of Community legitimacy from the national democratic processes which selected the members of the Council of Ministers, if philosophically defensible, nourished practical problems. The Council met in camera and the reasons for its decisions were rarely clear to anyone beyond insider circles. Moreover, despite the importance of the new Europe, member state political life remained resolutely concerned with national matters. Domestic social and political forces did not invest resources in European matters and, partly in consequence, member state parliaments rarely discussed and debated European-level issues. This meant that connections between Council decisions and national democracy were more formal than real.

Finally, the place of the European Parliament in all this was confusing. The Parliament constantly agitated for increased power in the name of diminishing the EC's "democratic deficit." Such agitation proposed a radical redefinition of the sources of Community legitimacy, but there existed no genuine European political culture and polity upon which to base it. If Europe had a political culture, it was steadfastly one of a "Europe of nations." In legal terms, the new Europe was the product of treaties in which its national members delegated pieces of sovereignty. What the Common Market could do was spelled out in the Treaty of Rome. Everything not thus spelled out remained within the purview of its member states.

The Common Market serves the post-war boom

The new Community began as a narrowly trade-oriented adventure. The EC's designers nonetheless nourished hopes that the integrationist activists they were letting loose in Brussels, particularly at the Commission, would rapidly push to "Europeanize" more and more activities. There was thus deliberately inbuilt tension in Community structures between the original mandate and the institutions set up to implement it: the Commission was endowed, at least in theory, with the capacities to promote a broadening of this mandate. The decisive intervention of General de Gaulle in the mid-1960s made clear that such hopes and the hidden agenda of the founders' institutional engineering were over-optimistic. As EC institutions began to take shape and as the new Commission, led by a president, Walter Hallstein, with definite federalist goals, began to flex its muscles, the confederalist French President stopped things cold.[25] The outcome of this first encounter was what came to be called the "Luxembourg compromise" (1966), and it governed EC institutional life until the mid-1980s.[26] The Rome Treaty had foreseen flexibility in Council decision-making, such that on occasion specific nations might be outvoted. But from "Luxembourg" onwards each EC member acquired the right to invoke "national interest" on matters which it regarded as essential. This implied a need to seek unanimity on all controversial issues and that each member state had a veto. The Common Market thus became an intergovernmental operation. From this point no matter what measure the Commission proposed, the Council could stop the measure unless all member state governments wanted it.

General de Gaulle spoke not only for France. The coming of the Common Market occurred at the high point of Europe's postwar boom. To varying degrees all EC members were pursuing successful strategies of expansion in which national states played central roles as direct economic agents. A combination of Keynesian economic outlooks, welfare states as counter-cyclical regulators, highly institutionalized industrial relations systems, regional development policies, and "deepening" the domestic market for consumer durable goods placed most member state governments at the epicenter of economic and social regulatory mechanisms and made the maintenance of a range of intra-EC economic boundaries imperative. During a period when national trajectories in macroeconomic, industrial, and social policy were successful there was thus little real demand for any massive transfer of regulatory activities to a supranational level.

There were some important things which the EC could do, however. Predictable international trading arrangements, articulated around national states pursuing such national strategies, were essential for each country's success. The EC thus provided its member states with an important trading tool that they could largely shape and control. Simultaneously it provided a buffer against and a subsystem within the US-coordinated postwar system of trade and payments. The EC customs-free zone facilitated a substantial increase in inter-EC trade in goods in slightly over more than a decade before 1970 EC internal trade rose from less than 40 percent of total member state trade to nearly 60 percent.[27] This trade increase, in turn, brought increased growth.[28] The administration of a common external tariff provided some protection of this market from the harsh winds of open international trade.[29] Finally, making agriculture Europe's major common policy area – at French insistence – occurred at a moment when farming had to be modernized and the majority of farmers removed from their farms. If EC efforts could cushion these changes and, whenever possible, be assigned political blame for them, so much the better.

EC institutional and policy development thus "stalled" at about the level which European national capitalisms needed. The "Common Market" became a handmaiden to continental Europe's postwar boom, a useful tool for certain purposes, but unwelcome in other areas. "Europeanizing" economic processes which were essential components of member states' national strategies (the movement of capital, for example) was not on the cards. Moreover, frequent lamentations about the desirability of greater macroeconomic policy convergence were unmatched by action, since national control over macroeconomic policy was critical to the developmental models most member states were pursuing. The Commission learned to administer ably, particularly in agriculture, refining its skills at setting soybean prices, measuring carrots, and subsidizing tobacco fields. When it dared to propose more, it was frequently ignored.

The EC and the fate of the "Europe of States"

The early 1970s brought a rekindling of Europeanizing energies. The period was the last gasp of postwar optimism. The first, "Common Market" phase of implementing the Rome Treaty had been achieved successfully. Now, perhaps, it might be possible to integrate further the mostly flourishing EC national economies into a real European economic space, as the Treaty had foreseen. Beginning with the Hague Summit of 1969 (after General de Gaulle's resignation from the French presidency), plans were set out to "widen" by including the British, Danish, Irish, and Norwegians, and to "deepen" by giving the Community larger budgetary powers, foreign policy coordination (in European Political Cooperation), and to begin moving towards Economic and Monetary Union (EMU). Enlargement occurred in 1973 (only the Norwegians fell by the wayside)[30] and the Community did gain new financial autonomy, acquiring its own limited sources of revenue. Broader ambitions in regional and social policies and movement to EMU were frustrated, however.

The Community's 1970s failures occurred for good reasons. The trials and tribulations following expansion provide one set of explanations. The British proved particularly difficult to digest; Labor threatened renegotiation of entry conditions after the 1964 election and, more generally, British governments were constantly fighting about budgets and politics. Other, and perhaps deeper, causes of frustration lay in changing economic circumstances. The terrible, and oft-told, tale of Europe after the first oil shock in 1973 provides necessary background. Stagflation, high inflation which employment-destroying deflationary policies could not root out, was the rule. Productivity, profit margins, and investment levels declined. European industry began to lose competitive advantage.[31]

The essential point, however, was that Europe's 1970s failures were constructed of the same national materials as its earlier successes. The 1960s had deepened corporatist tendencies and statist forms of regulation. When economic circumstances began to change, initial responses were shaped by such tendencies. Organized labor had a clear interest in protecting jobs, postwar reforms in industrial relations, and social policy. The political Left, whose strength was based largely on labor, had its own large stake in postwar strategies. Capital had also come to depend upon the national state for favors, protection, and subsidies. Finally, state managers had their own interests to advance. Political structures and coalitions at the coming of the crisis therefore led national governments virtually everywhere towards *accentuation* of the specific developmental characteristics of earlier years.

One result, as the 1970s wore on, was growing disparity among EC economies. Another was a rise in protectionism. Because tariffs could not be raised within the EC's customs-free zone, there was a rapid spread of non-tariff barriers, often state aids to industry to save jobs. As the use of such techniques generalized the effectiveness of the Common Market as a trade area was threatened. Growth levels fell to half what they had been in the 1960s, international trade expanded less, while intra-EC trade expansion actually stopped. By the 1970s Common Market members had begun to *need* "more Europe," greater international coordination of monetary, macroeconomic, industrial, and trade policies. Convinced, however, that the national development strategies which had worked so well during the postwar boom could be revitalized, most member states still did not *want* more Europe.

The Common Market thus ultimately rose and fell as an instrument of a capitalist "Europe of States."[32] In this context the EC, an instrument of the national development strategies of its member states, began a downward spiral. The Common Market's most important independent policy area, the Common Agricultural Policy (CAP), fell on hard times. Price supports and export subsidies rapidly rationalized European farming to the point where butter mountains and wine lakes began to appear. In the process, the vast cost of the CAP became a painful EC budgetary issue. Britain in particular found itself paying more than its share of the bills for EC agriculture, setting off a ticking bomb in EC deliberations. Europe was not dead, but it had been reduced to a forum for deals in which member states sought narrow ways out of crisis.

There were glimmerings of promise, but they almost always came from non-Community and/or confederalist sources. The US-induced collapse of the Bretton Woods system made European monetary cooperation a matter of survival, leading first to the monetary "snake in the tunnel" in 1972, an attempt to peg a number of European currencies around a common exchange rate whose floating was regulated, and then to the European Monetary System (EMS) and Exchange Rate Mechanism (ERM) in 1979.[33] On the institutional front, in the mid-1970s EC member state leaders began twice-yearly summits, the European Council, designed to promote better coordination and give clearer direction to the Community.[34] Finally, in 1979 the first direct elections to the European Parliament were held and this, plus a minor increase of the Parliament's power in the realm of budgetary control, created a slight opening for new democratic hope.

Centrifugal forces had become menacing, however. Germany, the one success story and increasingly Europe's economic locomotive, proceeded to an intelligent program of industrial restructuring, but it coexisted in the early 1980s with the first years of a Mitterrand administration determined to construct "social democracy in one country," while the British began to implement Thatcherite neo-liberalism. In the midst of this the new Reagan regime induced the deepest international recession since the 1930s. Finally, the EC itself was virtually paralyzed by annual budget disputes. British governments demanded their money back, following a doctrine of "just return" according to which the financial contributions of member states should be roughly equal to funds coming back from the EC.[35] When others resisted, the British prevented them from doing anything else.[36]

The EC's supranational potential had receded. The European Parliament and others advanced ambitious plans to regenerate forward movement but they were quickly deposited in libraries. With certain prophetic exceptions, largely in industrial policy, the Commission proposed little and implemented less.[37] Brussels accumulated a veritable parts-bin of good ideas for European change which would turn out to be very useful for Jacques Delors and his Commissions in the later 1980s, but were shelved prior to this.[38] The precious little European action that did occur emanated from intergovernmental, not supranational, sources. Europessimism set in, twinned with rising neo-liberalism.

Europe Returns

Something extraordinary began to happen in the mid-1980s. The context around Community institutions began to change, the willingness of member states to contemplate European solutions to their problems increased and, most importantly, the European Commission came alive to reassert its claim as the "proposition force" for EC forward movement. In order to understand this last matter, we must first explore the workings of the Commission in somewhat greater detail.

The European Commission is an unusual institution. It is constitutionally endowed with a number of quasi-governmental powers but it is not a government at all. It is not the instrument of a party with a majority nor does it have clear lines of authority in which certain officials have ultimate decision-making power. Officially it is a "college" of 17 members, each appointed by his or her government for four years.[39] In principle every commissioner is equal. Each one is assigned a policy portfolio with administrative "services" (General Directorates or "DGs" – the French acronym) to supervise and is charged with nourishing policy developments from the policy areas covered by these services. Commissioners are quasi-ministers, responsible for overseeing and stimulating the administrative services which fall within their assigned portfolio. Unlike ministers, however, each commissioner is individually responsible for contributing to a collective and officially egalitarian decision-making process of informed argument among colleagues endowed with equal power. Nothing, or no one, in theory, "arbitrates" decisions.

The Commission does have a president, appointed separately and prior to other commissioners, by the heads of state and government. In formal terms this president is only a *primus inter pares*, with no special powers beyond the duty of presiding. This is a duty with more substance than chairing meetings, however, since the Commission president must coordinate the flow of business such that the Commission has a recognizable and coherent program. The president has traditionally had a somewhat larger personal staff – or cabinet – for such purposes, plus control over those Commission services whose main function is coordination such as the General Secretariat, and Legal Services.[40]

Armed with this official duty to preside and the small tools which come with it, plus the services in his portfolio, a president has limited resources to generate cooperation and compliance from fellow commissioners and little statutory leverage to shape the nature of Commission proposals and order them into a conscious strategy. The egalitarian structure of the Commission, in turn, has traditionally placed a high premium on seeking consensus in decision-making, to the point where there are relatively few formal votes. Everyone's cooperation is essential, no one can be coerced; deliberately forming cumulative coalitions to subordinate refractory commissioners is unacceptable. Commissions sink or swim on their abilities to act together.

Of course, the major reason the Commission has had difficulty in playing its constitutional "motor" role to promote "more Europe" is that member states have blocked it. However, a Commission may be unable to take full advantage of a completely favorable diplomatic setting for reasons having to do with its own shortcomings. Even from a strictly *internal* point of view, a Commission's capacities to act effectively can be quite variable. The appointment of commissioners by national governments is something of a lottery, for example. People can be sent off to Brussels because they are the best available or without particular regard to qualifications. A simple syllogism follows. There have often been external reasons that even a good Commission could not do much. It is also true, however, that when circumstances open up for a Commission to achieve important results, it may not be up to the task. For an occasion to be seized, the Commission must be able to focus its own efforts. The most important element in any Commission's ability to do these things is the leadership necessary to create coherence and singleness of strategic purpose.

Here lies the rub. Community crisis or stagnation can flow from two different and separate processes. The most familiar story involves inability or unwillingness on the part of key Community institutions, the Council of Ministers in the first instance, to respond to the Commission's initiatives. This may close the Commission's general political opportunity structure. Difficulties may also flow, however, from a Commission's own inability to endow itself with the internal capacities to play the motor role intelligently and effectively. In specific circumstances, both sets of causes are likely to co-vary. It will be difficult for a Commission to "transcend" itself in a frustrating broader environment and easier in a congenial one. And however favorable the external opportunity structure, the Commission as an institution must find ways to transcend its formal organizational structures to exercise fully the proposition force power and role with which the Community's treaties formally endow it. Since strong Commission leadership is not constitutionally empowered, it has to be improvised. One can conceive of many ways in which this might happen, but it is most likely that such leadership will come from a Commission president creative enough to generate the wherewithal to become something more than *primus inter pares*. What this means should be clear. For effective leadership to occur, a president must find ways to acquire power which he or she is not formally entitled to have.

The history of the Community prior to 1985 illustrated both sources of difficulty. Nothing worked particularly well in or for the Commission in the early 1980s. A very frustrating external environment meant that there was little point in generating great new initiatives and the Commission president, Luxembourg's Gaston Thorn, was unable, in any event, to generate the kind of Commission energy needed to produce such initiatives. In this context strong individual commissioners were sometimes able to muscle their favorite programs forward, but the body as a whole was stuck.[41] Because there was no overarching and focused Commission strategy the administrative services, perhaps the Commission's most important internal resources, were demoralized.

The European Council at Athens in December 1983 was a nadir. Against a background of paralysis on budgetary matters, everything seemed blocked and a number of key players began to talk about achieving their goals in other than EC ways. But the environment began to open up in the first half of 1984 under the French presidency of the Council of Ministers.[42] François Mitterrand clearly wanted to untie some of the EC's knots, in particular the chronic dispute over the famous "British Check."[43] Success in this area made fruitful discussion possible in a number of others, in particular enlarging the Community to Portugal and Spain. Behind the Mitterrand initiatives was a new French strategy to help regenerate the momentum of European integration in order to conquer new political power at European level, largely through political means, to compensate for the loss of national control which the French economic policy turnabout of 1983 implied.

In this context appointments to the Commission in 1984 were a matter of essential importance. This might be a major moment of opportunity, but success also depended upon the capacities of the new Commission. The new team did not look that different from its predecessors on paper, a mixed bag of relative unknowns, old EC hands including holdovers from the Commission under Thorn, not-quite-top-level national politicians, and other important figures for whom a distinguished exile had to be found. Both new French commissioners fell into this last category, soon-to-be ex-ministers from the Mauroy government which would end in July 1984 when nominations were first discussed.[44] Claude Cheysson, who had been Foreign Minister, and Jacques Delors would both be unemployed. Mitterrand persuaded Kohl to be allowed to nominate the new Commission president, who would be French, and he first floated Delors's name, but Cheysson's name was also in the lists. Margaret Thatcher and Helmut Kohl both objected to Cheysson. Delors was then named. The renaissance of European integration thus began partly from serendipity. Claude Cheysson was a committed socialist and a former EC commissioner, known for stirring moral speeches and policy-making ineffectiveness.[45] There is good reason to think that a Commission under Cheysson would have produced high-minded generalizations but otherwise have been ineffective. Jacques Delors was a different story. One final irony was that Thatcher, who fought most of Delors's program tooth and nail and was ultimately cast down because of this, was in large part responsible for rejecting Cheysson, who would have been much more pliable to her.

Jacques Delors was a good fit for the task of getting Europe up and running.[46] He was a front-ranking European political figure of proven strategic capacities and a convinced, very knowledgeable activist for European integration. He also had strong reasons to be unhappy with Community stagnation and a good practical sense of what might overcome it. Finally, Delors was imbued with great personal ambitions. Brussels was a test for him, as François Mitterrand undoubtedly had anticipated. Great success in Brussels was the only thing which could point him towards the French presidency. Delors had more subtle credentials as well. He had never fitted very well in the French Socialist Party dominated by hard-line Left rhetoric and commitments, was positioned ideally at the center of gravity of the EC's political spectrum which stretched from moderate social democracy to moderate Christian Democracy. Moreover, Delors's ideas were rather more German than French, which would stand him in good stead with the Germans. He believed in the centrality of a dynamic market for creating the employment and wealth needed for a moralized social order. He was no ultra-liberal, however, and did not believe that salvation flowed from letting market forces rip.

Delors was a good choice because of his practical approach to politics as well. Neither a technocrat nor the kind of manager who decided on the basis of briefs provided by a staff, he was driven by personality and character to strategize, to connect the present to what he believed to be a better future. He gathered facts, and tried to project medium-term goals to fit these facts. The European Commission itself was not an institution of day-to-day management, except for the CAP. The Commission's job was to create and promote plausible scenarios for Europe in the medium term, exactly what Delors was best at. In addition, Delors had little use for precooked global programs, like that of the French socialists in the 1970s, but remained a determined reformist, convinced of the utility of carefully located policy changes which would later "spillover" into other areas. He almost instinctively agreed with the logic of the "Monnet method."

Delors, not a spellbinding public speaker, was nonetheless an unusually effective political pedagogue. Starting with a complete mastery of his "dossier," anticipating every possible twist and turn, Delors could reduce his arguments to a short list of points for whomever was listening. He knew what he wanted, knew the complexities behind it and could almost always argue more effectively than those who disagreed. These rare skills stood him in good stead, whether in presenting a proposal to the Commission, the European Council or with ordinary television spectators. And, like all good politicians, he had developed the gift of knowing when to speak and when not to, when to move and when to stand still. Finally, *vis-à-vis* a painfully demoralized European Commission, his fervor, willingness to take risks, and ability to inspire people to work as hard as he did could only be mobilizing.

The first period: the White Paper and Single European Act

It remained for Delors to identify a strategy. This did not take long. The President announced the Commission's new colors in his initial speech to the European Parliament on January 14, 1985,[47] slightly over a week after the new Commission took office. "Is it presumptuous to announce, and then to execute, a decision to remove all the borders inside Europe between now and 1992?" Delors was quick to say that Europe could not modernize its productive structures simply by creating a "big market." All kinds of new regulatory frameworks would need to be devised as well.[48] Delors announced that by June 1985 the Commission would have something substantial to present to the European Council to begin "moving towards European Union."

From a strategic point of view the Commission needed to devise and propose a program which would simultaneously set a new agenda for the Community and be acceptable to the European Council and the EC's then ten member states. Here both the general *nature* of the program and the *way* in which the Commission formulated it were critical. It would be much easier to mobilize member states where they had already made general public commitments than on entirely new issues.[49] The actual nature of what turned out to be the Commission's White Paper on completing the internal market was thus critical. What it did or did not say, what it proscribed and prescribed, could either turn the Community around or recreate deadlock.

The "1992" program was the first substantial product of the new Commission. Just prior to assuming the presidency Delors, observing a traditional ritual, "toured the capitals" to poll EC governments about their preferences for future Community activities. He offered them four choices from the parts-bin of good, but unimplemented, ideas generated in the Community's recent past, including Economic and Monetary Union, defense and security cooperation, Political Union (renewed federalism), and, finally, completing the internal market.[50] Not surprisingly member states favored the last option, the least dramatic and risky. Even though the European Council had begun pressing the Community in this direction in 1982, the member states were skeptical that much would be done.

The Commission assigned Arthur Cockfield, the new Commissioner for the Internal Market and one of Prime Minister Thatcher's Commission nominees, the task of drawing up specific plans. A former chairman of the Boots pharmacy chain and a long-time mover and shaker in the British tax policy world, Lord Cockfield was a thoroughly liberal Englishman. In his most recent job as British Minister for Trade and Industry, he had acquired first-hand experience of the flowering of Europe's non-tariff barriers to trade. Cockfield, his staff and members of Delors's cabinet, François Lamoureux in particular, first drafted a Commission White Paper, *Completing the Internal Market*, a list of the 300 or so measures needed to eliminate physical, technical, and fiscal barriers to intra-EC exchanges of all kinds.[51] The aim was to unify 12 separate markets (eliminating physical and technical borders), largely through commitment to mutual recognition as a method for harmonization. The idea followed the *Cassis de Dijon* precedent from the European Court. The White Paper was written at breakneck speed – three months after January 1985 – and included a detailed timetable which scheduled, proposal by proposal, the sequencing of legislation to enact these measures, spread out over the lives of two consecutive Commissions (i.e. eight years), hence "1992". The document contained little Europeanist rhetoric, no prophetic visions, and no high phrases hinting at spillovers. It eschewed anything likely to inflame anyone's particular passions.

In the end the White Paper's fragmentation into dense paragraphs about technical problems and absence of supranationalist forecasting made it hard for anyone to disagree with. These deliberately designed chracteristics of the White Paper were of great political significance. Placing a time limit on the implementation of the White Paper created a slogan – "1992" – which simplified a very complex cluster of policy initiatives and was itself essential in generating interest and enthusiasm from a wide range of publics. The pitch was to suggest that the White Paper and "1992" were vehicles to "get Europe moving again," rather than technical proposals. As Delors was wont later to say, "people don't fall in love with a single market," but they could be mobilized by a simple slogan.

The White Paper also played carefully to broader political constraints. Its general content was "deregulatory" (the word "deregulation" was often used in Commission documents of the period), focusing upon removing barriers to trade. This tapped ambient ideological prejudices, of course. But it also appealed to the specific desiderata of key member states. The Germans would profit from opening up the internal market. The French wanted it as much to enhance their diplomatic power on the continent as for economic purposes.[52] It was the British, adamantly opposed to new cessions of sovereignty to the Community, for whom the deregulatory emphases of the White Paper were particularly well targeted, however.[53] The "more Europe" which the Commission had on offer was more market than political integration.[54]

Once the White Paper was published in early June 1985, a new stage opened. The Milan European Council in spring 1985 had been called to deal primarily with the consequences of the Dooge Report about reforming EC institutions commissioned by the European Council a year earlier. One of the report's proposals had been for a conference of member states to negotiate changes to the Treaty about such institutional matters. The Danes, Greeks, and British opposed this and the Commission itself was initially lukewarm, fearing failure and favoring a more pragmatic approach.[55] Milan's major conclusion was to call an "intergovernmental conference" (IGC) on the basis of Article 236 of the Rome Treaty. The IGC would be charged to elaborate a treaty on a "common foreign and security policy" and to modify the Treaty of Rome to change "the Council's decision-making processes, the Commission's powers of implementation and the powers of the Parliament." The rarely used IGC formula, which the Italians uncovered, allowed the opening of interstate treaty negotiations by simple majority.[56] Mrs Thatcher was furious when the Italian Council President Craxi sprung the option.[57]

The IGC formula itself presaged a major shift in the political opportunity structure of the Commission and its member states. Obliging reluctant member states to come to the bargaining table in itself raised the stakes, since beginning an IGC created an obligation to conclude, which simple Council deliberations did not. In ordinary cirumstances the Council could send a piece of important legislation into purgatory by not acting at all. The failure of an IGC, on the other hand, would be intepreted as a clear public defeat for the Community in general. The costs were thus raised for any single member state bent on preventing satisfactory outcomes. Moreover, the complexity of negotiating packages on the table at an IGC would be greater than that surrounding a single piece of legislation at the Council. Multiple issues simultaneously created new possibilities for favorable policy linkages.

At intergovernmental conferences governments are the only legal participants.[58] Luxembourg, during whose presidency the IGC took place, made the Commission more than a committed observer, however, by asking it to present a complete set of proposals for modifying the Treaty in the key areas.[59] The Commission's White Paper agenda then eclipsed the earlier Dooge Committee concerns about decision-making efficiency and the Commission thenceforth played a "determining role."[60] What occurred first was open-ended dialogue (around Commission-prepared papers) between the Commission and member states. The initial treaty proposals, which structured outcomes, came directly from the Commission, produced internally by Delors and a small group of individuals including Claus-Dieter Ehlermann, head of legal services, and Emile Noël, secretary general. Much of the prodding of the Commission's services and final writing was done by François Lamoureux of the Delors cabinet.

The events which produced the Single European Act – the IGC and the Luxembourg European Council of 1985[61] – thus flowed from detailed scripts written largely by the Commission. This remained true even after the first "dialogue" stage, when the UK and other hangers-back agreed to enter real negotiations, and member states took over.[62] The Commission, seeking EC forward movement, systematically raised the threshold, asking for more than it knew it would get. After all the dealings, both at the COREPER (the Committee of Permanent Representatives, composed of member state ambassadors to the EC) and at ministerial level, the Commission nonetheless still secured a great deal of what it wanted – enshrined in the final new proposals to modify the EC's existing treaties, the "Single European Act."[63]

Perhaps Delors's and the Commission's shrewdest move was to link completing the single market to a fundamental change in prevailing EC decision-making procedures (tying the Dooge Committee's concerns to the "1992" project). Because the internal market program was so ambitious, it argued, the rules of the Luxembourg compromise had to give way to decisions by "qualified majority" for most White Paper areas. The Commission won most of what it wanted in this quest for qualified majority, except on fiscal harmonization and environmental policy.[64] Henceforth in single market areas member states might very well have to accept legislation they did not desire. It was the Commission as well which found ways to link qualified majority with extending the powers of the Parliament. In those areas where qualified majority would be allowed the Parliament would gain amending powers.[65]

The Commission also proposed a newly extended list of EC "competencies" – new areas in which the Community acquired a legal basis to act: in research and development, regional policy ("economic and social cohesion"), the environment, foreign policy cooperation (the inclusion of European Political Cooperation in the treaty). Locating these new competencies in their own treaty clauses, rather than tying them to the internal market, opened up great new possibilities. Economic and social cohesion, for example, became a specific aim of the Community, obliging specific programs which were to be undertaken separately from the internal market. Extending the Community's "social" prerogatives, particularly in areas of workplace health and safety, was the only new competence which the Commission itself did not propose – perhaps because it was afraid of British reaction. But it was able to hide behind the French and the Danes, whose social proposals, somewhat watered down, were ultimately accepted by the British. There was even a premonitory clause about closer monetary cooperation. One did not need a crystal ball to understand that Delors and the Commission were engineering the conditions for future spillover with all this. Even for those areas where unanimity decision rules meant that little action was actually likely, placing a new competency in the Treaty was a strong foot in the door pointing to treaty change later on.[66]

During the very first year of Delors's presidency the Commission had moved from being a prisoner of governments determined to limit its autonomy, to the position of an entrepreneur able to pyramid its role as broker of a "12-level chess game" (the words were John Major's after Maastricht) into new powers of initiative. The EC's progress in the later 1980s was based upon a considerable shift in the configuration of Community institutions which created more space to resolve problems in a positive way. The most important change, of course, was the Commission's return to the center of the action, proposing new programs one after the other. The nature of Europe's "legislature," the place to which the Commission brought its proposals for approval, also changed. Until the mid-1980s the "small" EC's actions had been overdetermined by the Luxembourg compromise. Anyone could veto, or threaten to veto, change. By 1986, with the entry of Spain and Portugal, the Community had grown into a group of 12 members of diverse needs and interests. In this new setting, if the Commission did its political homework properly, sounding out "the capitals" and pinning down allies in advance, it could exploit a newly positive-sum decisional arena. The trick was putting together complex packages which simultaneously contained things which would appeal to differing member state interests *and* proposed further movement to supranationality. Jacques Delors proved very good at such things, developing a particular mastery of European Council settings, where fundamental mandates for the Community's future were set out, in the process.

High-wire acts: the inner life of the Commission and the payoffs of success

Delors's great gifts for strategizing and politicking on a continental stage were essential, but not quite enough to ensure success. The Commission's own administration was vital, and its cooperation had to be acquired. Simultaneously, the Commission's new strategies had to be put into the public's eye. These tasks were less spectacular than the great intellectual and political efforts needed to get Europe up and moving initially, but they were nearly as important.

With the arrival of the new Commission in 1985 the "Brussels bureaucrats" were challenged to emerge from their demoralization and torpor. The administrative services, working under great pressure, had to produce a wide range of concrete proposals to fill out the White Paper. And once this task had been completed it then became necessary to devise new proposals for the IGC, look forward to preparing the actual legislation needed to implement the White Paper and Single European Act, and begin thinking through the new policies (the budget, agriculture, implementing "economic and social" cohesion) that would follow these initial steps. Moreover, the services had to do all this while continuing a list of routine activities already complicated by the impending enlargement of the Community to include Spain and Portugal.

Mobilizing the Commission's services for the new strategy was complicated. They could easily have collapsed under the weight and complexity of the new workload. Delors's strategic and political leadership in the Commission was a gigantic precondition, but not a guarantee that the services would perform. Like any administration, the Commission's was subdivided into self-promoting and self-protective fiefdoms which had to be coaxed towards more effective collaboration, which a committed team of new commissioners might do. But the best-kept secret in the story was that of the Delors cabinet.

Given the collegial nature of the Commission, "cabinets" had come to play an essential role in its life. If each commissioner was responsible for a portfolio and the resulting proposals coinciding with one or several policy areas, decisions about whether proposals would become official Commission policy were made collectively by the entire Commission every Wednesday. Every commissioner thus had to be kept informed about the work of every other commissioner in order to decide what to say and how to vote on Wednesdays. Cabinets – small personal staffs of six or seven people – were the instruments which the Commission had historically devised to do such information gathering and coordinating. Each member of a commissioner's cabinet knew the commissioner's own area well, served as liaison with the services, and oversaw policy development in areas for which other commissioners were responsible, gathering intelligence, preparing and evaluating dossiers, and keeping his or her commissioner informed. Beyond this, cabinet members performed a wide variety of other functions connected to the preparation and coordination of Commission meetings themselves – often in the "special chefs"[67] meetings called for each specific policy proposal (where cabinet specialists get together), and, later, in the weekly "*Chefs de Cabinet*" meetings to review horizontally the upward flow of proposals before things went to the Commission. Cabinets could stop the forward progress of inadequate proposals, or winnow out prior to actual Commission meetings those proposals on which consensus existed – which were then accepted as "point A" matters, by staff alone. Finally, they clarified disagreement and conflict, where it existed, so that the Commission could discuss its options clearly when it met.

The president's cabinet, slightly larger, did all of these things for Delors but had a number of additional functions tied, in formal terms, to his responsibilities. Officially, the president's cabinet presided over the complex processes of policy generation and coordination which had to take place before anything actually reached the Commission floor. Individual presidential cabinet members thus organized and ran the various preparatory meetings on specific policy at cabinet level including "special chefs." Moreover, the president's *Chef de Cabinet*, along with the Commission secretary general (who himself reported to the president), organized the weekly *Chefs de Cabinet* meeting.

When Delors and Pascal Lamy, his *Chef de Cabinet*, "disembarked" in Brussels on January 6, 1985, the presidency was a weakened office in a weakened Commission. The previous president, Gaston Thorn, had not been a strong leader and the Commission had been run, in a somewhat divided way, by a group of commissioners: Lorenzo Natali, François-Xavier Ortoli and Etienne Davignon. Behind these stood Emile Noël, the Commission's eternal secretary general, who held all the strings and knew all the secrets. The administration itself was in an advanced state of demoralization.

Pascal Lamy undertook his new job of organizing the Commission to support Delors's strategy, using methods which he had mastered while working in Paris earlier with Delors in the Ministry of Finance. Over the years these two extraordinary men had developed a clear division of labor and label. Delors was the commander in chief: visionary, intellectual and a statesman. Without his contributions, little or nothing would have occurred. Lamy was the general who drilled the divisions into line. He looked the part, tough as nails, a parachutist out of uniform. Moreover, a graduate of Paris's prestigious École National d'Administration and Hautes Études Commerciales, France's most respected business school, he

was as intellectually gifted as any of the first-ranking statesmen and ministers he had to deal with. The Delors presidency depended as much on the
symbiotic relationship between Delors and Pascal Lamy as on anything
else.

For the first year or so it was quite unclear whether Delors's strategy
would get off the ground and, connected to this, whether Delors and Lamy
would be able to get the Commission machine to produce. The "house," as
the inhabitants of the Berlaymont were referred to, had to be mobilized to
a much higher level of activity and achievement than it had been accus-
tomed to providing. The president's cabinet was the main mobilizing tool.
For a while, from all accounts, it was a blunt instrument indeed. Cabinet
members mastered the Delors "line" to the point where they could persuade anyone in the house into accepting it, something which required
deep commitment and endless hard work. They also had to pressure other
cabinets and the services to produce the right kind of work. This often
involved refusing to accept what others came up with and fighting to the
end with them to make changes. When even these things did not work, the
Delors cabinet had no hesitation in bypassing other cabinets to establish
and use parallel networks to obtain what was needed. Part of the approach,
inevitably, was to inspire fear, particularly about job security. To get the
machine moving, one of the cabinet's original members later noted, "we
had to be a gang."

In fact, at this point Delors and his cabinet were performers in a political
high-wire act. Delors had to promote an exceptional mobilization of internal Commission resources to produce the outpouring of new work needed
to provide the detailed proposals which were needed for a credible
reassertion of the Commission as a proposition force in the Community
system. This task was further complicated by the assertion by Delors of
exceptional new presidential leadership prerogatives. Delors's strategy included elevating his own position well beyond what the Commission's
institutional configuration formally allowed.

There were risks in this, as there were in the other dimensions of
Delors's strategy. Other commissioners and the Commission's services
might rebel and block the internal mobilization which was a necessary
condition of Commission success in the external world. Delors could be
incredibly demanding, in keeping with his Jansenist severity. He expected
his Commission colleagues to contribute as much effort as he did and to
produce work of the highest quality. The major secret of his domination
over the Commission was intellectual. He knew all important dossiers as
well as, or better than, the colleagues directly responsible for them. In
Commission meetings those who did not meet his high standards or who
disagreed but were unable to make their cases rarely escaped unscathed.
Moreover, to Delors the reward for hard work was to be found in the work
itself. Those who expected presidential "stroking" were disappointed. In
addition, during the touch and go moments that occurred in this delicate
first period, the president often gave in to mood swings, sometimes retreat-

ing into silence, sulking, and occasionally even exploding with anger. To make things even more complicated, Delors was subtle enough to know all of these things about himself in order sometimes to use them tactically. Finally, Delors was someone who ultimately thought through and decided things on his own. This solitary style, in which Delors opened fully to few peers (Pascal Lamy was one of them, along with other trusted members of his staff) meant that Delors, love of sports notwithstanding, was not really much of a team person.

The reasons the first period was a high-wire act are not difficult to understand, therefore. The Commission and its services had to stretch themselves beyond their limits to produce what Delors deemed necessary. On top of this Delors and his staff insisted on a strong presidentialist redefinition of Commission operations, which had little formal constitutional support. Commissioners and key administrators were aware that the potential payoffs of success might be great for the Community: enhanced Commission importance and a reinvigoration of the Commission's internal purpose. This fed willingness to go along with new initiatives, methods, and work rhythms. But payment would later be demanded, and its most acceptable currency would be the rewards of political success which would enhance the status of everyone in Brussels after a decade of decline. Without success within a reasonable time, however, there could have been a withdrawal of cooperation. Internally, Delors's position depended on the production of a payoffs to "the house" from external accomplishment.

Even with excellent Commission proposals and EC member states disposed to treat them seriously, every effort had to be made to "sell the product." The Commission had to elicit targeted support from important constituencies beyond the governments of member states for "1992," the Single European Act, and the new Commission itself. For the Commission, decoding and working the complex dimensions of its political opportunity structure thus meant going beyond the Commission and Council to generate support. Business support began to come in as soon as it looked as if the White Paper–Single European Act program was serious. European business had been looking for options of the potentially market-stimulating kind that "1992" promised.[68] Business and economic policy elites also proved particularly sensitive to the Commission's own efforts to argue in favor of the "1992" program in high intellectual terms through what eventually became the "Cecchini Report," a panoply of studies by economists about the "costs of non-Europe" – i.e. what EC members would lose economically if they did not go through with "1992." Hundreds of specialists were mobilized to do this work, a tactic which itself brought a significant number of policy intellectuals behind the program. Moreover, the Cecchini Report was published in a number of different ways, both scientific and "vulgarized," and it made a big impact.[69]

Labor support was more problematic given the liberal nature of "1992." Completing the Single Market was likely to threaten jobs in the shorter term before its promised longer-term positive effects took effect, as the

Commission's own data demonstrated. Jobs had become scarce throughout the Community. Official unemployment had risen to nearly 10 percent while the workings of social programs masked even more unemployment, perhaps 5 percent.[70] Moreover, breaking down barriers between national markets opened up prospects for "social dumping," the great fear of labor movements in Europe's more prosperous areas. Multinational corporations could indulge in "regime-shopping" by relocating or situating new investment in those areas of the Community with lower social overhead costs or, conversely, national governments might engage in competitive dismantling of social policy schemes in order to create incentives for corporate regime-shoppers. A wide range of nationally based regulatory and social welfare programs might be undercut.

Delors and the Commission worked hard on labor, in particular by promising the opening of "social dialogue" at European level: one of Delors's very first acts was to convene the so-called Val Duchesse discussions among "social partners." With labor Delors could also play on the studied ambiguities of his own position: "1992" was a liberal program, but Delors himself was a social democrat known for his strong advocacy of negotiation. He had intimated, beginning with his speech to the European Parliament in January 1985, that completing the Single Market would necessitate "flanking" programs, including social programs, and labor was attentive to this. Finally, labor leaders were hostage to Delors to the degree to which they were aware that they were unlikely to get a better deal or a more sympathetic leadership than from him.

The European Parliament was also a useful resource. Like the Commission itself, it was biased by function towards advocating "more Europe." The moderate increase in power which the Single European Act brought to the Parliament – the "cooperation procedure" – enjoined the Parliament to be more responsible than it had been earlier. Interactions around amendments, which involved increased Commission day-to-day attention to the Parliament and an intensified web of communications between Brussels and Strasbourg, moved the Parliament further into the Commission's camp on most proposals. Commissioners regularly appeared at Parliament discussions and the Commission met once a month in Strasbourg during the parliamentary plenaries, at huge expense in terms of transportation of papers and people. Delors in particular paid very close attention to parliamentary leaders, many of whom he knew from his earlier service as a Europarliamentarian or from French politics.

One paradoxical feature of the general political environment also facilitated the Commission's position. Skepticism about the Community was so widespread in the mid-1980s that there was a tendency to discount the importance of any new Commission initiatives. Many believed that even if something like completing the Single Market was announced, it would probably not amount to much. Thus Altiero Spinelli, one of Europe's grand old federalist figures, commented, after the Single European Act, that the "mountain has given birth to a mouse." This kind of attitude could work to minimize opposition to Commission plans. When the Act was presented for ratification to the French Parliament, for example, then Prime Minister Chirac, a Gaullist whose party bristled with anti-Europeanists, judged that so little was likely to follow that it was not worth spending political resources opposing it. Had Chirac, and a number of others like him, anticipated the burst of Community activity which did actually follow they would almost certainly have approached things differently.

The most important source of support for the Commission's new policies was good economic luck, however. At about the point when awareness emerged that something new was happening in Brussels, European economies started to improve. This was more coincidence than cause and effect, but coincidence with a powerful positive return for "1992" and the Single European Act. Europe's new activism could then be associated with a renewal of growth, prosperity, and job creation. It had always been much easier for Europe to move forward when economic success created a positive-sum game, and the years after 1986 were to prove no exception.

Russian Dolls

By 1987, when the ratification of the Single European Act was completed, the Commission had "returned" and the EC was headed smartly forward. The Commission had skillfully blended a mobilization of in-house internal resources, shrewd understanding of the political opportunity structures which it faced, smart politics inside the broader Community system, and a good reading of the external world into a major increase in its own credibility and resources. As all this occurred the Commission began to reap the rewards of success in terms of an increased store of new resources. What would it do with them?

The Delors strategy involved much more than simply succeeding at this first round of policy innovation. François Lamoureux, Pascal Lamy's second in command during the Maastricht period, summarized the Delors team's approach as a "Russian doll" strategy. "You take the first doll apart," he said, "and then, inside it is another one, which leads you to another and so on . . . until it is too late to turn back." The Russian doll metaphor implied iterated episodes of strategic action to seize upon openings in the political opportunity structure, resource accumulation through success, and reinvestment of these resources in new actions to capitalize on new opportunities. There was a certain "double or nothing" dimension to the next stage after 1987. The basic approach remained the same, but there was to be a significant change in direction. The White Paper and Single European Act sought to use the Community's traditional trade-market orientations. With the move to Russian dolls the Commission shifted its targeting subtly towards state-building.

The Delors package

The most significant Russian doll was the *paquet Delors*, the most underdiscussed major event in Europe's post-1985 renewal. Its preparation began in 1986, even before the ink of signatures to the Single European Act had dried. It originated in a confluence of three separate sectoral discussions inside the Commission. The EC faced a financial crisis in 1987 which necessitated changing the budgetary system. Next, the Structural Funds (a set of budgets dedicated to regional development policies) had to be reformed in the light of the Act and its new commitment to "economic and social cohesion."[71] Finally, the chronic financial bleeding of the CAP had to be confronted.[72] The originality of the Commission's approach, really Delors's own contribution, was to join these three problems into a single proposal first presented by the Commission in February 1987.[73] The dense text exemplified the approach of the Commission under Delors to agenda-setting. The package sought first of all to raise general member state commitments to the Community. Simultaneously it began to shift the policy grounds of these commitments towards political institution building. Finally, it sought new financial resources to enhance the position of the Commission itself within the broader Community institutional system. The major political argument for this complex proposal, endlessly and effectively repeated, was that the package was necessary for the successful implementation of the Act.

First of all, the Delors package involved a five-year commitment to a greatly enlarged Community budget. This projected various expenses, including those for the CAP, and pledged Commission observance of strict budgetary discipline. In exchange for this pledge the Community received increased and changed "own resources,"[74] making the Commission more like a real government in its budgetary latitude. Moreover, more resources of its own predictably supplied over five years enabled the Commission to avoid the terrible annual intergovernmental money fights which had paralyzed everything in the very recent past. The package also proposed certain changes in the CAP that began breaking ground for the fuller CAP reform that would be implemented in 1991–2. It also included a five-year program of guidelines for "capping" CAP spending, which kept incessant budgetary squabbles over agriculture off the table until 1993.[75]

The package's most important proposals were on "economic and social cohesion," that is, a new commitment to bringing Europe's less developed areas to levels comparable to those of its rich core. The reform of the Structural Funds – the Regional Development Fund (ERDF),[76] the European Social Fund (ESF), and its agricultural counterpart EAGGF (European Agricultural and Guidance Fund) – partook, in part, of a logic of "side payments" built into the Single Market deal. Spanish and Portuguese EC membership coincided with the Single Market program. The two new Iberian members felt entitled to specific help and, more generally, the completion of the Single Market would initially hurt the poorer regions of the Community more than the better off.[77] Beyond this dimension, however, the change in the Structural Funds brought the first really substantial European-level commitment to planned redistribution among member states. The workings of three separate Community instruments along with the activities of the European Investment Bank (which could provide loans) were to be coordinated in order to target a set of prior objectives. They included, in order: aid to less developed regions in the EC (largely in the South); reconversion activities in regions with declining industries (which included important areas in the North); programs to overcome long-term unemployment (for adults over 25 unemployed more than a year); help to enter the labor market for unemployed young people (under 25); and development/structural adjustment in rural areas.

The budget for such aid was to be doubled over the five-year period to 1992, when it would amount to 25 percent of Community spending. Most important, the funds thus made available were to be used in a planned way. Pluriannual programs would be shaped and overseen by the Commission in accordance with the new principle of "subsidiarity," i.e. policy worked by the most efficient level of government closest to the constituencies touched by it. The use of structural funds would be decided following contractual negotiations between the Commission and member states. The Commission would set out the general criteria for directing aid to regions within member states which fitted the objectives listed above, and the development of specific programs would follow specific new principles.[78] The sums involved, if modest in absolute terms, would be substantial in relationship to the investment needs of poorer EC countries.[79]

Political "packaging" was most significant in this Russian doll. The various measures proposed were not to be seen as discrete and separable. In his speech to the European Parliament in February 1987, just after the package had been made public, Delors announced:[80]

in economic terms, it is self-evident that a large market without internal frontiers could not be completed or operate properly unless the Community had instruments enabling it to avoid imbalances interfering with competitiveness and inhibiting the growth of the Community as a whole . . . the ship of Europe needs a helmsman . . . The large market without internal frontiers cannot, by itself, properly be responsible for the three main functions of economic policy: the quest for greater stability . . . the optimum allocation of resources to obtain the benefit of economies of scale and to stimulate innovation and competitiveness and the balanced distribution of wealth allowing for individual merit.

If commentators tended to overlook the meaning and importance of the Delors package, EC heads of government knew that they were being asked to ratify a major change in the rules of the European game. The Delors package was the first real test of member states' willingness to implement the Single European Act. A great deal more money would have to be provided and on radically new terms. Prior to this point member state doctrine on financing Europe involved a rule of "just return." Each country should receive approximately what it contributed and should have reasonably clear control over the circuits through which its money flowed. The Delors package asked that a genuine transfer of resources be accepted. It also asked that the Commission be granted a large measure of new autonomy in targeting and distributing the new budget.

The British refused to sign when the plan was first raised at the Brussels European Council in June 1987. The dramatic failure of EC leaders to approve the program at Copenhagen in December of the same year brought the Community very close to a new period of crisis. This time it was not only the British who held back. French Prime Minister Jacques Chirac, to take but one example, opposed doubling the Structural Fund budget. France, he argued, should gain as much as it paid, otherwise Europe was not worth it. On the other side, Spanish Prime Minister Gonzales denounced such intergovernmentalist calculations. The real "hero" in the success of the Delors package, which finally came at the February 1988 European Council, was President Helmut Kohl, who, with Delors himself, was able to twist arms at the last minute and carry the day, largely because the Germans were willing to subsidize the new financial arrangements.

Economic and Monetary Union (EMU)

Economic and Monetary Union was the highest-stake Russian doll. Pushing for EMU at the Hanover European Council in June 1988 – only short months after the *paquet Delors* had been finally, and painfully, passed at a special Brussels European Council – Delors arranged matters strategically the way he liked them.[81] There were strong arguments in favor of some kind of EMU as the logical complement to and culmination of the Single Market. Moreover, on the basis of such arguments the Community had made all kinds of solemn commitments to EMU over the years, especially between 1970 and 1985, which it had then shelved. The EC's file of overlooked promises was Delors's favorite place to find new things to do. It was hard for member states to refuse what they had solemnly committed themselves to earlier.[82] The campaign began in 1987 when the June Hanover Summit, at Delors's request, made him chairman of a committee to report a year later on EMU. The report, submitted to the Madrid European Council in June 1989, was a highly polished document setting out a step-by-step path towards EMU and involving a new conference to renegotiate the EC Treaty. The Madrid European Council gave EMU a good head of steam. The Delors Report was warmly welcomed, much as it stood, and a set of Community bodies were then asked to set up EMU Stage 1 and begin preparations for the new intergovernmental conference.[83]

The deeper logic of the EMU Russian doll was crystal clear. Pooling monetary and much economic policy sovereignty would necessitate supranational control over a wide range of economic matters. The single currency, when it came, would completely remove the tool of currency revaluation from national policy-makers, even if use of this tool had already been severely constrained by EMS. Underneath, to be sure, were questions of relative national power, and German pre-eminence in particular, in the dealings that would determine the directions of supranational monetary policy. Beyond this the need for stringent economic and budgetary convergence among EC countries (inflation levels, interest rates, budget deficits, levels of national indebtedness) dictated very large additional supranational constraints on national economic policies. Implied in EMU were further discussions and policy changes concerning economic and social cohesion since, as with the Single Market, EMU would *a priori* favor the richer and economically stronger EC members. The South (Spain, Portugal, Greece, parts of Italy, and Ireland) would need special help to insure that EMU did not block an already rocky developmental trajectory.

The social dimension

Russian doll III was even more controversial. In the neo-liberal atmosphere of the mid-1980s proposing social programs would have been problematic. Growing awareness of the potential redistributive effects of the Single Market, particularly on the part of trade unions concerned about "social dumping," made new initiatives to "organize" Europe's social space conceivable, however. The success of "1992" made them politically possible. The Social Charter, like almost all of Delors's Commission's propositions, had precedents from the early 1970s. The actual notion of a new *socle* (foundation) of social rights was first proposed publicly by the Belgian Minister of Labor during the Belgian presidency of 1987, but the Delors team had discussed such matters at length already. Delors then took the notion to the 1988 Stockholm Conference of the European Trade Union Confederation (ETUC). This speech summarized the President's thought on the "social dimension" in general. Renewed economic activity due to the Single Market was the *sine qua non* of European success, but, to cite Delors, "it is not a question of . . . simply creating a free trade zone, but rather an organized space endowed with common rules to ensure economic and social cohesion and an equality of opportunity in the face of new opportunities." The "social dimension," to Delors, included "economic and social cohesion," an essential tool to prevent social dumping, Community legislation where needed (in health and safety), and "social dialogue." Most importantly, at Stockholm Delors first spoke of a set of basic social rights as "one of the . . . major axes of European social space," clearly implying that these rights would be enforceable.[84]

The Economic and Social Committee and the European Parliament then debated an enforceable bill of social rights.[85] In the meantime an internal Commission think tank, the Groupe Lacroix, worked through the issues and Patrick Venturini, future social policy advisor in the Delors cabinet, was charged with producing a proposal on social matters.[86] The Marin Report – after Commissioner Manuel Marin – indicated the general directions which would be taken,[87] recommending a flexible "middle way" involving regional policies, some Community efforts to promote social policy harmonization and, most importantly, renewed "social dialogue."

The Social Charter of May 1989, which resulted from all this, was a "solemn commitment" on the part of member states – only 11, given furious British opposition to a set of "fundamental social" – and essentially wage-earners' – "rights."[88] It contributed no new legal value to the Treaty of Rome and the Single European Act. In the Commission's strategic logic, rather than creating new obligations the Charter should open the way to make good the unfulfilled social promises the Community's treaty base already contained, as clause 28 of the Charter clearly explained.[89] It was to redeem the limited social policy promises made first in the 1970s and extract as much policy mileage, and legitimacy, from existing legal prerogatives as could be extracted.

The Action Program which followed to operationalize the Charter proposed a flood of new Community legislation, some 47 different instruments to be prepared and submitted to the Council by January 1, 1993.[90] The bulk of proposals for "hard" Community action involved living and working conditions, freedom of movement, worker information, consultation and participation, equal treatment, and health and safety. In the areas of broader social policy (after a caveat that given national systemic differences "there can . . . be no question of harmonizing"), there were proposals for "recommendations" (i.e., non-legally binding opinions) on convergence of objectives in social protection and Community minima in social assistance directed to the poor. In the same register there was a proposal for a Community "opinion" (again non-binding) on appropriate minimum wage levels.[91]

The Social Charter had a number of political logics. It was partly to serve the Commission's general political and resource-mobilizing purposes by calming some of the fears which "1992" aroused in the European labor movement and, in the process, to help the Commission acquire labor support for its strategies. Moreover, to the anticipatable degree to which Community action could not be produced in support of Social Charter promises, the Commission could count on a substantial mobilization of indignant voices (including the large socialist bloc in the European Parliament) to spread the message about Social Europe. Here the Commission was hoping to generate the kind of public pressure for a future change in the European agenda which would be needed towards greater Community activism in social policy. This, in turn, would ultimately be helpful when the time came, as it would, to propose changing the Treaty, to allow for qualified majority Council voting across the board on social matters. Ever further into the future, it might help in opening the door to discussion about granting the EC new legal prerogatives in social policy. Finally, persistent British blockages on social matters, as well as on other issues, would isolate the British (important for the Commission's position in the internal politics of the EC), make Prime Minister Thatcher domestically vulnerable, and lay the ground for an eventual British turnaround.

Sturm und Drang over the Social Charter tended to obscure the Commission's other major social policy priority. The Single European Act included a new Article 118b stating that "the Commission shall endeavour to develop the dialogue between management and labour at European level which could, if the two sides consider it desirable, lead to relations based on agreement." The relaunching of social dialogue was in fact Delors's first social policy step, taken in January 1985.[92] The exercise was initially about confidence-building: belief in the desirability of flexible decentralization of capital–labor dialogue and in the superiority of negotiation over administrative coordination was at the very core of Jacques Delors's political philosophy. Delors's hope was thus to engage employers and unions in habits of discussion which, in time, might create mutual respect and trust and eventuate in more substantial "contractual" conclusions. In addition, the process might help transform the actors themselves into agents with the power to deal. There was considerable distance to travel here, since neither the ETUC nor UNICE, essentially Brussels lobbies, was empowered to negotiate.[93] The initial Val Duchesse discussions among UNICE, the employers' association, the ETUC, and the public sector trade association, thus did not get very far.[94]

Social dialogue was relaunched again in 1989 in the context of the new Social Charter *élan*. A "steering group" of top-level representatives of the different professional groups was thenceforth regularly convened by the Director General of DG V (the Commission's social policy administration) initially to talk about education and training and, more broadly, the evolution of the EC labor market. The steering group was also consulted on Social Charter proposals. Discussion quickly ran up against the participants' contradictory purposes. The ETUC wanted concrete proposals while UNICE insisted upon broad principles.[95] Moreover, all actors were obliged to keep their eyes on what was going on socially in the member states before saying much of anything, since imprudent remarks at European level could upset delicate, and more essential, discussions at national level.[96]

Strategies, tactics and overloaded tables

The "first period" and the Russian dolls moment demonstrated the fundamentals of the Delors's strategy. An opening existed in the political opportunity structure around the Commission to mobilize resources and allow the Commission to take advantage of the insititutional variable geometry built into the Community's treaty-constitution. It was necessary to begin with proposals which would tap most of the open dimensions of the opportunity structure and create forward momentum. With its liberal and deregulatory overtones, "1992" was important both in itself and as a launching pad. Its success was immediately cashed in on new initiatives: the Russian dolls. These proposals, which could be presented as contiguous with the Community's traditional mandate, in fact bore more "state-building" and/or supranationalizing logics and involved more explicit transfers of sovereignty.

Delors believed that regenerating European economic activity through the Single Market program was a matter of survival or decline for Europe. Without new investment, growth and job creation flowing from the enlarged and re-energized market nothing else could follow. But Delors also believed that the new market could produce few of these desirable things on its own. The *laissez-faire* approaches of Anglo-Saxon liberalism missed an essential matter. Markets existed within specific broader "models of society" which moralized individuals and structured preferences. The "1992"–Russian doll strategy thus involved both reinvigorating the market and consolidating a "European model of society."

This notion of a European social model – a humane social order based upon the mixed economy, civilized industrial relations, the welfare state, and a commitment to basic social justice – had its roots in the Social Democrat–Christian Democrat mainstream of continental European politics. The conviction that European capitalist societies both were and ought to be different was shared in this mainstream. It was also the core of the political project to which Delors had devoted most of his life. In it societies were more than markets, citizenship more than consumption, and government more than an economic traffic squad. People belonged to moralized collectivities which negotiated with one another for the good of all. Citizenship involved solidarity with others. Government, beyond stimulating economic activity to provide welfare, should craft a wide range of public goods, not only because of market failures and "externalities," but in response to demands of solidarity.

To Delors, enhancing the "European model" was also a logical concomitant of the Single Market program. The quest could thus be expressed both in arguments about "oughts" and about specific programs. In Delors's own words:[97]

> the implicit philosophy in European construction is much more dialectical than people ordinarily think. The competition which will be developed by the large market will also promote cooperation. And like competition and cooperation, liberalization and harmonization will go together, creating the conditions for a new regulation of the totality which will be created.

The list of Russian dolls thus followed. Social and economic cohesion was needed to promote economic convergence and prevent disruptive social dumping. At the same time, it embodied new commitments to interstate regional solidarity to serve as a precedent for breaking with earlier EC member state egoisms. Economically, the social dimension was a way of regulating the consequences of the Single Market to prevent the emergence of unfair trade in the labor market. It was also an avenue to greater dialogue and negotiation between employers and workers on European level, a way to counteract market-based tendencies undercutting industrial relations systems on national levels. The CAP needed more reform because of the waste and trade distortion which it promoted. But it also needed to be changed because of the centrality of rural development and the unique contributions of farmers to European society and ecology. New Community initiatives in research and development and environmental regulation were needed to enhance competitiveness. But they were also to reinforce specifically European cooperation in industry.

Delors was indeed a federalist, but knew full well that the earlier federalist dream of a "United States of Europe" was no longer plausible. Any new Europe would be complicated juxtaposition of different jurisdictions of a model quite unprecedented in the annals of federalist development: the ill-defined, originally Catholic, notion of "subsidiarity" was incorporated into the Delors vocabulary quite early on. Combining both market-building and state-building strategies was thus for constructing a supranational European state on the model of the nation state, whatever Delors's British critics thought. It was rather more motivated by urgent concerns to make sure that the European Community became something more than a simple market.

Delors could not have known that the project was located on sandy soil. A Cold War international setting had been stable from the Community's founding and Delors, like everyone else, assumed that this setting would persist. In "Western" Europe there were 12 EC members and a limited number of other, quite small, nation states, mostly members of the European Free Trade Association (EFTA) with the credentials to be EC members. To the East lay "existing socialism," appallingly inefficient and oppressive, to be sure, but cordoned off from the West and stabilized by Soviet power in what everyone assumed was a quasi-permanent way. In turn, Western Europe and the EC were protected from it by NATO and American power, likewise seemingly eternal.

The collapse of existing socialism after 1989 disrupted expectations in important ways. The EC had just pushed its accelerator to the floor, "1992" and the Russian doll proposals were using up most available energy. Applying the brakes – easing off the Delors proposals in order to confront new international problems – could well undermine EC efforts to strengthen itself internally and "deepen." On the other hand, should the EC be unable to give sufficient consideration to new international problems EC success at self-strengthening could become sadly irrelevant. Dramatic changes in the EC's back yard introduced political complexities that, in turn, could create new risks for the very delicate political equations upon which Delors's strategy was premised. Enough major proposals for change were already on the table in 1989 to saturate the EC's political agenda and exhaust the Commission and its resources. Intergovernmental conflicts about every one of the Russian doll priorities were intense, and many of these conflicts also crossed the Commission itself. Allies might be available for many, if not most, of the specific pieces of the strategy, but there was no chorus of approval for the strategy as a whole. Coalitions had to be built with care and with a constant eye to the future. Precipitating a front of opposition which might bring everything to a halt was a constant danger. With the coming of new international problems, there was danger that the EC might sink under a load of too many priorities, there was great danger of institutional and political overload.

Jacques Delors acknowledged the changing situation as early as his January 1989 speech to the European Parliament.[98] The Community needed to be reconstructed, he underlined, but this task would henceforth have to proceed in an uncertain context. Europe needed to be redesigned, including those areas of Western Europe which did not belong to the EC and the Europe beyond the Elbe which had earlier been beyond the EC's purview.[99] The best approach, Delors later advised, would be to build a "European Village" around the Community "house." For the Community to be able to sustain its place at the village's center, however, the first order of business was for the EC to "deepen and endow itself with the means of its ambitions."[100]

To Delors, priorities were clear. What had been initiated in 1985 had to be continued and completed. It was also imperative to respond to international change, however. The Commission's 1989 proposal to the EFTA countries for a European Economic Area (EEA) provided one approximation of what the EC's response might be. EFTA, founded at the same time as the EC, was a simple free-trade zone which deliberately rejected both common policies and supranationality.[101] The success of the "1992" program forced EFTA members to seek some alignment with the Single Market, despite philosophical differences with the Community.[102] The EC, given its size, strength, and prestige, was in a position to dictate conditions. The EEA was thus conceived as an antechamber to keep EFTA countries, suspected of an excess of devotion to free-trade zones and insufficient zeal for integration, from applying for EC membership.[103]

Coping with the travails of the ex-socialist countries of Central and Eastern Europe (CEECs) was the most troubling new problem for the EC. The EC began its new Eastern relationships with a coup. Following skillful maneuvering by Delors and Pascal Lamy at the top, the Community was given responsibility for coordinating G-24 (the OECD countries) and Community aid to Poland and Hungary at the July 14, 1989 Paris G7 Summit, a task later expanded to include the rest of the CEECs.[104] The Community then elaborated its PHARE program – Poland and Hungary: Assistance for Restructuring Economies.[105] The Community quickly negotiated its own cooperation agreements with these countries and, in addition, played a central role in the founding in 1990 of the European Bank for Reconstruction and Development to channel private investment funds and additional technical help to Eastern Europe.[106]

The issue posed by German unification, which Delors saw coming long before the fall of the Berlin Wall, was not "Eastern Europe" but the place of Germany in the Community.[107] This led him to take what will almost certainly be seen, in retrospect, as his single most important step of the post-1989 period. He took the lead in welcoming German unification. British Prime Minister Thatcher and French President François Mitterrand were both much more cautious, and Delors had to use his full powers of persuasion. In his annual program speech to the European Parliament in January 1990 Delors, citing precedents in the German Basic Law and the Treaty of Rome, announced that East Germany was "a special case . . . There is a place for East Germany in the Community should it so wish." In the complicated negotiations inside the Council that followed several Foreign Ministers opposed Delors's "special case" position, asserting that East Germany should fulfill the conditions for joining the Community like any other membership candidate. The next step was to prepare the way for what would become the "five new *Länder*" to be integrated immediately into the EC. Hard work by Helmut Kohl and Delors plus the results of the East German elections in March 1990 allowed the Delors line to win over considerable opposition.

When the five new *Länder* became part of the Federal Republic later in the year they were also integrated into the EC.[108] Under Delors's leadership Commission staff had by then worked out a package of EC policies to help this integration. Most of the *acquis communautaire* could be applied immediately. The main areas where special help and arrangements were needed were in trade with COMECON countries, agriculture, and the environment. When COMECON collapsed the first problem became less important. The agricultural situation was more complicated, given the CAP. The former East Germany received special quotas until the end of 1992 to help change its agricultural structures, despite the fact that EC farmers were unhappy about it. The environmental situation in the former East Germany, which turned out to be catastrophic, meant that the five new *Länder* were granted derogations from EC environmental requirements for five years. The huge task of legislating all of this towards the end of 1990 became one of Delors's most important priorities.

The wisdom of Delors's course on Germany seemed self-evident. A Germany anchored at the center of the EC was the *sine qua non* of the Community's future. And it was essential for the development of the EC to enhance the commitment of the Federal Republic, rapidly becoming the EC's dominant member, to the Community's future.[109] The Community's destiny and the future of Europe more generally would have been bleak indeed if the Federal Republic were to become a free, newly nationalist, political electron. Quite as important, Chancellor Kohl's gratitude for the Commission's help in the painless entry of the new *Länder* into the EC would be political cash in the bank.[110] That German unification would be hugely costly, in large part because of hasty and inadequate conceptualization by the Germans themselves, took nothing away from Delors's audacity.

All these initiatives were meant to be congruent with Delors's strategy. Because of the end of the Cold War opportunities existed for Europe to occupy new international political space. It might be possible to parlay these various new Western/Eastern Europe dealings into an enhancement of the Community's foreign policy capabilities.[111] The EC's external trade and aid prerogatives provided bits and pieces of foreign policy, although primarily economic. European Political Cooperation was the closest Europe came to common foreign policy in other areas, but it was completely intergovernmental.[112] The G-24 task thus presented a *de facto* foreign policy role which allowed the Commission to agitate for *de jure* changes towards a genuine common foreign policy. Here the Commission was being eagerly prodded forward by the French and the Germans, each for their own reasons, leading to a decision at the Dublin European Council in June 1990 to call a second treaty-changing IGC on "political union" alongside the EMU conference, with political union to include foreign policy.[113] Key EC member states usually held important foreign policy matters to be the very core of national sovereignty. Thus any hopes by Delors and his member state allies that the EC might acquire substantial new prerogatives in this area were very optimistic. Even before this became clear, however, there was considerable danger that the Community's table had been overloaded with too many priorities.

2

Inside the Berlaymont

**A Lexicon of Descriptions of the Cabinet of
Commission President Delors**

"Can't imagine what Delors would be without his Cabinet." (David Williamson, General Secretary of the Commission)

"a gang"/"commandos" (several times, even from inside the cabinet itself)

"practitioners of Rottweiler politics" (a member of a British cabinet)

"always two or three lengths ahead of everybody else" (another *Chef de Cabinet*)

"kneecappers"(an experienced Commission official)

"they have a will to control everything" (another *Chef*)

"Napoleonists, becoming Bonapartists" (Commission official)

The Delors strategy began in the mind of Jacques Delors, but its success also depended on the successful mobilization of the resources of the European Commission. The Commission's administrative "services" – the General-Directorates and other administrative units – despite their reputation as a massive and powerful juggernaut, are quite compact. Its members are by and large a talented group, well trained intellectually and recruited from the EC's member states through a stiff competitive examination process.

Despite the Tower of Babel possibilities of an administration attracted from the four corners of Europe, Commission activities had become remarkably coherent by the early 1990s. Nonetheless the small size, relative fragmentation of departments and nationalities, and the checkered history of the Community itself meant that there had been few guarantees in 1985 that the Commission's apparatus would perform to the high levels of dedication, energy, and productivity that Delors's strategy demanded. His own presence and power were the key to this change, but his secret instrument was his cabinet.

January 1991

The Berlaymont in 1991 was a gigantic monument to 1960s post-Bauhaus modernism and a certain epoque in the European Community's life, the right place for an EC which, until very recently, had been unsure what it was and wanted to be. The building had never worked. People who had spent their entire careers in it still had trouble finding their way around. Its elevators were slow, it had long, dark, and gloomy corridors covered with artificial-looking but real wood panels, its windows couldn't be opened, and the air conditioning made people dizzy. The top floor, number 13, was better maintained and airier, and one could see almost the whole of Brussels from its windows. The European Commission lived and met on the thirteenth floor. And there, every Thursday in the Commission's small dining room, the cabinet of Jacques Delors met for lunch, usually smoked salmon and other fish, salad, and fruit, washed down with a middling Bordeaux.[1] Then coffee, cigars and cigarettes.

The first of many cabinet lunches I attended was in January 1991, on the second day of the Gulf War. People straggled in from their various meetings until eventually there was a full house (minus Delors himself, who rarely attended). Things began, as they always did, when Pascal Lamy, the *Chef de Cabinet*, started talking. In his mid-40s, balding, slim, and athletic, Pascal doled out his political shrewdness with verbal parsimony, precision, and an irony variously humorous or simply sharp. The moment made it inevitable that the first subject would be the War.[2] "Insider" information from corridor gossip and diplomatic cyphers machine-gunned around the table.

Pascal then asked me to introduce myself and I did, rather timidly. My introduction turned out to be the first part of my field work. Some cabinet members were skeptical and, I suspect, a little fearful of an outsider breaking into their privacy. As I had the blessing of Delors and Lamy, they may have thought that I had to be up to more than I admitted. Moreover, they were busy with more tasks than they could possibly handle and wary of having to pay attention to a curious intellectual tourist in their midst. François Lamoureux, Pascal's Number 2, was especially agitated. He, for one, did not want to be the object of anthropological investigation. "I don't like to think about being watched like an ant at work," he said. This reaction frightened me a little, because François was a key figure, but it pointed to something more important. No one, including François, had been consulted or even informed beforehand about my arrival, despite the fact that the arrangements had been in the works between Pascal and myself for the better part of a year. Nothing could have better illustrated the total authority of Pascal Lamy and this, it turned out, was a fundamental insight into how things worked in the Berlaymont.

The discussion of my role was thankfully brief. There was a more important task on the agenda. Over lunch the previous week Delors had announced that the time had come to begin thinking about another item on the "after 1992" strategic agenda. After the two intergovernmental conferences (IGCs) which had just opened (on Economic and Monetary Union and on Political Union), it would be necessary to present a new budgetary package for the first post-1992 years. In Delorist terms the team had to prepare for a new "*grand rendez-vous.*" It was an in-house orthodoxy that the original *paquet Delors* of 1987–8 had been quite as important as the Single Market program itself in getting the Community going again, involving, as it had, substantial new commitment to Europe where it would be felt – in the pocket. The second Delors package was likely to be quite as important.

Delors's announcement of the need to get things going on it was typical of the way in which new strategic initiatives were begun. The President had the basic idea and had mentally worked through outlines and timing. This done, the cabinet was charged with working out the essential details. Thus Pascal had asked Jean-Charles Leygues, reponsible for budgetary issues, to prepare initial thoughts for this week's lunch. Jean-Charles had more questions than answers at this point. The first Delors package had given the Community space to grow during the implementation of the 1992 program, specifically by buying a degree of annual budgetary peace. What would be appropriate for the second package was less evident, however, in part because of uncertainty about what would come out of Maastricht. Demands on Community resources for international expenditures had begun to change in 1989–90, in part because of a vast expansion in aid for Eastern Europe. How much would this amount to in the five years after 1992? What would it do to the Community's more traditional aid needs for the South? Next, expanded commitment to "social and economic cohesion" had been an important Delorist innovation, laying a strong foundation for intra-EC solidarity. A new package would have to reinforce cohesion, but how much growth could one count on? The major budgetary item for the Community was the Common Agricultural Policy. Here again, however, reform proposals in the works could change the picture. How much could the Community raise its claims for revenue under various "own resource" categories (the revenues which it was specifally allocated such as percentage of VAT, percentage of GNP), before member states became upset? And what kinds of revenue-raising innovations would give the Community more budgetary autonomy, a key Delorist objective? Jean-Charles provided a good, if abstract, picture of the situation, but not much of a precise guide. Everything would depend upon how successfully the "after-1992" agenda emerged from the two IGCs that had just begun. Vast uncertainties existed, then, but Delors had ordered last week that a new "package" had to be designed – and so it would be.

The smoked salmon had been consumed along with just enough Bordeaux to stimulate the palate without cutting into the afternoon's productivity. Pascal lit up his Cuban Monte-Christo cigar, one of the perks of office. There were only two cigars on the table, the other for Jean-Luc Demarty, the cabinet's agriculture specialist.[3] Everyone else who indulged did so with a cigarette. As the room filled with smoke, it was time for the last ritual of the lunch, a review of Delors's schedule for the next few weeks. Delors travelled a lot and Pascal always required the particular cabinet member in the policy area addressed by a presidential trip to do the preparatory work. This was a way of sharing out the President's company and stimulating specific policy linkages between Delors and his team. As Pascal went down the list, day by day, those who were responsible checked in and added information where necessary. In fact, these days there was not much to talk about. Delors, along with much of the cabinet and other Commission members, would go to Strasbourg the next week for the monthly European Parliament plenary session, for debate on the Gulf War and for Delors's annual program speech.[4] Otherwise, the President had a light schedule. He had decided that it would be wise to lie low during the Gulf War.

Meeting the "gang"

Who were the members of the cabinet? What did they do? How did they talk about their work? Trying to pin them all down for initial conversations underlined how incredibly busy they were. Everyone was constantly tied down in meetings during "normal" working hours, coordinating, organizing, networking, and presiding. With few exceptions, my interviews started after 7:30 in the evening. The period from 7:30 until time to go home, which was almost always later than nine o'clock, was a precious moment for the cabinet. This was when they could consult among themselves, touch bases with Pascal and François, catch up on evolving "dossiers," and do the writing which was a central part of their work.[5] There may have been a few overpaid and underworked Eurocrats at the Berlaymont, but they included none of the people I observed. At top levels of the European Commission people did little else in life except work from early morning until late evening. Delors, who worked all the time at a frightening pace, demanded that everyone around him – and his cabinet most of all – should do the same. Moreover, he judged his colleagues not only on the number of hours put in, but on the quality of their "product."

The Delors cabinet – like most top Commission staffs – was overwhelmingly male. There was only one woman when I arrived, and another joined later.[6] Members ranged from mid-30s to mid-40s in age; cabinet service was a young person's game. It was three-quarters French, with one German, one Dutchman, and an Englishman, and carried on its internal business in French.[7] Despite public rumors, the cabinet was not a colony of *énarques* – elite French civil servants.[8] With certain exceptions, the others, including those who were French, had been Commission civil servants recruited by Pascal because of their mastery of "the house." The career ambitions of cabinet members matched the need among commissioners for people who knew the ropes and were willing to work that little bit harder to get the job done. Successful performance in a cabinet usually meant rapid promotion on the Commission's career ladder. Moreover, cabinet service was the central way in which up-and-coming younger Eurocrats got to know one another "transversally" beyond the administrative services where their careers began. The Delors staff was a mixture of two generations. A minority, including Pascal and François, had been around from the very beginning in 1985. In 1988, after the hard days of the Single European Act and the *paquet Delors*, there had been a major turnover, when most of the others had joined. Beyond the fact that being a presidential cabinet member led to quick exhaustion, 1988 had brought the beginning of a shift in strategy to an "after 1992" focus, precisely when the public itself was just coming to understand "1992."

I resolved to interview everyone I could as quickly as possible during these first days. As luck had it, François Lamoureux was first. François, a *Bordelais*, as the magnificent framed poster of Bordeaux's baroque *quais* behind his desk announced, was a lawyer in his mid-40s who had taught at the University of Metz before moving into the Legal Services of the Commission in 1978. He was also an experienced socialist politician who had served for a while as assistant mayor of a suburban Parisian town.[9] A member of the cabinet since 1985, François had a rare mix of gifts: crack legal skills, a solid political sense, and energetically pugnacious devotion to the Delors cause. He had been a central player in hammering out the Single European Act. He assigned me to read the bulk of Delors's speeches after 1985. If I wanted a short cut into what the cabinet had done over the years, this was the best way, he claimed. I found this puzzling. For most complex political operations reading a collection of speeches would provide a very misleading guide to events. I did what I was told, nonetheless, even though it took a week of very late nights. François was right. Delors's strategic ideas and announcements, along with cogent and persuasive arguments to support them, were all there.[10]

"Our first task is to free up time for the President," François announced. "The President is an intellectual who needs lots of time to read and think," plus constant written nourishment through memos and reflection pieces. Thus a full year before the formal proposals for the Delors's second budget package would be needed, Delors had clear ideas about what he wanted. But he needed the cabinet to flesh things out, work out the technicalities and give the suggestions that would refine the line. To do as much of the hard policy development work as it could, the cabinet would also have to dig down into the Commission's administrative services, mobilizing the experts and coaxing them towards the product Delors wanted. They would also have to work on conceptualizing the product, however, sending Delors think-pieces to stimulate his own larger reflections.

According to François, the cabinet also deflected conflict. "The President doesn't like conflict." François was himself one of the cabinet's more prominent "conflict takers," in part because he relished it and because he was often in a position where conflict was likely. He "followed" the two IGCs, more specifically the Political Union negotiations. On his desk were piles of typed documents, full of scratched-out paragraphs, which were the beginnings of Commission submissions to the Conference on Political Union. François's main job then was to generate these documents. He was also in charge of coaxing the hundreds of pieces of the Single Market program out of the administrative services and through the Commission. Finally, he kept a particularly watchful eye on the "competition policy" area, particularly on Community regulation of mergers and acquisitions, an area fraught with disagreement. As assistant chief, he also stood in for Pascal when necessary at weekly *Chefs de Cabinet* meetings and in forming the Commission agenda.

Joly Dixon, Delors's right-hand man on EMU, was next. Pictures of his children covered the walls of his office. Both Joly and his wife, a member of the cabinet of Ray MacSharry, the Agricultural Commissioner, worked brutal hours and, he reported, the pictures were there to remind him that his family existed. Joly looked the part of the sole Briton in the cabinet, tall and slim with reddish blond hair, inclined to tweeds and sweaters. A no-nonsense economist from the Midlands with a decidedly social democratic indignation, Joly had been an academic before joining the EC civil service in 1975. He then went on to serve in the EC delegation in Washington before joining the Delors cabinet in 1987. The choice (Pascal's) was a good one. Joly could function creatively in the rarefied world of international money managers, central bank governors, and finance ministers from which EMU had to be teased. He also acquired a few other important areas of cabinet responsibility beyond EMU, including oversight of the European Investment Bank and Eurostat, plus involvement on the money side of various aids to Eastern Europe. When we first met he was thinking about how to get aid effectively to the USSR.

Joly existed a little separately from the rest of the cabinet. His official title was "advisor" to Delors, indicating greater career distinction and higher pay than a simple cabinet member. And as the only cabinet Anglophone he was separate for another obvious reason. In our first discussion he confessed to feeling often as the "token," an outsider in a thoroughly French setting. His functions were technical and self-contained, and this set him apart as well. EMU was something of a parallel circuit; as this was Delors's most cherished after-1992 project, Delors was personally involved every step of the way. This placed Joly in a more direct relationship with the President than most of his cabinet colleagues. Joly thus had a clear sense of where strategic leadership came from – "the President is the source of everything, the creator of our lines."[11]

Lodewijk Briet, a Dutch lawyer, was in charge of competition policy, a central, if underpublicized, dimension of the Single Market program. The Treaty of Rome had given the Commission power over a range of legal matters pertaining to anti-competitive practices – various antitrust issues and state aids to industry used as unfair subsidies – to which new powers over mergers and acquisitions had been added in 1989. Since 1985 the area had come alive, with ever more vigorous enforcement of the rules and rapid accretion of jurisprudence tied to the dismantling of private-sector monopolies and government policies to give national industries a head start. Lodewijk had been recruited to the cabinet in 1988 out of DG III, the Internal Market administration, where he had worked on intellectual property law. He had earlier worked in the Frans Andriessen cabinet when Andriessen had run agriculture and also spent time in Washington DC, where he had polished his elegant English and developed a love for North America.

Literally hundreds of new cases in gigantic file folders piled up on Lodewijk's desk every week, mostly routine. A few contained potential legal problems and, more importantly, some others threatened the interests of member state governments. It was Lodewijk's job to help make sure that the Commission avoided legal problems and took care not to stir up undue conflict with member states. Lodewijk, before we had talked about anything substantive, announced that he would be leaving in a couple of months. In a tone of passion and anger, he averred, "the job is impossible, George. I have 5,000 infringement cases to deal with," pointing to the piles of paper on the table, "and I have to master them all, because I preside over the special chefs every two weeks. I go from eight in the morning until nine at night, and I don't get any weekends either. There has been a huge increase in the quantity of work. We have got too much to do." He felt unsupervised as well. "The worst thing is that there is no coordination at all, we never get together, and there is precious little bilateral contact either, until there's a problem . . . We're supposed to understand the President's thought and strategy on our own, but this isn't always easy . . . I very rarely ever even *see* the President."

Lodewijk was uneasy. He had had some problems with Pascal and François over positions to take on important cases of state aids to industry – French cases in particular (over large fines to Renault and Pechiney, among others). Commission competition policy was part jurisprudence and part political realism. The Commissioner in charge of Competition Law, Sir Leon Brittan, was a convinced neo-liberal with a strong staff of ideologically motivated and talented assistants who were attempting to push Commission competition policy competence as far and fast as they could. Other Commissioners and their staffs, including the Delors team, had to try to protect their "national interests" (represent the positions of the member states of their origin) against Brittan's efforts. Jobs and political positions were at stake in such matters. Conflict over competition policy was endemic and Lodewijk was not particularly well placed to deal with it. More of a liberal free-trader than anyone else in the Delors operation, he was more sensitive to the arguments of Brittan's staff. And he was not French, which made him less comfortable in the cabinet in general and less sensitive to the complicated problems which France might have in the new liberal climate. Lodewijk was frank with me about his feelings. "We're supposed to win, and we usually do. Part of this is because we're better than most of the other cabinets . . . But we're supposed to be tougher than the others, too. This means we have to fight *all* the time. I find it hard to fight all the time."

Patrick Venturini was formerly an important researcher for the French trade union in which Delors himself had been active.[12] Patrick handled social policy for Delors and also had to cover education, culture, and audiovisual policy (about which he had known nothing when he started). He had originally come to Brussels to join the Commission's internal think-tank, to work on what subsequently became the Social Charter.[13] In 1987 he was brought into the cabinet to draft the final Social Charter document for the Madrid Summit of 1989. After this Patrick had been a strong advocate, initially against Delors's inclinations, for an action program of legislation to give some legal teeth to the Charter. The action program involved nearly 50 pieces of Community legislation, which meant that Patrick was quite busy. The business was trying as well, since most of his proposals ended up stuck on the Council table because the British prevented passage (most social policy matters had to be passed by unanimity). Social policy, like EMU, was both very close to the President's heart and an important part of the after-1992 agenda, which meant that Patrick had reasonably frequent access to Delors. He also produced regular "information notes" for Pascal, to communicate the substance of developing policy dossiers and their stage of preparation. Here, Patrick commented, there was real space for personal initiative. If he thought that Delors should know about something, or simply thought that he might be interested, then he felt encouraged to engage in commentary and reflection.

Patrick, the father of two – soon to be three – young children, was discomfited by the "jailhouse" side of cabinet work. As he put it, "this is a very lonely job." Partly to humanize his surroundings he liked to have fresh cut flowers on the table in his office. Patrick suffered from an absence of general information and felt somewhat isolated. There was a first tier of cabinet members who had portfolios of breadth and, in consequence, were involved with a sufficiently large range of networks to give them a very great "horizontal" vision of what the Commission was doing, but Patrick was in a second tier with a specific "turf" and much narrower vision. Pascal did not believe in extra meetings to ensure circulation of synthesis and analysis through the team because he thought it took time away from more important things and might encourage grousing and, in any event, Pascal's greatest gift was synthesis and analysis, which he could do for the group better than it would ever be able to do for itself.

What did Patrick do? First of all, he oversaw the "cooking" of policy, tracking policy papers every step of the way through the administrative services. This meant, to begin with, shaping their production as early as possible and "animating" the necessary exchanges and discussions. To do this Patrick had built and cultivated multiple networks inside the Berlaymont. Connected with this, he said, he also "stopped balls before they get close to the goal," reflecting the interest in sports he shared with Delors. Nothing which did not meet his political, intellectual, and literary standards was to be allowed to get through the layers of Commission deliberation. Patrick's description indicated what very quickly became clear from observation. In many circumstances the Delors cabinet played the central role in producing policy papers and proposals, sometimes down to the activities of detailed drafting and wording. Patrick saw this as his crusade. This was in large part because General Directorate V, the social policy directorate, was notoriously ineffective. Moreover, it "had been a union lobbying organization, old style. It's taken quite a while to get them to understand that the world has changed and to get them to do work which is up to our new standards. Now we're almost there, and I'm pleased."

Jean-Luc Demarty, the cabinet specialist for agriculture, was heavily involved in very complicated tractations with the Commission. Delors was pushing for a major reform of the CAP. Jean-Luc was thus perspiring over the last stages of preparation for an important Commission seminar on the Sunday after we met. Demarty was another member of the second "wave" of the cabinet, imported from the agricultural forecasting unit of the French Ministry of Finance to undertake CAP reform. He was also responsible for transport, energy, and fishing. Demarty spent a great deal of his time giving me lectures on the intricacies of the CAP, which I needed desperately; I suspect that he did this a lot, even to Commission insiders. For decades the CAP had been the EC's main supranational substantive policy area. Its annual pricing round regularly brought groups of farmers to dump loads of potatoes in front of the Berlaymont. Nonetheless agricultural policy was both full of arcane subtleties and a policy ghetto. By far the largest single group of EC civil servants was involved in it, but everyone else tolerated it in order to do more interesting things. François, for example, reacting to my confession of interest in CAP reform, let loose a stream of cutting remarks about out-of-touch carrot-counters and milk-mountain climbers. "Pascal and I are modern," he said, "and agriculture is the past."

However much agriculture may have been "the past," putting together reform proposals was an essential matter, tied to fundamental budgetary issues and international trade, and had been underway for more than a year. Jean-Luc implied that the Commissioner for Agriculture, Ray MacSharry, another figure with whom Delors did not get along too well, had not been very helpful.[14] The bulk of the hard work had been done, at the behest of Delors and Demarty, by the powerful Director General for Agriculture, Guy Legras, another French import known as a skilled negotiator. CAP reform was especially controversial and would have to be handled carefully. Once the farmers got wind of what was up there would be a fight. The CAP was a quasi-corporatist operation, farmers were well organized, and the agricultural vote was still critical in a number of member states. Jean-Luc thought that, at best, getting the whole program through would take a year. In the meantime the biggest part of his job would be explaining and selling the deal to farmers, particularly in France. The phone rang at the very moment when we were talking about this, so I could listen to Jean-Luc "selling his product" to none other than the president of the French farmers' union.

Jean-Luc was of the "lonely work" school of cabinet life. Like Patrick, he lived uneasily with hypercentralization through Pascal and the lack of "coordination." A former Leftist, he had memories of 1968, which allowed him to coin the best definition I would hear for the cabinet's form of organization: "*autogestion militaire*" (military self-management). The cabinet was completely centralized around Pascal, hence the military side. But Pascal expected his charges to make their own energetic and creative ways in their assigned areas, the self-management dimension. Jean-Luc concluded that, in his eyes, the most important gift needed was "physical resistance."

Jean-Charles Leygues was the most difficult cabinet member of all to contact, and the reasons for this were not mysterious. Jean-Charles had a huge policy portfolio, including budgets, personnel, industrial policy, regional policies, research and development, and a host of other central things. If Pascal coordinated the Commission's life in general ways and François organized things in large areas like the Single Market and the IGCs, Jean-Charles was the key day-to-day "fixer." He was indispensable for his far-flung networks and ability to untie the complex knots of EC administration. Some cabinet members felt somewhat claustrophobically slotted into narrow areas, but Jean-Charles was everywhere. Like François, he was a French provincial, as the exquisite satellite photograph of his native Périgord on the wall communicated. He had studied and taught for a while in Bordeaux before joining the EC civil service in 1971. From there he had been omnipresent in Brussels: at the Council Secretariat-General, the Commission Secretariat-General under the legendary Emile Noël, in the Pisani cabinet and, finally, in the Budget General Directorate, which he ended up practically running. He had joined the Delors team in 1987 to work out the practicalities of the *paquet Delors* and had been devouring jobs ever since.

Overcommitment had its price, I sensed. Jean-Charles's historical description of the first Delors package and summary of where things stood with the second was interrupted by phone calls every two minutes. Jean-Charles was simply too busy to discuss the inner life or the organization of the cabinet. Moreover, he pointedly wondered how anyone else could be any different, given all that needed to be done. He was curt. "Look, I know that we all work harder than anyone else, but there are good reasons for it. The President is not an easy person to work for, but he has historically important things to do. We have to produce so much and so fast in order to make these things happen. We have to be a length ahead of everyone else, to be better, know more, stay longer, fight harder, to make sure that Delors's strategy becomes reality. If any one lets down, then the whole thing could unravel." The speech had the rhetoric of the tough football coach. Jean-Charles was to be observed rather than talked to.

Jerome Vignon, the guiding spirit of the *cellule de prospective*, the Commission's internal think-tank, was "para-cabinet" Jerome was a graduate of the prestigious French École Polytechnique and a practicing Catholic. He spoke with a timbre and intonation so close to the President's that when you heard them in another room it was hard to know who was saying what. Jerome was an intellectual who always sought the deeper logic of shorter-term events. A member of the original cabinet until 1987, Jerome quickly became an essential source of ideas about the general nature of Delors's strategy. It was not difficult to understand why he had shifted out of the cabinet, however. It would have been be harder to find two people so temperamentally different as Jerome and Pascal. Jerome was gently contemplative, and idealistic, with an almost academic bent. Pascal was a tight coil of activism and realism – even if, deep down, there were very strong convictions.

Jerome's *cellule* was an experiment worth watching. Officially it was the long-range planning shop for the Commission as a whole, charged with exploring major trends like biotechnology and immigration. But it was also part of the Delors machine, a place where the Commission President could subcontract parts of his operation of intellectual exploration to people he trusted. This side of the *cellule* was clearly perceived and resented as such in a number of Commission quarters. Beyond explicit planning activities, Jerome also thought that the *cellule* should link the intellectual world with the Commission. One of Jerome's colleagues, the eminent Louvain economist Alexis Jacquemin, was thus putting together an economic policy seminar which would invite such luminaries as Michael Porter and Jeffrey Sachs to give talks in the Berlaymont, which would be widely attended. A big conference on "European identity" was also being planned for later in the spring with Jurgen Habermas, Charles Taylor and Jean-Marc Ferry, among others. Jerome believed that such high-level adult education would tempt the Eurocrats out of their offices and engage them in thinking about broader matters. Putting together these two realms – practical planning for policy purposes and outreach-linkage to the wider world of ideas – would not be easy, as Jerome knew.

Pascal's Team

It did not take much time in my first cabinet *tour de piste* to discover how central Pascal Lamy himself was. Everything seemed to be routed up to

Pascal just as French trains all went through Paris. Pascal then rationed what went on to Delors himself. If the cabinet was Delors's key team in helping the Commission to produce what Delors wanted, then Pascal was its star player and its coach. The Left Catholic son of a suburban Parisian pharmacist, Pascal "made brilliant studies" as the French would say, flying through Sciences Po into the École Normale d'Administration (ENA) – the place where France's elite civil servants hone commitment to public service and learn to analyze everything in ten minutes and two points. Elite France is a small world. At ENA he graduated second in a class with Martine Aubry, Delors's daughter. Delors himself was a professor at ENA during this time. Pascal also "did" HEC, France's elite business school, giving him more credentials and contacts plus a sharp sense of the private sector. After ENA Pascal put in his time in the provinces as an *inspecteur de finances* before being appointed to direct a French government agency to shape up and save firms moving towards bankruptcy.[15]

Along the way Pascal joined the Socialist Party, and when the Left came to power in France in 1981 people who combined his gifts and his politics were unusual. When he became second in command in the cabinet of the Minister of Economy and Finances, Pascal's symbiotic relationship with Jacques Delors began in earnest. Delors, with Pascal's help, was then central in moving the Left towards France's fundamental shift in economic policy in 1982–3. After 1983, Pascal became Number 2 in charge of economic matters in Prime Minister Pierre Mauroy's cabinet. Then when Delors was named Commission president in 1984, he recruited Pascal to run his staff. Lamy had other choices, but Delors's vision for Europe was too tempting to turn down.[16] Pascal and Delors were thus in it together from the very beginning. Even before his official arrival in Brussels in early 1985 Pascal had assisted Delors in planning which commissioners would do what and what line of attack to follow to relaunch Europe.

Pascal, who confessed to being a St Simonian, radiated the self-containment of someone who believes that superior effort and lucidity can engineer positive changes. His asceticism and discipline are extraordinary. After reviewing his appointment book I discovered that he was rarely in on Thursday mornings. His secretary told me that Pascal ran in the woods around Brussels every Thursday to clear his head and keep in shape. And then she recounted the legendary story of Pascal appearing at an important meeting half an hour after finishing, in reasonable time, the Brussels Marathon. The way he ate was another demonstration: carefully planned, nothing rich, nothing extravagant, everything designed to pack in the power.

Pascal was a very busy man and I learned not to corner him until I had a long list of serious things to talk about. For our first big conversation after my initial *tour de piste* he had his suit jacket off and was wearing a navy blue "Team 92" sweater.[17] He was relaxed, smiling, smoking a cigarette, with his feet, in black boots and argyle socks, propped on the table. His eyes gave away delight in the games of power. I asked him a few leading questions, mainly about the history of the cabinet, and chatted a bit about expanding my interviewing travels beyond the cabinet itself into the "house." I needed his permission and help to do this and he granted my request. He was concerned, however, to correct my first impressions about the degree of conflict in the Commission. The Commission was a college, he underlined, and consensus was the central to collegial decision-making. The ultimate purpose of the cabinet, however tough it had to act to achieve it, was to forge solid agreement. Pascal's subtext was not meant to be a small lesson in the EC's constitution, however. Like everything about Pascal, it was political. The Commission had a particular place in the Community, to propose new policies. But for Commission proposals to stand a chance they had to be built upon consensus, on the sharp focusing of its resources and ideas. The Commission, and particularly its administration, represented a formidable array of intellectual and political firepower, but without such focus the Commission would be unable to play its role fully in the broader EC institutional system. Pascal was amazingly cooperative and helpful, but in an interesting way. He gave me what I asked for and spoke frankly. But it was my job to work out what was going on. If I needed something, it was up to me to find out how to get it, including from him. He communicated more in fewer words than anyone I had ever met, so that in this meeting (and all our subsequent ones) my long agenda of subjects was used up in about half the time I had expected. His silences were quite as meaningful as his words. They provided hints about where to go. But conversations with Pascal were demanding. One had to be a sharp, informed, listener. It crossed my mind how difficult it would be to work for a man who expected so much of those around him. After we finished with this meeting, or, rather, when I had run out of issues to raise, we walked down the long thirteenth floor corridor to the elevator. Pascal Lamy also walked twice as fast as I did!

Building the cabinet: principles

Pascal had built the cabinet to fit Delors, the Commission, and himself, in that order, but with emphasis overwhelmingly on fitting Delors. In Pascal's words, "as far as I'm concerned, the important thing was to have put together a high performance tool crafted to fit Delors's hand. Delors is the key. The lock was designed to fit the key." François Lamoureux put things in another way. "On the one hand there is a 'Delors system,' a statesman with political intuition who works and imposes his political choices, sometimes penetrates into details and gives instructions. On the other there is a 'Lamy system' to feed the President with ideas, carry out his instructions and protect him."

The cabinet was structured fundamentally around Delors the intellectual, strategist, and politician. Delors's scenarios were the key to everything else, and behind them lay enormous personal investment. Delors constantly scanned his environment through voracious ingestion of dossiers, personal contacts, careful analysis of the press and public documents and, finally, an explicit search for pertinent "intellectual" materials which often led him into conceptual areas where one rarely found most politicians. Pascal carefully structured the cabinet to facilitate all these activities. While many, if not most, major politicians were "managers" working off the conclusions of meetings and staff consultations, Delors's approach was more private. He did enormous amounts of reading, reflecting, and synthesizing that demanded the liberation of great blocks of time and space. Thus the cabinet, and Pascal himself, quite consciously protected Delors from an inundation of paper and appointments. This role had become progressively more vital as the international importance of the Community increased, and Delors became a statesman preoccupied by international issues. In consequence, an important part of the task of making the Commission work properly fell upon Pascal and his cabinet team.

When François suggested reading Delors's collected speeches he had pointed me to the wellspring of cabinet life. The cabinet's action was conceptually structured by Delors's evolving thought, and its most complicated tasks were to derive practical policy solutions from a given general presidential "line" and develop the arguments necessary to implement them. The work of assimilating and "translating" presidential strategy into specific policy areas was paramount for every cabinet member. Each was also responsible for providing Delors with substantial thinkpieces ("notes to the file" and "notes to the President") which explored the contexts and practical applications of Delors's more general ideas. The cabinet also had limited but real strategic initiative itself. Sometimes the presidential line was quite general, leaving room for creative translation into policy proposals, for example. And at times the specific meaning of a general line might not be completely clear, perhaps because Delors himself was inching forward towards new ideas. At these points Delors could be sphinx-like in his ambiguity and particularly open to suggestions from the cabinet.

The cabinet's "protective" role had another dimension. Delors, Pascal said, is "an old trade unionist who believes that discussion, even tough discussion, which leads to deeply shared conclusions is what binds people and allows them to move forward together." Delors had the capacities to produce ideas to connect the present and the future. These ideas and Delors's own ability to persuade others to follow them were the point of departure. Inside the Commission, however, the cabinet often served as Delors's "hard discusser," a collective vanguard for assuming some portion of the harshest day-to-day political and policy struggle of the Commission. Delors was not a great devotee of in-fighting. Because the cabinet could be more hard-nosed in its approaches to promoting the strategy, he acquired a freer political hand to be more conciliatory when final bargains had to be struck. The President was well placed to strike such final bargains. He stood at the exact center of Europe's, and the Community's, political core of social democrats and Christian Democrats. In any immediate sense partisan alignments of commissioners were an unreliable predictor of Commission behaviors. Liberals disagreed with liberals and social democrats with social democrats. But there was an important distinction to be drawn between a continental Christian Democrat with liberal economic proclivities and an Anglo-Saxon liberal ideologue. Christian Democrats, however liberal, were more open to arguments about the need for collective goods and social services, for more "organized European space," in Delorist terms. Delors could thus speak a commonly shared vocabulary, an important asset that the cabinet could help ration and protect.

Delors's hard-won eminence in the European Council was another fundamental political strength in his Commission leadership which his cabinet could use. He had very quickly developed a special relationship with the European Council which, over time, led to a *de facto* change in the workings of EC institutions. European Council meetings were special events to map out future EC priorities. The negotiations, carefully prepared in advance, were organized such that only two delegates from each member state and the Commission could actually be present in the room.[18] This setting placed great weight on the skills of the leaders themselves. Jacques Delors was as able as the best among them, and it fell to him to introduce and structure the debates. As François noted, Delors had a "magic recipe" for presenting himself on Friday morning as the resident expert and emerging by Saturday noon as a stateman and sometimes the "savior of the meeting." The European Council and its members came to depend upon him, in a way which granted him great power in its outcomes. From the point of view of the rest of the Commission this new, hard-earned, role made Delors the spokesperson for the EC's ultimate mandating institution, a decisive internal advantage. Delors's cabinet also acquired important power from this in its internal Commission dealings. It was itself implicated in the preparation and exercise of the President's European Council role and thus acquired an "inside line" to the desires and pulse of EC summits which was an important intellectual and political advantage "in house."

Managing other commissioners and the Commission administration was the second major concern in Pascal's cabinet design. European commissioners are appointed by their national governments according to standards which may not always have the effective and energetic functioning of the Commission at heart. Commissioners thus may be highly competent, industrious, and experienced, but this is not always the case. And they may be more or less gifted for "collegial" processes. Cabinet staffs were likely to reflect the adequacy of a commissioner's own fit with his job with some were more focused and hard-working than others.[19] In brief, there was great variability in ability and energy at the top of the European Commission. The success of Delors's strategic endeavors depended upon the coherence and quality of the Commission's production. Delors's own pre-eminence and capacities for persuasion were, as always, the central factor in

producing these things. But the President's cabinet was the major compensatory mechanism for generating high quality work when presidential
leadership was not quite enough.

The Delors cabinet became, in addition, an all-purpose agent for generating administrative performance. The Commission's administration was
very good. But like all administrations it was prone to self-protective conser-
vatism, jurisdictional feudalization, and inadequate comprehension of the
importance of political priorities. Moreover, the White Paper, Single European Act, *paquet Delors* and myriad other changes had produced an ava-
lanche of new responsibilities. Administrative habits ordinarily change less
rapidly than politically determined priorities and goals, and this disparity of
rates of change can be costly to strategy, whether through the workings of
inertia or through active resistance. Moreover, shifting priorities had sometimes made earlier administrative divisions of labor obsolete. Delors's cabinet was often called upon to create linkages between services which might
have occurred automatically in a more stable situation, for example. Finally,
there were more occasions than anyone wanted to admit where an administrative unit simply did not work well (there were a few entire DGs like
this). Where this was the case the President's cabinet had to intervene to
help do the actual work.

Pascal's own strengths and style constituted the third structuring principle. Pascal was, of course, constantly available to Delors. He was also the
central conduit from the Commission and its administration to the President. This meant gathering in and synthesizing huge amounts of material
– paper, conversations, ideas for Delors's consideration. The demands on
Delors's time plus his intellectual capacities meant that these syntheses had
to be completely focused and concise, yet subtle and elaborate. Delors's
reliance upon Pascal to communicate what was essential in a timely way was
huge. Not surprisingly, watching Pascal do anything, such as working
through a dossier, was to observe a rare model of efficiency, concentration,
and economy of gesture. Listening to or reading his subsequent reactions
was even more impressive.

Still, it took time for Pascal to do his jobs of feeding Delors with the
information and analysis he needed and systematically "double-checking"
and supervising all the dossiers concerning the Commission and Community. And while doing these things he had also to intervene in policy
progress as needed, calling in various high administrative figures for brainstorming and coordination, and be accessible to individual cabinet members, which he was, fastidiously. It was a matter of principle and good
administration for Pascal to be as available instantaneously to Delors and to
his cabinet colleagues as they were to him. Dossiers, papers, notes, and
documents submitted to Pascal were rerouted, turned around, and commented upon with lightning speed and efficiency.[20] The telephone and
intercom (the "bigaphone" in cabinet parlance) were central tools in this
quasi-instantaneous accessibility and responsiveness. Pascal was constantly
telephoning his colleagues, day and night, either to prod them or to

respond to their queries and calls. François Lamoureux commented that Pascal "would pursue me to the ends of the earth by telephone, but I could always get to him as well, whatever the difference in time, and he never complained."[21]

Pascal also had to be able to take sufficient distance from daily matters to anticipate the development of strategically essential dossiers by the cabinet and services. This often meant alerting staff: commissioning "think work" by Jerome and his *cellule de prospective*; calling "transversal" *ad hoc* task force meetings with high administrative figures to scout out future policy territory; and, more generally, assigning tasks and stimulating activity on issues often long before they were made public.

Pascal was "operational" as well as a manager and strategist. Together with the Commission Secretary-General David Williamson (who reported to Delors via Pascal, which gave Pascal some control over his actions) he planned the Commission's program, from its annual program to the specific agendas for the Commission's weekly meetings.[22] At the weekly meeting of *Chefs de Cabinet*, the final policy development filter before the Commission itself, he also played a central role. By *Chefs de Cabinet* his team members had already done their best, prior to and during the various "special chefs" processes, to generate quality policy and a consensus conforming to presidential strategy. But at the weekly meeting Pascal stood as the last barrier to inadequately executed and/or politically disagreeable work before it was passed upwards to the Commission.[23] Here he really was the ultimate gatekeeper, prepared to deflect matters in graceful ways or, if this was not possible, to fight hard. Even when he was not intervening decisively in the proceedings or crossing the room to phone, simply observing him sitting portentously next to Williamson was enough to demonstrate his power. Others around the table either awaited his cues or more rarely prepared, reluctantly, to do battle with him. From Delors's point of view, the success of this gatekeeper work was primordially important. The Commission was a difficult place to manage conflict when it did occur. Any political resources which Pascal and his team could save by the prior resolution of potential conflict were useful for other purposes.

Pascal's operational reach stretched well beyond the Commission room. Over the years, Delors, with Pascal's advice, had very carefully replaced a considerable number of high Commission officials, directors general and division heads, in critical areas. Needless to say, the criteria of choice had been competence plus agreement with the Delorist strategy. These people had power bases and ideas of their own, of course, but they were also indebted to Delors and Pascal and this made them particularly amenable to Pascal's concerns. Delors and Pascal were concerned, of course, with being able to get their way when they really needed to, but quite as much with having key people they could trust, and in whose abilities they had confidence, to call together for strategic discussions and idea production.[24]

Beyond the Berlaymont, Pascal's official charge as the President's "sherpa" for G7 meetings (the annual conclave of the leaders of the seven most industrialized societies plus the EC Commission president) and his informal position as Delors's collaborator placed him in front-line diplomatic networks. For example, when, during spring 1991, the Americans went on a minor rampage against Commission proposals for a common foreign and security policy, Pascal packed his bag and slipped off to Washington to explore matters with his friends "at State." And his contacts and friendships with leading figures around François Mitterrand (Elisabeth Guigou and others) and Helmut Kohl (Joachim Bitterlich) were constantly in play in fine-tuning the Franco-German "couple" to the melodies that the Commission hoped to play. Pascal's experience in such activities also made his reflections on the international ambition of the Community essential. Defining this ambition had been *the* intellectual and policy task of the Delors presidency at least since 1989.[25]

The French comparative advantage: Matignon and militantisme

Pascal needed lots of personal space to oversee the flow of Commission business and to perform his operational tasks. The strongly hierarchical cabinet structure which he had created responded to this need. Authority and directive power rested firmly and decisively in his own hands. Cabinet members had direct access to Delors when he dealt with their specialty areas, depending upon his priorities of the moment. But in ordinary circumstances they all reported individually to Pascal, who filtered, organized, and criticized, at times quite severely, what came at him, passing what was needed on to Delors. Moreover, the system was accompanied by an almost total lack of explicit collective coordination. Simultaneously, and paradoxically, cabinet members had a large degree of operational autonomy. In between Pascal and this individual autonomy there were no general, formally organized, intermediary levels beyond the weekly lunch. And given the total absorption of Cabinet members in their work, there was little informal socializing.[26] Cabinet members encountered and communicated with one another "horizontally" in task-oriented meetings, around targeted problems and policy areas, and through Pascal.

Despite the Pascal-imposed hierarchy of organization, the cabinet was not a classic "staff and line" organization. Each cabinet member had a different portfolio, in all cases larger than any individual could possibly handle. Pascal believed that small size and overload were important virtues which kept people striving and stretching. But there was a rough division and internal ranking between more generalist and "horizontal" portfolios and those which involved detailed policy oversight in specific areas. Pascal was the only general, but the cabinet had colonels with broad field responsibilities and lieutenants with more specific tasks. The Commission and its services were not particularly good at collaborating across different sectors in policy development and responding to urgent demands. In response, Jean-Charles Leygues's portfolio stood out for its horizontal breadth and

François was heavily "transversal" as well. Jean-Charles, François, and Pascal were all specialists in teasing strategically desirable policy products out of administrative and political complexity, inertia, and querulousness. Joly Dixon, sitting atop the EMU tree, and Bernhard Zepter, Delors's foreign policy advisor, had their own important bailiwicks with considerable "horizontal" purview (in Zepter's case, perhaps a little too much, given the complicated and not overly efficient ways in which foreign policy matters were administratively divided up in the Commission).[27] The lieutenants tended to be relatively more specialized in in-depth technical knowledge in narrower areas: agriculture, competition law, social affairs, the environment, and relations with the Parliament, among others. For lieutenants, where frequent participation in the cabinet's flexible system of functional area groups was somewhat less likely, the possibility of relative isolation increased. Bruno Dethomas, Delors's press secretary, observed that "this sort of arrangement can weigh rather heavily on some of my colleagues, I think, since they're all on their own a lot of the time."

Being "all on their own" was part of the design. Pascal had little use for modern "human resources" or "group" mechanisms of coordination and solidarity maintenance for his cabinet. One of the leaders of Martin Bangemann's cabinet, well versed in the latest in business-school jargon, averred that "there are two German cabinets in the building. One of them is Prussian, and it isn't ours."[28] Indeed, in the abstract, such a system of "*autogestion militaire*" could have had problems of insufficient communication and information flow. Bruno Dethomas, completely in awe of Pascal, wondered nonetheless whether this extreme "verticality may block our vision of things, our ability to see the whole picture as clearly as we should." Pascal, however, had built-in strategies for avoiding such dangers. The unfolding presidential strategy served as *the* anchoring point, an evolving text that centered everyone on the tasks of assimilation, interpretation, and translation into policy detail. What Delors said and did and the nature of Delors's production were sufficiently general and clear to provide a set of shared and unifying outlooks. Pascal himself supplied the rest of the glue, through his own work. His extraordinary gifts at rapidly assimilating and synthesizing a huge range of materials and his remarkable commitment to responsive availability allowed him to direct his colleagues and arm himself with a wide vision of the place of their work.

There were even deeper reasons for Pascal's deliberate neglect of general intermediary "coordination." On a personal level the absence of explicit solidarity-creating and "coordinating" group activities gave Pascal himself more space. In addition, it also made it virtually impossible to engage in collective nourishing of moods and second-guessing: cabinet members groused, criticized and, on occasion, felt sorry for themselves, but kept it all inside. Avoiding explicit "group forming" general mechanisms (all-inclusive group brainstormings and morning collective discussions, for example) also saved a lot of time. Adding additional meetings to the schedules of already overloaded people would have been a tricky and

expensive matter. Ultimately, however, Pascal's wisdom was to build
his cabinet around the kind of person who could sublimate the inevitable
discomforts of cabinet work and had the internal resources to start, sustain,
and satisfactorily complete complicated institutional struggles, and who
could assume full personal "implication" in Delors's strategy.[29]

In fact, there was a model for all this. Pascal had brought from Paris the
"Matignon" system, down to some of its smaller details but with the important exception of size.[30] As Pascal noted, "I chose a small team, where
coordination would happen as a matter of course, rather than a large one
which would have created coordination problems." French prime min-
isteral cabinets are constructed around loyalties to their leaders, not to
legal principles and administrative abstractions. Commitment to the particular mission of the *patron*, Delors, insured the bulk of necessary coordination and solidarity.[31] The *directeurs* of such cabinets, in addition, are easily
the equivalents of ministers (or European commissioners, when trans-
ported to Brussels as *chefs de cabinet du président*). Pascal's stature as *chef*, in
this model, flowed not only from his explicit political activities, but quite as
much from his capacities to mobilize administrative machinery to push
certain lines, stifle others, encourage some and frustrate others. Moreover,
to the redoubtable effectiveness of the Matignon system, moved to the
Berlaymont, Pascal added his own extraordinary capacities.

"Matignon organization," Pascal himself and the quality of his team gave
added comparative advantage to Delorist strategy. But there was a further
"French" accent to the cabinet's work which became clear from answering
the question of why individuals were willing to accept the demanding kind
of "implication" of working with Delors and Pascal. It certainly did not hurt
anyone's professional biography to serve in the Delors cabinet. But there
were easier ways to advance careers, especially for individuals of the calibre
who serve in the cabinet. Jacques Delors is inhabited by deep spiritual
motivations; he has a *grande mission*, in other words. Pascal's secret was
to have built the cabinet to mobilize individuals who were themselves
motivated by similar inner-directed moral convictions. The cabinet was
premised on tapping deeper sources of cohesion than any "teamwork"
managerial technique would elicit. Ultimately it was tied together by
what specialists on France, particularly the French Left, would call
militantisme.

In French political life *militants* were imbued with a particular political
style in which agreement on principles and strategy existed *prior to* any
administrative action. Cabinet members were believers and dedicated activists for the cause, not simply civil servants. The Delors cabinet thus started
from a solid foundation of crack administrative and political professionals.
Then these very able people deployed a "line," Jacques Delors's strategic
concerns, in the way political activists often do. They armed themselves *a
priori* with the very best arguments to advance this line plus the best cases
against any and all conceivable arguments that its opponents might invent.
With these weapons at hand, they then deployed an activist's energy to fight

the good fight. When asked about the main source of their motivation, cabinet members themselves provided answers which confirmed this *militantisme*. They were obliged to work harder, understand things more fully, and be better prepared, down to the smallest details, than "the others." As Jean-Charles and others constantly reminded me, to be a cabinet member meant always being a "length ahead" of everyone else and willing to take whatever risks necessary to make the presidential position prevail. "Delors is an extraordinary person and this is an extraordinary moment when we can make a clear contribution to the construction of a new Europe."

What made such cabinet *militantisme* doubly effective was the way that Pascal had structured its regeneration and reaffirmation into day-to-day processes. Partly as a function of the construction of individual portfolios, partly because of the large number of high priority items on the Delors agenda, each cabinet member dealt every day with matters which were central to the success of presidential strategy. Cabinet members were thus constantly aware that if they did not use every talent and effort to overcome the immediate problems of their own daily work the entire strategy could well be compromised.[32] In large part this also explains what made cabinet decentralization, which often left members painfully alone with their tasks, tolerable. Decentralized though the actual work of cabinet members may have been, policy interdependence for the success of the total strategy created a "team."

Militants use everything they have to win. What resources did the cabinet bring to bear to succeed? The best answers to this question came from other cabinets and the administrative services. Delors's pre-eminence was always first on the list, the major cabinet resource. This resource was not only in the mastery of Delorist strategy, but also in the benefits which the Delors cabinet gleaned from its closer attunement via Delors to the workings of other European institutions, in particular the all-important European Council. Next, the superior level of preparation and stronger commitment of the Delors cabinet were widely recognized. Here the "Frenchness" of the cabinet was oft cited, if rarely loved, in full acknowledgement of the comparative advantage of what I have called "Matignon plus *militantisme*." Respondents' definition of this "Frenchness" usually began with universal recognition of the cabinet's high levels of French administrative professionalism.[33] Cabinet "Frenchness" also had a political dimension. The cabinet's high levels of strategic conviction and energy made it virtually unstoppable. The contrast here was between a strongly *deductive* political style in which first principles and ideas are assumed and the more *inductive* approaches of other European administrative and political traditions. Respondents almost always noted that administrative cultures based on traditions of inductive discussion and/or *a priori* commitment to compromise and splitting differences were simply outclassed. Knowing what they wanted, having complete personal commitment to achieving it, knowing how to argue for it, and knowing how to use the "house" to tease out agreement with it: these were the cabinet's real resources.[34]

Knowing what they wanted and knowing how to argue for it tied the cabinet back to Delors himself, who was a combination of political intellectual and "hands on" operator. His constant strategic quests were fed from the outside world and by concepts and facts gleaned from evolving policy dossiers. As one former cabinet member told me, "Pascal is constantly asking for 'notes,'" memos of a think-piece kind. Everyone in the cabinet was aware that the exchange of information and ideas which they organized with the President went beyond simple "staff work." It constituted an ongoing debate between themselves and Delors, which was likely to have operational consequences. The exchange went in both directions, of course. Ideally, while the President's voracious intellectual appetites were nourished, the cabinet's awareness of the different dimensions of the President's strategic thinking and its evolution was simultaneously enriched. Delors's working methods were such that "notes" might not elicit responses at all, or if they did, not until much later. Moreover, the demand from the President and Pascal for notes which conceptually transcended simple briefs constantly obliged cabinet members to maintain reflective distance on their own, and the cabinet's more general, work. This demanded intellectualizing of a particular kind. The ideas in circulation could be grandiose and ambitious, but they had to practicable and solidly grounded in the deep logics of EC and European development. Delors, with the help of Pascal and the cabinet, was scanning his environment for intimations about what the future might and could be, not looking for interesting abstractions.

Generating Presidentialism

My ultimate purpose was to "follow" as many of the "hot dossiers" on the Delors strategic agenda as I could, from presidential strategy through the cabinet and Commission. But during my first weeks, as I settled into the arduous tasks of reading mounds of documents and going to lots of meetings, I also interviewed people far and wide inside the Commission; well over a hundred long interviews with members of other cabinets, a number of administrative directors and directors general and assorted others. I followed a "snowball" method of tracking down names, assisted by Pascal. What I was after were perceptions of the President and his cabinet, which almost everyone had to offer in abundance. Using my interview notes, I could then begin a preliminary mapping of the ways in which Pascal's team seemed to work.

Almost everyone I talked to beyond the cabinet began by describing the Commission and the President's cabinet's relationship in paradoxical terms. They would start with a pious description of the Commission as an egalitarian college in which conflict was minimized. They depicted its methods of producing policy in historically consecrated terms – ideas percolating up from the workings of the services to reach the point of Commission decision. Then they usually acknowledged that this system did not necessarily guarantee general policy coherence, let alone conformity with presidential strategy, and that anyway this really was not a very accurate representation of what happened. Those who had been around for a while added that the Commission's pre-1985 legacies had made the administrative services shy about making any important decisions at all. On the other side of the ledger, they all noted that presidential cabinet members were dedicated instruments of the Delors presidency and quite ferociously devoted to the production and implementation of an explicit strategy in arenas where other actors often had divergent interests.

Pascal himself always insisted upon the weight of consensus, often comparing the Commission system to that which existed in French governmental practices. The President and cabinet, rather than working against the system, he claimed, won the system to their sides. But institutionally, the Commission's president had few explicit political powers and procedural resources to pursue a strong strategy. Moreover, implementing a strong strategy involved sorting out a wide range of conflicts about its actual content. Delors's and the cabinet's problem, crudely stated, was thus to make the Commission function more like a real government and less like a college, while simultaneously preserving the collegiate forms and ethos. The college system itself worked to moderate conflict. By placing an ultimate premium on achieving consensus it discouraged the kind of oppositional obduracy that the adversarial structures of most governments encouraged. Collegiality more generally meant that actors (whether commissioners, cabinets or services) had to conceive of their interventions, however conflictual, in terms of contributions to an eventual consensus. There was thus little point in assuming a persistently negative or oppositional stance. All cabinets, including the President's, were aware that their central political function is to "get rid of the dynamite" and "keep blood off the Commission floor," to have their fights and then to close on agreement, even when they had lost.

Virtually everyone agreed that the most important reason for the ability to achieve consensus over time was that success created a massive payoff which encouraged everyone to be willing to accept further presidential initiatives, enhancing the stature and power of President Delors, raising the costs of opposing his positions, and creating new openings for the maneuverings of his cabinet. This payoff was particularly important to commissioners who, whatever their personal hesitations about the Delors strategy, found themselves "carried" by it to public prominence. Success gave the services additional incentives to cooperate as well. Psychologically it enhanced their sense of engagement in important activities while, in many cases, it increased the practical clout and resources of particular bailiwicks. There was also a common "in-house" argument about the manifest differences in collegial spirit and cooperation between the first and second Commissions under Delors's presidency. The first, the argument went, started from a low point and rose collectively. Movement from the White Paper through the Single European Act and the *paquet Delors* demonstrated that the Commission had initiated a strategically serious and sustained campaign to end Europessimism and relaunch the Community. The second, after 1989, was composed of commissioners who inherited from the first "situational rents" of increased visibility and importance. Thus, the argument continued, the second had a number of commissioners with less collegial commitment and *esprit de corps* and higher expectations of their due than had their predecessors. This meant that the cabinet's consensus-generating job was becoming more difficult.

The President's *de facto* power and prestige, derived from a record of success, was an important tool for the cabinet in more specific ways. I have already mentioned its ability to invoke superior knowledge of the workings and meanings of the European Council. Beyond this cabinet members could use or imply the argument that "the President wants *this*," which they apparently did with some skill. This line of argument, my sources were quick to note, could be particularly effective, used sparingly, because of its very ambiguity. It could be a signal to others that their commissioners would have to fight it out in Commission with a powerful president if their opposition to his position persisted. At the limit they might also have to face a Commission vote in which they could risk being marginalized. This was an important weapon, since the President's intellectual and political skills contrasted with those of his colleagues, if anything, even more favorably than those of his highly gifted cabinet did with theirs. Or it could be used as a lever to prod other cabinets as far as they were willing to go toward a very strong position in order to then allow the President to compromise at a lower, but still high, level. This was a "bad cop, good cop" routine, with Delors being the good cop.

Conflict thus kept creeping back. Sources repeatedly underlined the specific roles of Pascal, assisted by David Williamson, as the final tough "gatekeeper" in and around the *Chefs de Cabinet* meeting every Monday. Pascal's "bad cop" toughness in stopping inadequate or unpalatable proposals from going forward, or in setting up Commission debate on them so that Delors could then be more conciliatory, was legendary. One member of Brittan's cabinet, the group which was the most consistent target of Pascal, noted that "we have to fight all the time."

There was much more to the success of Pascal's machine than smart politicking and toughness, however. To get what it wanted the cabinet had to place a presidential strategy spin on the work of others unwilling to, or incapable of, providing it on their own. It had to be a "gatekeeper" to stop low quality and/or politically unacceptable work from moving forward. And, finally, it had to be able to generate almost *ab initio* the kinds of work which would advance the strategy when other commissioners and the services did not themselves produce such work. Ultimately there were not many subtle formulas for producing the right kinds of dossiers when others were reluctant to accept the presidency's superior argument. A former cabinet member with whom I talked, who had been the designer of one of Delors's most important initiatives, announced that the commissioner with whom he worked most often "was quite incompetent. He couldn't do anything right. I had no choice but to 'violate him,' to go around him and work directly with his own administration. Otherwise we just couldn't have gotten what we needed." He continued, revealingly, that "the President advised me not to do it . . . and I had to learn over time that most often when he said that he really meant that I *should* do it, but without causing too much trouble . . . And in any case I couldn't get the work done that he demanded without doing it." Jean-Charles Leygues was unafraid to general-ize about this, noting that "in the college system 'violation' is necessary." Another presidential collaborator averred that "my colleagues have to know how to administer kicks in the butt." François Lamoureux added a further refinement about such matters: "One has to know the President well enough to know whether when he forbids you to act like this it is a yellow or a red light. It may then be necessary to know how to play hardball without invoking the President's name at all."

To achieve its ends the presidential cabinet had to be willing to break through official chains of command and responsibility. "Reaching around" commissioners and/or their cabinets was common practice. The same was true of "reaching into" those administrative services whose leadership was refractory or left something to be desired. Although rarer, there were even cases of "reaching into" the intimate workings of other cabinets on essential dossiers. Needless to say, such activities did not always please people. Other cabinets and directors general complained about Pascal's team "having to know everything," having "no concept of subsidiarity," "giving lip service to collegiality," "drilling people into line," being voluntarist and making per-sistent efforts to "explain that others' ideas are bad." Another common grievance was that the cabinet persistently used its official control over the production of internal documents, particularly the minutes of meetings, to "shape things up in the President's favor." Finally, the tactic of manipulating the actual times of meetings, of which many on Pascal's team spoke almost proudly, caused some consternation. The famous occasion when Jean-Charles called a special chefs meeting to begin late on Friday afternoon and be kept in session until after midnight, by which point everyone had become amenable to his arguments, was legendary.

What was most extraordinary, despite widespread awareness of the cabinet's hard-nosed methods, was the degree to which these various prac-tices, if often resented, seemed relatively uncontroversial in the larger scheme of things. The conflict which they created ultimately was buried in consensus – hence the persistently garbled narrative which I received when I asked about conflict. One practical reason was that the Commission lived constantly with the pressure of urgent deadlines and the necessity of re-sponding rapidly to unforeseen events. In a complex administration, wide-spread acceptance of the need for rapid and flexible coordination in the development of policy can thus be understood, especially since the President's cabinet did have a legitimate coordinating role to play. Still, the pressure applied by Pascal's team, on top of the frenetic nature of Commission activity flowing from the objective increase in tasks, created frictions which had to be managed successfully. Indeed, doing so was one of the cabinet member's more important skills.

Inducing complicity seemed to be the essential tool. With certain exceptions, the documents and policy proposals which reached the Commission table and then "went public" were always labelled as products of the services and commissioners in whose areas they fell, however much the President's cabinet had actually intervened in their gestation. Even when cabinet actions breaking through official chains of command were received negatively, they had to be tolerated because ultimate success enhanced the reputations of those who had been manipulated. If the product was recognized as good, only the President's cabinet would know how much of its quality was due to its own work. In practice, the competence and clout of the Delors cabinet had consistently been high enough that anticipating the accolades of policy success became an important reason for the victims to accept their fate. In eliciting complicity the cabinet followed two basic rules. In general, it was wise to avoid too much of this kind of activity except for very good reasons. Here Pascal's team may, on occasion, have been too "macho," but its discretion was impressive. It lorded over the "house" in fact, but those lorded over were allowed credit for what the lords accomplished.

The year of all the dangers

Jacques Delors had a vision and a strategy. The Community had a brief window of opportunity to "deepen" itself before a menacing international market system dominated by the Americans and Japanese crashed in on it. As the Commission President never ceased repeating, Europe faced a choice between survival and decline. What was at stake was a model of society whose disappearance from the globe would be a historic catastrophe. Europe needed to become vastly more competitive economically while simultaneously reconfiguring its social policies and methods of political decision making. Delors wanted to use the European Commission to promote such large goals.

Delors, Pascal Lamy, and the rest of the Delors team were about to face the greatest challenges of the presidency, however. Most of the other players around the Commission had by now come to understand the Russian doll principles of strategic logic which had been so useful in the 1980s. Everyone would henceforth be on full alert to decode any new commitments, seeking the implied futures which they might structure. Such general wariness would make the IGCs on EMU and Political Union which were beginning in January 1991 very tricky propositions for the Commission.

Moreover, the post-1989 international environment within which these conferences would occur was itself highly unpredictable. Finally, the Commission and the Community had a huge number of balls in the air – the 1991 Commission agenda, as Delors usually announced with a certain tone of contrived astonishment, had 11 major priorities. For Delors 1991 was meant to be *the* turning point, the moment when EC deepening became irreversible. The stakes were very high for everyone, therefore, but particularly for Delors, his team, and the Commission.

3

"After 1992" Begins

Pascal wanted me to check in with Delors before being allowed to roam the Berlaymont. I had met Delors, of course, but this time, however, I dropped into his Berlaymont office at eight p.m. It was a quiet time, particularly on this snowy evening in January 1991. Almost everyone had gone home, or was in the process of trying to do so – streets were clogged in a Brussels quite unprepared to handle snow. Delors's office was at the very top corner of the thirteenth floor, with broad windows across the two back walls. His big desk, piled neatly with colored dossiers, faced black leather couches around a glass and chrome coffee table. At the end of the desk was an EC flag and a television set.[1] Delors was his usual impeccable, elegant self, a burgundy pullover over his shirt and tie, every hair in place despite a working day which had already lasted 12 hours. When Pascal and I walked in he put down his papers, walked around the desk, and sat down on the couch. Delors and I shook hands and began polite conversation.

The storm came with an abrupt change in tone of voice. "At any moment now we could be brought down by crisis . . . There are at least three different matters which could stop us tomorrow . . . Europe has had ten years of success, five years of crisis and seventeen years of stagnation." An anguished Commission president then proceeded to talk non-stop for nearly an hour. The three dangers were the Gulf War, the reform of the Common Agricultural Policy, and the perennial matter of the Community's "seat" (the official location of its major institutions). In each case the threat was division of purpose among member states and possible decline in their commitment to the new Europe. The Gulf War threatened Delors's cherished goal of a common European foreign and defense policy. CAP reform, whose design had been accelerated in the wake of the collapse of Uruguay Round talks at Huysel only weeks before, was fraught with pitfalls. The "seat" dispute – the Parliament, backed by Belgium and a few others, wanted to move to Brussels from Strasbourg – portended additional conflict. Delors spoke as if his life's work were threatened.

At one moment of opening I interjected that the theme of the "European model of society" held great appeal, that perhaps things could be held together by talking more about it. After a quizzical look, Delors went back to his Hamletesque speech. I inferred from Pascal's silence that responses were not expected. Perhaps this was one way Delors thought through his problems. Whatever the process, however, the President was absolutely right in his premonitions of crisis. The good times were over. "After 1992" had begun, and it would not be easy.

The complex talks which would eventuate in the Maastricht Treaty began in this Brussels winter of 1991. Two separate intergovernmental conferences (IGCs) had been convened under the same Article of the Rome Treaty which had been used to call the Single European Act negotiations in 1985. The actual meetings were convened across the street from the Berlaymont in the Council of Ministers building. For each IGC the member state ambassadors to the EC (COREPER – the Committee of Permanent Representatives) plus Commission delegates would prepare the ground week by week for the full ministerial meetings held monthly. The EMU conference had a strong starting point, the 1989 Delors Report. The IGC on "Political Union" was more of a "mixed salad," to quote a Commission delegate who added, "and we don't know what sauce it will be served with." Its agenda was much less clear. Prospecting for a Common Foreign and Security Policy (CFSP) was one item. Treaty changes to enhance the Community's "democratic legitimacy" (code for giving the European Parliament more power) were another. Reviewing and adding to the competencies of the Community and changing its decision-making rules was a third matter. Finally, there was a grab-bag of issues under the rubric of "internal and judiciary matters" (which covered drugs, terrorism, illegal immigration, organized crime, and the like).

EMU Up and Moving

EMU was the most important Russian doll, the next step in the direction which Delors had helped the Community to choose in the 1980s. The 1992 program, the European Monetary System (EMS), and the liberalization of capital movements taken together pointed towards an end to national exchange rate autonomy and a transnational economic policy center. The proposed monetary union, which would eventually give Europe a single currency (the ecu – European Currency Unit), would demonstrate the irreversibility of Community integration, cut transaction costs, and make money market speculation based on exchange rate uncertainties a thing of the past. A common EC economic policy arena, economic union, was intended to facilitate the EC's international dealings, promote new efficiencies, price stability, low interest rates, and prudent public finance practices. Jacques Delors often argued the case backwards as well, asserting that without EMU the achievements of the Community would be at risk.[2] Excessive exchange rate fluctuation could unravel the EMS, disrupt the Single Market, and lead member states or the EC to reimpose controls on capital movements. Either way, EMU was a big deal – a major new pooling of sovereignty and a huge step towards integration.

Beginnings

Mid-January 1991: the IGC had just opened and a great deal was on the line, but Joly Dixon was quite calm. Joly was Delors's right arm for EMU, and EMU, more than everything else, was Delors's baby. A lot was at stake. "The President's in charge of everything, as you've undoubtedly heard from everyone," Joly noted, "but he's *completely* in charge of this . . . I helped to put together the dossier, to get the services to produce, and I talked it through with him when he asked me . . . but basically he writes almost every word of the documents that count . . . Delors is really a world class intellectual on this monetary business – along with almost everything . . . here his experience makes him a professional the equal of anyone else." A call from Delors interrupted at this point. Joly's "*oui Président*" was followed by silence while Delors explained his concerns. He was worried that yesterday's Spanish announcement of a new plan for a "hard ecu" rather than a single currency might provide grist for the British anti-EMU mill. But neither Delors nor Dixon knew yet what the Spanish plan actually was. Joly was to find out and produce a quick memo.

The story of EMU which Joly told me explained his calm. EMU had first been seriously raised in the Werner Report of 1970, composed in the wake of the 1969 Hague Summit to discuss the Community's next steps after its "first stage" of creating a customs union and the CAP.[3] In March 1971 members had further announced "their political will to establish an economic and monetary union," and some initial steps had been taken, for example, the 1972 monetary "snake in the tunnel" (an early effort to tie EC currency fluctuations together in a systemic way to gain greater stability as the Bretton Woods system collapsed). Momentum, as well as the Werner Report and the monetary snake, collapsed when these same member states followed individual national trajectories in the face of disturbing new economic circumstances.[4] Then the EMS, with its Exchange Rate Mechanism (ERM) for promoting a zone of monetary stability, was established intergovernmentally by French President Valéry Giscard d'Estaing and German Chancellor Helmut Schmidt in 1979, to salvage what remained of the snake-like system. Full EMU had long since been placed back in the closet, however.[5]

Delors, the Commission, and the European Council had brought back the idea of EMU with the Single European Act's commitment to "enhance the Community's monetary capacity with a view to economic and monetary union."[6] It was this, a suggestion by French Finance Minister Edoaurd Balladur in 1987, and parts of the architecture of the original Werner Report that Delors used for his 1988 proposal to the Hanover European Council,[7] which Joly Dixon had been brought into the Delors cabinet to help prepare. At Hanover Delors was made chair of a Committee on EMU which, at his urging, was composed of Central Bank governors plus three eminent university economists.[8] The Committee would have low start-up costs, since everyone knew everyone else. More importantly, from Delors's strategic viewpoint, politicians would be kept at arm's length until the bankers had formed their own opinions.

Delors had managed from the outset to put his hands on all the EMU levers which mattered. In the critical preparatory phases in 1988 and 1989, he, Joly, and a small number of others quietly supervised the construction of the new EMU proposal. The hard work was done in Brussels, which Delors and Joly then brought once a month to the cosseted quiet of Basel to prepare what would become the Delors Report. Delors, Dixon, and Jean-Paul Mingasson, eventually appointed Director General of the Commission's Budget Directorate, worked closely with the two *rapporteurs* of the EMU Committee, Gunter Baer and Tommaso Padoa-Schioppa, both sure friends, to shape the Committee's proceedings to the President's liking. Back in Brussels, a slightly expanded, but still miniscule, Commission team met around Delors almost every week to plot their tactics – included were Jean-Louis Dewost, Commission head of legal services, Claus-Dieter Ehlermann, initially Commission press secretary and then head of DG IV, the Competition Policy Directorate, Mingasson, with François Lamoureux serving as all-purpose quick writer of texts. The Delors Report, along with almost everything else which followed, was, in Joly's words, "totally *ad hoc*, not drafted by any DG," and largely untouched by the full Commission itself. Mingasson added that Delors "spent a huge amount of time on the dossier . . . he always knew where he wanted to go."

After initial brainstorming, the Central Bank governors reviewed papers which they themselves wrote about their preoccupations, which Delors and his team used to move them towards consensus on what the Commission President himself wanted.[9] The Werner Report's three-stage architecture – roughly speaking a first stage to promote economic, and monetary convergence, a second to build new institutions, and a third to found monetary unity – was on the table from the beginning. By spring 1989 a fully drafted report was on the table. Even the Bundesbank's Karl-Otto Pöhl, a critical player, had moved closer to Delors's positions and the governors, including the Governor of the Bank of England, were fully on side for a Delorist report. The small team around Delors continued to be the source of impulsion. But as Jean-Paul Mingasson noted, "Delors corrected all the sentences ... there wasn't a phrase in the final paper which he didn't author."

When the Delors Report went to the Madrid European Council in June 1989, it was a highly polished document. EMU stage 1, which involved the promotion of economic convergence among EC member states, would begin in 1990, when the capital market liberalization of the "1992" program would come into effect. Moving to the other two stages necessitated prior modifications of EC treaties, rather more to get member states to declare irrevocable commitment to the entire EMU process than to polish the proposals themselves, however. While the Report included no fixed timetable for stages 2 and 3, since much would depend on the results of economic convergence, the ratification of these new treaty changes would be a symbol of the irreversability of the entire process. This commitment was an essential signal to the international financial community that EMU was serious. In stage 3, when exchange rates would be definitively fixed, Community rules in macroeconomic and budgetary matters would become binding.

From Delors's strategic perspective EMU was simultaneously market-reinforcing and "state building." A federal European System of Central Banks, with the status of other Community institutions, was needed to run monetary policy. Macroeconomic policy coordination, the basic dimension of economic union, would involve procedures and rules to monitor and control member states' behaviors, including their budget deficits and medium-term fiscal outlooks. The Report implied that the Community might even acquire certain powers of compulsion. The tasks of coordinating monetary and economic dimensions called for institutional changes as well.

Margaret Thatcher came to the June 1989 Madrid European Council, where the Delors Report was to be considered, determined to oppose every piece of federalist pretention, however minor.[10] Felipe Gonzalez, Spanish Prime Minister and Council President, had to use all his skill on the British Prime Minister (and Danish Prime Minister Paul Schluter, who supported her). Delors was demonstrably unhappy about the compromised wording of the final communiqué, but there was a touch of maximalism in Delors's petulance. The Madrid European Council gave Delors's EMU plans a good head start. Gonzalez managed to tempt the British, who might otherwise have caused an EMU crisis there and then, to sign the Madrid conclusions.[11] The British insisted upon hedging any future agreement but the EMU process based upon the Delors Report would go forward.[12] Everyone knew that the British would eventually oppose EMU, but later was better, since they would almost certainly be more isolated later than at Madrid. The Madrid summit also helped to clarify the German position. The German Central Bank was very worried about potential loss of its power in EMU, and its capacities to put obstacles in front of EMU were considerable. Nonetheless at Madrid Kohl had overridden Karl-Otto Pöhl, Bundesbank President, and this was an important sign. The Madrid European Council gave Delors's EMU plan a good head start.

Madrid assigned a "high-level committee" appointed by ECOFIN (the Council of Finance Ministers)[13] to report about procedures for "mutual surveillance" to reinforce coordination of member state economic policies, enhanced collaboration between Central Bank governors, and the operationalization of EMU stage 1. The ECOFIN Committee also circulated a questionnaire to scout areas of agreement and contention prior to the opening of the IGC. The Strasbourg European Council in December 1989 then decided to begin stage 1 in 1990 and agreed under Article 236 of the Treaty to call the EMU IGC (the British alone opposed). Because of forthcoming German elections, however, it was left to the second half of 1990, and the Italian presidency, to start the conference.

From Strasbourg onward the preliminary EMU propositions derived from the Delors Report were passed on from the Community's Monetary Committee in July 1990, the European Parliament committee on economic, monetary and industrial policy in September, and to Italian Finance Minister Guido Carli, acting President of ECOFIN, in October. In the meantime, in August British Chancellor John Major had outlined the UK's alternative proposals for a "hard ecu" rather than a single currency in stage 3, staking out the British position and giving the pro-EMU team ample time to organize against it. All the while the Brussels team around Delors and Joly worked steadily. Jean-François Pons, a newcomer to DG II, but an experienced practitioner in the rarefied world of international monetary operations, noted that Delors used his small working group as a place "to figure things out." Sometimes he would submit an idea and let the group knock it around. At others he would listen to the group debate specific technical matters. "Delors was usually quite open on these issues," said Pons. Always he would take the group's offerings away with him to reflect upon in private, undoubtedly late at night in his office, alone on the thirteenth floor. And the President went everywhere he could to shape the public discussion, giving periodic full reports to the Commission, which itself published a communication on EMU in August, and to Parliament. The Commission's administration also produced a long technical justification of the plans, modelled on the earlier Cecchini Report.[14]

When the Rome I European Council (the first of two Rome European Councils, on October 27, 1990) officially called for opening the IGC on December 14, 1990, its mandate – which the British refused to sign – was quite pointed.[15] Economic union would combine "an open market system that combines price stability with growth, employment and environmental protection . . . dedicated to sound and sustainable financial and budgetary conditions and to economic and social cohesion." Monetary union would involve creating a "new monetary institution" – this exact wording would turn out to be very important – to support price stability and "the general economic policy of the Community." It would also eventuate in irrevocably fixed exchange rates and a single currency. Stage 2 would start on January 1, 1994 – after the 1992 program had been completed, the new treaty ratified and as many EC members as possible had joined the ERM. The "new monetary institution" would be set up at this point to strengthen monetary policy coordination, develop the mechanisms for a future single monetary policy, and oversee the development of the ecu. Three years after this, at the latest, various conclaves and evaluations to decide when to go to stage 3 would be held.

The high politics behind the EMU debate had in the meantime become clearer. Delors wanted EMU because it would be a step towards European union, a giant new pooling of sovereignty. The French, following François Mitterrand's "Europe Option," wanted to gain politically what their weakness made impossible economically: part of the control over European monetary and economic policy from the Germans. The British were opposed because of EMU's supranational purposes and because they did not want to lose the pound sterling. The Germans were hesitant because they knew what the French and the Commission, in their different ways, were after, while the Bundesbank feared loss of control over German monetary policy.[16] Finally, EMU would be a considerably better deal for more prosperous areas of the Community: adjustment costs would be greater for the EC "South," with EMU's strong "price stability" commitments particularly burdensome.

The bargaining table

The publication of a complete Commission "Draft Treaty" on EMU, in December 1990, demonstrated how completely the team around Joly and Delors dominated preparations for the IGC. The draft treaty had been written completely outside regular channels by Delors's small group and put into final legal language by François Lamoureux.[17] Despite the fact that it was never officially seen by the full Commission it would serve as the centerpiece for negotiation among member states. Preparation had been so thorough and politically astute that by early January when the IGC sat down, few surprises were likely. Where member states had problems, Delors was aware and anticipating what to do. This was why Joly could be so calm!

Luxembourg would preside over IGC sessions until the end of June, when the Dutch would take over. The Luxembourg strategy was to produce a polished product by June as a testimony to their Council presidency.[18] There was danger in this way of proceeding, however, since premature conclusion-seeking could precipitate sharp confrontations before they needed to happen. Compounding this danger, from Joly Dixon's point of view, was that much of the actual work of organizing and writing up the Luxembourg "non-papers" (diplomatic usage for preliminary draft papers) would be done by the Secretariat and Legal Services of the Council, responsible for the organizational work of the Conference. Between Commission and Council staffs there were differences of approach and interest. The Council administration reported to the member states. The Commission was supranational. The negotiators from the Commission, according to Joly, had to keep the Luxembourgers under control and prevent the Council administration from straying from the original proposals.[19]

Differences among key players came out quickly during the first sessions of the IGC. At the first full ministerial negotiations in January, for example, the post-Thatcher British announced their opposition to a single currency and any schema which included an "irreversible" process leading to it.[20] To avoid being isolated, however, John Major had instructed British delegates to participate loyally, even where they disagreed on first principles. Their hope was to move EMU away from the model set out in the Delors Report. The Germans were wary of any European Central Bank System (ECBS) which would take on monetary and exchange rate responsibilities during stage 2. Moreover, they were opposed to the "new monetary institution" even being called an ECBS "to avoid any confusion with a Central Bank." National Central Banks should retain their full independence during the transition period, the Germans announced. Behind this was Bundesbank insistence on retaining full autonomy for much longer than the Delors Report anticipated. The Spanish initially played into the UK's hands by proposing a "hard ecu" for the second stage, to be replaced by a single currency in stage 3.[21] The French minister presented a full French draft treaty which sought more directive economic policy power for the European Council than had the Delors Report.[22] Other delegations raised "social and economic cohesion" issues, the distinct possibility of a "two-speed EMU" which some member states would not be ready to join, and "democratic accountability."[23]

Joly tried to put this initial diversity into perspective. "We'll be in a woods and trees period for a while . . . Everyone will posture and empty the filing cabinets." He added: "It's a ritual . . . all negotiations are like that . . . At first everyone tosses everything that runs through their mind on to the table and there's static. Then, after a bit, the differences that really count will come clear. Eventually, towards the last few sessions, they'll split their differences and we'll have our text." January and February 1991 were clearly high "static."

The second ministerial meeting in February brought at least one clarification. The British nourished the hope of reopening important matters which the Rome European Council meetings had officially closed, tempted by the Germans, who insisted that the Rome II European Council conclusions (Rome II in December 1990 had set out guidelines for the EMU negotiations) to mean that no new ECBS was called for in EMU stage 2. The language of Rome II called for a "new monetary institution" and not specifically an ECBS, making this interpretation plausible. The other ministers strongly reiterated that the European Council had granted a mandate to establish a single currency and single monetary policy, and the British were stopped.

Not long thereafter, however, the press began to talk of a "warming up" between the UK and Germany – Helmut Kohl and John Major were becoming fast friends, reporters claimed.[24] Major, who had not shifted basic British EMU positions one iota from those of his predecessor, had decided that UK tactics should change from predictable Thatcherite nay-saying to a more subtle game. As Joly remarked, "it was always easier with Mrs Thatcher. She would put her foot down and isolate the Brits . . . We could then ignore them and go about our business . . . But now that the Brits seem to want to play the game for real, things are getting a damn sight more complicated." Delors recognized the new complexity but concluded that Major's desire to put Britain "at the heart of Europe" was a change of tactics within Thatcherite continuity.[25] The issue became important with indications of rapprochement between Kohl and Major. For Kohl, meeting Major half way was partly "Europeanism" to encourage Major's new tactical openness. But it also might help the German negotiating position. Threatening to play the card of tactical alliance with the UK in dealings with the French was a good way of avoiding consistent imprisonment in the famous Franco-German couple.

Further disagreements came out during February's EMU discussions to define the "economic union" dimension and arrangements for promoting economic convergence. There was accord on general guidelines for "mutual surveillance" and the establishment and oversight of convergence guidelines. The Germans, unwilling to grant any supranational authority economic policy power, were adamant that such guidelines should exclude growth targets. The major convergence issue was keeping member states from running excessive budget deficits.[26] Delors seized the occasion to lecture the ministers on the dangers of placing too little weight on the "economic" and too much on the "monetary." The proposed ECBS could not be effective if commitment to macroeconomic policy objectives was purely verbal. EMU could not afford to be indifferent to underemployment, regional imbalances, incoherent economic structures allowing some member states to wall off their stock exchanges and banks from the market, and the effects of different approaches in industrial relations. Furthermore, he added, "can this kind of restricted EMU stand up to the questions which European peoples will raise through their democratically elected parliaments?" For Delors the Community had to have its own instruments of economic policy, just like member states.[27]

The first full German submission to the IGC on February 26 contained a small bomb. The Germans wanted to postpone creating an ECBS until the beginning of the third stage of EMU. The Delors Report had suggested the ECBS start with an "apprenticeship" role during stage 2. The Germans proposed instead a Council of Central Bank Governors, renamed in some decorous way, for the much narrower task of promoting monetary policy coordination. In addition, they wanted passage to EMU stage 3 to be considered initially three years after 1994 and be decided by the Council unanimously determining that a majority of EC members had met the desired convergence conditions. This meant that EMU, when it came, would be a "two-speed" affair. Only those who passed this first convergence test would become charter members.

Delors's angry public response accused the Germans of backtracking on the Rome II European Council conclusions. Moreover, "unidentified sources" from the Berlaymont intimated that Kohl had been manipulated by the Bundesbank. Kohl remained calm, however, announcing that "Jacques Delors is much too intelligent to make such a foolish statement." The Germans, Kohl said, had agreed to establish a "new monetary institution" at Rome, exactly as the European Council conclusions noted. They had never intended this to mean a European Central Bank, however.

The first EMU watershed had been reached. However indignant Delors sounded, everyone knew that the Germans would get their way. They needed time to digest unification. Moreover, Kohl needed something concrete to give to a Bundesbank at war with him since unification. The Commission game from this point on, hence Delors's theatrical indignation, was to restabilize the Germans to avoid new retreats, above all to prevent them from sliding towards British positions. Not having a central banking system during stage 2 was a step backwards, but the real purpose of establishing the new bank at stage 2 had always been to have a concrete symbol of commitment to EMU irreversability. There might be other ways of doing this. Nothing in the German document indicated that the commitment itself was threatened. As for a two-speed EMU, formalized in the German proposal, everyone had known that it was on the cards for some time. Joly Dixon, ever cool, analyzed the German paper as more of a bump in the road, something that one always encountered in tough negotiations, rather than a bomb.

Delors and Joly flew to Strasbourg in March to report on EMU to the European Parliament. The President tried to stress the importance of keeping the development of EMU within the time limits set by the Delors Report. Stage 1, already underway, was critical.[28] The essential thing was to have hard-nosed processes of "multilateral surveillance" over member state policies.[29] Multilateral surveillance was "getting off to too slow a start . . . the ministers haven't yet been open and frank enough with each other to make it work." There were a few bright signs. The first surveillance meeting had targeted the Germans, who had responded with positive changes. The problem, Delors noted, was that "the Finance Ministers are negotiating on EMU as if the first stage didn't exist at all. But unless we can succeed at the first stage . . . I really cannot see how there can be a second or third stage." All member states were participating constructively in the discussion, Delors noted. Major's new cooperativeness was a welcome change and "there has been progress," a last swipe at Mrs Thatcher.[30] The

British Prime Minister had a timing problem, however, since he could not ask the House of Commons to approve an EMU plan which bound Britain to a stage 3 which included a single currency. "The Commission will do everything it can to seek out a consensus at the intergovernmental conference." As I knew from Joly, Delors was already cooking up a scheme for a British "opt out" of stage 3.

On the plane back from Strasbourg Joly Dixon was eager to amplify. The Germans, he said, were hesitant about the loss of economic policy autonomy that hard formulations of "economic union" implied. In fact "the Germans don't want economic union at all." It might give other, "less responsible," countries power to override the Bundesbank. The specter of having to bail the Italians out of their huge deficit at the cost of German price stability stalked Bundesbank corridors. At the very least the Germans wanted a completely independent European Central Bank. Moreover, they did not want it to happen anywhere near as quickly as the Delors Report did. Kohl, Joly added, "hopes for some important new powers for the European Parliament to come out of the Political Union talks in exchange for EMU . . . He's afraid that EMU will look completely elitist." The French, on the other hand, very much wanted the beefy economic union which the Germans rejected and hoped to bargain for it in exchange for a small deal on parliamentary power, about whose extension they were quite cool. "The Germans will do as much as they can to limit this, but they won't be able to stop it completely."

The Spanish, Irish, and Portuguese – the South – wanted "to be bought, just like in the Single Market." The problem now, Joly indicated, was that "they don't have very much to give in exchange and there isn't much left in the till to pay them." This was why Delors had warned that if the South pushed up the cost too much, negotiations might collapse and everyone would lose. Finally there was the UK. Joly was suspicious:

> I don't know what the new game, Major's game, will really turn out to be. They want a treaty they can sign without joining EMU, that's for sure, but what this means I can't figure out yet. One thing is pretty clear, however. Since Mrs Thatcher has gone the Brits are trying to break their isolation, fishing for allies . . . The Germans look like the best bet. The British under Major could be a lot more mischievous than they ever could be under Thatcher. She usually maneuvered them into a corner. Everyone could then take for granted that they wouldn't deal and ignore them. [Despite all this, Joly concluded:] I'm not worried too much . . . We've managed to set the tone and the limits of the debate . . . Now we've got to be quick and nimble, play as best we can . . . We've got the advantage of knowing more about other people's points of view than anyone else [he noted]. The President watches and thinks about the basic strategic issues all the time. He is very good at knowing how to play the ministers, when to intervene, who to collar in the corridors, things like that . . . And he isn't worried too much either. He thinks we're almost there . . . the final negotiations will be on details and labels.

[Joly was more worried about other matters:] The fly in the ointment is the damned Political Union Conference. It's a messy talk shop, it's badly organized and we don't really have good clarity on what our target is ... Things are moving too fast ... There's always the possibility of *that* mess feeding back on EMU.

Political Union

The issue of "political union" had many antecedents, particularly in the repeated requests of the European Parliament for institutional reform. It had returned to the agenda partly as the result of growing concern about the Community's foreign policy weakness and the collapse of "existing socialism" after 1989. Delors had been prescient about this in his January 1989 speech to the European Parliament. The Community had to focus ever more energy on becoming an international political actor but henceforth the context would be more uncertain.[31] For the Community to sustain its place, its first order of business to pursue its strategy of deepening. Among other things this meant strong new state-building efforts in the foreign policy realm.

The Strasbourg European Council of December 1989 debated the political and institutional implications of EMU for the Community at some length. Delors had taken up these themes and suggested that they be addressed by an IGC in his program speech to the Parliament in January 1990. Then at the Dublin I European Council in April 1990, Helmut Kohl and François Mitterrand jointly asked to open another IGC on "political union," to address four objectives: "democratic legitimacy, institutional effectiveness, the unity and coherence of the Community across economic, monetary and political areas," and the definition and implementation of a "common foreign and security policy" (CFSP).[32] In May of the same year Spanish Prime Minister Gonzales proposed adding another objective, the elaboration of "European citizenship," and a first preparatory interinstitutional meeting (Council–Parliament–Commission) was held to survey the issues. Dublin II in June officially decided that this second IGC should run parallel to the one on EMU. In addition to foreign and security policy, the conference would discuss new EC "competencies" – areas in which the Community would be empowered by treaty to act. It should also define the meaning of "subsidiarity," the EC's new buzzword for relations among different levels of political authority. And finally, under the umbrella of "democratic legitimacy," were grouped a possible extension of the powers of the European Parliament, reinforcing the democratic credentials of other EC institutions, and promoting greater national parliamentary involvement in EC matters.[33]

No one had really had enough time to give full thought to this long list of contentious issues in the few short working months between Dublin II in June and the official opening of the IGC in December 1990.[34] Council,

Parliament, and Commission were able to narrow down differences about the general purposes of the new IGC by the Rome II European Council in December, but precision was lacking.[35] The meant that serious Commission agenda-setting for the second IGC was not possible: nothing comparable to the Delors Report on EMU had set out the parameters of the talks. Indeed, Delors was able to generate the Commission's preliminary opinion only by mid-October, after which it had to gather together and write down its ideas at breakneck speed.[36] It took until well into March 1991 to produce papers in due legal form.[37] When Commission proposals arrived in time to be read carefully they usually brought added value. But they had to share the table with a huge number of similar papers from member states.

Making some order out of the general political union fell to the Luxembourg presidency. As on EMU, the Luxembourgers were determined to "make their mark" by having a draft treaty on the table for the European Council in June. The Luxembourgers were not overly endowed with global statesmen. Joseph Weyland, the permanent representative, was a respected journeyman, Jacques Poos, the Foreign Minister, was not held in highest esteem in diplomatic corridors, and the Prime Minister, Jacques Santer, was far from a heavyweight. This endowed the Council Secretariat, the Commission's administrative rival, with greater power than anyone on the Delors team was happy to see.

From Delors's point of view the setting was dangerous. The backbone of his strategy was to build on enthusiasm created by "1992" to propose new "state-building" programs to create a European "organized space." The "political union" issues were at the heart of state building. EMU had been carefully and skillfully prepared, and, perhaps more important, involved a set of issues which fell largely under traditional Community trade-market purview; "political union" had barely been set up at all and it sought to break new Community ground. Through no fault of its own Delors's team was thus moving into the central phase of its strategy without sufficient preparation. In the best of circumstances shifting the EC mandate from market to state building would have been a difficult thing to do.

Only a very few people actually participated in writing the Commission documents for political union. In this the process resembled that of EMU.[38] At the heart of the operation was a steering group of four or five people which met virtually every day. David Williamson, the Commission Secretary-General, coordinated in-house resources and kept the paper moving. Jean-Louis Dewost, head of the Commission's legal services, was the language specialist. The two others were Claus-Dieter Ehlermann, veteran of the Single European Act and one of the elders of the house on treaty matters, and Riccardo Perissich, the director general for the internal market and industrial affairs. The motor was François Lamoureux, who dealt directly with Delors and was also the link to COREPER. Pascal was always in the background, if only because he might have to argue the case for the group's products at the all-important *Chefs de Cabinet* meetings, but his role was relatively restrained. Delors, who shaped the original strategies, often attended the weekly meetings, listening quietly and taking his thoughts back to the office for late-night reflection in order to produce ideas and instructions for more precise drafting.

There was something quixotic about François's political union job, but then there was something of the European knight-errant about him anyway. François, who combined a gifted legal mind and a quick pen, did a huge amount of the Commission's text drafting. He had amassed plenty of experience at cranking out Commission negotiating positions during the very compressed run-up to the Single European Act in 1985. He also had a sharp political mind, useful for arguing the texts through various levels of Commission preparation, and an explosive temperament. François communicated the threat of attack even when he wasn't actually attacking, which more often than not he was. This rare combination of skills and character traits was particularly useful in the special chefs meetings through which each text had to pass. Here the papers from the core group had to confront representatives of the entire Commission for the first time, and, given the enormous rush, it was important not to become bogged down. François, who thought through all of the angles, often felt personally impugned when people disagreed. And when he did explode – regularly – people tended to run for cover. Most of the time this was productive, but it did not make François the most popular member of the Delors staff.[39]

On specific issues the responsible commissioners were brought in and their DGs mobilized to produce ideas, even though François had no compunction about short-circuiting commissioners and DGs to find the right people to get the right product as quickly as possible (another habit which did not endear him to everyone). There were regular complaints, some on the Commission floor itself, about lack of consultation. But as Claus-Dieter Ehlermann noted, "this is a very unusual procedure, totally *ad hoc*. The papers aren't really drafted by any department. The hierarchical procedures of the services are simply too slow." François was more conspiratorial. "No one is supposed to know about our little group," he whispered to me. A short walk down the corridor was all I needed to discover that everyone did.

Even if François and his group worked relentlessly, Commission control over the first stages of the IGC was limited. Where the Commission had submitted its proposals early it was able to shape initial discussion to a degree, but it had not had enough lead time to do this in most areas.[40] Thus the first weeks of talking about political union turned into a nervous review of kilograms of paper coming from everywhere about virtually everything. Sometimes, on important matters, discussions began even before a Commission paper was ready, as was the case for discussions of "democratic responsibility" of the Commission, which involved nominating Commission members, social policy, and foreign and security matters. At the same time the member states emptied their filing cabinets, not always to the point of central issues. Papers about "tourism," "youth," and the like appeared. The weekly transcripts of the negotiations grew thicker and more time-consuming to read. One day Pascal summoned up his heaviest *basso profundo* irony to remark on the gigantic tome under my arm: "Oh, you're still reading those things. They're so full of irrelevancies these days that I file them right next to my wastebasket." Whole forests were being consumed to produce EC transcripts even though it remained difficult to distinguish woods from trees.

The Common Foreign and Security Policy (CFSP)

Easy consensus might be reached on a few matters, putting vague words on to the notion of "subsidiarity" for example, but more difficult issues of political union quickly mired in disagreement. Foreign and security policy was the most important example. Developing a CFSP was Delors's own most important single concern.[41] From 1989 onwards he had been training himself, in inimitable Jansenist ways, in world statesmanship, while seizing every opportunity to advertise the Community as an international player. For some time he did not have much help beyond Gunther Burghardt, former cabinet number two and key operative in European Political Cooperation (EPC), and Pascal, engaged in similar training. Delors was limited in foreign affairs officially to the Commission's legal roles, in foreign trade matters for example, and his activities in these areas sometimes annoyed the commissioners whose formal job it was. Commission foreign policy officially fell into the bailiwicks of Frans Andriessen, Abel Matutes and Manual Marin. Delors and Andriessen did not hit it off and the relationship had not been warmed by Delors's growing success at becoming the Community's foreign policy "head of state." The other two, whose portfolios (in Mediterranean and development affairs) overlapped, did not cooperate easily. Beyond this foreign affairs were almost arbitrarily divided up within and among different administrative services.[42] The foreign policy specialists in the Delors cabinet had complex problems to deal with, in consequence.[43] Through all this the President was haunted by a vision of the Community as a "big Switzerland" with gigantic economic power, few diplomatic and no defense capacities.

Since few things came closer to the heart of national sovereignty than the conduct of foreign relations and defense policy, by the time that the IGC opened Delors and the Commission had reconciled themselves to the fact that in both foreign policy and defense areas "supranational" would mean intergovernmental rather than federal. The next best thing to federalization was "binding intergovernmentalism," a confederal solution in which the Commission would acquire a significant role. In foreign policy the hope was to turn EPC, presently a talking shop which generated no obligation, into something more constraining. The strategy aimed first to make the European Council responsible, following the rule of unanimity, for defining areas of "essential common interest" in which there would be a common policy. Decisions about executing specific policies within these general areas would then be taken by the Council, using a formula for reinforced majority voting. Within these general areas of essential interest member states would be obliged to act in common and support specific actions decided by the Council. The "proposition forces" in all this would be the Council presidency and the Commission, acting together. In the security area, the aim was to integrate Western European Union (WEU) into the "European Union" (the proposed new name of the Community) and transform WEU from a symbolic empty shell into a real defense planning and coordinating agency as rapidly as possible. WEU would thus become the defense arm of the EC.[44]

Even if confederalist, these were ambitious goals. It was the Commission's job to push member states beyond where they might otherwise go, and, quite as important, to point them to the specific tracks which would allow greater movement later on. The buzzword was to create "evolutive" structures. The issue was whether member states would be willing to follow the French, Germans, and the Commission in a generally confederal direction and, if so, how far. Another open question involved the kind of structures which could be agreed to. Would the Commission itself be able to get a large enough foot in the door? Finally, would there be parallel developments in both foreign policy and security?

The relative slowness of the Commission in putting together its formal proposals (available only on February 28, 1991) was not quite as significant here as in other areas. The Franco-German couple had already set out the confederalist terms by joint declarations well before the IGC itself had opened.[45] Nonetheless the coincidence between the start of the IGC and outbreak of the Gulf War caused larger problems. The Gulf War stengthened the case of advocates of a Community CFSP, since its absence when the war began deprived Europe of considerable voice. On the other hand, divisions among member states about the war were substantial.[46] The disparate display provided strong ammunition to those who claimed that a common foreign and defense policy was inconceivable because of differences among member states. Moreover, it also made the Franco-German alliance shakier. Mitterrand wanted – in true Gaullist fashion – a strong foot in the door towards a genuinely autonomous European foreign policy and defense position, a point of view which Delors shared. The Germans, concerned to bury their growing power in something European and worried about the effects of the end of Cold War on Europe's international position, had been playing two hands at once: the EC in economic matters and NATO in security affairs.

The first full IGC discussions of CFSP began in late January 1991 on the basis of answers to a questionnaire distributed to COREPER by the presidency.[47] From this and the third ministerial meeting the following week, clear differences appeared around the central issue of which common foreign policy areas would be Communitized and how they might be designated. The British led the foot-draggers, willing to continue the discussion but completely skeptical. They rejected anything more than a cosmetic rearrangement of existing EPC and hoped to separate foreign from security policy to block relative European defense autonomy from NATO. The British had allies. The Atlanticist Dutch, for example, were afraid of "big country" domination and did not want the European Council making fundamental decisions. The French and the Germans stood their ground, however, supported by the Commission and Delors.

On defense and security policy, the ministers had to discuss a new paper from French and German ministers Roland Dumas and Hans-Dietrich Genscher that went considerably beyond the original Kohl–Mitterrand statement of 1990 on the prospective relationship between WEU, the Community, and NATO.[48] Would WEU become a Community institution, part and parcel, with substantial new powers? Or would it be a "bridge" between the Community and NATO, perhaps charged with thinking about the "out-of-area" European matters which NATO could not contemplate? The French were the strongest advocates of the first position, backed by Delors. The British pushed for the second. There were enough indications of Mitterrand's Gaullism to know where the French wanted to go, even though it was usually disguised in talk about the need to prepare for the likely US retreat from the continent. The British, for their part (and they spoke for the Dutch and the Portuguese), wanted to humor the French to give the Americans enough time to reconfigure NATO for post-Cold War purposes.[49] WEU would, in this view, become the long-sought-after burden-sharing "European pillar" of the alliance. When things were posed in such ways the Germans became uncomfortable, caught between two competing visions.

All of this created a fluid negotiating situation that allowed an important background player, the United States, to move its pawns. US policy in Europe was at a critical juncture. The end of the Cold War meant an important drawdown of US NATO forces. This, in the context of a re-nascent Community, could mean a decline in US influence over the course of European events and, perhaps, a "new world order" not to the Bush administration's taste. The US thus undertook to influence the EC's discussions. NATO Ambassador Taft, in a major speech to the Institute for Security Studies, announced that "we support a European pillar . . . but it shouldn't overlap with the Alliance. Instead it should work inside the Alliance for Alliance missions and outside of it only where it desires to undertake new missions." He added, menacingly, that "US public opinion will not understand any proposal which aims at replacing NATO by a different mechanism assuming its fundamental roles of deterrence and defense."[50] The speech, followed by a flurry of US diplomatic activity, could not have been clearer. The US was willing to accept WEU as an EC "bridge to NATO," but not as a potential alternative to NATO. The Americans hoped to encourage the British and squeeze the Germans. Meanwhile, they were taking concrete steps to make the French–Commission option less viable by encouraging an acceleration in NATO's strategic re-evaluation – itself pointed towards developing a rapid response force for European out-of-area problems and security contacts with Eastern European countries.[51]

All this made the Delors staff jittery. François, in touch with all the contradictions in the IGC and diplomatic circuits, simultaneously had to put the finishing touches to the Commission's own CFSP paper and push it through the Commission. The Commission had to put out the strongest position it could, both because intelligent maximalism was its institutional duty and because Delors saw the issue as central to the Community's future. Yet because the Commission's paper was late entering the fray and the positions of reticent and less maximalist member states were already evident these reticences found their ways into the Commission's own debate on the CFSP paper. François had to work very hard, and his passionate explosions became more frequent as a result. "It's unbelievable," he said. "Here we are in Europe, and there aren't enough real Europeans to go around. One third of the Italians are not Europeans, nor half the Dutch and most of the Portuguese and Greeks. The British want to become the 51st American State. It's pitiful."

The cabinet lunch on Thursday, February 22, took place on the day after the Commission finally passed the CFSP paper. The CFSP had reached the Commission table at the same moment as the Commission's annual ordeal of CAP price-setting. This year's agricultural debate had been even more painful because Delors had been defeated by Agricultural Commissioner MacSharry.[52] "It was great, they spent three-quarters of an hour debating the price of tobacco, and this was after the milk subsidies and the wheat prices, so we got the treaty by them pretty quickly. They were all exhausted," said François, beginning his recounting of the CFSP. François thought that agriculture was a waste of time, so his irony was heavy.

Most of the cabinet was only dimly acquainted with the CFSP proposal, so François went into detail:

> We've been working on it for nearly a year in our small group . . . [that is, the "steering committee" plus Gunther Burghardt] . . . and I wrote the whole thing myself . . . It was only when we knew what we wanted to go that we brought in the Andriessen, Matutes and Marin cabinets, who edited a few things . . . the Marin people were no use at all . . . We tried to set up a genuine Communitarization of foreign policy. The European Council will identify applicable areas by unanimity and then the Council will work via qualified majority to create policy. And we were careful not to set out an *a priori* list of areas where the CFSP would work. We avoided the list Rome II set out last year in order to prevent member states fighting about it at the IGC.[53] First get the treaty, then we'll specify the areas . . . The most important thing is to link foreign policy and security. We judged that we needed a mutual assistance pact, and we knew that it wouldn't be much use to have one until we had a common military operation, so to get both we imported the mutual assistance clause of the WEU Treaty. The Community will simply absorb WEU, and this, in turn, will give the Community a common position in NATO.

Pascal added, "if this works, it will feed back on foreign policy. It's the same people, after all, who will sit in the Council of WEU and decide on the common foreign policy. And they won't be able to sit in the Council of WEU without considerable unity, by definition."

Pascal felt that there wasn't much point in worrying about the "plumbing." "The most important problem is one of ambition. If we can take a big step now, the specific arrangements can be worked out later. And we should remember that the mutual assistance clause of WEU is stronger than the one in the NATO Treaty." Gunther Burghardt had recently visited NATO and reported his astonishment at discovering that "NATO has no new ideas, there's an opening for us." Jerome Vignon was quick to note, however, that the UK's position on the CFSP "was a regurgitation of the American position." Pascal added:

> our hope has to be that the UK will ultimately go along in order to demonstrate their new-found Europeanism, that the French will be able to overcome their insularity on defense issues and that the Germans will follow the French . . . the Germans like the defense idea already, however, since they're worried about "out-of-area" capacities in the rest of Europe . . . This is the first real response to Bush and Baker . . . but we're going to have to work hard on the Americans. [Pascal would shortly take a quick trip to Washington to lobby his State Department friends.] They're afraid the we're pushing WEU as an alternative to NATO. We have to tell them over and over that building up WEU and taking it into the Community will strengthen NATO.

The Commission paper, late as it was, helped clarify the discussion on the CFSP. It remained to be seen, however, whether the Commission's proposals would stand up in the face of the deep interests of member states and the evident antipathy of the Americans. In a situation of negotiations like the IGC it would have been unreasonable to expect results to match the Commission's proposals. In realistic terms, the central question was how well the Commission could shape the negotiating agenda to produce results which, in time, might lead to what the Commission desired. The second principle of Delors's method was to get key actors into a position in the present so that as things developed in the future they would have difficulty *not* fulfilling the Commission's scenario.

Delors himself had been deliberately lying low during the Gulf War. As he told the *Wall Street Journal,* "I decided that I should refrain from any activism, and show by my silence that the Community didn't have the power that would allow it to speak."[54] He chose the security issue for re-emerging, on March 6, after the end of the Gulf War, in the lair of the "enemy," the International Institute for Strategic Studies in London.[55] The speech, carefully worked over for weeks, was vintage Delors, straightforward, pedagogic and lucid, meant to raise the level of debate on the CFSP without pulling any punches.[56]

The Gulf War has provided an object lesson – if one were needed – on the limitations of the European Community [he began]. It is true that giant steps have been taken along the path of economic integration, and the last two years have seen advances on foreign policy cooperation. But the Community's influence and ability to act have not kept pace. [The Gulf War illustrated the Community's weaknesses in the security realm.] . . . once it became obvious that the situation would have to be resolved by armed combat, the Community had neither the institutional machinery nor the military force which would have allowed it to act as a community. . . Are the twelve prepared to learn from this experience?

We are building a *community* whose member states jointly exercise a measure of pooled sovereignty through fully fledged common policies . . . [Because of these foundations, the Community] is now moving towards political union. Europe's ambitions lay at the heart of the matter . . . Europe must want to be European . . . Can the Community consent to spending so much time and effort, can this be justified to the general public, unless it is part of a grand design? [Yet certain member states] stick to the traditional view of national sovereignty . . . there are also friendly powers which seem to fear the development of a European identity. [The US (the case in point)] has nothing to gain from a politically impotent and economically subordinate Community.

A common defense policy will be meaningless unless it reflects two types of solidarity: unity of analysis and action in foreign policy and a reciprocal commitment to come to the aid of any member state whose integrity is threatened. [The current institutional setting was less and less adequate to the task.] This is why the Commission . . . proposes a single center . . . and why it proposes that all provisions relating external aspects – foreign policy, security, economic relations, and development cooperation – should be brought together in one title of the treaty. [The European Council would agree on the essential interests member states share and would] defend and promote together. [As a dynamic built up,] people will come to see the need for this missing ingredient, the means of defense . . . [Taking over the mutual assistance clause of the WEU Treaty was the best way to do this.]

[What should the new WEU be?] . . . a forum for increased cooperation . . . a bridge to the Atlantic alliance, or . . . a melting-pot for a European defense embedded in the Community, the second pillar of the Atlantic alliance? . . . The second option is the only one compatible with my argument . . . These plans, even in outline, have caused concern across the Atlantic . . . The United States has stressed three demands: no internal bloc, continued globality of the allied response, no weakening of command structures . . . The existence of an internal bloc should not be a cause for concern [unless either the US rejects] the political integration of Europe, which would be unacceptable . . . or because there are doubts about Europe's commitment to the alliance. [These doubts were wrong,] since the new Europe would be willing to shoulder a larger burden than before. [There would be no contradiction between continued "globality" and] the Community determining its own course of action [on matters outside NATO's scope].

[Concluding, Delors asserted that] there is no point in seeking refuge in discussion about how to proceed in an attempt to escape the basic issue of what we intend to do together. Once again history is at our door. We will be judged by the answer we supply to the simplest of questions: "What destiny are we proposing to the people of Europe? What destiny and what ambition?"

Democratic legitimacy

The IGC negotiators also had to sort out the issue of "democratic legitimacy," in particular the powers of the European Parliament. The Germans, most directly engaged, reasoned that the large new poolings of sovereignty in EMU and the CFSP could not be sustained without greater democratic control. The German position was supported by the small countries, which saw federalization as a way of blocking intergovernmental approaches which handed power to the largest member states. This position was bound to elicit strong opposition from two of the latter, the UK and France. The British wanted to stop further accretion of power to European levels in general. The French wanted more European confederation mainly to maximize their own influence. The Commission was a strong advocate of federalism and thus in favor of more Europarliamentary power, but not at its own expense. The European Parliament obviously wanted more power: Jean-Pierre Cot, head of the European Parliament's Socialist Group, announced early that the Parliament would refuse to approve any new treaty which did not do this satisfactorily.[57] The Parliament's stridency bolstered Commission commitment, since the Commission needed the Parliament to pressure member states on other matters.

The new Europe had a chronic problem of democratic legitimacy. Brilliant in most ways, the "Monnet method" politically had a "stealth" side to it. The Community's founders had never been confident that the response would be positive if Europeans were asked clearly whether they wanted European integration. From its origins EC Europe was an elite operation. The Commission, the EC's constitutional "proposition force," was appointed by governments and accountable to the Council of Ministers. The Council thus became the EC's legislature, controlled by these same heads of government, who were careful to meet out of public view. The European Parliament had originally been a symbolic appointed assembly with little power. Whatever legitimacy the Community had derived from the democratic parliaments of the member states which appointed the governments from which the Council of Ministers emerged.

Observers had commented on a "democratic deficit" from the beginning. In the 1970s, however, the appearance of the European Council and an elected European Parliament made matters more complicated rather than better. The European Council worked as secretly as the Council of

Ministers. The elected Parliament, still with very little power, could never quite behave like a real parliament – even though it came to contain serious people who did serious work. Its new popular base encouraged it to agitate for an increase in power, however, and it became an ever more eloquent advocate for confronting the democratic deficit.[58] The Parliament could gain more power only at the Council's expense, perhaps becoming a "co-decider," but the EC's derivation of democratic legitimacy from national parliaments would then become more questionable. Furthermore, a parliament with greater powers would be a *federal* parliament, but the Community had not made any conscious decisions to become the Federation of Europe. The fundamental problem however, was that there was little Community mass political culture or debate.

Thus by the later 1980s the European Community had become a complicated political system. Delors was a real democrat who gave full attention to public and parliamentary venues for explaining Community policies and seeking support. He nonetheless had to generate his resources and do most of his political work in the EC's elitist world. The consequences of the Single European Act had made this elite system even more vulnerable. Qualified majority Council decision-making on Single Market matters meant that member states could be overridden, a step towards federalism. Giving "cooperation" to the European Parliament on Single Market matters was meant to compensate for this change, but it muddied the waters. The implementation of the Single Market program meant that Community policies of much greater scope and impact would touch ordinary Europeans in new ways. The IGCs were working on even greater EC policy power, through EMU in particular. A "European Union" which stretched into vast new areas would sooner or later run into serious political problems. New doctrines of democratic legitimacy had to be devised and supported by new institutional structures. The conventional wisdom was that the way to achieve these goals was to reinforce the powers of the European Parliament. It was this conventional wisdom – however flawed – which guided the IGC.

The IGC first approached the easiest problems. The Commission was traditionally vulnerable to "Brussels bureaucracy" accusations. Little could be done about the fact that governments appointed commissioners.[59] New democratic legitimacy in the matter of appointing commissioners thus came down to giving some right to to the Parliament to approve new commissions proposed by the member states. This would be consistent with a number of other existing parliamentary powers: even if it had never done so, for example, it could censure the Commission and demand its resignation. By early March, a somewhat amiable discussion had come close to consensus on the European Council submitting the name of the Commission president-designate for consultation by the Parliament. Then there would be a procedure for parliamentary approval of the entire new Commission. There was also talk that the Commission's term should become five years, instead of four implying that the president's renewable term would become two and a half years, thereby coinciding with the life of the European Parliament.[60] No doubt these changes would make the Commission more responsive to Parliament and vice versa.[61]

This was a small matter compared to the issue of the actual legislative powers of Parliament. François and his little group energetically attacked this problem. The strategic problem, from the Commission's point of view, was first to design a system of co-decision, then secure as much real co-decision from the IGC as member states would give, and, thirdly, to make sure that all this was not done at the expense of the powers of the Commission itself. François's group first tried to define the specific legislative areas in which co-decision should happen. This was a priority because the Parliament and everyone else would be swamped were co-decision to occur for all, or even most, Community legislation. In the parlance of the debate, democracy would undercut efficiency. The Commission team thus invented something they called a "hierarchy of norms," which distinguished between legislative instruments – which the proposal called "laws" – and regulatory acts. "Laws," really framework legislation concerning principles and general orientations, would be submitted for co-decision by Council and Parliament. These laws, once passed, would be operationalized either by the Commission or by national parliaments, depending upon quidelines that the legislation itself set out.[62]

François was quite taken with this idea – largely his. There were problems from the beginning, however, even inside the Commission. When special chefs considered in early February there was widespread resistance, despite François's sometimes passionate efforts. The Scrivener cabinet expressed its fear that "laws" would diminish the role of the Council.[63] "The Brittans" opposed as well, perhaps because the British government preferred cooperation as it was. The MacSharry cabinet worried that the Council would no longer be able to fix agricultural prices. When the proposal went to Commission similar difficulties arose. Brittan claimed that the hierarchy of norms proposal would completely modify the legislative process, be perceived as an attempt by the Commission to increase its own power, and was not really a priority. To avoid a difficult vote Delors sent the proposals back to François. A modified version was finally passed and sent to the IGC by the Commission on February 27.[64]

When the Commission presented its "hierarchy" paper on March 6, it included agricultural prices as "laws" and was very careful to deny that it sought new powers. Skepticism was widespread, however. The French were gentle compared to the Germans, who dismissed the proposal as of "centralizing inspiration." The Danes saw it as a huge threat to the Council, which might then become a "disabled veteran of the institutional war." Except for the anti-federalist Danes, however, the smaller countries were nowhere near as hostile as the larger. The Commission's defeat was not of overwhelming importance. What mattered most was securing genuine co-decision itself. The existing cooperation procedure allowed the Parliament to give an opinion on certain kinds of Commission legislation before the

Council reached its "common position" and then to propose amendments and reject these common positions. At the end of the procedure, however, the Council had the sole right to decide, if decision rules varied depending upon what Parliament and Commission had done.[65] As the IGC began to discuss how to "consider" developing co-decision there was a range of positions on the table. Most of the schemes either advocated a system of paper shuttling through different readings in both Council and Parliament or a "committee of concertation" which could intervene if disagreements could not be overcome. The final matter of substance – which the Commission's ill-fated hierarchy of norms proposal tried to address – was to determine which legislative areas would be covered.[66]

It was evident that transparency would not be among the purposes co-decision would eventually serve. The Parliament's own proposals, which advocated Byzantine dealings among Commission, Council, and Parliament about amendments and decision procedures, would have given Parliament a little more power, but at the cost of further confusing the public. Only a constitutional lawyer would have been able to follow what would have resulted.[67] The Commission's paper was not that much better. It proposed a complex "two-reading" co-decision procedure only slightly less bewildering than that proposed by the Parliament.[68] The Commission's proposal also insisted on the continued active presence of the Commission throughout since there was some possibility that member states might seize the occasion to exclude the Commission and make co-decision into a strict Council–Parliament affair.[69] Preventing this exclusion may well have been François's deepest concern.[70]

There turned out to be deep disagreements about the desirability of co-decision in general which transcended all the lawyerly debate. A number of member states – Italy, Belgium, the Netherlands and a few others – were friendly. The Germans, the strongest advocate, even proposed that the Parliament might be able to request the Commission to legislate and if the Commission either refused, or failed to act within six months, the Parliament could then propose its own project.[71] Fundamental opposition to co-decision and insistence upon the continuation of a modified cooperation procedure came from Denmark, Portugal, and the UK and, on different grounds, from the French.

Competencies

The next issue on the table involved extending Community "competencies" and changing their decision rules. *The* basic principle of the EC was that it could act where Community treaties permitted and, moreover, only in the ways specified. It had been a consistent goal of the Delors presidency to expand these areas and introduce qualified majority Council decision-making into as many as possible. The Commission, finally, had an interest in clauses about "European citizenship" and "subsidiarity." Delors,

François, and their team had thus been busily putting out papers on competencies since December 1990, in health, culture and the protection of cultural patrimony, energy, the environment, economic and social cohesion, research and development, and the "social dimension." They had also produced papers on "trans-European networks," which would allow Community-sponsored infrastructural programs in transport, telecommunications, energy, and vocational training. Commissioner Karel Van Miert was in the process of generating two more proposals on transportation and consumer rights, despite François's efforts to keep such decentralized Commission proposing under tight control.[72]

A great many Delorist ambitions thus remained to be confronted. The research and development proposal, to a lesser extent the energy proposal, and the trans-European networks clause were to be parts of a Community industrial strategy. The goal was the growth of high value-added, competitive firms with European outlooks and consistencies. Delors wanted to develop Community public policy which would encourage genuinely European industrial leadership, particularly in "strategic" high-tech industries. In research and development the Commission wanted to eliminate some of the restrictions in scope and program development in the existing treaty clause – which had been one of the major Delorist victories in the Single European Act.

The other major Delorist strategic concern was social policy, in both "economic and social cohesion" and "social dimension" areas. The Commission wanted to modify and complete Single European Act "cohesion" clauses by expanding regional redistribution to include not only the dedicated structural funds but also general Community policies like the proposed trans-European networks and environmental policies. Here "cohesion" might allow the EC South to receive some further redistribution in compensation for the relative cost to them of the EC's ambitious environmental goals and vocational training. But the Commission's proposal was in trouble even before it was tabled. The South, led by Spain, wanted clear "cohesion" obligations in the new treaty in other places, particularly in EMU, and in ways which would oblige the Community to make big new budgetary increases in the Structural Funds. Delors feared that this could cause difficulty and preferred to hold off until the *paquet Delors 2* was presented after Maastricht. For the Spanish, however, "bird in the hand" theory dictated holding up the IGCs rather than waiting until later.[73]

François and Patrick Venturini had had some difficulty in generating the right kind of "social dimension" paper, so it came in rather late. DG V, through Patrick's ministrations, had begun to change from being an administration "captured" by traditional trade unionism towards becoming an advocate for the "social partnership for competitiveness and dialogue" approach which could help build credibility for an expansion of the Commission's social policy role. Nonetheless, one early version of the social paper had to be completely scrapped because it was too old fashioned. The new one was gestated largely in meetings between François and Patrick.[74]

The text proposed broadening the Community's social policy purview within the "wage-earners' rights in the Single Market" perspective and expanding qualified majority voting. Both these changes would have created much broader scope for legislative action – even though largely to implement the 1989 Social Charter and Action Program. The major innovation lay in the proposed "social dialogue" clause (Article 118b), which would have allowed the Commission to turn agreements reached by the "social partners" at European level into binding framework agreements. This proposal was connected to a new paragraph in Article 118 which enjoined the Commission, prior to proposing legislation, to consult with the "social partners" to ascertain whether they might negotiate a framework agreement as a substitute for legislation. The carrot and stick logic was clear. Employers and unions, who had had no success at reaching agreements in various EC venues, would have to try harder or else be threatened with Community legislation. And if they did negotiate, the results could acquire the force of law.

Unlike other competency questions, social issues were extensively discussed in early April. The Commission's text and a number of others were closely examined. The French, Belgians, Italians, Dutch, Greeks, and Danes all favored the Commission's proposals. The Germans were against them and their use of qualified majority, proposing instead a "reinforced qualified majority formula."[75] The Spanish favored "pragmatism . . . a step-by-step" movement. The South did not want Northern labor market and social policy standards imposed before it caught up economically. The British position was that the Treaty needed no change in the social area; it was fine. There was irony here, since the British had always fought tooth and nail against everything "social" which had been produced under the existing Treaty.[76]

The Commission's "citizenship" proposal was a pure example of the Russian doll strategy. Felipe Gonzalez had first broached the possibility of putting European citzenship in the treaty. The Commission endorsed this as a way of "developing feelings of belonging to European construction." In the Commission text European citizenship incorporated the protection of the fundamental human rights contained in the Council of Europe's Convention of Human Rights, affirmation of EC prohibition of discrimination on nationality grounds, plus an enumeration and definition of rights and correlative duties in the civil rights area – travel and residence, political association, voting and eligibility for candidacy in local elections. It also affirmed social rights and duties "in a larger sense, as defined in the EC Treaty's social dispositions and the Social Charter," plus cultural and environmental rights. Finally, it enjoined equal protection of EC citizens outside the Community. The Commission's proposal was daring in its inclusion of social as well as civil rights, and it clearly was meant to be evolutive, such that new dimensions of European citizenship could be added later. But the discussion on citizenship, whatever the Commission wanted, would take time to decant.

Early strategic thoughts

In late February, just after the Commission had finally approved its "big" IGC documents on the CFSP and co-decision, Delors met with the Bureau of the European Parliament. Among many old friends and allies he was particularly frank. On CFSP he insisted that giving the Community a security component should be the central point, but worried about British and Dutch opposition to the Commission's WEU proposals. He expressed concern about British opposition to any binding common foreign policy and the reluctance of small states either out of fear of reinforcing the big-state-dominated European Council or because of neutrality. The one issue which loomed as a potential problem for both IGCs, he noted, was "social and economic cohesion."[77] If the Spanish insisted too much on cohesion, the IGC might be disrupted. I was sitting across from Enrique Baron Crespo, President of the Parliament and influential in Madrid, and could see that this message, meant for him in particular, had been received.[78]

Delors and the parliamentarians worried most about co-decision. Everyone seemed to reject the German suggestion for a committee of conciliation of 12 Europarliamentarians and 12 ministers – which left out the Commission. The Commission text had not yet been discussed by the IGC and Delors did his best to explain the "hierarchy of norms" passages. He warned, however, that the French "phantom of a Congress was still lurking about" (the Congress was a new Europarliamentary organ composed of national parliamentarians). Here as elsewhere, the French wanted to roll back movement towards federalism in the interests of confederalism and intergovernmentalism. "This would be something like a two-story hotel. The first story would have the Council and the Congress, with a waterfront view. The second story, where Commission and Parliament would be together, would get a view over the parking lot." In the discussion which followed the federalist maximalism of most of the parliamentary leaders came out quickly, particularly with reference to Parliament's own powers. Delors did not hesitate to inform them that their desires, which he shared, were likely to remain unfulfilled, particularly on co-decision. The message was that the Commission's positions would be as good as the Parliament could get and the Parliament would be wise to support them.

What dangers were on the horizon? The first was pressure by certain countries – unmentioned but mainly Anglo-Saxon – to "relax the elastics," slow down the negotiating schedule and push back deadlines for putting new institutions into place. "History demonstrates that the timeline is critical. If we don't quickly renegotiate our marriage contract" – a favorite Delorist metaphor – ". . . it might not happen at all." The second big danger "is the risk that we'll come out of this with three different Communities, what we have now plus EMU, a separate deal on the CFSP, and a third in the judicial cooperation area. This would be bad enough, but there would then also be a serious problem about the "gray zone' between them."

A few days later there was an "interinstitutional conference" on political union in the Council room across the street from the Berlaymont. These periodic conclaves brought the Council, parliamentary leadership and the Commission together to compare notes on the progress of negotiations. There was much diplomatic *politesse* on the floor, and, for some time, not a great deal of substance. Jacques Poos, the Luxembourg Foreign Minister, who was presiding, tried very hard to steer the discussion towards CFSP, where progress had been made, away from co-decision, which Parliament wanted to talk about. Parliamentary leaders, having taken some of the hints offered by Delors, took a hardline position on co-decision and expressed anxieties about the prospect of "three communities." The discussion quickly became surreal, however. Parliamentary leaders talked sharply to central points and the ministers dispensed airy and pious rhetoric in response. Delors was present but silent – it was Frans Andriessen's official job to speak – and looked ever more discomfited, reviewing a gigantic dossier about something else, which François ostentatiously delivered to him in the middle of the British minister's speech. At one point the Commission President stood up, walked over to me and commented, loudly enough for everyone to hear, "you know what a high mass is, don't you . . . well here we've got a high mass without any faith."

François summarized his view of the state of play on political union in early April. "The fundamental question mark concerns the *nature of the Community* which will come out of treaty revision," he began. The real fear was that the existing equilibrium among Community institutions might be upset, with "the Council being the beneficiary . . . to the detriment of the Commission with a few little improvements for the Parliament." On CFSP, the debate lacked ambition but had the advantage of "integrating defense" and foreseeing qualified majority voting. The Gulf War was the cause of the first, but there was an "easy fix" on the horizon. The new treaty would establish a long-term common defense objective and put off serious commitments until a second IGC in 1996. Furthermore, the IGC had postponed the issue of achieving coherence between the Community's common foreign economic policies – a Commission matter – and the CFSP. "In general, one could ask if the member states, resigned themselves to talking about defense again in 1996, aren't dropping their ambitions below the conclusions of Rome II." François did not think that things were going too well. He was quite worried about the Franco-German couple in particular. It had taken the lead on the CFSP, but divisions over co-decision seemed to be growing ever larger. The Benelux countries were also divided over co-decision, even if they could be relied upon to defend the Commission against the European Council. Spain "is isolating itself with its demand to subordinate everything else to getting more money . . . but episodically supports France in trying to prevent a reinforcement of Commission power." With one exception, the other member states had little weight, even Italy. And, as if to leave posterity a note about his own fallibility, he announced that "every day Denmark becomes more Community minded."

4

Organizing European Space

It was cold and foggy in Brussels on the early March 1991 morning when our little group met at the Brussels airport. "The President," who, over coffee, ordered me not to call him that since "in France there are thousands of Presidents" (leaving me at a loss to know how to address him), was to give a speech on agriculture to an elite of French farmers assembled in a "National Convention on the Future of France's Rural Space." Spring was in the air when the plane landed in Bordeaux. The setting was comfortable for Delors. The meeting would be chaired by a fellow "European," Jean-François Poncet, and take place in political territory controlled by another friend, Jacques Chaban Delmas.[1] Delors was worried, however, and spent the brief trip poring over his speech text, crossing things out and writing in the margins. On the plane were Jerome Vignon, Jean-Luc Demarty, Bruno Dethomas and Christine Verger (Delors's cabinet advisor on Parliament and relations with France), who all had helped prepare the speech. Delors was venturing into a lions' den. French farmers were the major obstacles to CAP reform, and CAP reform was a central element in Delors's "after-1992" strategy.

The speech began with a classic Delorist theme.[2] "The renaissance of the rural world is an issue of civilization" for rural settings were a basic dimension of "the European model of society." Europe's cultural and environmental backbones were rural. Farmers were "producers of goods, creators of civilization and gardeners of nature." What was happening to the rural world? In areas close to cities land speculation and the chemical intensification of cultivation were real dangers, Delors announced. In "classic" rural areas there was depopulation, an absence of career opportunities for young people and few local resources. And in deep rural regions there was poverty and slow desertification. The EC's responsibilities, and the CAP's deeper purposes, should be to restore rural development, Delors said. There followed a long justification of CAP reform. The proposed reform, a "workshop" to which contributions were welcome, would address farmers in their dual roles as producers and agents for rural development. French farmers, Delors asked, should reflect about the continuation of a system which created incentives to pollute. They should think as well about how EC aid should be distributed across different types of farms, about a limited international opening of European markets, about the declining agricultural population and its consequences for rural development and about how to create incentives to high quality, environmentally friendly farming. Its earthy subjects notwithstanding, Delors's speech was lyrical, full of passion about the importance of a certain kind of rural landscape and society to Europe. It was also very abstract.

We all then went to lunch at Chaban's City Hall. Delors sat at the head table with Chaban and Mme Chaban, the archbishop and the prefect. Chaban's "cellar," allegedly the best in all France, lived up to its advertising. After lunch Delors came over with a great smile, and asked what I had thought of the vintages – a Bordeaux *grand cru* and then a Sauternes. My enthusiasm touched his patriotism. He then asked Dethomas his opinion of the speech. Bruno replied, "it isn't quite there yet." This was what Delors thought as well. Persuading French farmers to change the CAP would not be an easy thing to do.

On the plane back, after devouring *l'Équipe* – France's "Sporting News" – Delors came back to chat. What would now happen with CAP reform? "It's prepared . . . but now it has to marinate for a while." What about the Commission? Delors did not mince his words. "Many of them are not very good . . . and most are living off our earlier successes . . . Not very many of them are ready for the burdens of making a Community go forward, and there really is no collegiality. They're into attacking me . . . and the situation is such that I've got to compromise rather than strike back." Bruno thought that Delors was too quick to compromise. Delors nodded, then continued, "but you know, the small politics of the Commission doesn't do much for me. It is the hard intellectual work of figuring things out and trying to communicate that really motivates me."

The "1992" program, the relaunching pad of the Community after 1985, was concerned primarily with revitalizing European market activity. Jacques

Delors was no rigid liberal, however. To him markets were social construc-tions that gained their vitality from the people who contributed to them. Their energy, skill, and willingness to cooperate were as much, or more, the results of the social arrangements within which the market existed than of the market itself. Europe's own historic success had been largely because its market had been framed by a "European model of society" – extensive social services, civilized industrial relations, negotiated transfers among groups to sustain solidarity, and efforts to steer economic activity for the general welfare. The Community's destiny, as Delors never stopped repeat-ing, was to be not only a market but also an "organized space." For this reason the backbone of Delors's strategy was to promote state-building programs on the back of market-building successes. Among the more important dimensions of state-building were reforming the CAP and trying to endow the EC with a coherent and aggressive industrial policy. While all of the spectacular negotiating events that led to Maastricht were going on across the street, inside the Berlaymont the Delors team was busily trying to "organize Europe's space."

Farmers, Americans and the CAP

The Common Agricultural Policy (CAP) had been a great EC success story. It was designed when European agriculture desperately needed moderniza-tion. Europe had been a net importer of food, technologies were backward, and a high percentage of member state populations still lived on the land. The CAP set out strong new incentives. It had created a unified EC agricultural market, protected EC agriculture from international competi-tion, developed a system of price supports and market intervention to maintain farmers' incomes, and encouraged them to invest and change. The CAP had also slowly acquired a "solidarity" dimension with its resource transfers from better-off to poorer regions. In time the CAP helped reconfigure European farming. Europe's farmers rapidly became as pro-ductive as any in the world. Rural populations declined steadily. The CAP also became the EC's major common policy and largest budget item, for a long time the major glue of the Community and one foundation of the Commission's role.

The CAP's success had perverse consequences, however. Excessive use of chemicals polluted the soil. Higher capitalization, the concentration of landownership, and increasing mechanization led to the depopulation of vast territories. Eventually increases in production ceased to increase agri-cultural incomes.The combined price support-trade protection system led to overproduction. Finally, excess production, purchased by the Commu-nity at EC prices, was subsidized for resale on the world market – "dumped," in other words.[3]

Recognition of the need for CAP reform grew during the 1980s. Efforts were made to oblige farmers to bear some of the costs of surpluses through changes in the price-setting system and constraining CAP budgetary guidelines designed, in theory, to bring European farmers closer to real market conditions.[4] Further actions had been necessitated by a major Community budgetary crisis in the mid-1980s prompting the measures contained in the first Delors package.[5] The fundamentals of the original system were basically untouched, however, and beneath the surface were growing conflicts between the interests of European farmers and international pressures. In particular, as the 1980s progressed the United States pressed ever harder its objections to the international trade consequences of the CAP. The Americans claimed that the EC's subsidized exports unfairly seized market share and lowered prices. No one, including the Americans, was particularly virtuous in such struggles among rich countries over shares of the world market, but the threat of trade war was real.

The opening of the GATT Uruguay Round negotiations in 1986 put the CAP on a collision course with the Americans. Agreement on basic definitions for the Round took a while to establish – including whether or not agriculture should be included – but American pressure on EC agricultural policy, supplemented by that of the so-called "Cairns Group," an association of non-big-power agricultural producers led by the Australians, was unrelenting.[6] The major issue was export subsidies. Even though the EC publicly announced that the basic terms of the CAP were untouchable, it was evident that either the EC would have to reform the CAP or the Uruguay Round, scheduled originally for completion at Brussels in December 1990, would fail. The Brussels meeting, at the Heysel Conference Center, was a disaster. The organizers tried to link agriculture to other GATT matters, but the Americans and their allies would not hear of it. When the EC made some desultory offers on agricultural trade the others walked out. The handwriting was on the wall for the CAP.

In fact, internal Commission discussions about CAP reform were well underway. Delors had sounded the alert in early 1990 and set out initial lines of thought. Jean-Luc Demarty, Delors's agriculture expert, had then begun working with key people in DG VI (agriculture) including Guy Legras, the Director General, Michel Jacquot, Demarty's predecessor in the cabinet and head of the EAGGF, Jerome Vignon, and Pascal Lamy.[7] The first full brainstorming had begun in June 1990, prodded forward over the summer by budgetary problems, with serious conceptualization starting in September. Policy development lines went from Legras and Demarty (with Delors calling shots in the background) to MacSharry – who, Demarty suggested, "was not really an intellectual" and then back to Delors.[8]

Jean-Luc, in his initial reflections in October 1990, concisely listed the CAP's central problems. First was the coexistence of high levels of protection against grain imports with the absence of protection on substitutes for grain products – something which seemed esoteric but was behind the oilseeds dispute with the US.[9] The second was more obvious. The CAP subsidized farmers in proportion to what they produced. Despite efforts in the 1980s to "modulate" such things, 20 percent of farmers produced 80 percent of the goods and received 80 percent of the support. Jean-Luc added further that "the Community has lived to this point under the illusion that it could end these problems by conserving the existing CAP's essential provisions . . . All that was needed was to negotiate protection on grain substitutes from the Uruguay Round" in exchange for some reduction in EC subsidies. This would not work – the Community was asking its trading partners to solve the CAP's problems rather than changing the CAP. Even were these neighbors foolish enough to accept this it "would only grant a brief respite after which the internal and external dysfunctions of the CAP would have to be faced in much worse conditions than today," ultimately "destroying the Community's agricultural competitiveness." Jean-Luc did not mince words. The old CAP had reached a point of no return.

The answer in the area of large crop production (cereals and oil-producing plants), central to the problem, was a system of "deficiency payments" rather like the American one. Income support would come from direct public subsidies and farm goods could then be bought and sold at real market prices. EC prices would then move closer to world prices and EC goods would circulate on the international market on the basis of competitiveness, not subsidy.[10] Deficiency payments, as direct public subsidies, could also be adjusted to encourage certain kinds of farming, extensive vs intensive, for example, or smaller vs larger. Moreover, it would also be possible to tie deficiency payments to land set-asides, to gain new control over production levels. Finally, the waste of supporting commercial middlemen could be minimized. There were risks, however, and the biggest was financial. To sustain existing levels of support through the new system, the CAP's budget would rise by 7 to 9 billion ecus. This could not be allowed, but it was an indicator that reform, at least in the short run, would not save money. The Commission would have to find acceptable ways to absorb any additional costs because otherwise there would be some danger of member states opposed to the reform beginning to "renationalize" agricultural policies to take up any slack. The second risk was more obvious. As Jean-Luc put it, "EC farmers (in particular the French) are very attached to the system of 'double prices.' " The largest farmers, with the most to lose from a new system, French grain farmers in particular, would be against it.[11] Maneuvering through the minefield of farmers' mobilizations against reform would demand great skill.

The first public indication of what was to come was Delors's November 1990 speech to the Assises du Monde Rural in Brussels, organized by a conglomerate of farmers' associations. As was his wont, Delors was at his most lyrical when discussing the EC's most down-to-earth-subject. His purpose was to "engage two discussions . . . on rural life and on the future of European farming agriculture." He thus focused more on Europe's space than on farming per se. A period marked by struggle against scarcity now had to be ended, since its policies had come to threaten the very existence of Europe's countryside. "We must change our behaviors." In the countryside there was "desertification and bad fallowness" that could eventually lead to the destruction of Europe's beauty and geographical equilibria. The "blind intensification" of production that polluted the earth had to stop. These were "not technical issues, but fundamental social problems." There were "imbalances between different regions, between the rural and urban worlds, and between generations . . . [constituting] an intellectual, as much as a political, challenge, for us all."

To Delors rural development was not simply economics: "The market cannot take care of all of the economic and social needs of a society, and it cannot take charge of . . . public goods, invisible goods that we can only get collectively." The future of the CAP was inseparable from the "collective good" dimension of the rural world. Secondly, "the equilibrium of the basic triangle" – market unity, Community trade preference, and financial solidarity – had to be maintained, "but not as it is. Community preference cannot be permanently ensured at the level it is now." The final messages were generally, but passionately, communicated. The Community's agriculture had to recognize international interdependence. Solidarity and rural development were key dimensions of the CAP. Rural incomes, Delors claimed, should henceforth be based on production and on rural development. The "how to produce" should become as important as "how much to produce." "If you conclude, after having listened to me, that today's policies should stay on course, then our discussion will have been in vain . . . in the absence of . . . [outside] . . . pressures, the continuation of existing policies even for five more years will lead to results that you will regret."[12]

The Uruguay Round collapse at Heysel in December was a disguised blessing, since the GATT negotiators were really not ready to deal on a wide range of things, and loud disharmonies on agriculture were a convenient shield. For Delors and his team, the collapse granted precious time to get CAP reform through the Commission and then win Council approval. Neither task would be easy. Delors's own scheduling foresaw approving the reform in time to fold its budgetary consequences into the second Delors package, in the aftermath of Maastricht, much as the first package had followed the Single European Act. There was bound to be real struggle over its contents, but all of its different elements would take on much more significance as part of a campaign for the Council to "make good on Maastricht" than they ever could separately. Moreover, when serious commitments had been fully made on CAP reform – spring 1992? – it would then be possible to deal more effectively on the Uruguay Round. More was at stake than the size of carrots, therefore!

Delors, Demarty, Legras, and MacSharry had an initial program by the time the Heysel confrontation occurred in December 1990. Its first dimension would involve changing internal market operations through the introduction of deficiency payments across the range of large crops (grains, oilseeds). These payments would vary inversely with the size of the farm to discourage intensification and promote extensification. Obligatory land set-asides were included. Other major product areas – milk, beef, sheep, and goat production – would also undergo profound market structure changes (price falls and quota changes to discourage overproduction plus bonuses for extensification). Things like sugar and wine were excluded, perhaps to avoid loading too many issues at once on to the French, Germans, and Italians. Under the rubric of rural development there would be new measures to protect the environment. There would also be early retirement program for farmers (at 55). Direct income supports for certain kinds of smaller farmers were to be expanded.

Once on the table, Jean-Luc thought, the reform would almost certainly grant the Commission more maneuvering room on the Uruguay Round front, both internally and externally. The fact that CAP reform was in progress would set limits on external pressures while the need for CAP reform to succeed in the Uruguay Round would work internally. There were dangers, however. The effects of "modulation" (the scale of support sliding as farm size grew to over 30 hectares) would be difficult for certain member states with large farms. Jean-Luc, in daily touch with the French, thought that 50 to 60 hectares would be more judicious. The FNSEA, France's powerhouse farmers' union, opposed reform altogether and without sweetening the pill it could cause serious problems. The rural development measures proposed did not articulate very well with the workings of the existing development fund (the EAGGF) and this might cause problems. But the major issues were political. The reform was "on a collision course with those with interests in intensive livestock production (the Dutch, the Danes, the West of France, Northern Italy, and Belgium), the port of Rotterdam – whose prosperity was partly built on agricultural trade – and big grain growers in the UK and the Paris region."

The next step was to persuade the Commission to accept the reform. Delors, Legras, and Jean-Luc made a deliberate decision to short-circuit usual Commission procedures. Rather than having reform percolate upward through the cabinet system, where there was solid risk of heavy politicization, conflict along national interest lines, a rash of amendments, and perhaps even sabotage, the project went first to a Sunday seminar of the Commission. The "seminar" tactic was to generate commitment on principles prior to getting into detail. What would then follow, if things went as planned, would be the publication of a Commission think-piece on the basic lines of reform, without details. This then would be the text which would "marinate," in Delors's words, provoking debate and discussion among member states, farmer interest groups, and other concerned parties, to scout the terrain, uncover dangers, and flush out enemies. After an appropriate period, the Commission would then propose its detailed reforms, which themselves would marinate for another few months. Jean-Luc estimated that the entire process would last at least one year.[13]

Jean-Luc helped prepare Delors well for the seminar, held in January on the first weekend of the Gulf War. The pair anticipated major debates on the principle of modulating income supports to size of farms and on budgetary matters. On something as politically loaded as CAP reform commissioners had to speak their national pieces, and such would be the case on modulation. The British, Dutch, Danes, French, Spaniards, Portuguese, and Italians all had reservations and wanted to protect the positions of larger farmers. The principle of differential treatment was also rejected by economic liberals like Sir Leon Brittan and Frans Andriessen. Only the Dutch completely opposed deficiency payments, however. There would evidently have to be a compromise on modulation, raising the cut-off point to include more farmers (indeed it seemed that this cut-off point had been deliberately set low to serve as a later bargaining chip). The budget issue would also have to be addressed. The reform was almost certain to cost more, rather than less, in the short run. Projected outwards in time, though, it would cost less than continuing the existing CAP. Demarty thought that it should be possible to argue that the macroeconomic gains of bringing food prices down to consumers would offset these budgetary charges.

Jean-Luc concluded that "the Commission debate is not likely to be easy. But no commissioner will be in a position to propose an alternative vision adapted to the problems of agriculture." The "reflections paper," debated in great haste at its February 1 meeting, at Ray MacSharry's insistence, was the actual document to be "marinated." It was very general and addressed the impasse of the existing CAP.[14] Its last few pages presented the outlines of reform, but it went out of its way to confront the argument that "modulation of support in function of the size of holding would be discriminatory and non-economic," trying to pre-empt the budget issues by making the best case for strong reform. It concluded that "the status quo is the one option that [the Commission] considers not to be viable."

Commission debate was difficult, as anticipated. Leon Brittan proposed an amendment softening the language on modulation, Bruce Millan indicted the proposal for insufficient attention to regional disparities, Carlo Ripa di Meana accused it of insufficient attention to the environment, while Frans Andriessen had a full list of objections, including disagreement with Delors's "rural preservationism." This dimension of the program would later come in for its share of public debate. British minister John Gummer, not a mincer of words, mocked the program for turning farmers into "museum curators," while French Agriculture Minister Louis Mermaz let it be heard it would please Delors to see farmers dressed up in seventeenth-century costumes. Still, the proposal passed.[15] So far, so good. In early summer 1991 the Commission produced its more precise paper. The real discussion would occur only after Maastricht, however.[16]

Organizing the Market?

It was inevitable that Jacques Delors's strategy for Europe would include industrial policy. Exposing Europe to the cold winds of international competition would not by any means guarantee the general welfare. Important industrial sectors were ill-prepared to cope with greater international openness and the international market itself was sometimes unfairly stacked in ways which could offer European firms up for sacrifice. One of Delors's more fervent "organizing space" hopes was thus to use Community "public goods" to strengthen European industry in its new, and threatening, global setting. Not everyone agreed with Delors, however. The British were the most articulate and doctrinaire liberals among member states, but the Dutch, Danes, and the Germans shared at least some of their attitudes. More generally, the high tide of 1980s neo-liberalism had brought a theoretical assault on virtually all forms of public intervention in the economy. Strong liberalism therefore had the intellectual upper hand.

Trying on industrial policy

Delors was frequently visited by the captains and generals of European industry. A select group of them thus alerted him in spring 1990 to the clouds gathering around European electronics. Olivetti, the big Italian firm, was in serious trouble, partly because of overadventurous takeover policies. Bull might well already have gone under without the deep pockets of its owner, the French state. Dutch Philips, the heaviest hitter, was shaky enough to contemplate pulling out of many of its electronics activities altogether. Siemens, the German giant, was suffering from the purchase of ailing Nixdorf and was negotiating with IBM for new strategic alliances. Thomson, the other French giant, was barely holding itself up through defense contracts. ICL, the main British company, had been bought by Fujitsu. In general, profitability had declined dramatically and international competition, particularly from the Japanese, threatened European survival in key product areas. Worse still, Europe's troubles were set in the generally ominous situation in electronics internationally. Even the large American and Japanese companies were feeling the pinch. After years of great growth, a shakeout was at hand. Finally, general trends meant that it could coincide with a recession.

Most of the big European companies had developed as "national champions" in sheltered national markets and through protected public purchasing, during years when American and Japanese firms were accumulating gigantic resources and internationalizing their scope. Would it be possible for the Europeans to become effective multinationals, or would the Single Market, by making them vulnerable to the more powerful and maneuverable Americans and Japanese, end up destroying them? Quite as important, was there any specifically "European" solution to their problems or would the end product be an industry dependent upon and subordinate to the Americans and Japanese – if there was an industry at all? Finally, what should and could the Community do? Delors's corporate visitors proposed expensive bail-outs and protectionism and intimated, *sotto voce,* that if the companies sank into deeper trouble the Community might be held responsible, with dire consequences for business confidence in the Commission's efforts.

The situation called for some kind of EC action. Although arguments about "strategic industries" had fallen out of fashion, electronics was clearly special. Electronic technologies affected other industries. It was not only the European firms that were at issue, but much about the European economy more generally, since Europe would be more dependent without a solid electronics sector. And whatever Delors felt about "strategic industry" arguments, he had to pay attention since the companies in the worst condition were in the French public sector.

Jean-Charles Leygues, the in-house fixer and jack-of-all-policy-trades in the Delors cabinet, oversaw industrial policy. When the alarm first sounded Jean-Charles set DG XIII, in charge of high tech and research, to think about what the Commission might do. The Commission had few recent industrial policy precedents to guide it, however. Delors and Jean-Charles had the very good idea, therefore, to start the appropriate Commission administrative services at work on a general document on industrial policy. With a general Commission position on industrial policy in place, it would then be much more legitimate to turn to electronics more specifically. "It was Jean-Charles who brought industrial policy out of the closet," noted the author of the industrial policy paper, a high-level Eurocrat in DG III, the Internal Market administration. The author's boss, Director General Riccardo Perissich, a veteran of Commission internal politics, was skeptical about EC industrial policy prospects. But he was also a shrewd politician whose high Commission post had come from Delors.

The more DGs involved, the more complicated it is for the Commission to produce a coherent piece of work. Industrial policy touched a large number of different Commission administrations. Jean-Charles could thus be found everywhere, managing the complexities of interservice coordination. It was during the gestation of the industrial policy paper that Jean-Charles convened a meeting, cited as the very symbol of how the Delors cabinet did things. The legendary meeting began late on a Friday afternoon and went on until 2 a.m. the next day. Jean-Charles got his way.[17] The final document, *Industrial Policy in an Open and Competitive Environment,* was published in October 1990.[18] Its line was clear. Firms were the key actors who made the final decisions: there could be no question of substituting public action for firm decisions in old-fashioned *dirigiste* ways.[19]

The new "Community approach" should involve "horizontal" coordinating policies to act on the environment within which firms made up their minds. The Community should begin by guaranteeing a genuinely competitive environment for firms by aggressive competition policies to hinder protectionist public policies and private market power. Community policy should also involve promoting a stable macroeconomic environment. In addition, the Community ought to act diplomatically to make sure that the workings of the broader international market were fair. Finally, it should use the tools which the EC already had at its disposal to ensure a high level of education, and promote "economic and social cohesion" and extensive environmental protection. Aggressive implementation of the Single Market program was perhaps the most important tool, but there were others, like "developing the technological capacity of the Community" through research and development. Then there was a coda: "The experience of the 1970s and 1980s has shown that interventionist sectoral policies are not an effective instrument for structural adaptation." However, "in the past, particularly difficult problems of adjustment have been dealt with at Community level, steel, textiles and shipyards, for example. Likewise, the Community has and should continue to pay particular attention to the areas which play a central role in the development of Europe's economy and industry such as telecommunications, semi-conductors, aeronautics, and the maritime industry."

Subtexts abounded, as Jean-Charles had intended. The Commission bowed and scraped towards the liberalism underlying "1992". Then it invoked the latest in trendy arguments to justify "framework" public intervention to promote smarter firm decision-making.[20] The deepest text, however, argued against the initial bowing and scraping and for the rehabilitation of the idea of industrial policy, albeit in redefined form. As Jean-Charles repeated many times, the Community "had to combine competitiveness and a real European texture . . . and not become a sieve through which international waters can flow at will." Jean-Charles had thus placed enough references to specific threatened sectors to establish a precedent for a sectoral focus. He wanted a door opened wide enough to slip through when the time came.

Electronically speaking . . .

In the meantime DG XIII had been working away on an electronics document. What could the Community do? This was what Jean-Charles had charged the high-tech specialists in DG XIII to explore. Their first draft was produced in mid-November 1990. The paper posited electronics as a "strategic industry" in crisis which needed exceptional derogations from the competition-focused policies of the Single Market program. If firms in electronics were not in a good position to make the right decisions it was for reasons largely beyond their control.[21] The paper then proposed accelerating technological innovation in part by spending more EC money on research and development programs – a "second generation of EC Research and Development."[22] The Community should also take the lead, *à la* MITI (the Japanese Ministry for Trade and Industry), in promoting strategic initiatives beyond research and development, using the new "Trans-European Network" programs, targeted training efforts to upgrade human resources, and responsive attentiveness to imperfections in international markets. The paper also proposed that the EC should make efforts, backed with carrots and sticks, to get the companies together and to cooperate in "European" ways.

Given the prevailing climate in the Commission, the document was triply flawed. It was "techno-yuppy," in the words of one critic, positing that industrial success was based upon technology rather than the market (the draft barely discussed the market at all). It was also producer, rather than user, centered. Moreover, it was much too clearly enamored of "the bigger the better" solutions. There was indeed something very Colbertiste about it. All of these things opened DG XIII to the accusation of being in the companies' pockets.[23] Finally, the paper was more political than factual, arguing for its preferred solutions without providing the information necessary to understand why they made sense. The paper's broader faults were a real problem for the Delors team, but the proposal to get the companies together under Commission auspices was what Jean-Charles, Lamy, and Delors most wanted to see.

The hard problems appeared during the first full interservice discussions about the document. The most hostile response came from the competition policy team at DG IV. Because of its function, its commissioner, the redoubtable Sir Leon Brittan,[24] and the centrality of competition policy in the Single Market program, DG IV saw the return to industrial policy advocated for electronics both as a "turf" threat and as an initiative cutting to the liberal antitrust heart of the renaissance of European integration. Its early January response to the draft thus subjected every specific suggestion to withering criticism. The paper's proposals for industry-specific measures, which did not demonstrate why electronics merited special consideration, contradicted the earlier industrial policy document. The paper, furthermore, made little mention of the role of enhanced competition for industrial success. Indeed, DG IV rejected the very concept of a strategic or basic industry. Perhaps the most important DG IV conclusion, however, was that there was no evidence that EC help would change anything.[25]

Perissich's DG III evaluated the electronics paper in less ideological ways. It asked for more facts and arguments, for a better job in analyzing priorities and timing, and expressed strong reservations about the notion of sectoral crisis. Better analysis was needed of international competitive conditions and the financial problems of the industry – what the markets looked like. The draft was also weak on the articulation between technology and the market, in particular the implications of the Single Market, and on the logics of international technological and industrial cooperation. DG III, unlike IV, did not object to the high-level meeting between Delors and the chief executives (CEOs) which Jean-Charles wanted to promote.

Jean-Charles had his work cut out. He had a political task, first of all, to make sure that DG XIII did not create a united front of opposition which could sink everything, including Delors's planned meeting with the CEOs. Fortunately, Martin Bangemann, the commissioner in charge of DG III, and Leon Brittan, who, with their services, would have had to form such a front, did not get along particularly well. It also helped that most of the other commissioners' cabinets involved had a national interest stake in putting up a good front on electronics. Jean-Charles's skill was central, however. He had a deep and long knowledge of the Commission which endowed him with an extraordinary ability to work a plurality of networks – he could call on the French and other national "mafias," on the socialists, and various technicians with common interests across departments. They all had to take him seriously because of the power which flowed from the enormous breadth of his presidential portfolio. There were very few people in the upper reaches of the Commission whose path Jean-Charles did not cross sooner or later, usually sooner, and most would need his help on something, sometime. Jean-Charles's counterparts understood these games, they trusted him and, most of all, they knew that he knew his dossiers backwards and forwards.

Eventually 15 redrafts of the original paper, and many more meetings, were needed to end the messy row. DG XIII's team tried to limit access of other services to the redrafting of the paper, and then sent its strongest representatives in force to meetings, often including Director General Michel Carpentier and three or four other high-level officials. This infuriated DG IV, which often received documents only minutes before meetings opened. DG IV's group, a stronghold of lawyers (one avowed that it didn't "take anything seriously if it is not a case"),[26] was handicapped by an absence of sectoral economic knowledge, which meant that it had little positive to contribute. This allowed Carpentier to discount it as "negative and unhelpful." Perissich's internal market team, the other major player, countered Carpentier's team in the "incessant meetings" by sending its own experts well armed with alternative texts.

The play of commissioners' cabinets complicated things still further. It was the cabinets' job to hammer out the best deal they could for their commissioners, to produce a presentable document at the same time and, by engaging in most of the bloodletting themselves, to keep blood off the Commission floor. On electronics, they were wired. As a high DG III official noted,

> all of us were getting incessant instructions on what to do from cabinet members, not even from the *chefs de cabinet* either. And they kept introducing fundamental changes into the document. This kind of thing has the effect, over time, of "deresponsibilizing" the services, we lost our willingness to take risks and think things through . . . Furthermore, the cabinets are always pursuing their own national interests, so that the dossier became heavily political.

As the weekly meetings went on and on, "shadowed" by an even larger number of informal dealings, "the Brittans," generally acknowledged to be the best staff in the Berlaymont (except for Delors's), played very tough. Katherine Day, the Brittan frontperson and one of the relatively rare female cabinet members, stood her ground with great tenacity, arguing against "producer-oriented" proposals and those "in this building . . . who haven't caught up with what has happened in the real world" (DG XIII).[27] Then the main target became Delors. "The Brittans" knew that Jean-Charles was not the same as Michel Carpentier, but they also knew that Delors's team needed the electronics paper to open high-level dealings with the companies. This step, in their minds, would almost certainly be followed by "sectoral intervention." From this it was an easy jump to labelling Jean-Charles a "closet interventionist." And, of course, the Brittans knew that behind Jean-Charles stood Delors. At their most uncharitable, they intimated that the President and Pascal were motivated by French concerns and that much of the electronics stir was directed at getting either direct EC help for, or EC blessing for a French bail-out of, Bull.[28]

Dénouement

It was customary for Jacques Delors to meet every six months with the directors general of the services, partly to fill them in on the state of play in the capitals, the Council and the international arena. The occasions were assemblies of the entire general staff of the European Commission, a group of distinguished, sophisticated middle-aged males – there were but two women.[29] On this last day of February 1991 there was some uncertainty in the air, given the convening of the IGCs. More specifically the Commission President was worried about electronics. Delors had himself been attending the regular meetings of Bangemann's cluster of industry and technology commissioners – the next level above the melee I have been describing – and was his usual well-briefed self. But as the paper-drafting exercise drifted on and acrimony spread the President grew impatient and decided to stir things up with the Directors General.

Delors began in his ordinary soft tone, running through a few small matters before repeating his regular litany about the Commission's "many tasks, *eleven* priorities, in fact," referring to the gigantic Commission program for the year. The storm began abruptly, however:

> Simplicity is the best way . . . If I could hire and fire here, I'd go after at least five or six of you . . . I know which ones among you don't take me seriously and those who do . . . I know who you are. We shouldn't live at the level of rumors and backbiting. We should be able to rise to the high level of the tasks at hand. I see everything and I think about what I see. In a government I'd be able to remove people. But here you're all barons, it is hard to shake you up . . . But I'll get to you nonetheless.

Pascal, who had come in the door as the tirade started, glanced across at me and buried his head in his papers.

The august Directors General began to squirm in their chairs. Delors went straight to the point:

> It will not do to make light of industrial policy. The Community is not, and will not be, a free-trade zone. It is up to us to make a European organized

space . . . There are some of you who seem to have barely progressed beyond the stage of elementary school. DG III and DG IV are worse here than the others . . . You should know that I have no intention of letting you get away with it. I've only one and a half years left to my term, but I'll take care of you, you can be sure of it.

The impeccable Perissich and Ehlermann sat tight and tried to maintain their composure. Both had reasons to be deeply hurt.[30]

Almost as quickly as it arose, the storm subsided. Delors turned to complaining about his Commission colleagues in the later stages of the Gulf War[31] and interjected his speech about the Community's "sixteen years of stagnation, ten years of progress, eight years of crisis."

Delors was capable of such semi-public black moods but I could not quite sort out the layers of meaning of this particular event. He was someone who avoided conflict, often using Pascal and his cabinet to initiate and "take" confrontation inside the Commission. Partly this was smart politics, but there was more. Delors had difficulty controlling the measure of his reactions to those who fell short of his own high standards. Wisely, he knew enough about himself to avoid the potentially costly hurts which might be inflicted if he did lose control. Moreover, the particular day had not gone well. Delors was furious about having just lost in Commission on the issue of agricultural prices. There was another line of explanation, however. One of the targets of his outburst, who knew Delors very well, was certain that the explosion was contrived – "acting" was the term used. Delors, the argument went, played on his reputation for awesome volatility to make subordinates do things that they otherwise might not be willing to do. In this version the fury was a gesture, needed from time to time, to get the machine up to speed again. One thing was certain: Delors had a tight time limit for a meeting with the electronics CEOs and he needed a document. "Kicking" DGs III and IV publicly was a short cut to end the text torturing which had been going on. It worked. The paper began to approach its final form very quickly.

The new paper, titled *The Community's Electronics and Informatics Industry*, began with a long bow to the earlier industrial policy paper. It then moved on to a well-argued and easily readable factual description of the European industry, outlining its strengths and, more important, its weaknesses compared with the Americans and Japanese. The section detailing the international market context contained the "hook," the idea of historically created market imperfections.[32] In both American and Japanese cases public authorities had played a central role in establishing viable bases – MITI planning for Japan, defense spending for the US. Moreover, in both cases there had been specific financial structures to make plans work. The results were mature, globalized electronics sectors. In Europe, without a genuine Community market, national champions had been unable to develop the economies of scale and technological synergies for effective global stature. The hook caught in the next section. European firms were in difficulty largely because of global market failures traceable to the differential roles of public authorities in the past. European firms were badly placed not because they had themselves made bad strategic choices on an open market but because European markets had given them the wrong signals. The situation in which the European firms thus found themselves was therefore not primarily their responsibility. Making them pay the full costs of it would lead to a giant sacrifice of European industrial potential.

"The measures to be taken . . . are in the first instance . . . the responsibility of the firm decision-makers themselves, and of their capacity to take advantage of the new opportunities which the creation of the Single Market presents." But "applying the principle of subsidiarity," it was up to the EC and its member states to "contribute to ensuring them a favorable environment, considering . . . what is at stake for the entire collectivity . . . in electronics and informatics." Proposals for action included company involvement in the proposed trans-European networks in telematics (linking different national and EC administrations), "distant education" (open universities and home training), transports, public health, and the environment. Proposals on technology included a "second generation of technological research and development" which moved from the "precompetitive" towards projects much closer to the market itself. Extensive training programs were also needed, along with strong EC competition policy to ensure a level playing field in the international market.

At the special chefs meeting, the next-to-last preparatory meeting before the paper went to Commission on March 26, when all commissioners' cabinets had a crack at the document, the final version was introduced. Jean-Charles was candid about it:

> For the President, this is just the beginning of a *démarche*. The document is nothing extraordinary, but it should open up the discussion that he wants . . . The paper is pragmatic . . . political . . . it isn't meant to be a technical exposé and it isn't a legislative proposal . . . The Commission has to send a message to the firms. It should be clear, first of all, that the Commission is no dupe. National champions don't fly any more . . . But we have to show that we are open to dialogue. If we don't do this then we risk providing an alibi to those who want to turn back the page and pump up their national champions . . . or those who want to ally with the Japanese and the Americans . . . Basically what we're doing is to try to get the companies to come out of the woods and announce their own strategies. Then, depending upon what they say, perhaps the Community can do something.

In the *tour de table* which followed the only discordant note came from Katherine Day, speaking for Leon Brittan, the only commissioner who had not been fully brought into the endeavor, who announced that "Sir Leon will not allow the Commission to get involved in sectoral industrial policy." According to the special chefs ritual outsiders who had not been in the flow of paper preparation anounced that their concerns had not been taken sufficiently into account – "social" Commissioner Papandreou's *chef* complained about the insufficient development of the training dimension, Regional Policy Commissioner Millan's respected *chef* argued that the document "missed the spatial characteristics . . . R&D is regionally concentrated," and Audiovisual Commissioner Dondelinger's delegate remarked that the document was weak on the software side. The prize for greatest exaggeration went to the Andriessen representative – assiduous throughout on behalf of Philips – who congratulated everyone present for their "excellent cooperation." At this point one of the Commission's industrial policy brains sitting next to me whispered, "greater cooperation than this and you're dead."

The end of a long game was in sight. The meeting with the CEOs which Delors and Lamy had been organizing was imminent, and the services were busy preparing options.[33] The Commission meeting was anticlimactic. Pandolfi, the commissioner in charge of DG XIII, presented the document. Bangemann stressed that it was not "sectoral . . . but rather the application, to a specific sector, of the general industrial policy which the Commission had earlier defined." Brittan was discreet, underlining his pleasure that the document did not suggest moving research and development spending towards product development.

The agony of producing a paper was the easy part. Only days after the Commission meeting French Industry Minister Roger Fauroux announced a new "engagement" of the French government on behalf of French electronics, involving roughly $1 billion in help. Fauroux further called for "a genuine European industrial policy," including a trade policy that does not turn the Single Market "into a field open to all winds," plus reinforcement of research support and cooperation between large groups. France, he noted, would be willing to renounce its own most important industrial policy prerogatives, but only if Brussels took up the cause. In the interim, the French had to do their duty as stockholder for French public sector groups.[34] The Fauroux communication revealed how much Delors had been under pressure from the French side. The French were determined to bail out Bull and Thomson whatever the Community did and were fundamentally skeptical that the Community would do anything at all.

At a rather gloomy cabinet lunch meeting on the day after the French announcement, Pascal, in his deepest ironic tone, allowed that "Fauroux isn't doing anything to help us, is he?" But the logic of things pointed in even more complicated directions. The French announcement indicated that Bull and Thomson (whose CEO was openly demanding protectionism)[35] were likely to prefer to go their own way rather than choose the "European" option which Delors desired. And heavy French state involvement was also likely to deter some of the other EC firms, particularly Siemens, which had an unhappy history of dealing with the French state, from "European" options as well. Philips had already expressed its skepticism.

Delors nonetheless carried on. With Bangemann, Pandolfi, Perissich, and Michel Carpentier he slipped away from the Berlaymont on a beautiful spring weekend to one of the world's best restaurants, in Saulieu, France, to meet with the CEOs of Philips, Olivetti, Bull, Siemens, and Thomson. François Lamoureux was humorously trenchant at lunch about the chosen venue: "If they were going to put on a show they should at least have done it in the cafeteria at minus one in the Berlaymont. It would have looked more democratic."

The press learned of the "secret" event through the companies. And despite a typical Lamy pronouncement that "we suffer too much from proclamatory industrial policy. We don't want to take the risk that the little bit of mayonnaise we have will turn . . . MITI doesn't call press conferences when it intervenes," almost everything that was discussed leaked. The companies, particularly the French ones, asked for trade protection and bags of money.[36] The Community countered by trying to persuade them of the need for a new grouping in semiconductor research and production "like the Airbus consortium" – the trans community alliance for commercial aircraft.[37] The plans which the Commission had brought involved combining research and development money, regional fund subsidies, incentives connected to EC procurement (largely for the famous "trans-European networks"), and a few other sweeteners into a substantially subsidized joint chip-making installation for the South of Italy.[38] In Pandolfi's words, "the time has come to reach a critical mass."[39] The Commission was willing to expend approximately $5 billion over ten years (a total of $18.5 billion including amounts the companies were already committed to invest) to get Europe into semiconductors, if only the companies in turn were willing to collaborate.

The story went on, in infinite complexity. The plot was simple, however. Three companies – Siemens, Bull, and Olivetti – were willing to talk about cooperation but each was simultaneously pursuing plans for strategic alliances with non-European firms, whether American or Japanese. Ultimately their choice was to "go global" by dealing either with a Japanese or American giant. In the minds of the company CEOs there really was no European option. Delors's hopes that a "European organized industrial space" could be forged out of a difficult situation for European electronics turned out to be overoptimistic.[40] The strategy which Delors, Lamy, and Jean-Charles had painfully worked out had at least one merit, however. It obliged the companies to come clean about their choices without the Community bearing the blame. This was small consolation.

Directing television

The high-definition television (HDTV) story was another case of trying to "organize" EC market space through industrial policy. The central issue was how to design EC programs to give Europe a better chance in the international struggle for domination over the next generation of television technology. When it had become clear, belatedly, in the mid-1980s that the

Japanese were about to monopolize HDTV through the definition of broad-casting norms, the EC had been shocked out of torpor.[41] It first engaged substantial research and development resources, largely through Eureka,[42] to devise a specifically European broadcast norm, HDMAC.[43] It then passed a Directive in 1986 that obliged high-powered broadcasting satellites to use an interim norm – D2MAC – receivable by both traditional TV sets and new "transitional" sets with rectangular screens ("16 × 9 s") to be produced by European firms, Philips and Thomson in particular.[44] The hope was to use the definition of a broadcasting standard to entice broadcasters and pro-ducers towards a specifically European HDTV system and encourage Euro-pean equipment manufacturers to invest in the new technologies. This norm-led strategy was meant to establish European pre-eminence in HDTV technologies, perhaps for once freezing out the Japanese.[45]

The 1986 Directive failed, however, because start-up satellite broadcast-ers in Europe did not transmit from high-powered satellites, sending out programs on medium-powered telecommunications satellites instead. This removed them from regulation by the EC's Directive and they broadcast using the old PAL system rather than D2MAC. However, because the Direc-tive expired after five years the Commission had to face the issue again in 1991. It thus asked for a new EC discussion document to begin reflecting on new Commission legislation. Delors himself had decided early on that the Commission needed a Directive that would compel broadcasters and pro-ducers to use D2MAC. Thomson, along with Dutch Philips, had invested a great deal in developing rectangular 16 × 9 TV screens in sets capable of receiving D2MAC so as to simulate true HDTV.[46] A lot of money was already on the table.

Patrick Venturini, whose main job was the "social" portfolio, had the HDTV dossier, and freely acknowledged, "when I got here I didn't know anything at all about this stuff. It's been on-the-job training since. But with Delors and Pascal you learn quickly, or else." As it turned out, it was not because of his recent education that Patrick got in over his head, but because of the nature of the dossier itself. Deciding what to do when the earlier Directive expired was programmed into the Commission's business, and discussions began first in November 1990 in the Audiovisual Group of Commissioners.[47] Initial meetings revealed that the conclusion Delors wanted would not be easy to reach. Conflicting interests in the television industry itself and the way in which it coincided with the national origins of the involved commissioners were the problems. Satellite broadcasters, whose PAL operations were barely surviving, would have trouble with the start-up costs of a new HDTV standard which would also make it difficult to keep their audiences (who would have to purchase or be supplied with expensive decoders). The major players were Rupert Murdoch's British B-Sky B, and Astra, a Luxembourg satellite company. Murdoch's interests in avoiding a new standard fit rather well with Sir Leon Brittan's liberal distaste for industrial policy, while Jean Dondelinger, the Audiovisual Com-missioner, was from Luxembourg. Program producers, who would initially have to produce HDTV-standardized material for a relatively small audience, existed in a hyper-competitive setting filled with aggressively marketed North American products. Filippo Pandolfi, an Italian, came from the country with the most successful producer of all, Silvio Berlusconi. Delors's views on industrial policy and the interests of Thomson in the new standard were clear. Frans Andriessen, peripherally involved through international affairs and ordinarily a strong liberal, was as beholden to Philips.[48]

It was hard to see how the Commission would be able to produce legislation upon which it could agree, let alone anything which the Council might pass. Initial exchanges in the audiovisual group showed DGs in profound disagreement.[49] At Commission level Delors and Andriessen wanted a new standard, Bangemann wavered, while Dondelinger and Brittan were opposed. Jonathan Faull, the Brittan cabinet member on the case admitted that "the standard proposed is at best *dirigiste*, at worst protectionist, and is evidently driven by Thomson and Philips. Eventually there will have to be a standard, but there is no good reason to make one now . . . let the market decide."

Patrick's first first step in sorting this out was to ask DG XIII to write a "pedagogic paper." The product was as producer-driven and technology-centered as the earlier electronics paper and caused a similar uproar.[50] Patrick asked for a redraft framed in terms of questions and choices about HDTV rather than conclusions, this time done by DG III rather than XIII. By this point, however, the Commission was besieged by lobbyists, among whom those from Rupert Murdoch's News International were particularly active. Jonathan Faull said that the Brittan office was receiving 50 to 60 letters a week, plus more direct contacts, with Pandolfi and Dondelinger the objects of unduly heavy persuasion.

To Patrick, settling on a standard was necessary to give the different components of the industry "a clear signal" to focus on the transition to HDTV. Without it efforts would be dispersed and synergies lost. This, he assured me, would be enough to lose any European advantage in HDTV and, perhaps, the European TV industry itself.[51] He was fond of citing the example of Philips, which had invented the video-recorder but lost out commercially because the Japanese had been able to impose the VHS standard. The situation was complicated, however, by an article which had appeared in *Le Monde* about American research on a digitalized HDTV signal which implied that the Europeans were throwing good money after bad on the analogic HDMAC.[52] Digitalization would allow terrestrial HDTV transmission (HDMAC was for satellites) and the Americans would then be comprehensive winners. Patrick answered that "digital research is six to ten years from succeeding. In the meantime we have to give our clear signal to European industry. If there is an industry, then it can work on digital. Without an industry it won't matter much."

"My strategy is to close down the range of choices . . . point everyone towards the new standard," Patrick announced. This was Pascal's approach in the *Chefs de Cabinet* meeting as well, when the initial document first rose towards the Commission.[53] Pascal suggested that all groups in the industry had to be consulted before anything could be decided. This took some of the heat out of the discussion. The Commission meeting followed the same line. The option that Pascal and Patrick personally preferred involved either a five-year phase-in of D2MAC or a "simulcast" approach that would oblige satellite operators to broadcast in D2MAC but allow them also to use PAL. The second was expensive, and the EC would have to provide large sums to sweeten the pill for producers and broadcasters. But if there was to be a European standard the EC would have to buy off those important interests in the TV industry who did not want it. The problem here, Patick averred, was that "the industry isn't really settled yet. Technology is flying, there is concentration going on all over the place, mergers and acquisitions, and the cultural context is unsettled. It won't be easy."

Others concerned did not agree. The satellite broadcasters were firmly against the new norm. They were without programs, equipment, and money and since growth depended on attracting new subscribers the added costs for new equipment looked to be a real threat. The Brittans had taken to referring to the proposed standard as "another Concorde." The Pandolfi cabinet was more technical, worried about digital doing to MAC what MAC had done to MUSE, the Japanese standard, and leaving Europe behind again. The Pandolfis, primarily responsible for the dossier, were nonetheless busily trying to pin down "burden-sharing" formulae.[54] Pandolfi's strategy was to call a conclave of various industry interests at the end of February 1991 to see how far they could be moved towards the Commission's position and what kind of legislation they would accept. He hoped to have the whole matter settled before the audiovisual council scheduled for May.

Patrick came out of the February meeting both puzzled and dissatisfied. "Pandolfi just let everyone talk around the table, he left things completely open to the groups. It was a bad method. When the Commission has problems it shouldn't leave it up to the industry to solve them." No consensus had emerged, not surprisingly, and a working group of representatives of different branches of the industry had been established to prepare another meeting at the end of March.[55] A questionnaire was then circulated to all of the actors.

The second meeting complicated things even more.[56] Behind an extremely fluid notion that agreement might be reached on "developing a new product and a new service" a deal was made to split the proposed Commission action into two separate instruments, the first a legally binding "Memorandum of Understanding" (MOU) defining mutual obligations among the different parties concerned, including the Commission, and the second a Directive on HDTV standards,[57] with the whole package scheduled to be finished for the June Telecommunications Council meeting. Patrick was skeptical, and also a little confused, because it was more and more difficult for him to find out what Pandolfi was really up to. The commis-

sioner for high technology seemed to have taken over the dossier all by himself, leaving his own cabinet and DG XIII largely in the dark. Patrick found this both strange and a violation of the ways in which commissioners were supposed to operate, but wrote it off to the personal inadequacies of Pandolfi.[58] But the consequence was that no one really knew what was going on. Most people had a reasonable idea what might be in a Directive since a draft had circulated three weeks earlier – an MAC norm would be defined, broadcasting in 16×9 would be in MAC, satellites would be regulated. But very few could figure out what the MOU would be, let alone how the two instruments would articulate.[59]

The fog lasted through the special chefs meeting in late May to prepare the June council, by which point there was still no Directive and no MOU.[60] Pandolfi's *chef* had to muster all his verbal virtuosity to get through the meeting, given the absence of hard information. He noted that the commissioner was still "consulting" and "negotiating" with the companies, a "positive result was certain, there was more agreement, the nucleus of a consensus was appearing." Patrick was quite harsh about the result, but powerless to do anything more than speak in stern tones. "What will be in the Directive? The last meeting of the working group was a catastrophe, what is going to be in the MOU?" After much talk around the table the representative of DG III finally announced that the documents in question could not be discussed because negotiations were still underway.[61] Patrick moved to adjourn until the next Monday, when the Pandolfis were enjoined to have the key documents. On the Monday there were no documents, however. After a discussion about the legal situation, Patrick, in the chair, announced, for the record, that he "found the procedures being used astonishing. The information changes from meeting to meeting."

Two weeks later there was a meeting of top-level officials at which a Directive proposal, close to the original draft, was approved, but no MOU. The Directive was needed, it seemed. "Without it, no one is likely to sign the MOU." Pandolfi ultimately brought a Directive proposal to the Commission on June 26, completely bypassing usual procedures to do it. PAL broadcasting would be allowed to continue, but strong financial incentives were proposed to promote simulcasting in D2MAC. New satellite broadcasting, all high-powered satellite broadcasting and all broadcasting for 16×9 TV would have to use D2MAC. Finally, all television sets with screens larger than 52 cm square would have to be equipped to receive D2MAC.

The rest of the story was anticlimactic. The Directive proposal went to the European Parliament in the fall, with Dondelinger also proposing the wide variety of support programs to producers and broadcasters that the proposed MOU needed to entice industry cooperation.[62] The Telecommunications Council finally discussed the proposal in December 1991, after Maastricht.[63] Pandolfi announced, first, that financial support for implementation would amount to 1 billion ecus over five years and, second, that the MOU would soon be signed.[64] The MOU was still on the cards, but unsigned, when the Commission proposed its action plan in April 1992.[65]

Three months later, just after the Danes had rejected Maastricht, the MOU approach was abandoned altogether.[66] The Commission turned instead to promoting a "declaration of intent" to be purchased, apparently, through bilateral deals between companies and the Commission. The Commission's own action plan had replaced voluntary industry cooperation as the motor for making HDTV happen in Europe. The action plan involved a big budgetary component which the British refused to accept.

The Americans were about to introduce a superior digitalized HDTV system and standard. Had the EC moved forward in the directions which Delors had set out in 1991 there would have been an enormous waste of money and the European TV industry might have been hurt. By July 1992 Patrick confided that "we were wrong in what we were trying to do . . . We shouldn't have been trying to impose our line the way we were. Pandolfi, whatever he was up to, really saved us from a situation which might have been very difficult."

The Other Industrial Policy

Competition policy was a central, if underpublicized, dimension of the Single Market program. The Treaty of Rome had given the Commission legal authority over a range of matters pertaining to anti-competitive practices (various antitrust issues and state aids to industry used as unfair subsidies) to which new powers over mergers and acquisitions had been added in 1989.[67] Ever since 1985 the whole area had come alive, with ever more vigorous enforcement of the rules, under Commissioner Peter Sutherland in the first Commission under Delors's presidency and then under Sir Leon Brittan after 1989. Jurisprudence had exploded, in consequence, and the Commission found itself investigating, inquiring, judging, and sanctioning violations.[68] Commission administrations, particularly DG IV, whose job it mainly was, constantly investigated complaints about abuses of market position and the effects on competition of corporate mergers – of which there had been a huge number in the later 1980s, in anticipation of 1992 – plus doing their best to make sense out of the complex and varied subsidies to national economic activities by member states in order to enforce Community rules. The basic philosophy of the Community was that the greater competition brought by a broader, more open market would lead to greater efficiency and lower costs. It was in the nature of things, however, for firms and other actors to seek shelter against the new market. Community competition policy was supposed to prevent this.

The Commission investigated, initiated legal proceedings, and meted out rulings and punishments. Doing all this in a serious way inevitably led to steady conflict, however; member states might be committed to the general logic of the Single European Act, but they could be counted on to try to protect national firms, employment, and economic interests when

they conflicted with competition law. Managing and containing such conflicts were almost as important as competition policy itself. The Commission did not want to have member states which had been alienated for
competition policy reasons lashing out in other critical Council decision-
making areas. More important, as with any genuinely supranational activities of the Community, the Commission needed to avoid clashes about
competition policy issues which would fuel public fury about "the Brussels
bureaucrats."

Disagreement crossed the Commission itself. Delors saw the Single Market as a means to "organize European space" across a wide range of areas
and believed that it would take specific policies, above and beyond the
Single Market, to encourage a needed "European" industrial fabric. Sir
Leon Brittan, who held the competition policy portfolio, was a genuine
neo-liberal to whom a fully open market was the only industrial policy. And
Sir Leon was a bulldog of a politician inside the Commission, determined
to struggle for his own goals, armed with the personal self-confidence of a
top class English barrister and backed by a top-notch cabinet.

Lodewijk Briet was in the middle of this when I first arrived. Every week
hundreds, sometimes thousands, of cases crossed his desk. Most were routine, but there were always a few which either bore potential legal problems
or which brushed the interests of member state governments. Lodewijk,
who presided over the bi-weekly special chefs meeting on competition
policy where Commission priorities were sorted out, had to make sure that
the Commission avoided legal problems and did not stir up undue conflict
with member states. Simultaneously he also had to represent Delors's own
inclinations about industrial and other policies and, finally, take into account the special political problems for Delors which flowed from lingering
French attachments to *dirigisme.* Lodewijk described Commission competition policy as part jurisprudence and part political realism. Sir Leon Brittan
and his staff of committed smart lawyers were always attempting to push
Commission competition policy as far and fast as they could. Other commissioners and their staffs, including the Delors team, sometimes disagreed
with this and had also to try to protect their national interests. Fighting over
competition policy was thus endemic.

Lodewijk was not a happy warrior. He was not French, even though like
most high Commisson operatives his French was perfect, and the Delors
staff operated on profoundly French principles which made all outsiders
feel a bit distant. Quite as important, not being French meant not being
able to apprehend fully the French national position on competition policy
affairs. He had thus had problems with Pascal and François about positions
to take on important cases of state aids to industry, French cases in particular. Lodewijk was uneasy about the separation of philosophical and juridical
principles from the rough-and-tumble which his job demanded. Pascal
Lamy put it clearly when he commented to me about Lodewijk that "he is
a very nice man, but he doesn't seem to like doing the political work that
someone in his position has to do."

Competition policy issues were so important – to everyone, not simply Delors – that great care was devoted to monitoring them. For Lodewijk this meant direct supervision by François Lamoureux and, at greater distance, by Pascal himself, primarily because of the many-tiered system of political dealing that such important issues involved. François "followed" Lodewijk in order to be able to battle for a better deal, over Briet's head, with his own adversaries in the Brittan cabinet, Jonathan Faull in particular. Pascal was always in the circle so that he, in turn, could go on a mission down the corridor to muscle "the Brittans" and, most importantly, to keep Delors informed. Delors himself conversed with Brittan regularly to keep their disagreements under control. Thus internal deals on competition policy were always being made.

As 1991 had turned, there had been more and more cases threatening important French vested interests, partly because the French were particularly invested in positions which skirted EC competition policies, and partly because Sir Leon Brittan and DG IV felt more emboldened to attack the heartland of *dirigisme*. This increased the pressure on Lodewijk, who finally decided to leave the cabinet.[69] His departure at the end of March was the occasion for something rare, a brief Delors cabinet social occasion, organized by Lodewijk himself in his small office at the close of the day.[70] Lodewijk had decided to leave in the best way he knew how, with a gracious smile, but also with an act – the little party itself – which underlined what he had found most lacking in his work. He would turn up, not much later, in an essential position close to Gunther Burghardt in the secretary-general's office working on the CFSP. It was Pascal's firm practice to make sure that those who had served well in the Delors cabinet should be well placed when they returned to "normal" EC life. His replacement, Geneviève Pons, fit the cabinet and job somewhat better. She was a young *énarque* whom François had been bringing up to speed over the winter.[71] Her training and background made her good at synthesizing huge amounts of material. Morever the commonality of culture between Geneviève and the leadership of the cabinet made communication easier.[72]

The constant skirmishing on state aids with which Briet and Pons were charged was tiring, but more or less routine. The Commission's new powers over proposed mergers and acquisitions had unprecedented implications, however.[73] DG IV had two "merger task forces" observing all substantial mergers underway, on the alert to find the Commission's first big merger control case. Important matters were at stake. The parameters of judgment in initial cases would become precedents for an entire body of subsequent law. In terms of industrial policy, what the Commission would and would not allow might determine what kinds of European-level large corporations could come into being. Finally, since the fate of large corporations was an essential matter to member states, where DG IV and Brittan decided to move would be a major issue for certain national governments. Thus it was no accident that François Lamoureux was on constant patrol.[74]

DG IV and Brittan, after screening dozens of potential cases, took a serious view of strategic alliance deals between Fiat of Italy and Alcatel-Alsthom of France, in particular the merger of Telettra and Alcatel – Telettra was the telecommunications subsidiary of Fiat. The merger would have moved Alcatel ahead of AT&T to become the leading provider of telecommunications equipment in the world.[75] DG IV and the Brittan team were tempted to make this their flagship case largely because Alcatel and Telettra together supplied 80 percent of the equipment to Telefonica, the Spanish telecommunications company. More importantly, Telefonica owned minority stakes in both Alcatel's and Telettra's Spanish companies, plus a small share in Telettra itself. Telefonica declared that these cross-participations would make no difference to its equipment purchasing programs, but DG IV was not convinced. Telecommunications markets remained largely national and the merger looked to tilt the balance of the Spanish market towards Alcatel, narrowing options for potential competitors.

François worked hard over winter 1991 to keep Brittan from bringing the case forward. From Brittan's point of view, the merger fit the new law's criteria because its potential effects on Spain, the most rapidly expanding telecommunications market in the EC, were sufficiently large. From François's point of view Alcatel, one of the successful private sector giants of French manufacturing, with the ear of the French government, was politically dangerous for the EC to take on. More fundamentally, although neither Lamoureux nor Delors had any sympathy for monopolies, they both believed that strong, world-scale European companies were the most important building blocks for a genuine organized European economic space. They had legal doubts as well, particularly about Telefonica's purchasing policies and the openness of the Spanish market to other big competitors like LM Ericsson and AT&T.

François thus had reason to argue, which he did with his worthy counterpart among the Brittans, Jonathan Faull. Watching François and Faull was like watching a very good sporting match between two first-rate legal minds with different political opinions. As François put it,

> I went at Faull legally first of all. He thought hard and gave me his answers and we went around again. But I introduced doubt into his head. He's a good lawyer and he knew that I had a point and he had to worry about the legal side of the first case. If it has flaws, then we're all in trouble. It's connected with the politics of things inside the Commission, too. If there are legal doubts, Delors can argue them and then Brittan may get beaten in Commission. Brittan doesn't want this to happen, especially on the first case. And Faull doesn't want Brittan to be beaten on Faull's advice. So I scared him pretty well.

Faull and Brittan hesitated, but something had to be done with the case since legal proceedings had begun and had to be concluded. The Brittan team also remained convinced of the danger to competition in Spain, even if it was reluctant to go to the wall with the case. Dealing, always possible in competition policy cases, thus became the order of the day. The threat of Commission action was sufficiently serious to bring representatives of the companies to Brussels armed with proposals to get the EC off their backs. After many meetings with Brittan and Faull in the middle, and François in the background, Telefonica agreed to sell its minority holdings in Alcatel and Telettra supplier firms to Alcatel, which had to agree to buy them to get the merger. For Alcatel, beyond annoyance, there was significant expense involved. It had to buy the shares at an agreed price far above any it would have chosen. A deal was nonetheless struck and announced on April 12, 1991.[76]

François and Delors had prevented Alcatel–Telettra from being the first case of a blocked merger. Faull and Brittan had saved face by obliging Alcatel to deal to obtain conditional approval for the merger – the Alcatel–Telettra case became the first conditional merger approval under the new 1990 merger control rule. Alcatel had had to pay dearly, but got the merger. Brittan and Faull were still on the alert for a good case to stop a merger altogether, so François had to stay on patrol. The CEO of Alcatel was furious about the cost of the conditions the Commission had imposed, and when, later, it was time for French CEOs to stand up and be counted on the Maastricht Treaty, he was one of the few to come out against ratification.

It took only a few short weeks for "the Brittans" to return to the attack. The case came on a different piece of the Fiat–Alcatel/CGE deal, a proposed takeover by Magnetti-Marelli (a Fiat subsidiary) of CEAC (an Alcatel/CGE affiliate) in the specific area of car batteries. The takeover was a mirror image of the Telefonica matter. It gave Fiat control over Alcatel/CGE's car parts division and would create the largest car battery group in the EC and fifth largest in the world.[77] The proposed group's European market share, only 22 percent, was not at issue. Its 60 percent share of the French market was the problem. The merger rule did not allow a concentration which would create a "dominant position in the common market or in a substantial part of it."[78] Sir Leon and his team had determined that this deal would indeed create a "dominant position" in a "substantial part" of the Common Market. The key to this was the designation of the French market as the "market of reference" for the application of the merger rule. Brittan had decided that in the area of car batteries there did not yet exist a full common market, only quasi-protected national markets, and that, furthermore, the only way to break down this fragmentation and promote a single European market was to refuse the merger of the top two market leaders in any national market.[79]

As the case rose toward the Commission neither François nor Pascal had to take the anti-Brittan position because Martin Bangemann and DG III were there first. Once again, motivations were complicated. Fundamental legal issues were involved, in particular the designation of "market of reference." Bangemann, backed by strong arguments about the way national markets worked, claimed that in this case the market of reference was the entire EC, not a national one. There were differences in selling prices among different national markets, but they were not so large as to indicate undue restraint of trade. If the European market were the reference point, the proposed group, with its 22 percent market share, could clearly not be considered a dominant player.

Beyond Bangemann's detailed arguments were considerations of industrial policy not unlike those of Delors in the Alcatel–Telettra case. The most important use of competition policy was to promote, not hinder, the development of world-class European firms. To Bangemann, Brittan's market of reference argument did just the opposite. The auto parts market was a critical element for the competitiveness of the European automobile industry more generally. Just as the car companies had to do enormous work to increase their effectiveness in the face of the Japanese, so to did the parts suppliers.[80] Preventing them from merging when merger made economic sense was foolish, he argued. Bangemann was also worried about an adverse ruling on Varta–Bosch, another auto parts merger with important German industrial stakes. The Delors team had an important interest of its own. Neither had much confidence, to begin with, in the Bangemann staff, even though François had taken steps to make sure that DG III did its work. The Bangemanns were notoriously sloppy, so the Delors cabinet had to cover for them. Deeper than this, there was a possibility that the entire FIAT–Alcatel/ CGE deal could fall through if, after the Alcatel–Telettra episode, the car battery case went against it. For French and industrial policy reasons, the Delors team did not want to see this happen.

The special chefs meeting on May 17, over which François vigorously presided, reviewed the issue. The Brittan/DG IV case was raked over the coals, not only on the "market of reference" point, but on a wide range of other issues having to do with the economic analysis of the industry and its markets. Seven cabinets (of 17) expressed fundamental reservations, two held back awaiting more information while François, for Delors, contended that insufficient interservice discussion had taken place to justify any conclusion. Other things being equal, Brittan was on the way to a defeat in Commission. This time, however, the Brittans showed no inclination to back down.

The *Chefs de Cabinet* meeting the next Monday morning was tense. Jim Currie, Brittan's *chef*, presented the best possible case well and was then besieged by counter-arguments led by the Bangemanns and the two Italian cabinets and followed by almost everyone else. Currie defended himself in ways that made clear that Brittan wanted this case to go forward, despite the wide range of reservations around the table. Pascal, who had the last word, listened quietly and counted potential Commission votes with a devilish gleam in his eye. He was absolutely certain that Brittan would be beaten in Commission and thought that this might have a tonic effect. Thus, rather than intervening to stop the case from moving forward he announced that the Commission "would profit from a debate on these questions."

Later in the day, while walking down the corridor of the thirteenth floor I encountered Sir Leon, with a wide smile on his face, walking jauntily towards Delors's corner office. This was clearly not the expression of a man about to be defeated in Commission. I concluded that the situation must have changed. Indeed, the corporate parties on the firing line had decided that they would prefer to deal: Fiat had offered to sell its majority share in another French battery firm and this was enough to get Sir Leon off the hook.[81] The merger was approved and later the German Varta–Bosch merger proposal was authorized under the same conditions.

Sir Leon's quest for a good first merger case was unrelenting, however. Only a few days later, in early June 1992, the Commission "opened proceedings" (beginning a four-month legal inquiry) on the proposed acquisition of the Canadian aircraft maker de Havilland by ATR, a French-Italian consortium composed of Aérospatiale and Alenia. De Havilland was a financially troubled manufacturer of technologically sophisticated and successful turboprop commuter airliners, the Dash 8 series.[82] ATR, the French-Italian consortium, made similar planes, the ATR-42 and 70, that had done well on both the European and North American markets. The Canadians were wary of the deal and held it up for much of the summer in a search for clarification of the European consortium's intentions.[83] Since there were strong divisions of opinion inside the Commission there was thus some hope that the Canadians would disallow the deal. This was not to occur, however, and de Havilland returned after vacation, therefore.

5

Reading the Non-Papers

... it's a bad period ... nothing's going well ... We're in the middle
of processes that will take time, lots of time, to mature ... But now
there's disentegration around us ... EFTA is falling apart, the Soviet Union is a mess ... In the international economy, on interest
rates and other matters, the Community doesn't look like it
exists ... We've got too many things to do and we don't do them as
well as we should ... There is an accumulation of sectoral problems.
The Americans are screaming about defense. Kohl and Gonzales,
who we really need, have difficult domestic situations ... The Luxembourg Presidency is pitiful, they're not moving forward on anything that counts. The internal market is inert, and the vital signs on
social policy are totally flat ... As for the Commission, Delors might
as well not make his grand gestures about collegiality, the others
could not care less ... The first Commission wasn't any better in
terms of quality, but at least they could remember that they began
from the bottom ... Delors should work on them more, but he
hasn't got time ... and they have a monumental capacity for not
doing anything ... In the intergovernmental conferences everyone
is undercutting everyone else. COREPER is full of people whose
goal is to bite everyone's ankles ...

But if you look at our strategy it is hard to see what we've done
wrong. If we hadn't had the intergovernmental conferences we
wouldn't be any better off on economic policy or on enlargement ... And now if we asked for the conferences we wouldn't
get them ... there's a *fin de règne* atmosphere, the conferences have
changed the timeline, the end of this Commission is now the conferences rather than the end of 1992 ...

We've been through other moments like this. *He*, he likes these
things. He's at his best in crises ... But when he's provoked them
himself. This is one he hasn't provoked.

Pascal Lamy, cabinet lunch, April 30, 1991

Spring had difficulty reaching Brussels in 1991. The *grisaille* which lasted
nearly through June was a reflection of the Commission's troubled times.
At precisely the moment when Delors had hoped to see Europe moving

smartly towards important new heights of integration, clouds were gathering. The all-important first stages of the intergovernmental conferences (IGCs) began to get down to the essentials in spring 1991. The Delors team had to expect less and less control over the agenda as member states started to hone their own preferences for the hard bargaining in store. What it had not anticipated was that these preferences were slowly becoming less *communautaire* and more national. Moreover, the IGCs themselves were deepening divisions among EC member states. As Jean-Charles Leygues perceptively put it,

> we're at the end of the Russian dolls period. Before we could count on being ahead of other people strategically. We knew what we wanted and they were less clear, partly because they didn't believe that anything much would follow from the decisions we asked them to make. Now they know that we mean business and they look for all the implications of our proposals. There are huge numbers of new things on the table and it will be much tougher going from now on.

The cycle of the Delors presidency, after five years of upward movement, was beginning to turn.

Reading the Non-Papers

The IGCs were the central agenda matter for Delors. But the outside world had begun to make the going treacherous. The post-1989 era, in what looked to be a European economic and political renaissance, clearly implied major changes in US–European relationships. Increased EC economic assertiveness, particularly on trade and economic policy matters, would threaten the US. The inevitable decline of the US European defense presence also implied declining US influence in the strategic-defense area. But the Gulf War gave the Americans considerably more leverage over Europe than they would have otherwise had, and they did not hesitate to use it. Thus as the IGCs picked up speed the US began to play the defense card. The key issue was NATO, important in itself but also the major source of US leverage over the Community.

The Gulf War left the EC divided. France, the usual protagonist on "transatlantic" matters, wanted a new Common Foreign and Security Policy (CFSP) to strike out in exactly the directions which the Americans did not want. The key to this was establishing an organic relationship between Western European Union (WEU) and the EC and then endowing WEU with some real defense roles. These were Delors's hopes as well, as the London speech showed. British pro-Americanism had been restimulated by the Gulf War. The UK thus argued that the CFSP should not compete with NATO and that WEU should be a "bridge" to the alliance rather than an organic part of the EC.[1] The Germans, largely absent from the Gulf War (even though eventually they had provided some aerial support in Turkey) were in a difficult position. In this context the historic ambiguities of their foreign policy, playing NATO against the French and the EC against the Americans, became more difficult to negotiate.

The Americans thus had space to work. As the CFSP came on to the IGC table the US tried to slow the development of autonomous European defense capacities. In official language, it wanted Europe to be a partner rather than a rival and limit any renascent WEU to the status of a European NATO pillar, with "out-of-area" capacities to be negotiated with NATO.[2] The Americans could be confident that the most Atlanticist EC members – the British, Dutch, and Portuguese – would slow CFSP deliberations until NATO itself had been able to clarify its own strategic outlooks in autumn 1991. The Delors cabinet was of two minds about the transatlantic consequences of the Gulf War. One line was cautious. The EC had held together in the Gulf crisis until the going got tough. With hot war, however, member states dispersed. The new divisiveness was disturbing, and the cards now held by the US were important. The second view was that the spectacle of European division and American power could well prove a stimulus to more energetic Europeanism in international policy.

The interim European Council meeting in Luxembourg on April 9 had been put off several times in the absence of a clear agenda. It was dominated by foreign policy issues. The French had managed to schedule a WEU meeting simultaneously, an astute coup to magnify Europe's movement towards a CFSP. The British were only the most vociferous in expressing their annoyance. Last-minute improvisation by John Major, without American permission, of a plan to protect Kurdish enclaves in Northern Iraq – replete with WEU transportation – prevented a fiasco. Everyone came out ahead, if breathlessly. The French could trumpet the first successes of a common EC foreign policy, the British could bask in their, rare, "good European" role while the Germans could be pleased not to be caught between the French and the British. The only grumblers were those who then had to organize the Kurdish enclaves. A harried-looking Joly Dixon, when asked the next day what he was up to, barked back, "trying to give money away, as usual." François Lamoureux, doing the legwork of piecing together the operation, commented "it's really crazy how hard it is to come by 150 million ecus for the Kurds."

The uncharted new international setting was slowly undercutting important parts of Delors's strategy. One major manifestation of this came from the ex-socialist countries of Central and Eastern Europe (CEECs). The PHARE program – Poland and Hungary: Assistance for Restructuring Economies – had gotten billions in aid pledged and organized. Cooperation agreements with these countries were already in effect. The European Bank for Reconstruction and Development (EBRD) had just opened with great pomp and controversy.[3] Trying to parlay such new West–East dealings into enhancements of the Community's foreign policy capabilities was a clear Delorist goal. The liberal economic shock therapy applied to the

CEECs was causing problems, however.[4] By 1991 the major consequence was that the economic and institutional bases of whole sectors of CEEC populations had been painfully undermined with little compensation beyond liberal rhetoric. The consequences, in terms of high unemployment, uncompetitive industry, ill-adapted institutions, and political volatility were inflammatory.[5] Meanwhile, private Western investment was very slow in arriving and the EBRD had difficulty finding a footing. There was mounting international talk about the EC's inward focus at a moment when the CEECs were in trouble.

The Community's great virtue was that it, perhaps alone, was willing to listen seriously to the CEECS. They would thus undoubtedly have come begging for more EC help, given the paucity of other doors upon which to knock. Inevitably, their first demand was for more money. Here the Community faced great resource constraints, especially given new commitments for aid to the USSR and, later, its successor republics.[6] In general, the Marshall-Plan-sized effort needed was clearly beyond EC countries. Even the Germans, who earlier might have been willing to give more, had begun to face the bottomless financial pit of unification.[7] Quite as important, the Commission had to tread carefully in order not to jeopardize prospects for the Delors budgetary package that Jean-Charles Leygues was busily "cooking" and which would seek substantially more money to pay for Maastricht.

The tasks at hand made such caution look small.[8] One important dimension of CEEC–EC discussion involved "association agreements" – or European Accords, as they were renamed to establish regular institutional contacts and a ten-year passage to free trade.[9] The Community offered asymmetrically favorable trade concessions to the CEECs, but with very real limits. Because adamant member state resistance squeezed Commission generosity downwards, there turned out to be restricted trade reductions for agriculture, textiles, and steel, just those areas where the CEECs had some comparative advantage.[10] Breaching the CAP's external protection to allow Eastern European farmers to sell their goods more freely within the EC invited serious trouble in a context in which the Commission's proposals to reform the CAP (vital to the Uruguay Round and hence to the EC's international standing) had already run into heavy opposition from farmers and agriculture ministers.[11] The steel and textile problems were localized in the EC "South" (Spain and Portugal). But obliging the South to make trade concessions also courted IGC difficulties, however, since the Spanish, self-appointed spokespersons for the EC South, had begun to play an extremely hard-nosed game about cohesion.

"Deepening," the Delors strategy, was beginning to be troubled by demands about "widening." Lech Walesa's visit to the Commission in early April was an abrupt reminder. Walesa dressed down the Commission for not helping Poland enough and protested against the limited trade openings proposed in the European Accord deals. Then he raged about rich persons' clubs to a packed post-meeting press conference. "We would not like the iron curtain to turn into a silver curtain separating a rich West from a poor East," Walesa announced, while threatening that if the EC didn't open itself up more "there would be a rush of ten million Soviets to Germany."

The initial European Accord drafts made no commitment to eventual EC membership, a question which was the most bothersome of all.[12] It was far-fetched for the poor and just barely non-socialist CEECs to pretend to full EC membership. This would have wiped them out economically as swiftly and surely as German unification had wiped out East Germany.[13] There were strategic problems here as well. Opponents of the entire Delors line, led by the British, wanted nothing more than a flood of new and difficult-to-digest members to drown federalist state-building once and for all. In addition, obliging CEECs to beg at the EC's door for the long years until they had accumulated the Community's stiff membership credentials would be politically unseemly and contribute to European instability.[14] Dissent about CEEC membership prospects had begun to cross the Commission itself. Frans Andriessen, Foreign Affairs Commissioner, thus publicly proposed that *à la carte* affiliations with the Community could be created short of full membership.[15]

The Commission and Community were walking a tightrope. Delors's strategy sought to accelerate integration of the existing Community beyond a point of no return by superimposing a state-building logic upon the underlying market dynamic of the "1992" program. A central pillar in this was establishing the Community's international role. Until this could happen, the EC had to confront a fast-moving environment without the resources to do so. To be sure, the Commission and its allies were trying to change this situation through the IGCs. But to the degree to which the Community was unable to act coherently in international politics it became more difficult to negotiate a new role at the IGCs. The Gulf War promoted divisiveness and, more ominously, the policy choices to cope with the CEECs were further divisive. In the background the great communist federations of Yugoslavia and the USSR were beginning to come apart. In Yugoslavia proclamations of independence from Slovenia and Croatia were being drafted, the federal government was preparing scenarios (including military action) to prevent them from becoming independent, and the French and the Germans – key to a unified EC response – disagreed. The French, pro-Serbian, wanted to keep the Federation alive as long as possible. The Germans, pro-Croatian, preferred it to break up.

Although by dint of Delors's far-sighted actions in 1990 the former East Germany was now a Community matter, things were not working out as planned on German unification either. The Bonn–Brussels axis had been strengthened by quick Commission action after 1990 and Delors and Kohl became fast allies as a result. And a Germany obliged by unification to spend and import more translated into gains for the recession-prone rest of the Community. As time went on, however, the costs of integrating the former East Germany turned out to be vastly greater than anticipated.

Anxiety about inflation, budget deficits, and trade problems led the Bundesbank to keep German interest rates high, dictating austerity to other European monetary authorities. Moreover, the efforts needed to get unification off the ground began to turn German attentions inward. Economic strains, anxiety about refugees and immigrants, East–West tensions, and disagreements between the government and the Bundesbank festered and began to sap the European and federalist strength of the Kohl government, with the threat of making the Bonn–Brussels axis ultimately less powerful and predictable.

There were other international problems. Common Agricultural Policy (CAP) reforms would ultimately provide the centerpiece of any new EC proposals for the Gatt Uruguay Round, and there was an unspoken hope inside the Berlaymont that a game of "chicken" could work to the Commission's advantage. The threat of trade war inherent in the GATT negotiations could lessen internal opposition to CAP reform while the gestation of CAP reform might give the United States pause before pushing too hard on trade. The game was risky and nerve-racking, however. The Americans, led by the redoubtable Carla Hills, George Bush's Trade Representative, seemed determined to push too hard, while the French, the main beneficiaries of the unreformed CAP, seemed equally determined not to yield.

The Commission's 1989 proposal to the European Free Trade Area (EFTA) countries to create a European Economic Area (EEA), another of Delors's international priorities, was also coming to a head. The EEA had been conceived of as an antechamber to keep EFTA countries, suspected of an excess of devotion to free trade and insufficient zeal for integration, from applying for EC membership.[16] The EFTA countries had first to negotiate with the EC as a single unit, thereby accepting supranationality in principle.[17] The Commission intended to socialize EFTA members towards eventual membership; thus EFTA would have to learn to be like the EC in order to play in the EEA. EFTA would also have to accept the entire *acquis communautaire* – over 10,000 pages of the EC's accumulated rules, regulations, and laws. After submitting to all these conditions EFTA members would get more or less full access to the Single Market, but without political control over future EC decisions.

Dealing with the EFTA countries should have been the easiest of problems, but by spring 1991 the talks had become very hard-nosed on the exact nature of EEA institutions,[18] complex opt-outs for special problems, the place of agriculture,[19] fishing rights,[20] and north–south transit through the Alps.[21] There was a particular problem over whether EFTA countries should be asked to accept the principles of "cohesion" and, if so, when and how. The Delors line, defended against almost everyone including DG I and Frans Andriessen, was that an EFTA regional fund contribution, which the Spanish were demanding, should be kept off the table for fear that EFTA would use it to corrupt the logic of negotiations, either through linkage with some other important issue or through direct deals with the EC

"South." Finally there was a problem of legal jurisdiction over EEA matters. The European Court had already begun to question the constitutionality of any "mixed" EC–EFTA arrangements in which EFTA would acquire even a minimal participatory role in EC juridical deliberations. Slowly but surely, however, progress was made. By the middle of Brussels' rainy spring things had narrowed down to fish, Alpine transit, and side-payments to the EC South.

The appearance of progress was misleading, however. EC success, which had initially driven EFTA towards the EEA, intensified EFTA desires to "get in," while the end of the Cold War dramatically recast the situations of Austria, Sweden, Finland, and Switzerland, whose neutrality had earlier been a barrier to EC membership. Finally, the stringency of the EEA structures pushed EFTA members towards demanding EC membership. Why should EFTA countries wait in an EEA antechamber where they acquired all the burdens of Community membership and few of the rights? There was thus a flood of new EFTA interest in Community membership. Austria had applied in mid-1989, Sweden was preparing for July 1, 1991, even though Community membership would involve a wrenching re-evaluation of a wide range of Swedish social and economic practices. The Finns, reeling from the collapse of their long-standing economic relationship with the Soviet Union, prepared to peg their currency to the ecu as a prelude to a Finnish application.[22] The Norwegians, who could not be refused if they applied since they had earlier been accepted, leaned in the direction of a new bid. Even the Swiss, celebrating the 700th anniversary of Confederation, began to think about joining. The perverse consequences of an EEA policy designed to stave off enlargement had thus put enlargement on to the table.

In the midst of all of this international complexity came troubling signs that the "1992" program itself was beginning to lose some of its luster. One of the more striking, and hilarious, signals came from the British press. In response to an administrative oversight (which originated in Britain itself) it looked momentarily as if Single Market harmonization of the use of artificial sweetener additives might entail banning the production and sale of prawn-flavored British potato crisps. There was much carrying on about "bulky Bangemann" (Martin Bangemann, in charge of the internal market, was a large man) who was attacking British lifestyle. He was "The Sour Kraut Who Wants to Ban Our Crisps." This might have been easy to overlook, given the British press's capacity for absurdities about the EC. But a number of less poetic ruffles from other countries about threats from harmonization – to non-pasteurized French Camembert, German pure beer, Italian pasta and the like – indicated that something more than the peculiarities of the English was at issue.[23] Everything here was connected to the Commission doing the enormous jobs which the "1992" program enjoined it to do, and any mistakes and oversights were usually easy to correct. But different member state populations were beginning to realize that "1992" would make important differences to their daily lives.

Open questions

François Lamoureux labored on in the vineyards of political union, pausing barely to express pleasure when *The Economist* called him the "Saint Just" of the Commission. At the top of his list was finishing the Commission's proposals to the IGC, prodding Commission actors to "get out the product and muscling his way through meeting after meeting." For François, the publication of the Luxembourg presidency's first "non-paper" on political union did not improve what was already a bad springtime.[24] The Luxembourg presidency, behind which lay the Council of Ministers' secretariat, was concerned with acquiring parenthood of an essential moment in European integration and wanted as much as possible of a new treaty on paper before the Dutch presidency began in July. This approach meant getting the initial grounds of consensus into a "non-paper" by April 1991, to point to "bracketed" controversies for resolution by the Luxembourg European Council in June.

Writing things down in hard language early in the game could crystallize matters prematurely and narrow margins for maneuver before they needed to be narrowed. For Delors the non-paper was a trial, primarily because of the "three-pillar" architecture proposed for "European Union." The Community plus EMU would be one, the CFSP operation the second, and intergovernmental cooperation on internal and judicial affairs (immigration, crime, drugs, terrorism) the third. The European Council would be the unifying element among the pillars and the source of general political directions. The Commission, Parliament, and Court would all see their powers confined to one part of "Union." Moreover, general preamble materials about fundamental principles of European integration would apply only to the Community. Behind this structure was an intergovernmentalist coalition between the anti-federalist French and the anti-integration British. More generally, as the IGCs claimed more areas for Europe, member state concern about remaining in control increased. Pillars were not to Jacques Delors's taste, however.[25]

The European Parliament's new "co-decisional" role was one item left open. But it was clear that co-decision would be limited to a relatively few matters (cohesion, research and development, the environment, and aid to developing countries) and that there could be some threat to the Commission's power in the ultimate conciliation procedures between Council and Parliament.[26] Worse still, on the CFSP the Commission's suggestions had been heard, but the text was "minimalist," in François's words. A two-level system was proposed. "Political cooperation" along existing EPC lines would continue. In the second level member states might define "common positions," with general objectives decided upon unanimously by the European Council and the Council of Ministers charged to implement. Within these "common position" areas member states would coordinate national policies but specific "common actions" could be decided by the

Council – with decision rules bracketed. Common actions would bind each member state.[27] The complexity of the procedures would make it difficult to create a dynamic towards common action and do little to promote new coherence in the Community's foreign political work.

Hard discussions about defense were put off; in particular the key matter of whether WEU would become the EC's defense arm was postponed until new discussions set for 1996. That this was a better outcome than the complete identity between EC defense and NATO that the British and Americans wanted was small consolation.[28] The non-paper contained vague language about compatibility between WEU-European actions and NATO obligations, but stated that the two things were separate. Moreover, it clearly announced future close association between the EC and WEU. And, despite the weakness of the language, it did set out a trajectory towards the real security autonomy which was Delors's objective.

The Luxembourg non-paper was a moment of truth for the Commission.[29] The Political Union IGC had been called very late in the day, catching Delors without time to do a great deal of preparation. The Commission had rushed out as many strong proposals as it could, even though one heard criticisms of François for moving too slowly. But limited speed was much less important than the constraints imposed by the timing of the IGC. The Commission could not really play its crucial agenda-setting roles, making the IGC a chaotic affair largely governed by the member states. Within these limits, Delors, François, and the Commission did what they were supposed to do. They demanded more than they would get, the Commission's job, going through the exercise energetically to push the member states beyond where they would have gone on their own. The roasting that the Commission and Delors were getting in the (particularly British) press indicated that they were scoring points. David Buchan, in the influential *Financial Times*, commented that "the Commission has, in the eyes of all EC governments, far overstepped the mark."[30] By making strong claims the Commission won a few important things (on the CFSP, for example, and on competencies) even though the bracketing of decision rules made the extent of success unclear, but lost on others, particularly on the general question of architecture for union (pillars were undesirable). A number of important matters, co-decision in particular, remained in suspense.

Toughing It Out

The Commission's real problem was neither propositional slowness nor excessive boldness, but, rather, the methods of the Luxembourg presidency. Had Commission proposals been given more time to decant, they might have progressed further. The Luxembourg non-paper distorted and shut off some important discussions. In this context, Delors realized that it would henceforth be impossible to struggle for everything the Commission wanted and it would have to limit essential damage by focusing upon a number of targets for action. The most important goal was to undercut "pillarization." Delors had three other priorities. First, he wanted to strengthen the defense clauses of the non-paper, building on earlier French proposals to make a stronger "evolutive" commitment to common defense. Next, in the social policy area he hoped to "re-establish the role of the social partners" by reinserting the "negotiate or we'll legislate" hook into the social area. Finally, on co-decision, Delors wanted to push hard to expand the number of areas to which co-decision rules would apply and make sure that the Commission was not cut out of final deals between Council and Parliament. There was thus a rapid internal discussion in the Berlaymont about the Luxembourg non-paper, beginning with François's small group, then to a large institutional "Group of 17," special chefs, and on the floor of the Commission itself. Cardoso, the Portuguese commissioner, commented upon the "unexpected acceleration of the expected calendar" and Brittan added, wisely, that the Commission had to be careful not to look as if it was interested only in protecting its own positions. In general, the Commission agreed with Delors's selection of priorities.

After the non-paper François Lamoureux was full of venom for the Luxembourgers, whom he labelled "*gagnes petits*" (those willing to settle for little). He had little more sympathy for the Council secretariat, which had its own goal of diminishing the Commission's importance. He, Delors, and the others steeled themselves for the hardball to come. The Luxembourg non-paper was by no means the last word, but they knew that the best they would obtain on political union would be clear "evolutive" indicators on structure, CFSP, and co-decision, rather than the breakthroughs for which they had earlier hoped. Now it mattered more to "get things on rails," in Pascal's words, but even laying rails posed complex negotiating problems. Ultimately, the key to trade-offs at a higher level than the Luxembourg non-paper were Franco-German differences. The French wanted a strong EMU and clearer directions on defense, but they were confederalist on structure. The Germans were federalist on structure and much cooler on EMU than the French. Here there might be room to deal. But the Commission had to be as tough as it could and François was worried about softness, particularly on EMU.[31] "It was exactly the same on the Single Act. Emile Noël wanted to give in," François reminisced. Delors had overruled Noël, with François as his hatchet man.[32] All of this was to signal Delors was prepared to brazen things out again, even if everyone around them was prepared to cave in. "We'll take it straight to the heads of state, if we have to," said François.

The negotiating table

Delors knew well that there was no way to replace the confederalism of the Luxembourg non-paper by a true Community "tree." At best he could help insert new language into the preamble of the new treaty to unify the three separate pillars into somewhat of a Community, building thereby a "temple." Discussion of "structures" at the fifth ministerial meeting in mid-May showed that, of those who spoke, only the British really favored the Luxembourg non-paper. The Belgians, Dutch, Greeks, and Germans sided with Delors, while the French and Italians were lukewarm.[33] Delors, François, Pascal, and others thus pulled all the strings they could find.[34] The Commission also quickly generated its own amendments to the Luxembourg preamble, including a reference to the "federal vocation" of European construction, submitted on May 21.[35] When the permanent representatives discussed this two weeks later the Italians and Spanish had joined the "unified" camp, and a majority of member states were against the simple pillar approach.[36] Delors's target was change by the Dresden meeting of Foreign Ministers on June 3. By then there had been some progress. Despite British, French, and Danish opposition, a new "hat" for the Luxembourg proposal was designed which moved in the direction of unification and embraced the "federal vocation."[37]

Delors then took the theme on the road, announcing to the European Parliament a week later that federalism was "the consummate form of democracy." Delors's success, in its turn, sparked another furious British debate in which Tory anti-Europeans, eager to narrow John Major's margin for maneuver in the forthcoming European Council, denounced Delors's plans for a "superstate." The British press went on about the "F-word" and Mrs Thatcher denounced what she foresaw as "the greatest abdication of national power and sovereignty in our history" to the House of Commons.

The problems which Delors, François, and the Commission found in the CFSP sections of the Luxembourg non-paper were even less amenable to tinkering than treaty architecture. From the outset the Commission had resigned itself to a confederal approach, but one in which the Commission had a presence and small "proposition force" role. The Rome II European Council had in fact sanctioned this in December 1990, announcing that the Council would be the one decision-making center, there would be a unified Secretariat (the Council's, in all likelihood), and that there would be a "reinforced role for the Commission." On defense, where national sovereignty was even more at issue and where high transatlantic politics were involved, interstate debates would be key.

The first full ministerial discussion on the CFSP in April revealed the extent of disagreement. The French were the major proponent of a strong confederal CFSP, strengthened defense provisions and a clarification of the relationships between the Community and the WEU or, rather, the absorption of the latter by the former. France's supporters (Spain, Greece, Italy, and, to a lesser degree, Germany) were more cautious about the EC–WEU connection and more "evolutive" in general. The smaller states, afraid of big state domination in confederal arrangements, were concerned to strengthen the role of the Commission in CFSP deliberations, encouraged in this by the Commission President. The neutral Irish particularly wanted to slow things down. The Danes, Portuguese, Dutch, and the UK all expressed strong pro-NATO objections to EC–WEU merger plans. The British did not want "Union" to have its own defense policy: WEU should be tied both to the Union and to NATO: the "bridge proposal." In addition the British wanted a clear statement about relationships with NATO. Delors himself argued very carefully that what was at issue was beginning a process of "Communitarization" of CFSP which should also be tied to the Community's foreign economic policies.[38]

Much of the action about the CFSP continued to be transatlantic. On April 17 Secretary of State Baker met with EC Foreign Ministers. He argued that European foreign and security policies should not weaken NATO, NATO's integrated military structure should be maintained, (new) European defense structures should be "open" to all the European members of NATO, these structures ought to facilitate the protection of vital interests outside Europe and, finally, that if changes to existing military structures were envisaged, they should be discussed within NATO as well.[39] The British were predictably pro-American in promoting such positions, while Dutch Foreign Minister Van den Broek was an additional US supporter of considerable importance, given that the Dutch would be Council president for the last stage of negotiations.[40] The Americans, fearing that EC deliberations might pre-empt the field, also put a rush on the NATO strategic review. The French seemed determined to promote exactly what the US did not want. The Franco-German miilitary corps was already in the wings, while the Americans were already conspiring with the British to set up a NATO rapid reaction force to counter it. President Mitterrand was upset about all this, and various, if not always coherent, French statements indicated his deep neo-Gaullist skepticism about NATO's future.[41] The French publicly announced that any moment of reckoning on defense was far in the future, but the Americans, undeterred, worked on the Germans to pre-empt Franco-German unity.[42]

The Copenhagen NATO ministerial meetings in June, attended by the French, cleared the air a little, pending fuller discussions on NATO strategy in the fall. For the Americans the key issue was to insure that NATO remained the central European defense organization, rather than becoming an intermediary between the US and an EC defense pillar. Provided this was clearly understood by the Europeans, the Americans were willing to allow the EC to move forward. French efforts to row against the current did not get far. The real problem was that Europe was not convinced about the need for a new defense identity. This gave the Americans considerable space to constrain EC action.[43]

The CFSP defense dimension was one of those "rail-laying" operations which Pascal and François were fond of discussing. EC members were unprepared to take decisive steps at this point and were vulnerable to American pressures. The best that could be done was to make sure that the "Union's" new treaty would contain language that could point the EC towards greater common action in the future. Thus when the Commission proposed its new amendments to the Luxembourg non-paper – which, despite problems, did propose EC defense – they were carefully targeted. The Commission recognized, first of all, that any future common foreign and security policy arrangements would have to involve "an adaptation of the preparation and implementation of common decisions and an eminent role for the European Council . . . But this adaptation . . . should not be pushed . . . to the point of challenging or breaking apart the existing model which has demonstrated its dynamism and efficiency to this point." The Commission stressed the role of the "Union," as opposed to the European Council, in defining and implementing the CFSP and very carefully reinserted the Commission into all of the deliberative stages which these tasks would involve.[44] Neither Delors nor François was under any illusion that the Commission's new amendments would actually settle anything. CFSP was a matter which geo-political elephants would decide and any deal would not come until very much later, probably during the final days of negotiation and certainly after NATO had concluded its own strategic review.

The Luxembourg proposal on "co-decision" was another sore point. Both the Parliament's hopes for new powers and the Commission's proposal about a "hierarchy of norms" to designate co-decision areas were set aside and it looked as if co-decision would be extremely limited. The Parliament was very unhappy and the Commission, both from principled commitment to greater democratic scrutiny and to consolidate its alliance with the Parliament, had good reasons to push harder. The non-paper also proposed procedures to accompany co-decision which, in certain circumstances, could lead to legislation being decided by a "conciliation committee" of the Council and an equal number of representatives of the Parliament. The Commission would be present, but without significant power. This constituted a major breach in the Community's existing legislative procedures, in which the Commission was empowered to prevent changes of which it disapproved.

The politics of co-decision were complicated. The British and Danes opposed co-decision outright. The confederalist French were lukewarm but knew that they would have to give something to the Germans in exchange for EMU, about which the Germans were increasingly less enthusiastic.[45] The Italians, like the Germans, were eager for co-decision, and many smaller countries favored it. But in general the member states had not yet made up their minds.[46] The most obvious result of the April ministerial discussions was, however, that the complicated rules which seemed to be emerging would be comprehensible only to constitutional lawyers. This was hardly a promising remedy for the Community's democratic deficit!

The immediate issue for Delors was that the Parliament and the Council might be preparing to deal at the expense of existing Commission prerogatives. Delors thus went to work at the April plenary session of the European Parliament, asking:[47]

How . . . does one explain this will to weaken one of the Treaty's institutions
– the Commission – on the part of certain founding member states of the

Community . . . ? . . . We are asking for the maintenance of the dispositions of the Treaty which allow our institution to ensure the continuity of Community action . . . If this deviation were to continue the Commission will have to assume its responsibilities . . . and I'll have to come back to you and ask . . . why you have accepted a system which, even if it partially increased your legislative power, diminishes the dissuasive capacity to censure and risks plunging Community institutional processes into endless palavering between Council and Parliament at the expense of efficiency.

To the press he denounced an "enterprise to demolish the Commission . . . which puts the Commission on the sidelines . . . We could then rename the Commission 'the group for preparing the common activities of the Council and the Parliament.' . . . I wish you good luck in finding candidates to preside this group. You can be sure that I won't be one of them."

At the May 15 Interinstitutional Conference on Political Union, which included Council, Parliament, and Commission, the parliamentarians pushed the ministers for clear responses to issues about the extent of co-decision. As usual the ministers did their very best to avoid giving serious answers. The discussion turned into a complete dialogue, however, as Delors and the other Commission representatives were silent, a Delorist tactic to emphasize Commission indignation. At the very last moment Delors intervened to announce how interesting he had found "the exchanges at this bi-interinstitutional conference. It is surprising that, once again, the Commission has been relegated to the end of the discussion." To express the Commission's position "with all of the necessary nuances" Delors announced a press conference immediately following where he publicly blasted the ways in which co-decision issues were being treated, and underlined the threats to Commission powers.

Dealing was hot and heavy from this point on. The Luxembourgers seemed determined to limit co-decision to a short list of matters.[48] But the proposed procedures grew even more complicated with the introduction of a "third reading" to follow any failure of conciliation. François rushed around Strasbourg during the June plenary parliamentary discussion just days before the European Council, in rare high agitational form, to corner people and argue about single words, fulminate about the results, and then go back to fighting about the same words. Finally, the Commission's right to withdraw proposals brutalized in the conciliation procedure was restored. Luxembourg produced a new proposal, which had become completely opaque to virtually everyone except François, Delors, and a few parliamentary leaders. But it was far from achieving general consensus at the sixth ministerial meeting just prior to the European Council.[49] From the Commission's point of view the worst had thus been averted, but resolution on co-decision, like the CFSP, would await later days of negotiation.

The Luxembourg non-paper's approach to social matters was also difficult for the Commission to accept. It cut back on new Article 118a coverage recommended by the Commission (which would have been been subject to qualified majority voting) and replaced the Commission's "negotiate or we'll legislate" clause in Article 118b with vague language about the desirability of collective agreements to help implement new Directives. Those who wished to strengthen the EC social dimension (the Belgians, French, Dutch, Germans, Italians, and Danes) disagreed about how much strengthening to do and about decision rules. Most favoring change also favored an extension of qualified majority voting, but the Germans wanted a special "reinforced qualified majority rule" in the social area alone (and, if this could not be obtained, they favored unanimity). The British refused *any* changes to the Single European Act status quo.[50]

The April meeting of the Social Dialogue *Ad hoc* Group underlined the complexity of the situation. The employers' federation (UNICE) had earlier submitted a position paper arguing that the EC should be involved in social matters only where the Single Market could not function without it. It should keep out of anything "quantitative in nature" (wages, hours, vacations, social security contributions, etc.) "or . . . strongly socio-cultural in nature" (industrial relations systems and "consultation-participation"), and/or "normally the subject of collective or individual bargaining." In the few areas remaining Community action should be governed by obligations to pursue subsidiarity. UNICE was playing its usual intelligent game of "slow-down and decentralize."[51] In contrast, the European Trade Union Confederation (ETUC) and the unions wanted more of everything in the social area.

The Social Dialogue *Ad hoc* Group was a Delorist pet project, established in 1989 after the Social Charter to regenerate moribund discussion among the "social partners." It included the UNICE executives, spokespersons for the public sector employers' group, and ETUC's top leaders. At the April meeting Jean Degimbe, DG V's Director General, for whom social dialogue was the last passion of a long career, presided, while Patrick Venturini sat quietly near him. The official agenda was to generate feedback to the Social Affairs Ministers' Council the next week, but it was pre-empted by the revised Luxembourg proposal with its modified "social dialogue" proposals to allow the "social partners" to ask the Commission to "recommend" to the Council that contractual "framework agreements" be legally binding across the EC. The new proposals had infuriated the European Parliament, which feared being cut out of the legislative role upon which its future was based, and this worried the social dialogue participants.

Successive speeches by Zygmunt Tyzkiewicz of UNICE and Matthias Hinterscheid, outgoing ETUC General Secretary, expressed concern about the Parliament's reaction. To both, the idea that the Parliament should feel that its legislative prerogative would be infringed upon by a legal "extension" of the results of collective bargaining implied that the Parliament was eager to replace collective bargaining with legislation. ETUC genuinely wanted a European collective bargaining breakthrough and was worried that the proposal might undercut its parliamentary support. UNICE wanted neither legislation nor collective bargaining, but thought that collective bargaining would be easier to stop than legislation. Neither major social partner really liked the Luxembourg proposals. This gave Degimbe the space to work on both UNICE and ETUC gently but carefully throughout the afternoon. What other choices were there, he queried? By implication, there was at least one, the Commission's. The ETUC favored the Commission's original "negotiate or we'll legislate" idea in which the Commission would signal its intention to legislate and then the social partners could bargain collectively to pre-empt legislation, not only because Patrick had worked long and hard with them about it. The ETUC was a weak organization that depended more on the Commission for support than on its national union constituents.[52] Bargaining results in Brussels could make ETUC vastly more important, and generate more constituent support. UNICE had a different agenda, of course, and had always refused to bargain at all. To UNICE "social dialogue" was meant to be just talk.

ETUC understood that the Commission's original approach could well provide the incentives for real bargaining which the employers had always lacked. Thus it was surprising to hear Tyzkiewicz announce that UNICE favored the Commission's proposal over that in the revised Luxembourg non-paper. Patrick claimed that this major change was because certain national employers' associations, the French in particular, had changed their minds about the utility of European-level bargaining. Conversations with UNICE people revealed another logic. UNICE felt boxed in. It preferred little change at all in the treaty, but had to act as if some change would be likely. It preferred the Commission's proposals to those in the Luxembourg non-paper because it judged that these proposals would make it easier to limit Community social action. What UNICE feared was a great extension of legislation in the social area, and the Commission's ideas were a lesser evil. When the Commission proposed to act in a social area, the "social partners" could then ask for a bargained solution to avoid legislation. To begin with, the organizational changes needed to give both UNICE and ETUC statutory rights to bargain would eat up a lot of time. In bargaining, UNICE could exhaust the statutory time limit before admitting that no solution was possible and then send the matter back to the Commission. At this point, the Commission would have difficulty legislating because the Council would already be alerted about the lack of consensus. Or in the worst case in which real bargaining was unavoidable, UNICE could bargain hard for a low-concession deal. Given the assymetry in eagerness to bargain between unions and employers the unions would want a deal more than any specific results. If UNICE stayed firm the results were likely to be harmless. The negative side of this for UNICE (the positive one for ETUC) was that for the first time UNICE would have to accept the principle of European collective bargaining. The April "social dialogue" thus revealed that the IGC negotiations had created a dynamic among the "social partners" which, in certain circumstances, might lead to symbolic breakthroughs towards European collective bargaining. Depending upon how the IGC developed, then, there might be a potential for new social policies. On the other hand, every IGC discussion on social policy indicated that the British would refuse any serious treaty change.

The unresolved issue of "social and economic cohesion" hung over both IGCs through the Luxembourg presidency. From the beginning the Spanish had railed against existing cohesion efforts and threatened trouble unless significant changes were made in the new treaty. Delors and Dixon had helped to calm things down in the early stages of the EMU talks. The Spanish returned to their quest with a paper to the Political Union IGC in March.[53] The paper was stridently negative about existing Community cohesion efforts, recalling the EC's repeated commitments to a territorially equilibrated economic union, particularly in the context of impending monetary union.[54] The contrast was striking, it noted, between such statements and "the circumspection with which we have approached the subject" in the IGCs. The Single European Act had failed to come through on cohesion and the EC budget had never been adequate to the task – total amounts were too small and revenue gathering regressive. "It barely takes into account the relative prosperity and the capacity for paying of different member states," the paper added. Given their agricultural structures the Spanish, despite their economic weakness, had come very close to being net contributors to the EC budget. Structural fund co-financing obliged recipients to produce substantial matching money to get EC help, which was difficult for poorer countries. Finally, narrow focus on infrastructure neglected spending on human resource development. The Spanish disagreed generally with the architecture of the Structural Fund reforms in the 1988 Delors package. In addition, they claimed that insufficient attention was paid to cohesion in other Community policies like agriculture, research and development, the environment, and transportation. EMU, with important consequences accentuating regional disparities, would add to such pre-existing difficulties. EMU convergence criteria would place greater strain on poorer EC member states while EMU itself would deprive member states of traditional adjustment mechanisms.

Even after treaty revisions, the Spanish contended, the EC would be more a Single Market than a truly integrated space, without the kinds of compensatory mechanisms federal states possessed. It would therefore not be able to perform the cohesion tasks that circumstances would demand. A new set of tools had to be devised that would include a progressive system of revenue raising where wealthy regions would contribute to the poor as a matter of course, a "new financial instrument" to raise more money, and major changes in the working of the Structural Funds. The Spanish also repeatedly announced that they would refuse a treaty which did not confront these issues.

Delors judged that insisting upon these issues could break up the IGC. Commitment to the systematic resource transfers of genuine federal states was unacceptable to those (not only the UK) for whom federalism was anathema. Massive new financial commitments would be resisted by almost all of the more prosperous Northern states in the midst of austerity programs and recession. Finally, the Commission was not pleased with Spanish criticisms of the Structural Funds. Publicly reopening the Structural Fund dossier could be a Pandora's box, leading to challenges to the whole idea of social and economic cohesion. And whatever the reality behind the criticisms (the Commission was itself unclear about this), the Commission wanted to keep the definition of future changes as much in its own hands as possible. On the other hand, Delors's tactic of trying to calm the Spanish with promises about great new generosity in the second Delors package was not going to work.[55] The Spanish realized that their power would be greater before, rather than after, the IGCs. Much would depend upon how strongly the other "Southern" member states (Greece, Portugal, and Ireland, with Italy an interested outlier) would support the Spanish. It might be easier to buy off the others than the Spanish, but even to do this would involve doing more on cohesion.

EMU – what really counts?

The difference between the Political Union and EMU IGCs was announced in the first paragraph of every set of EMU negotiating minutes in the opening rubric, "the state of the dossier." Here was repeatedly announced that "during . . . earlier meetings, the personal representatives examined articles . . . of the EEC treaty *on the basis of a Commission working document on the treaty to institute EMU*," with the "Commission working document" the "draft treaty" which Delors, Joly, François, and his "Group of Four" had produced in late 1990. The EMU discussions, although not free from disagreements, were orderly and well organized.

By spring a good deal of EMU discussion involving technical "banker's" debates had been decentralized to financial experts.[56] Agreement was also possible on issues like the need to intensify efforts towards economic convergence in EMU stage 2 through "multilateral surveillance." The first area of controversy concerned the date and processes of passage to stage 2 of EMU – 1994 or not, automatic or not. Both the Rome I European Council (October 1990) communiqué, which the Commission defended strongly, and the initial Luxembourg non-paper had announced 1994. A majority stood behind this, but Germany, the UK, the Danes, and the Dutch wanted to make this conditional on indices of success in convergence. The Commission, and the French, would eventually win the date struggle. Connected with this was whether or not the proposed European System of Central Banks (ESCB) would be put into place during stage 2 of EMU to "apprentice" towards full stage 3 powers. Here the Germans were adamantly against the Commission, insisting that Rome II had spoken of a "new institution" for stage 2, not the proposed "Eurofed." A subsidiary conflict occurred on what to call the "new institution." In general, the Germans wanted neither the substance nor the label of a new central bank.

The Germans were also arguing with one another about EMU. The Bundesbank, smarting from its defeat at the hands of Kohl and "the politicians" over unification, and strengthened by unification's ever more negative consequences, was resisting Kohl. Kohl, with a weakening domestic position, had to conciliate his enthusiasm for integration with the Bundesbank's obduracy. He thus announced publicly that EMU was less important than success on political union, particularly on co-decision. Delors and the French, who desperately wanted EMU, were warned to be very careful on political union to give Kohl room to maneuver. Moreover, the British, playing a careful negotiating game, were still trying to position themselves in an anti-EMU coalition with the Germans. The British had already announced that they would refuse to agree to a single currency and John Major was under huge pressure from the Tory Right to bring home an anti-EC triumph. None would be greater than defeat of the dreaded EMU, particularly through a deal with the Germans.

Six months before Maastricht was early to lay down a big bargaining chip, but at this point Delors needed to pre-empt an anti-EMU British–German coalition. At the "informal" May Finance Ministers (ECOFIN) meeting he thus proposed a new position on passage from stage 2 to stage 3. No member state would be obliged to move to stage 3, Delors proposed, but equally no member state could prevent others from moving to the third stage, nor could anyone be excluded if required convergence conditions had been fulfilled. This meant that the British could henceforth sign an EMU Treaty without being bound to proceed into EMU's third, single currency, stage. This left very little further space for Major to play a wrecking role in the EMU negotiations.

The larger British problem had not been resolved, however. Despite "moving to the heart of Europe," the UK was systematically opposing every proposal for significant change at both IGCs. The short-run effect was to diminish the high ambitions which Delors and his allies had for a new treaty. But John Major would eventually have to make a hostage of some other proposal to gain British acceptance of a total deal for domestic political reasons. For Delors, the one consequence of playing such an important bargaining chip at this early point was that he and the Commission were almost certain to lose something additional at Maastricht, with social policy being the prime candidate. The fact that the British were no longer likely to block EMU also meant that EMU opponents on the German side could no longer hide and would henceforth have to play an open slow-down game. The distinction between slow-down tactics and a veto by two key member states was life or death, of course. Moreover, there was hope that damage could be limited if Kohl secured enough out of the Political Union IGC.

By the sixth ministerial negotiations in early June, important EMU issues had been clarified, in particular the general outlines of what would happen in stage 2. The "new institution" would not be a European Central Bank sitting atop an ESCB "apprenticing" for stage 3 but would instead be a

Council of Central Bank Governors (although the name would later be changed to "European Monetary Institute"). During stage 2, strong efforts would be made to promote convergence and monetary policy coordination, while free capital circulation would be completely in place and national Central Banks would move towards statutory independence from governments. The Germans had won breathing space to put their unification house in order. But to get this space they had opened the way towards a solid EMU treaty and its full implementation. Stage 2 would be brief. First consideration of movement to stage 3 by the Council, working on reports from the Commission and the Council of Central Bank Governors, might come as soon as 1996. Several important matters were unresolved, however. Convergence criteria for passage to stage 3 and institutional linkages and role definitions between the European Council, ECOFIN, and EMU remained to be worked out. The place of cohesion awaited fuller discussion. The agency of EMU's "foreign policy" in international monetary matters had to be designated. Most importantly, how to move from stage 2 to stage 3 had not been decided. Still, the EMU train was picking up speed, and on the tracks which Delors and the Commission had laid.[57]

Joly Dixon was pleased by what had happened during the first few months of EMU negotiation. "We've made good mechanical progress," he noted, with reference to the complicated technical work which had been done about the "banking" side of the "new institution" and the institutional structures of the new banks. On the other hand, he regretted having lost on stage 2, since the "beauty of our original architecture" had been sacrificed in the interests of a somewhat "incomprehensible" interim arrangement, "but all is not lost." The deal with the British had disarmed the biggest time-bomb. "As long as they can sign without necessarily having to lose sovereignty" the British would be less of a thorn in Delors's side. The other major matter, besides movement from stage 2 to 3, was the actual meaning of the "economic union" side of EMU. The French wanted to gain some control over the Bundesbank and German monetary policy via EMU. According to Joly, French Finance Minister Pierre Bérégovoy was arguing strongly that a broader macroeconomic policy role had to be built into EMU. The Germans were adamant against this, arguing that the "Eurofed" should statutorily be even more independent of political control than was the Bundesbank. The French and Italians had protested, but there was little evidence of success in the final Luxembourg non-paper of June.

Joly was confident that there would eventually be a deal, although what kind was not yet clear. "So far there's no heat in the process. The combination of COREPER and the Finance Ministers is enough to talk the soul out of everything . . . We've got to get some steam back, because we can't go on beyond December." Joly himself was already pulling back. Central in the long process of agenda-setting and the very important maneuvers of the first months of the IGC that had zeroed in on final questions to be settled, he would henceforth play a diminishing role. Final matters would be decided only at the very top. "We've already settled the majority of the big issues," he noted. "For the rest, it will probably be the European Council's business, and for that it is up to Delors himself. The key will be playing the German card, through Bitterlich . . . Pascal's friend . . . and Kohl himself."

Delors brought the European Parliament up to date on EMU in June. The Commission was not always delighted with the discussion, he said, but it was going well. The first major problem was transition from stage 2 to stage 3. A short second stage, he noted, was the only way for EMU to become credible, otherwise what he labelled a "*cartel des nons*" of certain banks and governments would have time to sabotage the whole process. The second problem was "economic union." In Delors's words, "economic policy is not only monetary and budgetary policy . . . even if these days it may be fashionable to think so." EMU thus should be an instrument guided by broader policy outlooks. How this might happen and how it could be built into the treaty were essential matters. Speakers from the floor of the Parliament rose one after the other to express skepticism about further achievement here. Their views were rather self-centered. Christine Verger, the parliamentary affairs specialist in the Delors cabinet noted, "all they care about now is their own powers." But the deeper issue was clear. EMU would be a technocratic affair, "monetary and budgetary," in Delors's terms, run by bankers and largely beyond anyone's control.

Delors's speech to the Parliament was easy to deconstruct. To get the Germans to move ahead on a quick transition to stage 2 the likely trade-off would be an EMU apparatus only formally connected to the Community. This apparatus would be dedicated to monetarist "budgetarism" in which price stability and tightly constrained budgeting were the basic parameters of economic policy. Delors apparently believed that this trade-off would have to be made. It would be better for European integration to have EMU rather than not, even at this price. But the moment was one where an extended period of low growth and recession was opening and the cost could prove to be very high.

François Lamoureux tried to sum things up a few days later. "We've won one thing. There will be an EMU in the Treaty." But he was pessimistic about EMU. "We've lost the game on economic policy. Policy coordination, such as it will be, will be intergovernmental, our voice will be very small. More important, the 'budgetarists' have won." Like Joly, François was thinking about his next step. He had been asked by Edith Cresson, Mitterrand's new prime minister, to become number two in her cabinet. He was very flattered by this, of course, going on about "Edith this" and "Edith that," but he was equally flattered by the strong pressure which Delors had placed on him to stay in Brussels a while longer. He rationalized, "I'm a bit tired of being number two, why should I go be number two again in Paris?" In fact, Delors needed François a while longer. EMU was "on rails" but the political union talks were far from clarified. François knew all the details and all the people. Until that IGC reached the point that EMU discussions already had, François was essential.

Behind the Scenes in the Berlaymont

Jean-Charles Leygues broke some important news to the cabinet lunch on May 22. The Commission would have to leave the Berlaymont because unpleasantly high levels of asbestos had been discovered in the 25-year-old building. The asbestos was not dangerously carcinogenic, but over the years it had been progressively disintegrating and its capacities as a fire retardant had declined. In the event of severe fire the entire building might collapse. The situation was embarrassing, because no one was quite clear whether the Community's own environmental norms had been observed in building its own headquarters. The Commission's departure would have to be rapid, with packing and moving to coincide with Maastricht in December. Despite the hassle, it was hard to find anyone who would regret the building, which, when the news later got out, the press started to call the "Berlaymonster."

It turned out that the Berlaymont did not belong to the EC at all, but to the Belgian state, backed by a syndicate of investors which included the Citibank of New York. The most important matter that this raised, beyond indignation about the bad services rendered by the landlord (which quickly led to general cabinet grousing about the free-for-all of Brussels real estate) was that the Commission did not know whether the owner planned to renovate or tear down the building. This decision had important consequences for both the Commission's future lodgings and its budget. There was no other building large enough to house everyone, causing further concern about dispersing the administration across Brussels. Initial rumors that the Commissioners would end up in the same building as the Belgian secret police turned out, thankfully, to be wrong. Together with their cabinets, they would go instead a few hundred meters away into the Breydel building. There, symbolically, Delors would end up in the office once occupied by the Commission's first president, Walter Hallstein.

Screening

The Delors team had been able to relaunch European integration after the mid-1980s partly because of its skill at remobilizing the Commission's own administration. For a while it had promoted a "forced march" in which Delors, Pascal, and the cabinet had demanded higher quantities and qualities of work by themselves working harder, more effectively, and more strategically than anyone else. The Delorist momentum had also been infused with less regard for lines of command and administrative niceties than veteran Berlaymonters would have liked. This could work for a brief time, but for the new approach to work in the medium term, there had to be payoff for those making the extra effort, from the broader policy successes of the Commission's "product." Without a mobilized Commission, the "product" would not be good enough to achieve success. But without success there could be no mobilized Commission. This was one reason the first period of the Delors presidency had been very tense "in house." It was not until the passage of the Delors package in 1987–8 that there was clear internal support for the Delors strategy and method to insure peak Commission administrative performance. At this point there was a collective sigh of relief at the top, but no celebration, because the Russian dolls strategy involved reinvesting this new internal Commission goodwill in great new effort, lasting into spring 1991.

Delors, assisted by Pascal, used two interconnecting tools to make the Commission go during these years. First of all there was a gradual, but wholesale, change of administrative leadership at director general level which, in its wake, also brought considerable change in sub-leadership (down to unit head level). The new administrative leaders were almost all individuals with whom both Delors and Lamy could deal in confidence and who could be called upon whenever needed without undue concern for institutional boundaries. It would have been hard to fault the choices: Giovanni Ravasio to DG II, the economics section, Ricardo Perissich to DG III, Internal Market and Industrial Policy, Claus-Dieter Ehlermann to Competition Policy DG IV, Eneko Landaburu to DG XVI for Regional Policy, Jean-Paul Mingasson to DG XXI on the Budget, Jean-Louis Dewost to legal services, among others. All were smart, knowledgeable, hard-working, and independent (and many were French). That they owed their positions to Delors understandably made them more "flexible" for the Delors strategy than many, including their predecessors, might have been. Alongside this backbone of new leaders was the presidential cabinet itself, which perfected and institutionalized the mobilizing style devised after 1985. The Delors team was everywhere coordinating, arguing and insisting upon ideas, generating proposals, monitoring the work of others, obliging institutional "flexibility," and simply pressuring to get its way.

The Delorist leadership system thus reposed upon two complementary and interconnected groups of extremely talented individuals at the very top of the Commission administrative hierarchies. Both did a good job at the kinds of cross-divisional horizontal communication at which the Commission would otherwise have not been particularly gifted. The problem was that the rest of the Commission administration existed in an uncomfortable subordinate position. At upper middle levels there was a growing sense that the approach involved bringing in people from outside in ways that slowed, even blocked, prospects for promotions and careers. More generally, if "the troops" had indeed had their morale boosted by the Community's new success, their outlooks and the broader structures within which they worked remained largely unchanged despite all the new challenges and an intensified and changing workload. Moreover, "the troops" were in many ways the *object* of the new DG leadership teams and the cabinet. They were constantly under pressure to mobilize for new, urgent, purposes that they did not always understand. Thus beneath a certain relatively high level of administrative rank there was considerable alienation and resentment, if comforted by high salaries and tenure.

These matters did not pass unnoticed. An important figure in the Bangemann cabinet gently announced one day that he thought that the "human resources management" of the Delors team was behind the times in centralizing and commanding rather than decentralizing and eliciting participation. Another high official, whose job placed her in daily contact with a wide sample of Berlaymonters, was blunter. Pascal, she said, was a "paradigm of French administrative skill . . . he knows absolutely *all* the dossiers . . . but is still able to take his distance from things to reflect." His system, however, was "centralizing Bonapartism," even "Bonapartist becoming Napoleonic." Because of its top-down nature it worked to "deresponsibilize" people. In addition, everyone felt unappreciated for their exceptional effort.[58] She talked further about a "wearing out of power" which she felt in her colleagues. They seemed to be slowing down, not responding so readily to the various incentives to mobilize in the Delors–Lamy system.[59]

This was not the end of in-house problems. A whole set of difficulties were created because the Commissioners themselves were neither happy nor effective. The first Commission under Delors, which had ended in 1989, had worked reasonably well as a college. Jacques Delors, left to his own resorts, was something of a loner, not particularly good at generating help and comradeship among the rest of the Commission leadership. Yet the Commission functioned best when he could obtain such things. In that Commission he had gotten a lot from Arthur Cockfield who had an almost Dunkirk-like sense of Single Market mission, and Lorenzo Natali, with whom Delors had struck up a real friendship. Confidence and trust between Delors and these two men, both Commission vice-presidents, meant that information and burden sharing at the top filtered outwards and made collegiality effective. This, in turned, had allowed containment of the damage caused by the usual quota of inept commissioners and difficult personalities. Moreover, that first Commission had brought low expectations to Brussels and been elevated by the successes of Delors's strategy. It had become more collegial in consequence, not unlike a sports team that had found a winning formula.

The second Commission under Delors's presidency, in place in 1991, was a different story. Delors had no one like Cockfield and Natali to share burdens and help generate collegiality, in part a product of Delors's own success. That he had become much more than *primus inter pares* and was constantly playing on the world stage was resented. The general view was that the Commission was composed of people who took its new stature for granted. Pascal, as conversant with the vocabulary of economists as anyone, invoked the concept of "situational rent" to describe it. In consequence, the college, a delicate institutional form which depended on interpersonal harmony and willingness to assume collective goals, was riven by personality conflicts, individualism, and political disagreement.

The situation was most depressing among the Commission's most important members and its official vice-presidents, where collegiality ought to have begun. Delors respected Leon Brittan, the most effective commissioner besides himself, but disagreed with him about almost everything. Delors was a progressive Catholic and former French trade unionist, Brittan a neo-liberal British lawyer. Between them there prevailed a diplomatically regulated state of conflict. Brittan was careful to alert Delors, often in *tête-à-tête*, about the timing and targets of his next salvos. Delors then mobilized his divisions to spike the Brittan guns, or to batten down the hatches. Vice-President Frans Andriessen, a third-term commissioner and "Foreign Minister," deeply resented Delors's towering international presence, having spent the first Commission resenting Delors for other reasons. Martin Bangemann, another vice-president charged with the vast Internal Market portfolio, was brilliant but he waited instead until the very last minute to improvise responses to things. Henning Christophersen was a competent financial technician, but without much imagination. This was the Commission inner elite and they were all liberals, even when their political label was Christian Democrat. This was clearly a political problem for Delors, but limited by the fact that they disagreed as much among themselves as they did with Delors.

The second tier of commissioners during Delors's second presidency was even less promising. Ray MacSharry had become one of Delors's *bêtes noires*, to the point where Delors overlooked the agriculture commissioner's considerable merits as a negotiator. MacSharry's Irish provenance probably overdetermined his resistance to Delors's views on agriculture: he had ambitions in Irish politics and came from a farming background in a society with an extraordinary dependence on agricultural trade. Bruce Millan, the second British commissioner (a Labourite) worked hard and in principled ways on his regional portfolio, but was so little able to get beyond it, despite a very good staff, that he was referred to as "the accountant."[60] Similar things could be said of Antonio Cardoso e Cunha, in charge of administration. Filippo Maria Pandolfi, another vice-president did everything by himself and trusted neither his own staff nor his directors so no one ever knew quite what he was up to. Carlo Ripa di Meana, the other Italian, seemed to have decided that the only way he could advance his environmental portfolio, plus his own considerable personal ambitions, was to run a separate shop communicating with the others through press releases.[61] Of the two Spaniards, Abel Matutes was often out of town tending to business affairs and Manuel Marin, the Commission matinee idol (he was a young and handsome man), was unpredictable and moody. Jean Dondelinger of Luxembourg (audiovisual and cultural matters), Vasso Papandreou, the Greek socialist in charge of social affairs, and Christian Scrivener, the other French commissioner, were out of their league. Karel Van Miert, a Belgian socialist in charge of transport, was the only positive surprise of the second Commission, while budget commissioner Peter Schmidhuber was, in the words of someone who worked closely with him, "absent even when he was present."

The cabinet system and this indifferently endowed and uncollegiate Commission came together to create other perverse consequences. Horizontal relationships between Directorates General and their commissioners were always variable because commissioners were more or less capable of giving effective political and administrative leadership and the administrative services had their own interests to protect. But the combination of weak commissioners, the huge pressure of the Commission's policy priorities, and Delors's insistence upon strategic coherence made them even more unpredictable. Horizontal coordination was vital even if the apparatus did not itself produce it. This was the central reason Delors and Pascal had developed their inner circle of new and trustworthy directors general and why Pascal had designed the cabinet as he had. The short-circuiting of official hierarchies that resulted, however, tended to make those who ran them upset and uneasy.

Horizontal coordination through the cabinet system had become a problem. The system had been established to serve collegiality, help commissioners to maintain linkages with different constituencies outside the building, and "liaise" between commissioners and their assigned services. It had also become a setting for younger Commission functionaries to establish horizontal vision and set up in top Commission networks. But all this had become out of control. Cabinets meddled too much in the services' business. Sometimes skillful cabinets became "shadow cabinets" for their commissioners' administrations, undercutting the autonomy of the appointed leaders of Directorates General. Cabinet members, including the most junior of them, often reworked and rewrote the work of the services – sometimes "just for the fun of it," in the words of Assistant Secretary-General Carlo Trojan. The services were chronically annoyed about such things, never sure whether what they had produced would be taken seriously or tortured out of all recognition by cabinets.

Much of the Commission's post-1985 success could be attributed to Delors's system for mobilizing the Commission's resources. But it was highly contingent upon the presence of a few important people whose positions were not permanent. The succession to Delors, which had to come sooner or later, would bring a change in personnel, and could precipitate a rather dramatic deflation in Commission effectiveness. And to the degree to which the Delors system was precarious, therefore, such changes could quickly turn into a serious problem for European integration. Delors and Pascal would not have been themselves had they not already given serious reflection to such important matters. Little could be done about the commissioners themselves. The second Commission under Delors was well into a term which would expire at the end of 1992. It made sense to reflect upon how the "house's" subsystems could be redone, however so that new Commissions would face a very different environment in

which some of the Delorist advances, at least, had been better institut
ionalized.

The problem of cabinet meddling was but a small piece of this, to which
Pascal had an initial solution. Why not try to remove as much as possible of
the task of horizontal coordination from cabinet hands? Pascal thought
first of transferring much of it to the Secretariat-General, whose formal job
was to promote coordination. Whenever multiple services had to be
brought together to produce complex policy it would thus become the
Secretariat-General's job to do. This approach had the advantage of cutting
out cabinets, including the president's, until the penultimate stages of pre-
Commission discussion. The approach had been used with some success to
produce an industrial policy-style paper for the biotechnology sector. The
danger that the Secretariat-General might use its new power to strengthen
its own political position – in much the same way that the Delors cabinet
had used its coordinating power to push Delors's strategy – seemed minimal. The Secretariat-General reported directly to the Commission president and would be responsible to the Commission's annual program,
which spelled out policy priorities in a clear way. Beyond this, it would
always be possible to coordinate highly important policy development matters through task forces of high officials. Pascal had also been experiment-
ing with this method throughout the year by convening task forces himself
on problems such as aid to the CEECs and the Soviet Union and EC policy
towards Japan.

There remained the much deeper problem of Commission organization, however. One of the more important task forces which Pascal had
called together was charged with "screening" (evaluating) the Commission's own internal operations. There had been massive changes in the
Commission's tasks after 1985. Despite this there had been good political
reasons for not attempting to restructure the Commission earlier, despite
rising costs in rationality and efficiency. The Single Market program
strained the Commission to its limits. Delors's strategy needed a cooperative "in house" base for the huge numbers of new programs to be developed. Simultaneously restructuring the Commission could have created
uncertainties and undercut cooperation. But once the mountain of Single
Market legislation had been produced the rhythm of Commission work
would change. Monitoring and implementation would take on much
greater importance while the new tasks enjoined by the results of
Maastricht, whatever they might be, would call for refocusing. As this
moment approached Commission restructuring should become an essential job. "Screening" was designed to lay the groundwork for such restructuring. There was one further reason for adding restructuring to the
agenda. One battle to be joined after Maastricht would be over the *paquet
Delors 2* including, among other things, requests for increased funding for
the Commission for new personnel. To be plausible, these requests would
have to be backed by reasoned argument about changing Commission
needs. "Screening" was an instrument for developing such arguments.

The "screening" exercise itself was shrewdly organized. Each Directorate General was examined by teams of senior EC civil servants under a director. In all, 700 interviews were conducted with virtually all the upper-level functionaries (down to unit heads). The interview agenda contained a number of important questions about matters such as unnecessary duplication of support services, possibilities for decentralizing work to member states or contracting it out, budgeting and evaluation processes, and what to do about the Commission's computer and information-processing facilities. In almost all of these areas there was important information to uncover, like the waste that followed from each DG having its own public relations operations, for example, and the costs of the Commission's haphazard and inefficient information-processing policies.

Beyond this were larger priorities. One was to design an internal redistribution of personnel to maximize effectiveness within budgetary constraints, eliminating jobs in certain areas to create new ones where new policies demanded them. This was connected with the deeper matter of restructuring DGs to confront the Community's new tasks more intelligently. Like Topsy, the Commission had grown and changed. There were many too many Directorates General and equivalent units, 34 in all. A number were badly defined, at great cost to Commission effectiveness. This was most obviously the case in foreign affairs: three commissioners and two DGs plus the Secretariat-General and the Commission presidency all had hands in handling a multiplicity of tasks. The division of labor that resulted made little administrative sense, created endless territorial disputes and exhausted Bernhard Zepter, the Delors cabinet worker in foreign affairs. Even if Commission strategy were completely coherent, incoherence would almost certainly be created by this kind of organization. Structural Fund administration was similar – three of the five funds were lodged in different DGs, which ran them according to their own particular logic. There were also a number of units that were simply not very good at what they did. The "information" directorate, DG X, was universally perceived as inadequate, even when the tendency for sensitive politicians to blame public relations for their problems was discounted. DG V, the social affairs directorate, was not far behind.

"Screening" was hardly necessary to uncover the most important of these problems since everyone had complained about them for years. But the screening exercise and report, in the late spring of 1991, were a useful cover to announce important conclusions that were already clear in the minds of those who organized it: David Williamson, Carlo Trojan, Jean-Charles Leygues, and Pascal Lamy. They reasoned that since everyone denounced cabinet meddling, for example, it should be possible to propose reducing the size of each cabinet by one member. This would not resolve the meddling problem, even if it would oblige cabinet members to work somewhat harder to achieve the same level of meddling, but it would free 17 A-level (high administration) posts which could then be reassigned to a priority area.

Jean-Charles's own thinking demonstated how widely the net had been cast. Beyond the issues of too many DGs and too much duplication, there was a general problem of coordination. "There isn't satisfactory coordination in any area of Commission activity, and the 'culture of DGs or of dossiers' takes precedence over Commission culture," he noted. These problems were particularly acute in foreign affairs, the Structural Funds, and the complex budgetary control interface between the internal market, evaluation, and external matters. Moreover, there were "too many generals (A1s), colonels (A2s) and non-commissioned officers (unit heads)." Since they all had to have places, all kinds of useless positions had to be filled and there was extensive duplication of activities. Given the real needs of the Commission in new policy areas, some more effective system of rotation had to be devised.

The screening report and Jean-Charles's reflections both contained strong recommendations about major changes in the Commission's functional organization with policy implications. For the internal market area, for example, economic analysis DG II needed to be pointed towards sectoral, as well as its existing macroeconomic, approaches (connected with industrial policy). There were also large duplications of activities between DG XIII (high tech), a self-sustaining empire, and DGs III, IV and X (Internal Market, Competition Policy, and Information, respectively). It wasn't hard to detect Delorist intentions to remodel the industrial policy dimensions of these diverse DGs and put them into one place, probably DG III. At the same time there had been a proliferation of small units (DGs XXII and XXIII, the Consumer Protection Service and the Task Force on Human Resources),[62] to undertake horizontal coordination across other administrations that might have been better handled in other ways.

The list of criticisms was long and detailed. DG V needed more resources to handle its new social tasks. In "framework policy" areas (competency administrations whose task it was to produce broad "framework" orientations for Community action in research and development, environment, energy policy, and the like), there had been an explosion of new tasks with which the services had not yet caught up. Research and development, in particular, was spread across too many areas. Moreover, the accretion of new tasks had led to the employment of temporary workers, with serious perverse effects. There were so many temporary personnel in DG XI, which dealt with the environment, for example, that it sometimes acted like a colony of outside agitators from the Greens. In the Structural Funds areas a "culture of separate funds" persisted, despite the 1988 reform which had decreed targeted coordination among them all. In this area as well "the evaluation function does not yet exist," a dangerous admission. In the "common policy" areas of agriculture DG VI tended to do everything, rather than decentralize things to member states. The newer fisheries DG XIV had imitated the organigram of DG VI and created a number of empty administrative boxes. Finally, and most important, in foreign affairs, there should be a "triangular" redivision of labor from the existing dispersion into a clear area where foreign policy, strictly speaking, was made, another for foreign economic and commercial relations, and a third for cooperation and development activities with the less advanced areas of the world.

The screening conclusions were strong medicine for the Commission. Like all such exercises, its first function was to "marinate," socializing different Commission areas to the prospect of future change.[63] Little was likely to happen in concrete terms until after Maastricht. Delors's second Commission would terminate at the end of 1992, which made the second half of 1992 the most likely target for administrative reorganization, which would be carried out around the reconstruction of portfolios to be assigned to incoming new commissioners. There were some big ifs in all this. Real change could be worked only by Delors, yet Delors's term was scheduled to end in 1992. This would render him a lame duck just when it would be logical to proceed to administrative reform. Pascal and others had begun to circulate the rumor that Delors wanted to stay on for another term, partly to counteract such lame duck effects. But the purposes of the rumors were also undoubtedly to lay the foundations of an extension of Delors's tenure.

Even if the matter of Delors's tenure could be dealt with, reforming the Commission would demand relative external calm and lots of resources. The Commission's structures had not been rebuilt after 1985. The new Europe had been put together by a European administration from the 1970s. In time "the house" had thus settled into being run in the ways which Delors, assisted by Pascal, had originally designed around 1985. Urgent policy tasks continued to press, and performing them always seemed more essential than reconfiguring the administration, a time-consuming, draining, and probably costly exercise. The administrative reform scenario was constructed around a successful Maastricht to enlarge Commission reponsibilities in a number of new areas. This would oblige the member states to increase the Commission's budgetary base, and more money would make it easier to move people around. Even in the best of circumstances, however, it would be tempting to continue the Delors–Lamy trade-off of policy production by "forced march" without administrative reform, since there would be huge numbers of new matters to face. But what if Maastricht turned out to be less important than anticipated, and what if the member states did not want to find much more money for the Community budget? It was not impossible that the Delors presidency might then end without confronting the job of rebuilding the essential administrative tools for future Commission success. In the light of gigantic questions about Europe's international role, monetary and economic policy, and the democratic deficit, the job may have looked small. But the Commission's effectiveness was the very basis of Commission influence in the broader European political system.

6

Turning Point – Onward or Downward?

> How high are our ambitions? . . . Since the First World War our
> continent has been falling behind the rest of the world. History
> judges severely those peoples whose leaders, whatever their partisan
> affiliation, proclaim a universalist vocation but are willing to tolerate
> the absence of strong ambition implying economic, indeed military,
> power, at the same time as great generosity.
>
> Jacques Delors, October 1991

The wind had begun to turn. International uncertainties, in large part
stemming from the end of the Cold War, had begun to disrupt relative unity
of purpose among EC member states. The IGCs were providing very mixed
signals. Economic and Monetary Union (EMU) seemed likely to emerge
intact, but political union was a disorderly mess, likely to produce confusing
results. Delors's strategy had always been premised on building forward
momentum until finally there would be no turning back. On the evidence
from the first part of 1991, resources for new political successes would
clearly be harder to find. This meant that the strategic grounds for forward
movement would be difficult to map. Managing consolidation, rather than
breakthroughs, looked to be Delors's next challenge.

A Season of Turbulence

From the beginning of its Council presidency Luxembourg had been eager
to make its mark on the projected new treaty by the June 1991 European
Council. This eagerness was wildly optimistic. Some important things had
been decided on EMU (the "no veto, no coercion, no lock-out compromise" for the UK, for example) but even here there were large open
questions. Virtually everything on political union was open. The Luxembourgers had illusions about making their European Council a working
session to settle these matters. No one else wanted this, however. Ultimately
Helmut Kohl laid down that there should be no rush to decision.

There was small drama at the European Council. Delors and François
had gone on the road about "pillarized" Treaty structures and won eight

member states to their position. Thus the Dresden Foreign Ministers' Meeting prior to the European Council pushed Luxembourg to change its "non-paper" preamble towards a "temple." "Union" became the Community *supplemented* by the other two pillars, with language announcing that the two new non-Community pillars should enhance and not undermine the *acquis communautaire*, and that the Union should be served by a single institutional framework. One important additional feature was the notion that the "Union" had a "federal vocation."

The "federal vocation" caused a volcanic eruption in the House of Commons, the Tory Party and the British press. Indignant Euroseptics announced that federalism was a "matter of historical importance on a par with the Magna Carta, the defeat of Charles I and the battle of Waterloo." Mrs Thatcher denounced Delors's plans for a "superstate." The eruption was a symptom of the confusion that prevailed about EC federalism. British critics saw it as centralization and an indicator that the EC might be serious about being more than a market. The Germans understood it in terms of their own constitution, as decentralization. The French wanted a much stronger EC, but on a confederal basis. Delors had distinctive European state-building plans, but when he talked about federalism he sounded German. The smaller countries were divided, but a good many of them saw federalism as a way to limit domination by the larger states.

A European Council to be forgotten

When I remarked that nothing much had really happened at Luxembourg Pascal Lamy agreed, and added, "given what various people wanted, that nothing much happened was the best possible outcome." The European Council at Luxembourg was eminently forgettable. The 12 decided to use the Luxembourg June non-paper as a framework for continuing the IGCs towards Maastricht.[1] Delors presented a communication on "cohesion" with his customary skill and thoroughness at justifying regional redistribution, in a preview of the second Delors package.[2] The major surprise for the Commission at Luxembourg was a proposal from Chancellor Kohl to "communalize" matters of right to asylum, immigration and anti-criminal activities (advocating a Europol).[3] None of this improved prospects for Maastricht, however, and Pascal had resigned himself to a much weaker deal than Delors would have liked. "There are still a few bumps for EMU, but that looks pretty good, but for the rest, the best we can do is lay the rails and hope that the train will ride on them later on." François Lamoureux, more apprehensive, thought that there was considerable risk that EMU would emerge with a long, and empty, second stage which could bog down the entire process later on. On political union, "it will be a minimalist paper, I'm afraid. They're going to put off making any real decisions on the key matters – defense, co-decision, citizenship – until 1996."

The real event of the Luxembourg summit was the despatch of the "troika" (the Foreign Ministers of the present, past and future EC presidencies) to Yugoslavia.[4] The collapse of the Soviet Union's regional hegemony had been signalled, in general, in 1989. One of the many consequences of this was political instability in those national federations, including the Soviet Union itself, where communism had been the political glue. Yugoslavia, where Titoist communism had provided a means to unify one of the more nationalistically fractious areas of Europe into a federal republic, was a case in point. As the glue wore out, older national identities, hatreds, and irredentism came back.

Delors had postponed a scheduled diplomatic trip to Belgrade in May when it became clear that his presence might muddy an already unclear situation. Croatia and Slovenia were on the verge of proclaiming their independence from the Federation.[5] As things turned sour the Community had tried to exert whatever pressure it had through financial aid and promises about an association agreement. By late June violence broke out between federal troops and Slovenian militias, and signals pointed to eruptions between Serbia and Croatia. The Milosevic federal government had two options: first, to try to prevent the dissolution of the Federation and, if that failed, to occupy Serbian areas of Croatia by force. The Croatians were certain to resist. Everyone was aware, although not as acutely as they would become, that nationalistic hatred between Serbs and Croatians was close to the surface.

The problem from a Brussels point of view was that major EC member states disagreed about how to respond. German Foreign Minister Genscher strongly favored immediate recognition of Slovenia and Croatia, a course which would have invited Serbian military action. The French and others (particularly Spain, which faced its own regional nationalisms), favored dealing with the Yugoslav Federation even if a mask for Serbian regional imperialism. It would be easier to settle differences about territorial boundaries within an existing legal entity than among independent, possibly warring, countries. The French position was designed to have an exemplary discouraging effect on other federations from dissolving – the Soviet Union in particular. The British were skeptical about the Community doing much at all.

Yugoslavia was more than a device to mark a European Council with little else to say for itself. It was the first real test since the Gulf War of the EC's capacities to act internationally. Much was at stake. The test would be seen as a measure of the Community's ability to practice a common foreign and security policy. The communiqué from Luxembourg advocated negotiation within the existing constitutional order, respect for existing boundaries and human rights, particularly those of minorities, a deepening of the democratization process through further economic reforms, and a "search, through dialogue," for future structures for Yugoslavia. The Community, although divided on the subject, also suspended its aid.[6]

The Yugoslavia test would be extremely difficult for the Community to manage. Member state division made it virtually impossible to muster effective resources and the determination to act. It probably would have been necessary to project military force, or threaten credibly to do so from the onset of the situation, to oblige the potential combatants to negotiate. But this was completely out of the question. The British refused even to think about it – arguing that interfering in a civil war would be a dangerous course. The Germans were prevented constitutionally from using force and did not agree with the official Community position. The French, who might have been willing to think through this option, could not go it alone and, in any event, had a military apparatus which was singularly ill-conceived for what would have been needed.[7]

As conflict opened between federalist forces and Slovenia and Croatia, the EC invoked the emergency mechanisms of the Conference on Security and Cooperation in Europe (CSCE) and sent improvised mediating missions into the field.[8] On July 7 the Brioni accords ended the war in Slovenia and set out a series of conditions for peacefully deciding other matters, backed by an arms embargo and a suspension of EC aid to Yugoslavia. The Community at that point sent observers to Slovenia to police the deal. There wasn't much to observe and very little subsequently happened (the cease-fire allowed Slovenia to move towards quiet and successful independence later). This was perhaps just as well, given the rather complete lack of preparation of the Community observers. But allowing the Slovenians to bank on later independence foreordained the disintegration of the Federation and obliged the Belgrade government to mobilize to capture Croatian territory by military means, and the Yugoslav conflict was on.[9] Along Serbian – Croatian borders Serbian irregulars and the Yugoslav army invaded Croatia to reclaim Serbian areas, and the Croats fought back.

At the end of July the Community asked Serbia to allow EC monitors to enter these areas and the Dutch presidency began to organize a peace conference over which Lord Carrington would preside and which would be aided by an arbitration committee of notable jurists led by Robert Badinter. The initiatives were overshadowed by disagreement among member states about how to proceed.[10] Predictably, the protagonists in what was becoming "former Yugoslavia" quickly integrated the Community's peace-seeking activities into their war-making strategies. The result, by fall, was a seemingly endless series of Community-brokered cease-fires which were either used by different actors as staging points for their military goals or violated even before they had been signed, while the brutality and intolerance mounted. In effect, Community actions in Yugoslavia were rapidly undermining any credible EC common foreign and security policy. Even before Maastricht put legal words on paper, it was strikingly clear that the will for a real common policy was quite absent. In September Delors advanced an answer to his favorite query ("Will Europe be an adult or an adolescent?") about the situation. The "Community has behaved like an adolescent confronted by an adult crisis . . . If it had been ten years older, there would have been a European intervention force in Yugoslavia."

Yugoslavia was but one – very spectacular – symptom of the slippery nature of the Community's context, as the pattern of international perturbations from the spring persisted. Negotiations with EFTA marked time.[11] Negotiations with Poland, Hungary, and Czechoslovakia on Association Agreements bogged down as well. As the Czechs announced after one session, great progress was being made "except on the key issues."[12] Finally, in its last act before the summer recess, the Commission ruled on the Austrian application for admission, the very first step towards enlargement. Negotiations would have to await the completion of treaty renegotiations and the second Delors package, and then the Austrians would have to accept the Community as the new treaty defined it.[13] The Austrians didn't blink. Enlargement was thus on the horizon, with all the added complexity that it was bound to bring.

Despite Yugoslavia and these smaller matters, the inhabitants of the top floors of the Berlaymont (except Gunther Burghardt, chained to the mast by Yugoslavia) had hoped to have a normal summer vacation. The Commission, which itself lived by the "European Model of Society," officially observed an August-off schedule.[14] Nearly a year of 80- and 90-hour weeks of total concentration had taken their toll, even on tough characters like Pascal and François, and they were going to try to leave.[15] The issue of who would be around to provide a cabinet *permanence* always a difficult problem – was sorted out (amid moaning and groaning) at a cabinet lunch. Fabrice Fries, the youngest and freshest cabinet member, received the biggest part, with the rest divided up. Delors himself planned to observe the vacation ritual, although he was hardly a lawn-chair-and-detective-story type. He set out for his modest country retreat in Burgundy with two gigantic trunks full of documents and books and a fax machine for keeping in touch. While taking his leisure he intended to seek the intellectual and political core of the issue of European federalism.

For François Lamoureux, it turned out, vacation would mean a change. "Edith" – French Prime Minister Cresson – was sinking in Paris, amid innumerable public gaffes, difficult policy problems, and a staff that hadn't gelled. François was asked to lend a hand again and this time, in early August, Delors packed him off to Paris. Delors had become worried about the disorder of the Cresson operation. Then François might serve some useful purpose in Paris during the run-up to Maastricht. Finally, and most important, Delors now felt that he could do without François in the IGCs. This was a clear signal that what happened in the IGCs would henceforth be the business of top member state leaders. "Crunch time" was beginning and the field would be occupied by the elephants. What the Commission could do, barring last-minute maneuvering, had already been done. And all the last-minute maneuvering would be done by Delors himself.

The Commission's *permanence* was left in the hands of Karel Van Miert. The putsch in Moscow, which occurred on Van Miert's watch (and which abbreviated Delors's vacation), sent the Commission scurrying to generate and supply new aid to the Soviet Union in a belated effort to prop up Gorbachev, and Van Miert proved himself up to a very difficult job. Joly Dixon (who liked his vacations, alas) was quickly involved, dealing directly with Michael Emerson, the EC's new delegate in Moscow, who was operating frenetically out of a Moscow hotel room. Joly had to scrape up the money from different budgets and services. But he and Emerson also had to figure out how to give the Soviets, particularly the Muscovites, a large amount of food aid. There were great risks of the aid finding its way into parallel market circuits and feeding the growing Soviet underworld more than the Soviet people or, if it could be moved into the genuine market, of undercutting precarious legitimate businesses. For a moment the Community thus ended up giving out food by hand in white plastic bags.[16]

Dutch detour towards Maastricht

Delors and his team, not displeased to see the last of the Luxembourg presidency, had higher hopes for the Dutch. That the Dutch Foreign Minister, Hans van den Broek, was a convinced Atlanticist would undoubtedly be important to the Common Foreign and Security Policy (CFSP) discussion. But in general the Dutch, and Ruud Lubbers, the Prime Minister, had strong federalist inclinations, as befitted a small member state with vital economic interests in the Community. Moreover, on matters of treaty architecture the Dutch favored the "tree" over the "temple" model. When van den Broek first announced the priorities of the Dutch presidency he also included energetic action on Single Market matters, the conclusion of EEA negotiations, and CAP reform. Most noticeably absent, as Delors quickly announced, was concern about the social dimension.[17]

Negotiations on political union began on schedule after the Luxembourg European Council. Then came summer vacation. When Community activity resumed in early September, however, the political union talks did not start up again. The first two negotiating sessions were cancelled by the Dutch, pleading the pressure of urgent international matters on the Dutch presidency and the permanent representatives. Something else was going on, however. The Dutch, largely on their own (although encouraged by Commission insiders) had decided to prepare an entirely new non-paper. By later September this paper was circulating and the press filled with rumors about its contents. The Dutch were playing a dangerous game. The Luxembourg European Council had done very little, but it had announced that the Luxembourg non-paper should be the basis of subsequent discussions. If the Dutch effort departed too far from the Luxembourg non-paper (and why write another paper if it did not?), those who opposed the Dutch innovations would have procedural as well as substantive arguments on their side in rejecting it.

When it did come the Dutch non-paper caused a huge stir.[18] Its most important feature was the abandonment of the three-pillar formula. Although the former third pillar of "home affairs" (judicial and police co-operation) continued to have an intergovernmental spin, everything would be integrated into a single "Community" structure through a new pre-amble. Article 2 of this preamble committed the Community (and not the "Union" of three pillars standing separately of the Luxembourg non-paper) to a set of central matters, including the *acquis communautaire*, a CFSP with defense ultimately included, and strengthened protection of the rights and interests of nationals of member states.[19] The new non-paper also granted the European Parliament the right to reject legislation in large areas (ex-cept agriculture and commercial policy).[20] Delors, whose preferences had been written into the Dutch effort, was quick to note that 90 percent of the provisions of the Dutch non-paper were the same as the earlier Luxem-bourg document, but it was the remaining 10 percent that counted.

The "black Monday" ministerial meeting of September 30, 1991 moved the Dutch non-paper immediately into the dustbin. Emmanuele Gazzo, ultra-federalist patriarch of *Agence Europe*, the "bible" newsletter for EC watchers, went so far as to speculate that the purpose of the non-paper had been to "flush out" the various oppositions to the Luxembourg one to prepare the way for an easier deal. This was undoubtedly too Florentine, but the Dutch had managed to produce multiple coalitions against their work. Belgium, Germany, Spain, and the Commission delegations were willing to negotiate on the Dutch text. But seven member states – Denmark, Greece, France, Italy, Luxembourg, Portugal, and the UK – denounced the non-paper as "contrary to the conclusions of the Luxembourg European Council."[21] On the basic issue of treaty structure – the Dutch "tree" – only Belgium, Germany, and Italy were pleased. A different set of countries disliked the new CFSP proposals (where Dutch Atlanticism was clear). Yet another group rejected the increased power proposed for the Parliament. And virtually everyone was upset about process: the Dutch had wasted three months of their presidency to produce a new draft paper. Had the paper been accepted for negotiating purposes, it would then have taken many months beyond the Maastricht target date to work it through. As things stood the Dutch had forced the IGC talks on political union into a frenetic pace. Five weeks remained until the Foreign Ministers' Conclave in Novem-ber, when final negotiating matters would be set out. From the point of view of delegations unhappy with various parts of the Luxembourg non-paper, the Dutch procedure, by using up time which could have been used to hammer out new deals, guaranteed that most of the Luxembourg non-paper would be part of the final compromise.[22]

The return of industrial policy

Industrial policy was a matter that would not go away. The Commission could talk as much as it wanted about not having a "sectoral" industrial policy, for example, but it had to do just that for automobiles. For cars,

"1992" meant removing national protective barriers and replacing them with a common EC policy that would ultimately have to conform to international trade standards of openness. National protective barriers varied greatly across the EC member states, lower where they had no domestic manufacturers, higher when they did, and highest when the success of those manufacturers was strongly dependent on national markets. The industrial policy problem arose because dismantling national barriers and quotas might have meant being immediately inundated by Japanese cars.[23] The American example was clear for all to see, and important parts of the European industry were even less competitive than the American industry had been.[24] It was no exaggeration, therefore, to judge that the future of Europe's automobile industry would be largely a function of how greater access for Japanese imports could be arranged.

The EC thus had to do something to help its car industry after "1992", however liberal the prevailing ideological winds. Because unilateral external tariffs were taboo, help had to come by dealing directly with the Japanese, following the American example, but before rather than after the damage had been done. From the moment the issue surfaced in mid-1989, Delors was at the center of what happened, holding ten full meetings with the various commissioners engaged in the dossier (including Andriessen, Bangemann, Brittan, Pandolfi, Ripa di Meana, and Scrivener). François was deeply involved as coordinator, counsellor, internal negotiator, and all-purpose tough guy. And as the long negotiations opened up Delors personally oversaw everything. Andriessen and Sir Leon Brittan handled most of the "external" dealings with the Japanese through 1990 and 1991, while Bangemann was charged with the "internal" side, dealing with the European car manufacturers.

The internal problems were almost as large as the external ones. Andriessen was a liberal from a liberal country with no domestic car industry, not an inordinately skillful negotiator, and not on good terms with Delors. Brittan, beyond his liberalism, came from the major location of direct Japanese foreign investment in cars in the EC, which made him an interested party.[25] And as Bangemann ascertained, the European car industry itself, through its manufacturers' association, was the major agitator for help, or, in gentler language, a slow phase-in of more open trade. The French and Italian industries (Renault, Peugeot-Citroën, and Fiat) were particularly vulnerable because of very large stakes in their own heavily protected domestic markets and relatively weak export positions. In consequence they were more worried than the Germans. Fiat (whose Chair, Umberto Agnelli, was president of the European manufacturers' association) wanted to get the Japanese to agree to level off their exports to the Community prior to 1992, while Peugeot-Citroën advocated an extremely high basic quota. Both industries wanted a very slow reduction of quotas over a long transition period. The British, who had become, in the words of more than one French official, an "aircraft carrier for the Japanese," and the principal base for Japanese transplants (Japanese models assembled abroad), were much less keen on protection.

Finding common ground in these delicate international and European talks was not easy. Delors thus had good reason to take matters in hand. From the outset in 1989 his goal was a trade deal that could achieve consensus across this wide range of interests and be agreeable to the Japanese as well. He also sought to use the automobile question to open larger informal trade discussions with the Japanese. The approach that was defined involved a transition period beginning in 1992 during which there would be a progressively declining EC quota on Japanese cars. The actual quota numbers could be altered in accordance with varying market conditions and would take into account both direct imports from Japan and transplants produced inside the EC. It would be monitored over time, and adjusted if need be, by the Commission and MITI (the Japanese Ministry of Trade and Industry).[26] There was also to be agreement that the Japanese would not especially target the markets of those member states like Italy and France where quite high barriers had earlier protected territory for domestic manufacturers. But there were to be no restrictions on Japanese investments in automobiles in Europe itself. All of this had to be negotiated and introduced as the European car industry prepared itself for the Single Market, which implied considerable work on norms and standards, environmental regulations, reflections upon Europe's more general transportation plans, and research and development help for the car companies to adapt themselves to international best practices.

The trade deal struck on the last day of July 1991 represented a "consensus" worked out between MITI and the EC.[27] According to the "interpretative declarations" issued in Brussels, carefully edited by Delors, there would be a transition period to open trade in cars through 1999. During this period projections were made for the development of the EC car market with the total numbers of Japanese imports allowed set at slightly below the level of penetration in 1992 (from 11 to about 8 percent). Trade was to be "monitored" by MITI and the Commission and there were agreed methods to share market ups and downs between European and Japanese manufacturers. Japanese vehicles, imports plus transplants, were to rise to 16.9 percent of the EC market. Transplants were to be held to a level of 1.2 million. Finally, the Japanese agreed not to "target" specially those markets that had been strongly protected prior to "1992." The "hidden agenda" of the deal was to oblige the Japanese to invest in European production rather than in direct exports to Europe, another lesson drawn from the American experience. One codicil, negotiated by Delors during his trip to Japan in the spring, was a Japanese statement about a broader opening of their domestic market to European products in general.

The public vagueness of the deal was out of deference to the Japanese desires for discretion and to divide its European adversaries. Limitations on transplants disturbed the British and were difficult for the Japanese to admit publicly (thus agreed, they were never announced).[28] The French and Italians were not at all happy, for other reasons. The likelihood that they would progressively lose their protected domestic markets implied entirely new business strategies and massive structural adjustments. Thus Jacques Calvet, chief executive of Peugeot-Citroën, blasted the Commission and Community about its "hateful agreement," further fueling anti-EC sentiment in France in the process.[29] Commissioner Carlo Ripa di Meana, covering his Italian bets, dissented from the deal in Commission. The fact that the EC's trade balance with the Japanese was growing dramatically worse by the month also played a role in the outburst of anger. Delors's careful attention to the complex conflicts in cars paid off, however, despite these outbursts. Everyone ultimately accepted the agreement and a potentially explosive and dangerous situation, that could easily have been as damaging as that which would later follow the Blair House deal with the US on agriculture, was avoided.

The car agreement implied new EC industrial policy moves, and the Commission ultimately produced a substantial "industrial policy" package to help the car industry modernize during the transition period.[30] The proposal first suggested extensive industrial harmonization to make a genuine Single Market in cars out of the fragmented setting which existed. Then it advocated research and development help for transition to "lean production," extensive training programs for workers plus broader "active labor market" measures to facilitate labor mobility.[31] The paper's central focus, beyond inducing lean production, was on increasing productivity through promoting innovation and raising the workers' skill levels.[32] It thus inched towards the use of research and development money for product development, as opposed to "precompetitive" research, and sought to promote greater cooperation among the firms themselves.[33]

The EC was indeed moving towards a new industrial policy posture, with the automobile deal as model. The entering wedge was the need to modernize and adapt specific industries in the Single Market and the changing international trade setting which the Single Market brought. Whole industries, like automobiles, would otherwise be menaced with rapid decline. Commission "Communications" on the biotechnology,[34] maritime,[35] textile and clothing, and aeronautics industries, in addition to that on cars, all went in similar directions. These papers all stressed and elaborated the horizontal, framework perspective of the original industrial policy paper.[36] They repeated the incantations that it was not for the EC to help out sectors, but rather to shape broader market structures to allow firms to receive clearer market signals and respond in innovative, rather than protective and self-destructive, ways.[37] The major movement beyond electronics was less stress on industrial "hardware" and much more on investment in intellectual and human capital.

This movement in industrial policy came largely from Delors and his staff, leaning heavily on DG III, starting with Commissioner Bangemann and Director General Ricardo Perissich. Jean-Charles and François, backed by Pascal, were the central operatives. When François left the cabinet to work for Edith Cresson in August, Jean-Charles replaced him as number two in the cabinet, relinquishing his industrial policy responsibilities to a French newcomer, Jean-Pierre Jouyet. Jouyet, a young *énarque* politically close to Delors, had been head of the cabinet of Michel Rocard's Industry Minister, Roger Fauroux, where the "horizontal framework" approach had been discussed extensively.[38] It was Jouyet, with Perissich's DG III, who took over nursing what became a flood of new papers beginning in the fall of 1991. The process was not without problems, however. However much one talked about horizontal framework intervention to give clearer signals for firm decision-making the companies themselves almost always wanted traditional sectoral intervention, often simple bail-outs (this was evident in electronics and it defined the automobile case). Moreover, there was an internal Commission "policy legacy" that militated in the same directions. The high-tech DG XIII, sectoral-producer-oriented, with strong budgetary and programmatic resources in the EC's research and development programs, was a skilled, even feared, infighter for sectoral interventionist policies.

Not very many member states were eager to grant the EC room in the industrial policy area, making the "marination" of the Commission's new ideas a slow process. Some (the UK and other liberals) resisted for ideological reasons. Others felt that industrial policy should remain in the hands of the member states. Finally, Community resources in research and development programs, regional funds, harmonization, and the like, were relatively small. Even if they could be sensibly targeted, it was unclear whether they would make that much difference. The Commission's industrial policy "Communications, "therefore, were more bark than bite initially, encouraging those who had wanted to make industrial policy in the first place more than making converts. The EC, like a crab, sidled towards industrial policy, with sizable obstacles rendering its course even more sinuous.

Perhaps the most perplexing issue involved the Commission's own competition policy prerogatives. They were an essential part of industrial policy writ large in the "horizontal framework" argument, the key instrument for creating a genuine single market. But they had a life of their own. Competition policy, as promoted by Sir Leon Brittan and DG IV, was a liberal crusader whose logic sometimes contradicted EC level industrial policy (however "horizontal") as much as it did national-level intervention. On a strategic level, if Delors wanted to "organize" a European industrial space, Brittan, standing atop long-standing Commission prerogatives, wanted quite as much to "open" this same space. The complexities involved in trying to reconcile these different quests had become a central feature in Commission life.

Sir Leon Brittan, it will be recalled, had in late spring decided to make the ATR–de Havilland merger proposal the first case under the new merger control procedures. The Canadians had then decided to review the proposed deal, but any hope that the Canadians would resolve the matter had collapsed by early September. When Sir Leon communicated to Delors, in a letter dated September 23, that "we must *not* allow this merger to proceed," the case re-emerged. The shape of the internal Commission controversy over the judgment was predictably similar to that which had emerged when the case was looked at first time round. Brittan and DG IV contended that the merger would create a dominant position. ATR–de Havilland together would be strong enough to wipe out British Aerospace and Fokker, ATR's major EC competitors who, not coincidentally, were the major corporate objectors to the proposed merger. The argument was based on an analysis of market segments for turboprop planes broken down by the number of passengers carried.[39] Furthermore, the "dominant position" which the merger would create would make ATR–de Havilland strong enough to pressure airlines, undercut competitors, and then further expand market share rather than increase efficiency. Finally, the turboprop market had only a five-year expansion period before reaching "maturity." This made it impossible for any competitor to develop a competitive new product in time.

DG III led the opposition to Brittan, disagreeing with the method for assessing market share as prejudicial to the proposed new company.[40] Moreover, even if one accepted this unfavorable method, ATR–de Havilland would not hold a dominant position on the international "market of reference" (which counted), as opposed to the EC market. New entrants would not be blocked and airlines not appreciably constrained to buy ATR–de Havilland. DG III's underlying arguments were much broader, however. It argued that the industrial advantages of the merger were great, creating synergies in research and allowing better access to economies of scale. The merger would allow Europe to possess a world-class leader in commuter aircraft.

Michel Petite, who had replaced François Lamoureux following the case for the Delors cabinet, commented that "competition and industrial policy are on a great collision course." He couldn't understand why in an aerospace market which was obviously global the Community could "stand in the way of a European champion of daunting efficiency . . . the Americans never had any anxiety about allowing Boeing to acquire a dominant position in the jet market." Petite foresaw that Brittan would lose in Commission, however, because the "European champion" dimension to the proposed merger would prove seductive enough to carry the day. Intelligence work prior to the special chefs meeting pointed to a Brittan defeat as well, and special chefs confirmed Petite's optimism. Bangemann's and Van Miert's cabinets (Van Miert was in charge of transport) strongly objected to Brittan's proposal. Jonathan Faull responded very ably for Brittan, and he was supported by the Andriessen and Schmidhuber cabinets. A majority of the rest of the cabinets supported Bangemann and Van Miert. Christophersen, Marin, and MacSharry were undecided. Petite announced as undecided for Delors as well, but this was politics – if the President could avoid yet another conflict with Sir Leon, so much the better. Counting heads thus led to the conclusion that Brittan would lose by several votes. The *Chefs de Cabinet* meeting on Monday September 30 confirmed this.

For once Delors's intelligence was misleading. Unlike every company in Brittan's sights before it, ATR did not lobby hard. Neither did the French government. Henri Martre, the head of Aérospatiale (ATR's French parent company), did make a ritual pre-Commission visit to Brussels. He knew that the merger was in the line of fire, but brought no new proposal to Brittan, clearly violating the informal etiquette of such cases according to which companies under merger scrutiny were expected to offer something to get off the hook. Martre's performance mobilized a puzzled Sir Leon and his team to press even harder on other commissioners.[41] Brittan also lectured to anyone who would listen that the merger would cost jobs in the European aerospace industry. The logic of this, probably correct, was that ATR wanted de Havilland as a North American beachhead to which to transfer pieces of ATR production to satisfy North American local content concerns about the purchase of ATR aircraft.[42]

Martin Bangemann and his cabinet, in whose industrial policy dossier the matter fell, were charged primarily with organizing the opposition to Brittan. Bangemann's laid-back personal style was reflected in his team. Bangemann's *Chef de Cabinet* refused to interact in anything but German, which limited his effectiveness in the dense dealings among cabinet leaders that played such a central role. There were other people on the Bangemann staff, of course, but they were kept at a some distance from the main action by the *chef* and because of Bangemann himself. Bangemann was very talented, but not a detail person. He relied on his unquestionable brilliance to pull things out at the very last moment, often on the floor of a critical meeting itself. His staff was thus never quite sure what Bangemann needed and had difficulty in being very effective. All of this was important. While Brittan and his group methodically worked over his fellow commissioners for days on end, "the Bangemanns" did little or nothing.

The result was a shock to Delors. Brittan won nine votes and the merger was blocked. Beyond the other Commission liberals (Andriessen, Schmidhuber, and Cristophersen), Cardoso, MacSharry, Dondelinger, Millan, and Marin all voted with Brittan. For each of these commissioners Brittan's hard politicking had been central. Most said simply that they were giving way to the "commissioner in charge," although others, including Millan (a British Labourite with whom Brittan almost never saw eye to eye) and Dondelinger, indicated that they disagreed with Brittan even though "giving way." Manuel Marin, the swing vote, gave an utterly incomprehensible argument to explain himself, but seemed to have traded his vote for help from Brittan on a pending project to reorganize the European fishing fleet, an essential Spanish dossier. When it became clear that he would lose, Delors, as was his usual practice, abstained.

The defeat was the result of accidents and oversights that, for once, almost all played against what Delors wanted. Because of the ways in which Petite and Pascal had read the preparatory meetings, no special alarm had been raised. This meant that no one in the Delors team was backing up "the Bangemanns" or, rather, that no one was doing the work that the Bangemanns ought to have been doing. The departure of François Lamoureux to Paris was important. Michel Petite, his successor, was a Commission pro, but when the ATR–de Havilland case reappeared he had been on Delors's staff for only three weeks.[43] Delors and Pascal rarely gave clear signals on competition policy issues until the last moment because they knew that François had a procedure that he would execute whether they urged him to or not. Michel had not been broken in either to François's procedure or, more importantly, to the art of interpreting the absence of signals from above (that sometimes was a red light, other times not). Bruno Dethomas, who was very close to Delors, allowed "there was a bad evaluation of special chefs and the *Chefs de Cabinet* meeting . . . the various cabinet members were not in touch with their own commissioners, so it was difficult to know how they would vote." Delors was "angry about the bad risk assessment . . . he would have worked harder had he been alerted."

There was a ferocious outburst against the decision in France (and to a lesser extent in Italy).[44] French Finance Minister Pierre Bérégovoy denounced a "technocratic deviation . . . by high civil servants who, however eminent, have no business setting out political lines. Brussels . . . in the name of competition law that had nothing to do with the issue . . . has denied Europe the weapons to confront economic competition." Elisabeth Guigou, Minister of European Affairs, was more restrained, pointing out that the decision ran counter to the industrial policy guidelines that the Council had approved. Foreign Minister Roland Dumas brought the matter before the Council itself on October 6 and proposed that the Council reverse the decision.

It was a costly defeat for Delors.[45] For some time he had been topping all polls as a potential candidate for the French presidency. The little world of *présidentiables* in France was not one of fraternal comradeship, however, and the Commission decision on ATR–de Havilland brought out the long knives. The rapacity of the personal attacks against him was partly driven by rivals' desires to destroy him. Jacques Chirac attacked him for "choosing to abstain in a debate where the fundamental interests of France and Europe were at stake." Michel Poniatowski, Giscard d'Estaing's hatchet man, announced that "Jacques Delors played against Europe and against France." The most painful words came from the socialists, including Michel Rocard himself (Rocard apparently had opposed the merger when prime minister).

Such things hurt and infuriated Delors, both in his pride and because of the powerful anti-Commission, anti-Community tone of the French response. He knew better than anyone that the balance of public opinion in member states about the renaissance of European integration was delicate. In his October 6 press conference Delors thus pedagogically reviewed the legal empowerment of the Commission's actions and the institutional circumstances that led him to act as he had. "To the French, I say . . . if you want the construction of Europe it involves life together as twelve. There are advantages and risks to this. If you don't want this . . . then you should decide to get out." But then he underlined that there might be very little agriculture left in France without the CAP and that, moreover, in a long list of competition policy matters the Commission had been gentle with France. At no point, however did he show the slightest inclination to disagree either with Brittan or the ATR–de Havilland decision. Collegiality was too important.

The damage in France for the Community turned out to be much more serious than that for Delors. ATR–de Havilland fed the anti-European nationalism that would nearly torpedo the Community a year later on the Maastricht referendum. Pascal Lamy was philosophical. Rather than dwelling on oversights and mistakes he joked about how symbolic airplanes had always been to the French ("you have remember the Caravelle, and then the Concorde and the Airbus") and the ambiguities of French attitudes about the Community and especially the Commission. History showed that when the Commission's collective head appeared over the parapets the response had often been an artillery barrage from the French camp. The French expected Europe to be subordinated to their own interests. Pascal nonetheless worried about the effect of the decision on the IGCs. Had Brittan used ATR–de Havilland to force the French to back off on political union and bring them closer to the British? He concluded that "Perhaps it's a blessing in disguise . . . whatever else it does, it brings ideas about industrial policy up front. Our new formulae are being discussed." Indeed they were. *The Economist* warned gravely, the week following, of gathering strength in the camp of the dreaded interventionists.

The complex relationship between these "new formulae" and competition policy would persist. Just as ATR–de Havilland was coming on to the agenda in early summer 1991, for example, Brittan presented a controversial proposal for obliging public-sector manufacturing firms to provide extensive financial data in order better to track state aids.[46] The Commission was again deeply divided. It was finally approved, with Commission socialists against, in mid-July. Delors was concerned that suspicion of public firms was being stimulated and that the Brittan text might reinforce the position that the Commission was bearing down too heavily. Like Pascal, he was worried that this might be negative for the IGCs. Later, at the very moment when ATR–de Havilland was reaching boiling point, a quieter struggle went on about the deregulation of public utilities. Cardoso, in charge of energy, had proposed opening up protected national gas and electricity networks to "third party access." Brittan, part of the working group of commissioners involved, urged that it be done with great speed (Article 90, paragraph 3 of the Treaty would have allowed the Commission to begin deregulating immediately by Directive). Cardoso was willing to go slower (under Article 100a), but still move forward. Public monopolies in these sectors existed in almost all countries, they employed many people, and Europe was in recession. The matter would have been touchy in the best of circumstances. The French were particularly raw. And the IGC might well turn on what the Commission did before December.[47]

Countdown to Maastricht

The outlines of Maastricht were reasonably clear by fall 1991. From the Commission's point of view expectations had been lowered by what had happened during the first half of the year; in Delors's September words, "there is a large risk of modest conclusions." The Commission's major agenda-setting role had been played once its own papers had been discussed. Henceforth only Delors could really do much in his role as high-level negotiator. When the political union talks resumed in October, negotiators had to move fast. The fiasco of the Dutch non-paper had eaten up a lot of time and COREPER had to meet at least twice a week. EMU, as usual, would proceed more majestically.

Political union

The general institutional outlines for CFSP had been sketched in by Luxembourg. The European Council would define principles and common policy would be conducted by the Council and its secretariat (that would integrate the EPC secretariat). The Commission would be "fully involved" and the Parliament regularly informed and consulted. CFSP actions could take three forms: intergovernmental cooperation to achieve common positions unanimously (like existing EPC), "common actions" in general areas decided by the European Council, and in the security realm. The ill-fated Dutch non-paper had simultaneously proposed greater Communitarization and greater Atlanticism and when it failed it became clear that there would not be very much CFSP and that whatever there was would be intergovernmental.

Security and defense were the major open questions. Progress began with a joint Italian–British statement on October 4, 1991 in which the UK seemed willing for the first time to allow a serious security dimension, provided it could include language committing the WEU to act both as "union" defense arm and to reinforce the European pillar in NATO, a soft formalization of the "WEU as bridge" position.[48] This prompted the French and the Germans (who dragged the Spanish in), to issue their own statement on October 11 arguing for greater WEU independence from NATO.[49] The elephants still disagreed, but were drawing closer. The new NATO "strategic concept," approved in early November, was central.[50] NATO recognized WEU as a relatively autonomous European pillar of the common defense, a notion sufficiently ambiguous to support the UK's "bridge" idea and French–Commission hope for an "evolutive" position. Large open questions remained about decision rules for joint actions, including the use of qualified majority voting for implementation,[51] and about the final list of areas for joint action.

A similar pattern of movement to weak compromise could be seen in other areas. The British, Portuguese, and Danes had clearly stated their opposition to strong co-decision in early October. The concept of "Community law," last remnant of the Commission's original "hierarchy of norms" approach, was abandoned, necessitating a list of the specific areas where co-decision would apply.[52] Controversy persisted about the nature of the conciliation procedure for co-decisioned legislation, and the Commission, through David Williamson, continued to fight for its right to withdraw legislation that had been amended in ways to which the Commission objected. It was clear that Parliament would not be granted as much new power as it wanted. Everyone seemed to agree that an extension of the cooperation procedure was desirable, however.[53] The general logic of co-decision discussions pointed to a procedure that would increase parliamentary power in certain areas but at the cost of new institutional opacity. In particular, there might be a cumbersome third reading of legislation.[54] In other areas, what would go in the "third pillar" of internal and police affairs remained murky, while the British made abundantly clear that they were intent on blocking any change in social areas.[55] Under "competencies," agreement was close on the range of matters new and old to be in the new treaty. The remaining sticking point was the extension of qualified majority voting.[56]

Delors took a hard line whenever he could get a hearing. To the October interinstitutional conference, for example, he announced that "it is clear to me that nothing has changed since the Luxembourg European Council . . . not a single delegation has moved forward, not one."[57] He concluded prophetically that "we haven't ever talked about the effectiveness of the system that we will end up with . . . are we working inside a test tube or are we thinking about public opinion and European citizens?"[58] At the November ministerial meeting Delors again gave his "cohesion" pitch, this time detailing the likely contents of the Commission's coming budgetary package (including a new doubling of the Structural Funds). This was an effort to call off the Spanish, but the Spanish minister responded that Spain would not let Maastricht get by without treaty insurance on cohesion.[59] Delors's sternness, which suited his personality very well, was also a negotiating position. He knew that there wasn't much chance of pushing member states much further in these last weeks, but he certainly had to try.[60] He was also looking beyond Maastricht, as ceaseless repetition of the cohesion line made clear. If the Spanish succeeded in forcing the Maastricht European Council to include a strong new cohesion plank, this would imply many of the new budgetary commitments that he would propose anyway. If the Spanish did not win at Maastricht, arguing with them that they could leave the cohesion matter until the second

Delors package could help pre-empt Spanish threats to bring Maastricht down, provided other member states made a sufficiently serious commitment to the package later. Either outcome would make the post-Maastricht setting more promising for the Commission.[61]

Patrick Venturini, a soulful man, had been suffering throughout much of the year. Cranking out Social Charter and Action Program legislation (which all had to be in the pipeline by the end of the year) involved supervising production of a couple of dozen complicated pieces of legislation by DG V, which was not a very efficient operation. The worst part of this was that Patrick knew that virtually none of this production would become law. The British would block every proposal that demanded unanimity and contend that anything presented under qualified majority rules really belonged under unanimity. When these tactics were unpromising they doggedly tried to negotiate Commission proposals down to harmlessness.[62] Patrick thus found himself passing on proposals to the Council to see them shot down in flames.

An unexpected turn of events cheered Patrick up. When the IGC first discussed social matters in the spring, the Commission's "negotiate or we'll legislate" idea had been left in limbo. The Luxembourg non-paper had watered down Commission social dimension proposals. The Dutch social clauses discussed in early November were weaker than those in the Luxembourg non-paper. Despite the weakness of the Dutch proposals, they included an expansion of Community legislative purview compared to the Single European Act.[63] Employer worries about new social legislation grew, therefore, and UNICE finally concluded that a "negotiate or we'll legislate" clause might turn out better than a meager right to be consulted about Commission legislation. Employers could always slow down negotiation and bargain for the least damaging deals, while legislation was forever. And given labor's weakness, harmless bargains would not be hard to get. Discussions went on at the *ad hoc* social dialogue group, prodded on by Patrick and Jean Degimbe, Director General of DG V, until October 31, 1991, when the social partners wrote a joint letter to Prime Minister Lubbers urging that a version of the initial Commission proposal be put into the treaty proposals. The Dutch complied.[64]

Delors's victory here was significant. Social dialogue had finally produced something serious, thanks to the Commission's cleverly designed proposals. UNICE's strategic retreat was eased because the employers thought that the British would stop the passage of anything remotely resembling the October 31 proposals and, as a result, that little or nothing would come of their "deal" with ETUC, except, perhaps, that UNICE would win accolades for being cooperative. Maastricht would be a surprise in this respect, however.

The penultimate pre-Maastricht meeting was at Noordwijk in mid-November. Then the Dutch presented a full non-paper on political union that retained the basic three pillar structure of the earlier Luxembourg non-paper, tying the pillars through soft wordings.[65] The preamble announced that the "Union" would have a CFSP "eventually including the definition of a defense policy." The European citizenship clause was strengthened, as was the preamble proposal on "subsidiarity." Decision rules proposed in the "competency" areas, in particular for research and development and environmental policy, were unusual, however, to the degree to which co-decision and Council unanimity were associated. On CFSP the Dutch proposed that decisions to undertake joint actions be unanimous, those on "modalities for the implementation of a joint action" be by qualified majority, and the actual list of areas for such actions left to Maastricht. There was also limited Communitarization of the CFSP and the "third pillar" allowing the Commission a larger role (except over the police). The size of the Commission was to be reduced to 12 (with five additional junior commissioners a possibility) and the Commission's nomination was to be approved *en bloc* by the Parliament.

At Noordwijk the British, for the first time, accepted some form of co-decision, but "everything depends upon its extent," said Douglas Hurd, the British Foreign Minister. In the air was a deal between the reluctant British and the confederalist French to limit German desires for increased Europarliamentary power. The Germans were willing to allow this because the British seemed to be moving towards a more general treaty deal. The Spanish were for unanimity on environment and social policy, undoubtedly to prepare trade-off deals on cohesion at Maastricht. The British, Danes, and Portuguese balked at qualified majority voting for implementing CFSP joint actions, but the NATO summit in Rome had opened up the possibility of deal on defense.[66] The issues left open for the European Council were the social dimension, the final touches of legal cooperation in the "third pillar," competencies, the precise extent of qualified majority voting, final formulation of the CFSP and, as always, social and economic cohesion.[67]

On the eve of the European Council the Commission published its final positions on "the stakes at Maastricht." CFSP had pride of place. For the Commission, the concept of "joint action" was the "fulcrum of treaty reform, that which will progressively give a real foreign policy to the Community,"[68] but the excessively complicated decision procedures envisaged by the Dutch were unworkable and likely to discredit the Community as an international actor. The Commission was also concerned about the definition of common security concerns, interests, and decision-making, but above all about the WEU–NATO division of labor. Would WEU be an integral part of European integration, subordinate to the "Union," or a "bridge?" The Commission proposed a compromise in which the WEU–NATO relationship was acknowledged, but WEU's different ties with NATO and European Union were spelled out.[69] Commission fear of excessive "pillarization" was a final central concern. To the extent to which separate pillars could not be avoided, the Commission hoped for language that would pledge evolution towards one eventual whole Community.[70]

EMU

The Luxembourgers' major EMU accomplishment had been the "no obligation, no veto, no lock-out" approach to remove the British threat.[71] The new Dutch presidency set its sights on the remaining major problems, including passage to, and the content of, stage 2, movement to stage 3, and the "economic" dimensions of stage 3.[72] "Social and economic cohesion" was the most likely addition to this list, followed by democratic responsibility in EMU institutions.

There was persistent disagreement among key member states about EMU stage 2. The Delors Report and the Commission wanted EMU banking institutions (the European Central Bank and the European System of Central Banks) to be created in stage 2 to apprentice for stage 3. The Germans and the British wanted a glorified Central Bank Governors' Committee. The Germans argued quite sensibly that monetary sovereignty was indivisible, but everyone knew that they wanted to put off real EMU as long as possible.[73] British, of course, wanted a slow transition in the hope that there never would be an EMU. That the Germans would get their way was clear.

The Dutch also had difficulty finding agreement about movement to stage 3. Institutional matters like who would decide and how were problems, but the underlying issue was that a two- or even three-speed EMU was on the cards and an acceptable way of framing it had to be found. If, since the opt-out deal, the UK would be the second speed, the third would be composed of member states ineligible for stage 3 because they could not meet convergence qualifications. EMU had been defined to be largely about price stability. To get in, member states would have to maintain a level of inflation close to that of the best-performing member states, participate in the EMS "narrow band" for at least two years, build a "sustainable" government financial position (low annual budget deficit and debt as a percentage of GDP), and have long-term interest rates no higher than 2 percent above the three best-performing members. A number of important things were in dispute, including whether these convergence conditions were "criteria" or requirements, how strictly they should be interpreted, when the assessment(s) of these conditions would occur, how many "first speed" member states would constitute a critical EMU mass, and the role of those who could not join immediately. [74]

The Dutch prepared a new EMU non-paper for September. The January 1, 1994 date which they proposed for beginning stage 2 won easy agreement. At this point member states would begin making their Central Banks independent of politics, establish multi-annual convergence programs, and intensify mutual surveillance with an eye to eventual decision about stage 3. A European Monetary Institute (EMI) would intervene at this point to administer the EMS, run convergence programs and clear the road for stage 3, and then disappear at the beginning of stage 3. The fact that EMI would be *the* key stage 2 institution and that its days would be numbered by successful convergence obviously suited the Germans. The institution-building prior to stage 3 of the Delors Report was thus replaced by "confidence building."

The Dutch – developing a Belgian idea – then proposed procedures for moving to stage 3. A joint report by the Commission and the EMI to the Council before the end of 1996 would review performance on four key convergence criteria. While refraining from proposing whether the Council of Ministers or the European Council would then formally decide, the Dutch suggested that if a majority of member states were ready to go to stage 3, then the Council, acting unanimously on a Commission proposal, should fix a date for doing so.[75] But there was no definitive transition date. If things did not work out first time around, the procedure would be repeated in two years, presumably until the conditions were met.[76] The prospect of an indefinite postponement of stage 3 pleased the British and the Bundesbank. Delors and his team were deeply unhappy, along with the French. The actual procedures suggested by the Dutch would be modified, but their "two-speed" idea would stand.

In September the Dutch proposed giving a "derogation" (temporary opt-out) status to those who could not join in the first wave, postponing until later their confrontation with the convergence criteria.[77] This elicited a ringing denunciation from the Europarliamentary leaders at the September EMU interinstitutional conference. The Parliament was the last bastion of "Southern" efforts to moderate the stringency of EMU and engineer North–South redistribution of its adjustment costs.[78] Delors, who supported most parliamentary institutional positions, did not on the "two-speeds" matter. He knew that EMU itself was at stake. Delors considered that once the treaty was signed by all 12 member states it became a "Community endeavour." As long as those in the second tier were granted derogations promising eventual entry in exchange for good economic behavior, the EMU plan could work. Hence Joly Dixon's words after the September Foreign Ministers' meeting: "the idea of a two-speed Europe is dead . . . That is not to say that all must move at exactly the same time, but the move forward will be made by a Community decision of the twelve. There can be transition clauses."[79] Accepting the reality of two EMU tiers also served useful political functions. Candidates for derogation lost their major reason for pressuring to soften convergence criteria and for strong compensation to underwrite adjustment costs. This was essential for conciliating the Germans' strict demands on price stability and others' fears about vastly increased EC budgets. It also placed the second-tier candidates in a position where they would have to make strenuous efforts to bring their performances into line.[80]

The October meetings zeroed in on general economic policy commitments, convergence criteria, and the institutional workings of EMU. The first discussions to define "excessive deficits" were revelatory, since the tougher the excessive deficit clauses were, the more constraint would be placed on EC members' fiscal capacities. North–South divisions again appeared, with low-inflation, low-debt countries disagreeing with high-inflation, high-debt ones. The criteria proposed by the Dutch (annual deficits no larger than 3 percent of GDP and total debt of less than 60 percent of GDP) would stand. Procedures for monitoring and enforcing them were delicate topics, however.[81] The Commission and Council would propose desirable broad guidelines for member state and Community economic policies and the European Council would then consecrate them in a "recommendation." Commission and Council would then monitor the observance of these guidelines through "multilateral surveillance." Various mechanisms, ranging from public shame to outright penalties, were proposed to sanction those who strayed.[82]

The European Central Bank was to be even more independent than the Bundesbank, and this created a big problem of democratic accountability. Here the Commission essentially folded its tent, to the chagrin of the Parliament. Democratic legitimacy for the European Central Bank and EMU would flow primarily through national parliaments. As a result, there were few openings to include the European Parliament in the workings of EMU. The Commission's reticence here was part of a deal with the Germans, who were reluctantly willing to accept EMU as long as it had a banking system which was independent from politics. The Germans themselves knew that this kind of EMU was almost by definition undemocratic. Their conclusion was that the change would be sustainable only if the powers of the European Parliament were reinforced in the political union negotiations. The Commission and the Germans agreed that a trade-off on democracy would have to lay elsewhere than in EMU, but the trade-off was never really made. The European Parliament was given a token role in appointing the president of the European Central Bank and the right to receive periodic reports, but little more.

In October, five weeks before Maastricht, the Dutch produced their penultimate non-paper.[83] At this point basic decision rules for the passage to stage 3 remained in "square brackets". The date for passage would be set by the European Council after which the decision on transition would be taken by the Council, on Commission advice, which would determine who would be in and who would need a derogation. Transition would not begin unless at least seven member states were ready to go (the number was also a square bracket matter, however). The Dutch non-paper also attempted to narrow "opt-out" options for stage 3. The door remained much too open for many negotiators, however, and discussion continued. No ultimate date for full EMU was proposed, either. The possibility of an indefinite delay thus remained alive.[84] The major issue which the Dutch avoided was cohesion, and the penultimate ministerial meeting in November was largely taken up with it as a result, again because of the Spanish. Their well-rehearsed line was that rich countries stood to gain from EMU and the poorer ones to lose. For the poorer ones to accept this there had to be a payoff. This time the Commission worked on the Irish and Portuguese, perceived to be "softer" on this than the Spanish, to leave cohesion until the second Delors package. But the issue remained open.[85]

Certain important matters remained on the EMU table, then, necessitating final marathon ministerial meetings a few short days before Maastricht which settled on a fixed date for the beginning of stage 3.[86] The proposal to build in definitive "irreversibility" on EMU came from the French at the last minute.[87] If seven member states had fulfilled the convergence conditions by 1997 and there was a unanimous Council decision, EMU might then begin. But come what may, as long as a simple majority of the Council agreed and whether or not convergence targets had been met, EMU would come in 1999. The Germans had formal reservations about this, and specifics would be changed at Maastricht, but the timing dimension would stand.[88] The problem of finding a way to allow the British (and perhaps the Danes) to opt out without allowing generalized abstention was also resolved. A special opting-out protocol would be attached to the treaty for the UK alone.[89] Conflict about the Commission's role occasioned by another French proposal to limit Commission proposition force autonomy was largely beaten back by the Commission.[90] The Parliament did not fare quite so well and its EMU role remained miniscule. The expected struggle over which member state would host the European Central Bank then opened when the Germans announced that they wanted it in Frankfurt. Finally, the Spanish put the cohesion matter on the table – to be rejected once again.[91]

A Small Town in Limbourg

The Maastricht European Council, perhaps the most significant in EC history, opened on December 11 in Limbourg's small capital city. To keep European Councils intimate the 12 heads of government and the Commission president are allowed only *one* other negotiator in the discussion room, usually the Foreign Minister or, when specific policy areas are discussed, a technical minister. The intimacy of the setting contrasts with the regiments of aides on alert outside the meeting area: there were 96 high French civil servants alone at Maastricht. In ordinary European Council circumstances each leader would be well briefed on negotiating differences. For Maastricht, based on a full year of complex prior negotiations, great amounts of time had been devoted to "gaming" the talks. With huge issues at stake staffs had precooked schemes and turns of phrase for all of the most likely scenarios.

Thus there was not a great deal of space for political creativity at Maastricht and the logistics for seizing upon such space as there might be were very complicated. Information had to be passed from the two negotiators to staff leaders in the corridors who would then mobilize the right troops to produce materials. In order to communicate the substance of what was happening in the room, one of the negotiators had simultaneously to follow the talks and send out information to staff chiefs. Managing this kind of situation was difficult. If the proper information did not get out in an accurate and timely way the moment for decisive intervention might escape. Moreover, even when the information did emerge, work outside the room had to be done effectively, something which was not always easy with large teams in different places.

The Commission lacked the clout of a large member state but it could hope to compensate by using flexibility, shrewdness, commitment, and the wide-ranging knowledge which its nature and position granted it. The Commission's operation was a typically "Pascalian" creation, well engineered, organizationally light, quick and commando-like. There were but 30 Commission people in Maastricht, including the all-important secretaries, by far the smallest delegation. There were a few technical specialists, but the team's core was the half-dozen or so individuals who had overseen the Commission's positions throughout the long negotiation: Ravasio and Dixon on EMU, for example, Dewost of Legal Services, Van Solinge of the General Secretariat, Michel Petite on political union, and Gunter Burghardt on foreign and defense matters. This group, a small number of trusted operators from the Delors cabinet and the top of the Commission administration, had complete mastery of the dossiers and had brought argument and potential amendment texts for all predictable summit contingencies which could be thrown on the table on call, if needed.

The scene, typically, was built around Delors, the Commission's key negotiator, sometimes spelled by Andriessen and/or Christophersen, and seconded by David Williamson. Because of Delors's mastery of the range of dossiers, Williamson could function primarily as a stenographer. Williamson, an unusually quick-minded man, produced clear and informed notes almost instantaneously for Pascal, who then moved in and out of the room to give them to secretaries while barking marching orders into his walkie-talkie to specific members of his team. Arguments, ideas, and proposals in good treaty language were then passed back to Delors for use when the time came.

Maastricht brought few surprises. In political union the "three-pillar" structure so little desired by the Commission was confirmed, but with preamble language which might prevent it from being irreparable (Title I, Article C). The confederal pillar for CFSP emerged as anticipated: CFSP was essentially intergovernmental EPC writ large with confederal "joint actions" conceivable in four initial areas – CSCE processes, arms control and disarmament, nuclear non-proliferation, and the economic dimensions of security (arms and technology exports, etc.).[92] The decision rules for "joint actions" were restrictive and confusing: the Council still retained the power to decide, unanimously, what decision rules would be used case by case. The Commission's right of proposition, shared with member states and the Council presidency, was small compensation for such crippling procedures. Higher points included a relatively favorable resolution of the WEU–NATO problem which combined the "bridge" positions with relative

WEU autonomy. And there was commitment to a "common defense policy which may lead . . . to a common defense," a Belgian formulation that the British had earlier been unwilling to accept.[93] Finally, a reconsideration of CFSP was scheduled for 1996 as part of a larger review of parts of the new treaty. The "third pillar" of judiciary and internal affairs involved a long list of "questions of common interest" for regular discussion among member states.[94] There were also prospects for "Communitarization" of visa and immigration policy and, in passing, the European Council approved the establishment of Europol.

"Democratic legitimacy" included a reinforcement of the power of the European Parliament. A complicated co-decision procedure, including the third reading, was instituted for matters of the free circulation of labor, the internal market, framework programs for research and development, action programs on the environment, certain consumer protection matters, and trans-European networks. In addition, the Parliament acquired broader rights of advice and consent (*avis conforme*), rather more budgetary scrutiny, and approval over the Commission as a college (which remained at 17). The cooperation procedure was also extended.

There was a specific article (3B) on "subsidiarity," specifying that no action of the Community should exceed what was necessary to achieve the objectives of the treaty. And a new Committee of Regions was established. Clauses on European citizenship granted certain rights to "each citizen of the Union" (i.e. every member state citizen) including the right to vote and be elected in municipal and Europarliamentary elections, diplomatic protection when outside the Community, the right of petition to the European Parliament, and the "right to circulate and live freely on the territory of member states." These provisions were a mixed bag. Some – like European citizenship and subsidiarity – had great "evolutive" potential. Others, like co-decision, were small advances. Beyond the clear insufficiency of progress in "democratic legitimacy" (a very serious matter) the major problem was lack of transparency. By definition legitimacy was something granted by citizens. Maastricht's changes were more likely to produce confusion and incomprehension.

Under "competencies" the Spanish finally won concessions on cohesion: a new fund to help the "South" underwrite environmental and trans-European network expenses plus promises to reform operations of the Structural Funds. Clauses on research and development and environmental policy were strengthened to include qualified majority decision rules. Trans-European networks in transport, telecommunications, and energy could be decided by qualified majority, while industrial policy, with the objectives of competitiveness and accelerating structural change, was subject to Council unanimity. Other new competencies where language was generous but Community power minimal were in consumer protection, education, culture, professional training, and health. In general there were a number of matters which might "evolve" towards a much larger Community role in the future, depending on future political conjunctures. But member states were clearly concerned to limit Community incursion into important policy areas. From Delors's point of view this was a relative setback for "state building." EMU, the best-prepared matter on the table, went through without much controversy.

The biggest surprise of the summit came in the social area. The Dutch proposals on social policy involved an enlargement of the Community's social policy purview plus a version of the October 31 "negotiate or we'll legislate" letter from the "social partners." In their mailing, however, the Dutch indicated that they had another social text in their portfolio. This one, a considerably watered-down version of the first, anticipated British opposition. The Dutch had good reason to think that social matters would be the place John Major would draw his line, hence they had prepared a compromise to conclude the talks. But the Dutch had been wrong in thinking that the British would be willing to sign the compromise that they had prepared, even though substantively it would have allowed very little progress on social matters. Major needed a public Maastricht confrontation for his home crowd, something which would allow him to announce "game, set and match for the British." Thus he refused to deal on social issues and stood on keeping the treaty as it was. This provided an unexpected opportunity for the Commission. When it looked as if things might break down over social issues, Delors produced language and justification for what would become the "social protocol" to Maastricht, an agreement by 11 of the 12 EC members to work with the original Dutch social proposals. The British would not be bound by this and would be engaged in social matters only by pre-Maastricht treaty arrangements.[95]

In his cabinet post-mortem Pascal bragged about Delors's system, saying that "we were a good hour and a half ahead of everyone else." Being ahead mattered little unless the system came into play precisely at those rare moments when a suggestion or argument from Delors and the Commission might turn an issue around, however. Judgment about when to intervene had been left to Delors, of course, and he had chosen to be quiet throughout much of the meeting. He had intervened to get Spain and Germany together on "social and economic cohesion" – resulting in another protocol as well as the new cohesion fund – and to reinsert consumer protection into the draft. But the Commission's most successful intervention was on the social protocol, the product of prior brainstorming and quick action from the support team and smart politics by Delors himself. As had so often been the case for Delors's good ideas, it was the obliging Helmut Kohl, by this point looking for a semi-graceful way to end the talks, who placed the proposal on the table.[96]

The deeper logic of the events escaped few in the Berlaymont. Maastricht had been designed to pyramid resources from "1992" into a new great leap forward for the Community and integration – a very large Russian doll. Jerome Vignon, most faithful among the faithful and in close touch with Delors's priorities, announced over dinner on the evening after the summit that the deal was "*pas bon!*" Only EMU was a clear Delorist success. Next to EMU, Jerome thought progress in the defense area was the most important accomplishment. The weak foreign policy provisions might, at best, lay "rails." In the "rail" sense, he thought there were a number of other useful clauses in the new treaty – on citizenship and cohesion, for example. But the whole was "mediocre."

Jacques Delors and his Commission had hoped for a major "deepening" of the Community, one which would help Europe to cross the qualitative frontier towards definitive integration. Before Maastricht the Community had been member states willing to integrate when it served their interests. After Maastricht, Delors had hoped, these interests would be conceptualized *through* the Community. In 1991 there was not enough member state commitment to allow this great leap. This had been reflected in the negotiating strategies of the most important players. The British, central to the talks, had resolved to avoid isolation and then resist all attempts to extend the Community's reach. The French wanted a strongly integrated and "deepened," but confederal, Community where France could compensate for economic weakness by its political and administrative leadership (particularly through EMU). The Germans were firmly federalist, but hesitant – and divided – about EMU. While there were other important players, the logic of Maastricht was created largely by interactions among these three member states.

In a different context, in which the international setting had not yet been rocked by the end of the Cold War and the economic optimism of the later 1980s persisted, these interactions might have allowed different conclusions. In 1991, alas, they obliged a downward ratcheting of the great ambitions nourished by Jacques Delors and his Commission. The British had systematically undercut all state-building initiatives, federalist or confederalist. The weakness of CFSP was due primarily to this. The British and French, in turn, had combined to frustrate the strengthening of the European Parliament which the Germans wanted in exchange for their willingness to accept EMU. The British also encouraged the Germans in their desire to slow down the EMU timetable, in particular to eviscerate stage 2. The French were strong enough to insert an "irreversible" EMU timetable into the treaty, but this irreversibility, in legal language, might be reversible if facts dictated it. The Germans thus had not gained what they really wanted – greater European federalism and democratic legitimacy – and given what they were reluctant to give: EMU. This somewhat inequitable exchange was unlikely to make the Germans enthusiastic about their centrality in the EC and the role which everyone else hope they would assume as the generous bankrollers of Community Europe.

Delors had to report about the Maastricht deal to the European Parliament: a group who were even more dissatisfied with it than he was. The Commission's collective verdict was mixed, he announced: positives outweighed negatives. "Europe's relaunching is accomplished," he noted, because of success on EMU, defense, subsidiarity and, to a lesser degree, foreign policy, where the decision rules "won't make things easy." "For the optimists," he said the CFSP "provides a learning process . . . for the pessimists it demonstrates the absence of basic consensus." Subsidiarity "will take real discipline to work." There had not been enough extensions of qualified majority voting, important to the Parliament because they correlated with the new co-decision powers in the treaty. Continued unanimity on industrial policy and research and development were particularly damaging. On co-decision itself, Delors was ironic about a legislative procedure which allowed "nine different ways to deal with a proposal."

What was the likely balance of Maastricht? The Commission President was careful to underline the state-building dimensions of the deal. But to him, EMU was the real key, pregnant with spillover potential, particularly in the realm of industrial policy, a better CAP, and rural development policy. The economic and social cohesion protocol pointed towards the "new grand rendezvous" proposals of the second Delors package. The Social Protocol might make it possible to break the legislative and negotiating stalemate surrounding Social Charter measures. Delors reported: "Maastricht represents important progress . . . Nothing would have happened without the Single Act and '1992' program to begin with . . . but now making a single currency and a common defense can take over the momentum . . ." It all would "have been much better without the tripartite pillarization, but the various bridges introduced in the preamble, thanks to the Belgians . . ." made it less dangerous. Whether playing masterfully to the Parliament's critical susceptibilities or expressing his own deeper feelings Delors came perilously close to damning Maastricht with faint praise.

The parliamentary leaderships of each major group responded with a combination of self-interest and insight. Jean-Pierre Cot, Socialist leader, announced first that "Europe has kept its rendezvous," but then queried whether the product was up to the nature of the problems it was designed to solve. There were nonetheless the serious advances listed by Delors. "Then why should we be standoffish about this treaty?" Cot asked. This was a double-edged rhetorical query. Cot knew that the Parliament would eventually approve Maastricht, but the failings of the new creation in terms of increased democracy were serious. To Egon Klepsch, the Christian Democratic leader and next president of the Parliament, "the democratic deficit still obtains." Paul de Gucht, the Liberal spokesperson, worried that "Europe is integrating at a faster pace than it is democratizing." Such warnings about democratic deficit would be prophetic.

Last Sprint Towards European Union

History has many milestones and 1992 is one. It marks the culmination of the inspiring venture, the awesome undertaking bequeathed
to us by the founding fathers of the Treaty of Rome. It marks
the beginning of a new era, the era of Maastricht, and opens up the
horizons to European Union . . . My reaction to the signing of the
Treaty of Maastricht is to paraphrase what that great European Paul-
Henri Spaak said on the occasion of the signing of the Treaty of
Rome: this time we have not lacked courage, this time we have not
acted too late.

Jacques Delors

"We had bad luck with the Danes. The date was badly chosen and
the campaign was badly run . . ." but . . . "Europe has been built in a
St Simonian way from the beginning, this was Monnet's approach.
The people weren't ready to agree to integration, so you had to get
on without telling them too much about what was happening. Now
St Simonianism is finished. It can't work when you have to face
democratic opinion."

Confronting the Community's democratic deficiencies is long
overdue: "not that this is much comfort now, with the mess which
we face. The Commission has got to pull in its horns, be quiet
and careful . . . at just the point when good ideas are most
needed . . . and he [Pascal often referred to Delors as he], he's got to
lie low for a while while the shells fly around. He doesn't like that
one bit."

"Behind it all is 1989. The end of the Cold War has destabilized
everything . . . But I don't regret Maastricht a bit. Without
Maastricht . . . the Community might well have gone under in the
aftermath of 1989. Things would have been even more fragile, and
commitment to an EC solution to things even weaker . . . Europe
might well have broken."

Pascal Lamy (conversation with the author, July 1992)

How, then, can we explain the fact that all these achievements have
not made it possible at least to cushion the effects of the world

recession? Was the single market process merely a flash in the pan? *The truth is that although we have changed, the rest of the world has changed even faster.*

European Commission, *Growth, Competitiveness, Employment*

The Maastricht days symbolically coincided with moving out of the Berlaymont. Berlaymonters were to be dispersed throughout Brussels. Commissioners, their cabinets, press operations and key operatives in the General Secretariat would go up the street into the much smaller Breydel building. Delors and his team would exchange their big, bright offices for smaller quarters on the twelfth floor of Breydel. Delors himself would sit in roughly the same place where Walter Hallstein had set up the "Common Market" and later confronted the wrath of General de Gaulle.[1]

Business as Usual?

Maastricht was the culmination of years of hard work and personal investment, in particular by Delors and his cabinet. For some cabinet members it was also the time to move on. As Economic and Monetary Union (EMU) business wound down, Joly Dixon had turned to distributing aid to the former Soviet Union. He had known for some time, however, that he would become a director for international macroeconomic analysis in DG II, rejoining his EMU co-conspirators Giovanni Ravasio and Jean-François Pons (and Commissioner Henning Christophersen). Jean-Charles Leygues, putting the finishing touches to the second Delors package proposals, was also on the move. Jean-Charles, who had briefly succeeded François Lamoureux as Pascal's number two, would become a director in DG XVI (regional policy), where he would follow through key items of the package involving the Structural Funds. François Lamoureux himself had been installed for some time in a lovely office next to Edith Cresson's overlooking the Matignon garden in Paris.

Maastricht thus meant that the entire "senior" trio of Pascal's team was moving on. For Joly and Jean-Charles three years were enough. Their fatigue was evident. Joly, somewhat immune from the charms of French public service, was increasingly cryptic about the harshness of Pascal's system. Such sentiments were not in Jean-Charles's character, but he had undoubtedly had his fill as well. Service for Delors and Pascal had its rewards, among them promotion in the hierarchy of the Commission. Joly and Jean-Charles were cashing in. This kind of "reclassification" was also part of Delors's and Pascal's vision of things – what wasn't? – since it allowed them to place loyal people in key posts. Joly, Jean-Charles, and François, when he later returned from Paris,[2] would thus join a growing group of distinguished ex-presidential cabinet members in crucial positions where they could be called upon to do their duties by Delors.[3]

For those staying on after Maastricht, it meant moving on to the next pieces of Delors's strategy, mostly in preparation for well over a year. The second Delors package, Jean-Charles's assignment, would go public early in 1992. The agricultural budget component of the package would depend upon successful agreement of Common Agricultural Policy (CAP) reform, so Jean-Luc Demarty indefatigably carried on lobbying, particularly with the very unhappy French. Bernhard Zepter labored over the Uruguay Round in the hope that the GATT talks would prod CAP reform while, simultaneously, movement towards CAP reform would facilitate the GATT negotiations. The Commission had also been charged with producing a document on enlarging the Community for the Lisbon European Council (the Portuguese had taken over the EC presidency for the first time) and Pascal had convened a working group of the "usual suspects" to do the hard thinking. Jean-Pierre Jouyet, who became Pascal's number two after Jean-Charles left, was busily working on industrial policy problems, particularly on further conceptualization of the "framework-environment" approaches that had been under the surface of the electronics episode of the previous year. Patrick Venturini had the implications of the Maastricht Social Protocol to sort out.[4] Geneviève Pons continued day-to-day competition policy business while trying to move forward on the Commission's controversial proposal for a carbon dioxide tax, a major new environmental initiative which had caused the principal EC institutions to fall under siege to oil companies. Delors and Pascal had put Michel Petite, François's successor, in charge of a group to prioritize remaining Single Market measures with an eye to the "1992" deadline of January 1, 1993.[5]

Pascal's hard-nosed review of Maastricht in mid-December 1991 spotted new danger signs, however. The second Delors package was designed to play the same role as the first had after the Single European Act. Maastricht endowed the Community with a list of new things to do, and the package would present the member states with the bill for them. Not only would the new programs have clear costs attached to them, but the package would also attempt to increase member state financial commitments more generally while simultaneously expanding the Commission's own budgetary scope. Getting the first *paquet Delors* through the European Council had been the major triumph, and trauma, of the Delors's early presidency. Pascal had deduced from the atmosphere at Maastricht that struggle over the second could be even more difficult. Negotiations over cohesion had been tough. The Spanish hard line on the special cohesion fund and a new doubling of the Structural Funds meant that Delors could count on strong pressure for a hefty increase in the funds when the second package was debated. But the Germans, squeezed by the costs of unification, had expressed reluctance about yet again serving as paymaster-general for regional development. Pascal was mildly hopeful, because "we did get a commitment to the new package into the language of the cohesion protocol." But German reticence to take out the checkbook, the gesture that had made the first package possible, was a warning sign.

Pascal had picked up another warning sign. The Spanish had also exploded about Commission "meddling" in EC environmental regulation. This came on the back of British denunciation of Commission environmental regulation.[6] Pascal was apprehensive about member state backlash against the Commission in the offing. The Commission needed to be much more careful about things that might annoy publics and governments, "the Camembert and potato chip business." Jean-Charles agreed that the environmental matter was especially dangerous. Carlo Ripa di Meana, the environmental commissioner, was an uncontrolled cannon whose erratic actions had already been costly.[7] Moreover, Ripa's service, DG XI, had become a "Green lobby."[8] There was also a similar "research" lobby, DG XIII and its associated interest groups, which Jean-Charles believed capable of annoying member states.

Margins for maneuver had narrowed, Pascal thought. Public opinion was more attuned to the ways that new Community policies were actually touching real lives, and the Commission personified the Community. In addition, some member states were looking anew to the Commission to serve as a scapegoat for their economic and political difficulties. After Maastricht, as Europe had a greater and greater impact on ordinary citizens, baiting "Brussels bureaucrats" was likely to occur more frequently and with greater vehemence. Pascal wanted the cabinet to alert the rest of the Commission about this. Everyone needed to be more careful about observing "subsidiarity" and, above all, avoiding anything which might be construed as Commission meddling.

Budgets and farmers

Virtually everyone in Brussels greeted Maastricht as the *end* of a complex moment. Ratification of Maastricht would be unproblematic, they felt, because member state governments would not have signed without knowing that they could deliver approval. With Maastricht safely behind, therefore, and with Pascal's various warnings of possible bumps in the road ahead, Delors's team geared up for strategic business as usual. The first item on the agenda was the second Delors package, in the works since January 1991. Then, after Delors's appearance at lunch to announce the coming new "*grand rendez-vous*," Pascal had assigned Fabrice Fries, the newest cabinet member, to rummage through the records to write a paper on how the first package had been developed.[9] Fabrice's paper had then passed to Jean-Charles, who, among his other talents, was a budgetary professional.[10] Jean-Charles's initial think-piece, finished in spring 1991, went to Delors, whose thoughts became a briefer working paper for discussions led by Pascal with Jean-Charles, Jerome Vignon, and Jean-Paul Mingasson, Director General of Budget Administration (DG XIX). When Delors and this small group had agreed on precise directions the tasks of concrete drafting were delegated to the Commission services.

Jean-Charles's initial thoughts were a good reflection of Delors's strategic ones. The second Delors package should follow and build on the model of the first, which had tried to institutionalize innovations in budgeting and consecrate EC commitment to regional redistribution by reforming the Structural Funds. The second should further inscribe these commitments as part of the *acquis communautaire*. A new five-year financial plan would give the Commission relative budgetary autonomy and financial backing for Maastricht's priorities, with the Commission committed to strict observance of budgetary guidelines. There would be also a substantial increase in funding for "social and economic cohesion" both as a general deepening of regional policy and as a counterpart to the foreseeable adjustment costs of EMU to the EC "South."[11] Then there would be a substantial increase in the EC's "external" costs tied to Maastricht and foreign policy innovations.[12] A combination of new Single European Act and Maastricht policy competencies – research and development plus trans-European networks (which, combined together, looked like industrial policy) – had to be financed as well. The five-year projection for the CAP was the final major item.

In their early projections, Delors and Leygues were concerned to use post-Maastricht budgetary discussion to communicate messages about the Community's expanding responsibilities. The EC, said Jean-Charles, was "moving from specific to general competencies" in proto-federal ways. The best argument for the additional costs was that the Community's new roles supplemented and/or substituted for things which member states would otherwise do. "Subsidiarity" could thus be invoked to argue for substantially greater budgetary growth for the Community than for member states. Building the second Delors package around such arguments was essential not only to portray a more grandiose post-Maastricht Community but also because the distribution of costs and advantages of new policies "do not coincide either in the short or long term." Some member states would benefit more from what others would have to pay. Very good arguments were needed because, as Jean-Charles remarked, "member states have become more and more demanding about Community spending and the institution symbolizing it, the Commission." Jean-Charles's early work in 1991 also developed projections of different levels of Community budgetary ambition. A Delors package built around a "clear" commitment to strong new objectives would have an aggregate increase to 2 percent of GNP by 2000. A more "fluid," less ambitious approach, which Jean-Charles believed more realistic, would be 1.6 percent. The "fluid" approach would involve an increase of Community resources from slightly below 1.2 percent of GNP in 1992 to between 1.3 and 1.4 percent in 1997. Final projections depended upon Maastricht, of course, but even the "fluid" option, premised on a middling Maastricht result, demonstrated how overoptimistic both he and Delors had been in 1991.

The final Commission text of the package, entitled *From the Single Act to Maastricht and Beyond: the Means to Match Our Ambitions*, appeared in February 1992,[13] structured by Delors's and Jean-Charles's original architecture.

For economic and social cohesion, it proposed an increase in the Structural Funds, including the new cohesion fund, totalling 11 billion ecu over five years, close to the doubling which the Spanish wanted. For "external action," 3.5 billion (more than triple) was proposed. The CAP would grow by 4 billion, but decline as a percentage of the EC budget, from 64 percent in 1987 to 45 percent in 1997. Finally there was a grouping of horizontal internal policy budgets to promote "a favorable environment for competitiveness" at the cost of a further 3.5 billion. "Competitiveness means competition" and was determined, the paper noted, by "human resources, control over future technologies and better exploitation of the advantages of a large market." A case was then made for much more Community intervention through more and different research and development help, much greater EC involvement in vocational training (tied to the Social Fund, whose purposes would be turned towards training for new forms of employment), and the trans-European networks in transport, telecommunications, and energy. Here notice was being given of the last piece of the Delors strategy. On the revenue side, the proposal sought to raise the EC's "own resources" ceiling from 1.20 to 1.37 percent of Community GNP between 1992 and 1997, Jean-Charles's original "fluid" option.[14]

The reform of the CAP also moved forward on schedule. Delors's second package and CAP reform were, of course, connected, since EC budgets were contingent on the fate of the CAP. The original Delors–DG VI–MacSharry plans from early 1991 had been "marinating" through fierce lobbying, difficult Agricultural Councils of Ministers, price-setting marathons, and arcane debates about beef prices and milk quotas.[15] Behind all these things stood strong interest groups and important national stakes. Conversations with Jean-Luc Demarty reflected the rarefied nature of the agricultural world in their concentration on details of grain market prices and their interruptions by phone calls from various "presidents," usually of French farm lobbies.

By early 1992, however, Jean-Luc talked less of details and more about the race between CAP reform and the Uruguay Round talks. The Americans and their Uruguay Round allies were pressing hard on the Community, holding everything else hostage to progress on agricultural matters. EC insiders knew that the CAP reform had to be pushed through, and not only because the old CAP was wasteful and disruptive of international trade. Without a reformulated CAP to anchor its GATT bargaining positions – "beyond these lines we cannot go" – the Community would be persistently vulnerable. The reform proposals would bring EC agricultural prices closer to real world market levels and allow easier entry of Eastern European agricultural products, a medium-term remedy to one of the roadblocks to closer ties to the Central and Eastern European Countries (CEECs). Before final reform, however, the Commission had to cope with an agricultural world full of organized and shrewd people out for the best possible deal.

As deadlines approached in early 1992, Council meetings became edgy, reflecting basic differences among member states and the heat of electoral campaigns. The French were most vocal in defending the old system. There was also an implicit threat that some member states might "renationalize" parts of agricultural policy. The Portuguese presidency managed the discussions with some skill, however, and after more than a year and 16 Council sessions decision time came in the spring.[16] The divisions were quite predictable, between the British, Danes, and Dutch, the freer market side, against the French and Germans. Ray MacSharry and other commissioners did their best to mediate while carefully linking final compromise proposals with the annual CAP price marathons – real carrots and sticks.[17] The hardnosed discussion intermingled the future EC budget, world trade and the "raspberry regulation."[18] To quote a sharp-tongued journalist, the Council "resembled nothing so much as an Arab souk." Nonetheless, political agreement on CAP reform was reached on May 21, with protests outside the Council building underlining that the deal was serious.[19]

The new CAP would bring a reduction in guaranteed farm prices by product moving decisively towards world market price levels. Ultimately the EC would no longer dump excess production and distort world trade. The existing price support system for income maintenance would be progressively phased out and farmers would be compensated for declining prices by direct payments based on production factors (land, livestock), connected to a set-aside system, quotas, and bonuses to control production levels. As had been implicit almost from the beginning, the idea of "modulating" compensation for loss of revenue to size of farms, with smaller farmers fully compensated and larger ones paid less, was argued down. Finally, closest to Delors's heart, there was a rural redevelopment dimension, early-retirement subsidies, reforestation, and incentives towards more extensive and less polluting production.[20]

For all its messiness, the new CAP deal was a significant step forward. Its price was generalized income supports covering virtually all farmers, sometimes better than under the old CAP. The CAP budget would thus continue to grow. Given new budgetary techniques these supports became much more visible, however, perhaps establishing grounds for a progressive letdown of farmers' groups over time.[21] The stage also seemed set for clearer dealings with the US on GATT, as long as, in MacSharry's words, "our trade partners . . . recognize the extent of the step taken by the Community today and its contribution to the stabilization of world markets" The EC had done its bit, in other words. Others would have to be "prepared to be realistic, pragmatic and to pay in return for our contribution."

Headwinds

Initial Council discussion of the second Delors package in March and April revealed how difficult "business as usual" would be after Maastricht. The

British argued that the package was unacceptable. It was possible to meet some of Delors's targets without changing the "own resources" ceiling at all, they claimed, while most of the other targets, particularly those which sought to further entrench new Delorist increments of the *acquis communautaire*, were intolerable. The British were in a complicated position, however. The British budgetary rebate was also on the table. The British would find it difficult to take too hard a line on the new Delors package without getting into trouble on their "check." The Belgians and the Italians, both ordinarily staunch Europeans, agreed with the UK about holding down EC revenue growth.[22] The Germans, more and more constrained by their domestic economic situation, announced that it was inconceivable to have a Community budget growing twice as rapidly as member state budgets. The French, saving their firepower for final CAP confrontations, were prudent. Only the "South" really liked the package.

The debate showed the growing reluctance of more prosperous parts of the Community to underwrite solidarity and cohesion. Feeding this was the beginning of a precipitous economic downturn. The first Delors package had worked in part because EC economic growth had been greater than its projections had anticipated. For the second the situation was almost completely the opposite. The Commission's proposals, put together only a few months earlier, had been built on an assumption of an annual 2.5 percent growth figure. By the time debate on the second package opened they were already wildly overoptimistic and Commission economists were obliged to quickly go back and reconfigure things at a much lower level (1.1 percent for 1993).

Delors well remembered the complicated struggle prior to passage of his first package in 1987–8. The political situation then had been tense for a full year, with the future of Delors's presidency at stake, before a deal could be struck, thanks largely to German willingness to pay. In the later 1980s, however, the Germans were on top of the world and the European economy in an upswing. After the Foreign Ministers reviewed the second package for the first time in March 1992, Delors, in "tough it out" mode, noted cagily that there had been "no outright opposition" and added that the Community needed a clear decision by the end of the year. To those retreating from commitments to solidarity and cohesion he admonished that "we are building a community, not a financial clearing house or a baccarat game."

How far toughing it out could get was unclear, however. Skies were darkening dramatically. If there was one "law" in the history of European integration it was that forward movement correlated with economic optimism and crisis with economic difficulties. In 1992 the Germans were no longer on top of the world. Worse still, the EC's entire corner of this world faced huge economic difficulties. The long mini-boom which had carried Euro-enthusiasm after 1985 had ended. As the tables of growth and unemployment show, Europe faced a very severe recession, the worst in decades. Unemployment began to shoot up and analysis of it revealed that cyclical downturn was coming on top of the employment-reducing effects of the "1992" program itself. Companies were shedding labor as they restructured for the Single Market. The new Europe had long been sold, not least by Jacques Delors, for its ability to create jobs. It was now being lived as a job destroyer. Moreover, analyses showed that EC unemployment was substantially greater than in comparable economies elsewhere, in the US, for example. For some, obviously deep, reasons, Europe had been less able to create jobs than other regions, and this had become very costly and painful. And as the gloom of recession lowered observers pointed to the fact that the EMU proposals, with their stringent anti-inflationary convergence criteria, would make it even more difficult for member state governments to lower interest rates and go into greater deficit to stimulate economic activity. Even within such constraints, however, member state budgetary equilibria had begun to look much worse. Deficits shot up and cast new doubt upon whether the EMU convergence criteria were feasible at all.

Whether or not European integration was good medicine in the medium term for European peoples and economies – and the major arguments for Maastricht were medium term – EC policies had begun to touch the lives of ordinary Europeans in immediate, and quite negative, ways. If

Table 1: Annual percentage growth in large EC economies 1990–1993

Country	1990	1991	1992	1993
Germany	4.8[a]	3.7	1.4	1.2
France	2.2	1.2	1.9	1.6
Italy	2.2	1.4	1.2	0.8
UK	0.5	−2.2	−1.0	1.3
Spain	3.6	2.4	1.4	0.9

Table 2: Annual unemployment percentage in large EC economies 1990–1993

Country	1990	1991	1992	1993
Germany	4.9[a]	6.7	7.6	8.3
France	9.0	9.6	10.3	10.8
Italy	11.1	11.0	11.0	11.3
UK	5.9	8.3	10.1	10.8
Spain	16.3	16.3	18.0	19.3

[a] Pre-unification
Source: OECD, *Economic Outlook 52* (Paris: OECD, 1992)

the economic cycle was the central determinant of the political opportunity structure that Jacques Delors faced, the Delors strategy faced a new situation.

The Ratification Season

The edited Maastricht text was officially signed in February 1992. There were few celebrations on the streets of Europe, however. Most Europeans had but a hazy notion of what the text contained. Despite the editing, the Treaty's 250 pages remained "as readable as a London bus timetable," in the words of a British journalist.[23] As we will see, many of these ordinary Europeans were ready to conclude the worst. Moreover, there was little joy in Europe's capitals. Member states were nourishing their own doubts.

The Delors strategy had always had a British problem. That the British would continue to grumble was not surprising, therefore, particularly given the proximity of parliamentary elections. The Tories' miraculous but slim victory (a majority of 15) in the March 1992 polls complicated the problem further. Eurosceptics in Major's Tory Party, inspired by Baroness Thatcher herself, gained much greater leverage. John Major thus faced the worst possible results of his sinuous "Eurocourse" of "putting Britain at the heart of Europe" to give the UK greater influence against federalization and to promote a free-trade definition of the EC. The British had contributed more than anyone to the mediocrity of the Maastricht results. But this "success" had not been enough to deter Major's Tory opponents who believed that Major's strategy would make the UK a hostage of Delorist forward movement and that Maastricht demonstrated their case. If Tory Eurosceptics combined with Labour nationalists Major's margins would be small indeed. It looked as if Major would have to put on tennis whites for another "game, set and match" to ratify a Treaty whose minimalism he had so proudly defended only months earlier.

German support was particularly critical for Delors's plans. Widespread German criticism of the Treaty was thus as disturbing as the likely effects of the British election. The Kohl administration stood strongly behind Maastricht, but many Germans were worried about what they considered the Treaty's inadequate trade-off between greater EC democracy and EMU. Bjorn Engholm, Social Democrat leader and Prime Minister of Schleswig-Holstein, noted the "striking imbalance between EMU and Political Union," and raised the issue of whether Maastricht's cessions of sovereignty might not be an unconstitutional removal of power from German *länder* (a line which would eventually lead to litigation at the Federal Constitutional Court).[24] Each day the Bundesbank found new reasons to dislike EMU.[25] Recession hit Germany like a block of ice. In addition, largely due to unification, German budget deficit and inflation levels had both shot up to 5 percent. The combination set the Bundesbank's teeth on edge. More generally, German economists returned to their fears that EMU convergence criteria would eventually be softened to favor weaker economies, Italy in particular. When this happened, they said, Germans would have to pay the bills at the cost of their own domestic economic stability. *Der Spiegel*, *Bild* and others in the press also nourished a scare campaign about the loss of the Deutschmark. By June 1992, opinion polls showed that the majority of Germans disapproved of EMU and felt the planned pace of movement towards a single currency to be too rapid. Underlying much of this, yet again, was increasing German domestic anxiety about the political disruptions and costs of unification. Managing these tensions, along with a connected rise of anti-immigrant extremism, was becoming a very difficult task for Helmut Kohl. Kohl, a politician of legendary electoralism, had to begin thinking seriously about the nest of local, national, and European elections set for 1994, 19 in all, and would hardly be able to ignore mounting anti-EMU and anti-Maastricht feelings.

Certain of Maastricht's provisions were in conflict with specific clauses in the French Constitution.[26] Thus the Constitutional Council had to be consulted for a ruling and a suggested plan of what needed to be done.[27] Proposals for constitutional change then had to be voted by both Houses of the French Parliament, assembled together. Only after all this could the new Treaty itself be brought forth for ratification. Debate surrounding this preliminary vote thus provided an occasion to preview the state of French public opinion on Maastricht. The explosion which occurred was a shock.

That Jean-Marie Le Pen, leader of the extremist National Front, would label Maastricht "a crime" and that the communists saw it as a capitalist plot were predictable. What was shocking, however, was the virulence of anti-Maastricht feelings in different parts of the moderate Right.[28] Within the neo-Gaullists, projected to be the core of the French government after the March 1993 elections, there was a virulent anti-Maastricht explosion led by the redoubtable Charles Pasqua, a gruff national populist determined to steal back errant Right voters from Le Pen, and by the gifted Philippe Séguin.[29] There was also considerable anti-Maastricht sentiment within Giscard d'Estaing's UDF Party and even on the fringes of the ruling socialists themselves.

Denmark and Ireland had both called Maastricht referenda for June 1991. The Danes were unpredictable. The Parliament and major parties favored the Treaty, but Danish voters had very nearly voted down the Single European Act in a 1986 referendum.[30] The Irish would ordinarily have been a surer bet, with an economy so heavily dependent on the EC that ill humor about Maastricht could be very costly. The Irish Maastricht debate coincided, however, with a *cause célèbre* involving the right of a 14-year-old rape victim to travel to England for an abortion. The Irish Constitution forbade abortion and the Irish had insisted upon a protocol to Maastricht to maintain this prerogative.[31] The case underlined the lack of clarity of this Irish protocol. Would it or would it not allow the Irish government to prevent such travel? Despite an official declaration that the protocol was not meant to allow Ireland to refuse basic Community rights to freedom of movement, Maastricht came under attack from both sides. The Church argued that "free movement of people" would undercut the abortion ban, while feminists and others interpreted the protocol as an Irish opt-out to enforce the ban.

The ratification season thus began in a context of greater opposition to Maastricht than anyone could have anticipated. Yugoslavia further stimulated public doubt. Lack of member state agreement when the crisis first exploded in summer 1991 had led to a low common denominator consensus around a refusal to recognize the sovereignty of Slovenia and Croatia (obtained only through German abnegation in the interests of EC unity).[32] The influence the Community could bring to bear on the various Yugoslav actors was thus limited, and recognition of this, in turn, emboldened protagonists to discount Community pressure. Things then went downhill rapidly in autumn 1991. The Serbs correctly predicted international recognition of the Slovenian and Croatian independence and moved to occupy as much Croatian territory in Croatia as possible before the international community could react. This pushed the EC, the US, and the Soviet Union to propose sanctions (primarily oil and arms embargoes) as well as the preparation of UN mediation – on the way to the Vance–Owen peace mission. In the meantime the Germans pressed harder for official EC recognition of Slovenia and Croatia. Throughout the fall Gunther Burghardt worked tirelessly inside European Political Cooperation to prevent the Germans from acting unilaterally but by Maastricht the Germans were determined to act. On January 15, 1992 the EC prepared to recognize ex-Yugoslav candidates for independence, including Bosnia-Herzogovina (with the Greeks vetoing recognition for Macedonia) as long as conditions proposed by the French were observed.[33]

The collapse of the EC's non-recognition/mediation strategy helped prepare the way for the disasters which would ensue in Bosnia (ethnic cleansing, mass rape as a military tactic, and efforts to starve the Muslim population in the siege of Sarajevo). The horror of the events was understood by the public – the spectacle of Sarajevo slowly dying appeared nightly on television and the numbers of refugees rose into the millions. Sanctions imposed by the Community and others had little influence over the war, except perhaps to deprive the Muslims of access to arms. The events underlined Europe's failure. If the Community was of little use in dealing with situations like Yugoslavia then of what use was it more generally? More specifically, Yugoslavia showed clearly that Community member states were unwilling and unable to pursue a viable common foreign policy even to block barbarism in their back yard. Yugoslavia, at first an opportunity for the Common Foreign and Security Policy (CFSD), progressively destroyed the CFSP's credibility and damaged Maastricht in the process.[34]

The Danes say no

On June 2 the Danes voted "no" Maastricht by 50.7 percent to 49.3 percent, 46,000 votes.[35] There seemed no simple reason for this. The Danes, with

Europe's highest GDP, did very well out of the EC economically, particu-
larly out of trade in agricultural goods. Different Danes had rejected it for
different reasons, with a goodly proportion of serendipity to help them.[36]
The Danes clearly disliked the *political* side of Maastricht. Earlier Danish
discussions of the EC (in 1972 on membership and on the Single European
Act in 1986) had been about the Community's economic dimensions. The
Danish electorate received Maastricht as a change in contract with the EC.[37]
European defense, more intervention from Brussels, and transnational
economic policy through EMU implied a federal Europe which few Danes
– including many who voted "yes" – were eager to have. Beyond this the
"no" voters were a curious mixture. "Under-Denmark" (the poorer, the less
skilled, public-sector white collar workers) opposed the elites. Fifty-seven
percent of women voted "no," many out of fear for the future of the Danish
welfare state.[38] Finally, political extremes were against Maastricht: the Left
"1968 generation" (the peace movement, Greens, and feminists), and the
right-wing populists.[39]

The Danes also shared in the growing hostility towards political elites
apparent all over Europe. The Schluter government had been in power for
ten years, and it was perceived as tired and out of touch across a wide range
of issues, but particularly the EC. It was easy for "no" advocates to conflate
the government's difficulties with the EC's more general lack of democratic
clarity. A leak from Frans Andriessen's services commenting about the need
to reduce the Council voting strength of smaller EC members when the
Community enlarged did not help.[40] Coincidences played a role as well. Just
when the campaign was gearing up Prime Minister Schluter came under
the cloud of a corruption scandal (which would ultimately end his career).
Moreover, the Social Democrats, part of the governing coalition, were in
the midst of a leadership struggle and pressured for a very brief campaign
to prevent EC issues from hanging over their leadership congress. In consequence, they did not mobilize effectively for the "yes" side and two-thirds
of their supporters voted "no." The referendum campaign was also too
short to allow full debate and some projections showed that Maastricht
might have won had discussion continued for but a couple more days. The
eagerness of the government to distribute hundreds of thousands of copies
of the Treaty, unaccompanied by explanatory material to penetrate its
thickets, was also a factor. Finally, opposition was greatly strengthened by
the skillful presentation of anti-Maastricht positions by a "June movement"
of respectable intellectuals.[41]

Delors and his team had responded to the mediocrity of the Maastricht
treaty itself by gritting their teeth and plunging forward into the implementation of the various different post-Maastricht dimensions of the presidential strategy. The Danish "no" signaled a transition towards a new posture of
holding the fort. But the most immediate problem after the Danish referendum was to prospect for ways out of the situation that the Danes had
created. "To be and not to be, that is the answer" was the way Danish
Foreign Minister Ellemann-Jensen summarized the Danish problem. With-

out destroying itself, how could the Community allow the Danes to be both in and out of Maastricht Europe? Suggestions from many sources that the Danish result should lead to a renegotiation of parts of Maastricht were vetoed by Portuguese Foreign Minister Pinheiro, speaking for the Council. Delors's choice was to brazen it out until the Danes changed their minds. The line was quickly hammered out at an emergency meeting of EC Foreign Ministers on the margins of a NATO meeing in Oslo on June 4.[42] Maastricht was a matter of EC survival: the ratification process and normal EC life should continue, allowing the Danes to sweat out the implications of being forced out while the other 11 moved forward together. In the interim the Community would be attentive to new Danish suggestions and the Danes would gracefully be encouraged to hold a second referendum. The Danes quickly promised a White Paper for the fall and it was clear that they would ask for a set of *de facto* opt-outs from Maastricht. As long as this was carefully done the EC would find some way to oblige, without, of course, actually changing the Maastricht Treaty itself.

Delors would have to assume an unusually low profile for a while. The Commission was preparing a paper on subsidiarity to submit to the Council (to which François Lamoureux would contribute after returning from the Cresson fiasco in Paris).[43] It was pre-emptively useful to discuss this paper with as much seriousness as possible.[44] There was also new Commission talk about "renationalizing" certain policy areas. Most of the examples given of this (EC norms of drinking water, the issue of an EC passport) were not weighty enough to be persuasive, however. The only genuinely touchy issue mentioned was environmental policy, in particular the EC regulations on "wild birds" that had driven hunters to form their own political parties in Latin countries. The problem here was that EC environmental policy was as popular in most of Northern Europe (Denmark in particular) as it was mistrusted in the South (and in Britain, for different reasons). "Subsidiarity" was an essential subject for EC actors to clarify, but it was too elusive to help out much with the general public.

Success in the Irish referendum (69 to 31 percent) was minor solace.[45] The Lisbon European Council came and went as if everything was in suspended animation, only partly because of the ineffectiveness of the Portuguese presidency. Delors had already retreated on one important dimension of his second package, under huge pressure from the UK. The program would be spread over seven rather than five years, and during the first two, when the economic growth of EC member states was projected to be very low, the ceiling of Community "own resources" vs GNP would not be raised. Beyond this, action on the package was passed forward to the the the British presidency that would follow the Portuguese. This was not the only problem at Lisbon. The Spanish were upset because pressure on the Commission's proposals also involved threats to projected growth in cohesion spending. Perhaps Spanish pressure might help the Commission later, as it had during the Maastricht negotiating period? Discussion on enlarging the Community, based on a Commission paper, was inconclusive, despite

Delors's strong effort to get member states to take the institutional implications of enlargement more seriously.

The major problem in such uncertainty was the imminent British Presidency. British reticence on a wide range of pending issues, including Maastricht, was common knowledge, as was British desire to hasten enlargement and drown movement towards greater EC federalism in the institutional complexity that would certainly follow. The British were prepared with alternative definitions of "variable geometry," including a proliferation of different ways of belonging to the EC by opt-outs and partial memberships, that would progressively restrict full Community actions to a narrow range of trade-market matters. Moreover, the UK intended to be an activist president for its own agendas on such matters rather than seeking consensus. Finally, the British themselves had huge ratification problems. Major was committed to Maastricht, but faced a very rocky path to get the Treaty though the House of Commons. None of this boded particularly well for the Delors strategy.[46]

Le petit oui . . .

On the day after the Danish result François Mitterrand announced a French referendum on Maastricht for September. Since Maastricht could have been ratified by parliamentary vote alone (the two Houses of Parliament voted overwhelmingly for the pre-ratification constitutional amendments) his decision made sense only if there were other agendas. No doubt Mitterrand felt the renaissance of European integration after 1985 to be very much his work, and a successful referendum could restore its momentum after the Danish shock. Beyond this Mitterrand had carefully monitored the profound divisions in the French opposition which had emerged in earlier debate about modifying the Constitution. The neo-Gaullists and the Centrists were deeply split (half of the Gaullist deputies had voted against changing the Constitution). It was too tempting for Mitterrand, with parliamentary elections only six months away, to resist using a referendum to whip up civil war in the opposition in the hope of undermining its huge lead in the polls. François Mitterrand was willing to bet the future of the Community partly to shore up his own weak regime.

Mitterrand's early polling showed two-thirds favoring "yes," yet the aging President had underestimated the historical roots of nationalism, protectionism, and Jacobin *dirigisme*.[47] His administration had worked for nearly a decade to eradicate such outlooks but they had been restimulated by austerity, monetarism, rising unemployment, restructuring, and recession. In France, where executive power was more concentrated than anywhere else, the elitist and opaque nature of EC processes (the famous "democratic deficit") could be superimposed on to haughty Fifth Republic politics. As the Danes had already demonstrated, the moment partook of a more general crisis in relationships between European political elites and peoples. Finally, perhaps more than in any other large EC state, the various steps of the renewal of European integration had not been subjects of extended public debate. There was a profound thirst in France to talk about Europe, therefore, and not all the talk was friendly to Maastricht. The Maastricht referendum offered various national populist forces, both Right and Left, a golden opportunity to coalesce against the EC, Maastricht, and anything else which came to mind. The murky, complex Maastricht text was its own worst enemy. What Maastricht promised, already a great deal for nationalists to disagree with, was in the medium term. The French lived in a difficult present.

Opponents of Maastricht thus began with several distinct advantages and it took but a few brief days after June 3 for what Jacques Julliard labeled "the great national unburdening, the ball of the bitter, *kermesse* of the frustrated, carnival for complainers" to begin.[48] Everything in French politics came out, mainly against Maastricht. The independent Left and many others cursed the neo-liberal conspiracy. Communists talked about "Maastfric" (*fric* in French argot means money). Left Socialists, behind former Socialist Defense Minister Jean-Pierre Chevènement, marched against Maastricht for "Republican patriotism." The Right of the Centrists and the Right of the Gaullists articulated a soft national populism. The extreme Right National Front lumped Maastricht with the coming of immigrant hordes. The Greens divided and waffled, as was their wont, but mainly over specific reasons to oppose the Treaty. Substantive issues for the "nos" included Yugoslavia, the failure of social Europe, foreigners voting in French local elections, "Brussels bureaucrats," the menace to Camembert cheese, threats to French agriculture from the CAP reform, GATT and Eastern Europe, unemployment, the need for trade protection, fears about the loss of the franc, and the loss of foreign policy and defense autonomy. Finally, there was regicide in the air. Despite Mitterrand's efforts to distance himself from the vote, a huge majority of the French had concluded that *le vieux* had been around too long!

By the end of August polls were at 50–50 with "no" forces leading in momentum and energy. From this point the government, the pro-Maastricht opposition (around Giscard d'Estaing), and economic elites pulled out all stops. Prime Minister Bérégovoy and Jacques de Larosière, Governor of the Banque de France, warned that a "no" would precipitate financial disaster. Former Prime Minister Raymond Barre attacked protectionist and *dirigiste* revivals. Socialists and conservatives unusually spoke on the same "yes" platforms around France, amid great publicity. Great writers, actors, and intellectuals submitted full-page "yes" petitions in the daily papers. Jacques Delors averred that "if my work is disavowed, I'll resign." Helmut Kohl spoke on television, together with Mitterrand, about the need for Europe. The "yes" camp's central political claim was that French rejection of Maastricht would mean the end of European integration. Both sides invoked the German menace, the "nos" asserting that Maastricht meant surrender to German power and the "yesses" that Maastricht was the best way to contain this power. Maastricht had become the symbol of France's *de facto* loss of national control over its environment. The French were having trouble adjusting to a new world.

France's *"petit oui"* – 51 percent yes, 49 percent no – saved, but hardly endorsed, Maastricht. Like Denmark, the "tiny yes" was by and large rich, urban and well educated.[49] The "nos" were farmers – connected with the CAP; workers, particularly those in social crisis-ridden suburbs and declining industrial areas; lower white-collar workers and the less well-educated. François Mitterrand had – barely – won one part of his bet. Had France rejected Maastricht it would have been finished and the Community would have found itself in a black hole. On the other hand, he had clearly lost another. Maastricht had been saved by the Center-Right, its electorate, and its leaders. Mitterrand's enemies, Chirac and Giscard, ended up ahead of the game. The referendum call had done little in the short run to enhance the political fortunes of Mitterrand and his government. In the medium term, however, it was likely to consolidate an emerging cleavage in French politics which did not bode well for Europe. Protectionist national populists would henceforth confront elite internationalists advocating freer trade, austerity, and Europe.

François Mitterrand's "Europe option" had been designed in the mid-1980s to replace the French Left's nationalist, *dirigiste* social reformism. It would allow France to compensate for the loss of its national leverage by promoting the renewal of European integration. The vision implied quite precise economic policies. The core of German power was its monetary centrality. French success depended upon being able to win a piece of economic policy control from the Bundesbank, hence EMU, an essential piece of Mitterrand's strategy. But since price stability was at the heart of Bundesbank success, France had to restructure, become more competitive, and learn to play in the Bundesbank's financial league. In particular, French governments had to develop hard-nosed approaches to turn the franc into a strong currency, the *franc fort* policy, implying tough controls on budget equilibria and interest rates. The results involved sustained austerity, governmental abstention from efforts to stimulate growth (hence toleration of relatively high levels of employment), and retreat from major reforms. The Europe option thus enjoined sacrifices for the French, particularly the more "ordinary" among them.

The strategy assumed that renewed European integration would bring new growth. The inaccuracy of this assumption made the burdens even greater. The growth accompanying the first years of the Single Market program had then given way to profound recession and, in any event, had not been robust and job-creative enough to convince the French that the Europe option was paying off. The Maastricht referendum, "small yes" notwithstanding, was an indicator that the French judged the Europe option a failure. For Mitterrand, this was a devastating judgment on the most important part of his life's work.

For Delors the "small yes" meant that, in retrospect, the powerful Delorist movement towards Maastricht as a decisive political turning point had been miscalculated. Maastricht had been a turning point, but more towards a renewal of member state anti-Europeanism. Delors had been one of the original architects of the new French economic policies in the early 1980s and his career in Brussels had initially been Mitterrand's doing. Mitterrand's efforts to shape the intergovernmental context had always been a key element in Delors's own strategy and both he and Mitterrand shared a firm belief that EMU was the central element in Europe's future. To be sure, Delors's federalist state-building and Mitterrand's confederalism had often worked at cross-purposes. But Delors also shared the assumption that renewed European integration would bring a big payoff in growth and employment and the relative political failure of Mitterrand's Europe option underlined his overoptimism. Unlike Mitterrand, however, for Delors the "small yes" was better than a "no." It provided some margin to move forward and Delors had no other choice.

Under siege?

Everything in Delors's strategy was designed to interconnect and produce forward momentum. By autumn 1992 it seemed that everything had begun to connect perversely. The Uruguay Round negotiations were a further case in point. With the passage of CAP reform in the spring the Commission thought that it had established conditions for GATT success. The CAP reform would provide a baseline to constrain American demands and on the EC side the delicacy of the Uruguay Round negotiations would deter member states from attacking the CAP reform. When secret negotiations resumed in September 1992 there remained a few large issues. How much would compensation to EC farmers for the price cuts of CAP reform be exempted from consideration as subsidy? How much should the EC cut its subsidized exports and how great a subsidy could they receive? Finally, the difficult dispute with the US over subsidized oilseed exports had to be settled.[50]

The scenario was overoptimistic, however. Deep opposition to CAP reform and EC trade policy towards Eastern Europe, replete with tough street demonstrations by farmers, had been an important factor in the upsurge of "no" voting in the French referendum. The French government itself had but grudgingly accepted changing the CAP. With the Socialists in trouble and legislative elections set for March 1993 the Commission could not expect help from the French and it had been naive to think that the Americans would not push beyond limits set by the reformed CAP. The Bush administration also faced a difficult election. The talks were tough. The Americans were obdurate on the oilseeds matter (taking it to GATT arbitration, which they won).[51] On the EC side, the French Minister of

Agriculture threatened that France would not cooperate in reducing wheat exports. At the Birmingham European Council in October François Mitterrand refused to hear of concessions beyond CAP reform limits, as the French themselves had calculated them. France's largest farmers' organization growled that it had accepted CAP reform only to facilitate a Uruguay Round deal and that it would accept no further concessions to the Americans.[52] Delors was forced into the ungratifying task of keeping French isolation from going too far, trying, not always successfully, to get them to link agriculture concessions with other Uruguay Round areas.

An unfortunate explosion occurred on the November weekend just prior to the US elections. In Chicago, Ray MacSharry, backed by Frans Andriessen and British Minister of Agriculture John Gummer, came close to a deal on oilseeds with US Secretary of Agriculture Ed Madigan which would have unlocked the rest of the agriculture package. Delors, with the French at his back, had in the meantime telephoned MacSharry to warn him that the proposed deal went beyond CAP reform and the Commission's negotiating mandate.[53] Delors also announced that he would oppose the deal in Commission and was confident of winning, and that were the deal to go forward, it would be vetoed by at least two member states.[54] MacSharry promptly resigned from his role as oilseeds negotiator and, with Andriessen, went back to Brussels to confront the Commission President, with whom neither was on cordial terms. In the meantime the Americans announced trade-war sanctions worth $300 million on EC imports (200 percent import tariffs, mainly on French wine) to start 30 days later. Delors was outvoted in the Commission on the issue of the negotiating mandate. MacSharry then retracted his resignation, the oilseeds talks were resumed, and a deal was struck at Blair House in Washington on November 20. Each side made concessions on oilseeds and outstanding Uruguay Round agricultural matters (which both attempted to hide from potential opponents, with new ways of calculating).[55] Trade war was postponed and the way had been opened for a return to serious discussions at Geneva on the Uruguay Round as a whole.

The tactic of linking CAP reform and the GATT talks had worked. But the damage done to Delors in the process was substantial. Throughout the ratification debates Delors had been thoroughly tarred and feathered, painted as the "model Brussels Bureaucrat." His missionary-visionary pedagogic style, which had long stood him in good stead, was more and more denounced as imperious. Moreover, as ambivalence about the Community came to the surface Delors paid ever more dearly for his presidentialization of the Commission, both outside and inside the Commission itself. Uruguay Round infighting with MacSharry and Andriessen had incensed his enemies and allowed them to portray him as a defender of French interests. The British press was particularly murderous. The French denounced the Blair House deal and the Commission for allegedly having violated the CAP reform and also threatened to veto the GATT deal and undo CAP reform. Much of this was politicking toward imminent

French parliamentary elections, but it damaged Delors's position in French politics.[56] The Commission President had no choice but to lower his profile, while the Commission moved into retreat mode.[57]

The worst was occurring elsewhere. To finance unification in chaotic political conditions the Germans had run ever larger budget deficits, creating a risk of uncomfortable inflation levels. In response the Bundesbank played tough – the German discount rate and Lombard rates both reached their historical highs in summer 1992.[58] Meanwhile the Americans, running up to the critical 1992 election, pushed their own rates very low to stimulate the economy, leading to a declining dollar. Financial flows towards Germany and the dollar situation weakened other Exchange Rate Mechanism (ERM) currencies and pushed some towards their narrow-band limits. In consequence there was extensive Central Bank intervention and speculation on money markets. Because of the centrality of the Deutschmark in the European Monetary System (EMS), the Germans were forcing everyone else to pay part of the bill for unification.

Every member state that desired to keep its currency within the narrow-band fluctuation limits of the ERM was obliged to keep its own interest rates much higher than it would have liked.[59] In recessionary circumstances this made counter-cyclical stimulation nearly impossible. Maintaining high interest rates in summer 1992 was made more difficult because of the post-Maastricht political environment, which stirred up further turbulence in currency markets, particularly around the pound and lira.[60] A major ERM realignment might have stopped the problems quickly, but no one wanted this because of the serious negative effects it might have had for the French referendum campaign. Furthermore, many policy-makers, with their eyes on convergence criteria and the coming of stage 2 of EMU, had come to see the ERM as a proto-EMU with fixed exchange rates.[61]

On Black Wednesday, September 16, 1992, the British left the ERM after having invested huge amounts in support of the pound and pushing up interests rates twice (to 12 and then 15 percent) within hours.[62] The British had entered the ERM in 1990 at an exchange rate the Germans had thought risky. Moreover, there had been internal differences all along in the British financial and political establishment about ERM, exacerbated by the Maastricht negotiations and the ways in which ERM membership had helped frustrate slight movements towards British economic revival. The British thus used Black Wednesday to effect a competitive devaluation and rapidly took steps to stimulate domestic activity. The Italian lira dropped out of the ERM on the same day, the Spanish peseta was devalued within the ERM and the Spanish, Portuguese, and Irish very quickly reintroduced exchange controls.

EMS stability had been one of the rocks upon which Delors had built his EMU proposals.[63] EMU was to be built incrementally through enhancement of the EMS, particularly in the crucial stage 2, mainly about convergence, scheduled to begin in 1994. The crisis of September 1992 and its aftermath left the pound and the lira outside the system, the peseta and

Portuguese escudo devalued and menaced, and currencies of Finland, Sweden, and Norway – three EFTA candidates for EC membership – cut loose from their earlier pegging to the EMS. In January 1993 the Irish pound had also to be devalued. Even worse, in the wake of the September changes and the French referendum the franc itself came under speculative siege, saved only by huge joint German–French efforts.[64]

The autumn 1992 crisis demonstrated that it would be much harder than Delors had hoped to promote economic convergence and move towards EMU. Moreover, the changes in outlook accompanying the monetary frenzy would further dampen enthusiasm for EMU. Europe was close to the edge, indicated by the circulation of rumors in the autumn about Franco-German contingency plans for a two-speed EMU, enhanced by a well-publicized Mitterrand–Kohl *tête-à-tête* and a Delors speech in which he intoned that "if some countries are looking for alibis for delaying the Treaty, it may well be that others will take the lead." How far such plans had actually gone – some distance – was less important than the official provenance of the rumors. Footloose EC member states, like the UK (then exercising the Community presidency), were being warned against going too far. The events strengthened the hand of anti-EC and anti-Maastricht elements in Britain and reinforced John Major's resolve to pursue his own strategy of frustrating Delorist integrationism.[65]

A great deal was on the British presidency's plate. Major was in domestic political trouble, surrounded by Eurosceptics in his own party and threatened with defeat in the House of Commons on Maastricht ratification. After preliminary discussions in the House of Commons in which the government had won an important vote by a margin of only three, Major announced (without even consulting his own EC diplomats) that the British would wait to ratify Maastricht until after a second Danish referendum in spring 1993, effectively tying Her Britannic Majesty's foreign policy to the whims of a few Danes. Helmut Kohl's mood, darkened by British remarks about the Bundesbank's behavior in September, was not improved and the decision infuriated Mitterrand. French anger deepened when the British float-devaluation and subsequent stimulation policies turned currency speculators' attention to the franc.

Everyone was aware that the British presidency would try to stall agreement on key matters at the Edinburgh European Council in December 1992, almost a year to the day after Maastricht and a few short weeks before January 1, 1993, the official end of the "1992" period. From Major's point of view the moment was ideal to blunt movement toward a "federal" Europe, already slowed by post-Maastricht events. After years of being maneuvered about by Delors, the French, and the Germans, the British were regrouping to promote the EC as a simple free-trade zone. Finding words to facilitate another Danish referendum was Edinburgh's easiest task. The Danes had earlier produced a long paper that sketched out acceptable options.[66] The British and the Council Secretariat then came up with the formula of a European Council Declaration which would "apply only to

Denmark, to the exclusion of any existing or future member state." The declaration assuaged Denmark's anxieties about European citizenship rights, let Denmark opt out of stage 3 of EMU and a common defense policy, and allowed the Danes to submit important matters of judicial and internal affairs cooperation for domestic ratification.[67] The Danes would thus be asked to reconsider ratifying a treaty from which they had managed largely to extract themselves and their new referendum, in spring 1993, had every chance of being successful.[68]

Producing statements on subsidiarity was more difficult. The British first produced a list of pieces of Community legislation, including the bulk of Commission proposals in the "social dimension" area, which they considered illustrated violations of subsidiarity.[69] The statement finally proposed at Edinburgh was relatively inoffensive, however, stipulating that observing subsidiarity was a question of following certain general guidelines. Community action clearly allowed by treaty posed no problem. Where there was legal ambiguity the Community should refrain from action unless the issue was clearly transnational and could not be satisfactorily dealt with by member states and the advantages of Community action were clear. New consulting procedures were to be observed by the Commission prior to presenting new proposals.[70] The statement then presented an extensive list of matters which the Commission would undertake in 1993 in the interests of subsidiarity and "transparency." The statement provided sensible, if vague, responses to complaints and spoke directly to Danish concerns. But, as Delors and others pointed out, it was the complexity and democratic deficiencies of the Community itself (rather than subsidiarity and transparency) which were the fundamental issues.

The second Delors package was the key matter at Edinburgh. It had almost as much importance as the first had had in 1987–8. Without a substantial new budgetary commitment the implementation of Maastricht would be slowed, earlier commitments to trans-Community solidarity undermined, and the broader Delorist dynamic undercut, all primary British objectives. Moreover, if the second package could be scaled down and, simultaneously, enlargement speeded up, diplomatic and institutional complexities in the way of further EC "deepening" would be intensified.[71] From Major's point of view it was comforting that German money had become scarce, making scaling-down likely. On the other side, the Spanish were adamant about cohesion and increasing the Structural Funds. Mitterrand was in a genuine rage, announcing that if the British and the Danes would not play, the EC could go on, "at ten," without them. After the ratification season's turn towards making a scapegoat of the Commission, and the Uruguay Round imbroglio, Delors himself had fewer capacities to generate pressure.

Delors had earlier agreed, in the name of the deepening recession, that the initial Commission timetable be extended to seven rather than five years, with growth in the Community's "own resources" held off for the first two years. The British were after bigger fish, however, and had counter-proposed a seven-year scheme that cut back dramatically on the growth of "own resources" funding and the Structural Funds, while completely chopping budget items for "competitiveness" (industrial policy matters).[72] Their goals were ostensibly to hold EC budgetary growth to levels comparable with member states' and to block Delorist momentum to institutionalize a number of "creeping federalist" notions through the budgetary package. Delors went to battle against this as "contrary to the spirit of Maastricht" and found considerable support in the Southern countries whose cohesion funds were in the line of fire. The Spanish threatened that, if anything like the British proposal ended up on the Edinburgh table, there would be no deal at all. But when it turned out that the financially strapped Germans favored something like the British proposal, the Commission and the South had to split differences. There was a final compromise in which the "own resources" ceiling would rise from 1.2 percent of GNP to 1.27 percent in 1999 (vs Jean-Charles's original 1.37 percent figure for 1997), the Structural Funds would grow somewhat less than Delors had originally proposed and would be supplemented by the new cohesion fund. Moreover, there was some recognition that member state budgetary contributions should be progressive and tied to relative economic strength. The Commission's agricultural projections and its proposals on external affairs and administration were accepted more or less as drawn. Spending on "competitiveness" disappeared and the British "check" issue was settled the way the British desired.[73]

Given the EC's downward spiral, the important thing was that Edinburgh produced a deal on the Community's financial future. Moreover, even though the deal had been pared down considerably, it remained "evolutive." A set of programs would be sustained until the end of the century and the Commission's budgetary autonomy would be guaranteed. The deal on the structural and cohesion funds meant that the all-important commitment to regional redistribution would be sustained.

Things could have been worse. Edinburgh brought a number of less significant accomplishments. For example, the summit decided to begin negotiating immediately with EFTA applicants for EC membership. It also declared victory for the implementation of the "1992" program, even though it had to recognize that a number of matters remained unresolved, particularly in the area of the free circulation of people, perhaps the most symbolic issue of all.[74]

Delors was not the type to contemplate surrender, however much he was on the defensive. The Commission had to continue taking the lead in defining Europe's interests. As the Community's national economies sank into deep recession this meant producing tangible "European" recognition of these difficulties. The Community's means were limited, but they might be enough to provide an important signal to economic decision-makers that European economies were not preordained to go downhill. Thus the Commission proposed, and the European Council voted, an EC growth stimulus package at Edinburgh which allowed the European Investment

Bank and the European Investment Fund, under Commission supervision, to generate several billion new dollars in loans to support infrastructural projects in transport, energy, telecommunications, and environmental improvement. The proposal also came with much encouragement to member states and firms to expand their economies. Given budgetary situations and the high interest rates which the Germans were enjoining on everyone else, however, the gesture fell far short of what was really needed.[75] Moreover, even as it passed, everyone was skeptical that its implementation, which depended upon member states, would be undertaken seriously. But the gesture would have its consequences.

A Last Act in Character

January 1, 1993 was the official end of the "1992" period and the quiet way in which it passed spoke volumes about the state of the EC. The ambiguous state of "1992's" completion was one reason: there were delays in major programs like VAT realignment, incomplete transposition into member state law of important legislative measures, and problems in enforcing legislation already passed. Failure to remove airport passport controls by the target date was an index that free movement of people lagged behind the three other EC freedoms, another signal to ordinary Europeans that the EC worked more for business than for them. But larger clouds obscured the EC's recent accomplishments. Would Maastricht finally be ratified and, if so, what would it mean in practice? Could member state commitment to integration be rekindled? What would come of persistent monetary turmoil? Would Europe be able to regenerate its economic vitality? Delors and his team had little choice except to salvage what they could. Maastricht was the key element, the most that they were likely to get and the grounds for their holding action. But it was a perilous juncture, spirits were low, and both Delors and Pascal were going through difficult times.

Pascal Lamy often spoke of Delors's capacity to "draw on his batteries" in crises. "He likes crises . . . especially those which he makes himself." But now he was surrounded by a multifaceted crisis which he had not created, and his displeasure was beginning to show in greater moodiness. In part this was because of the French political situation. Although Delors claimed to be uninterested in the French scene, Paris was more and more troubling. He remained a conceivable future candidate for the French presidency but he had few organizational resources inside the Socialist Party, which would have to nominate him. The Socialists were busily tearing themselves apart and the only thing that remained relatively clear was that Michel Rocard was likely to be Socialist presidential candidate. In response, Delors had rather weakly founded yet another "club" of faithfuls, *témoins*, and courted a younger generation of *quadra* (40-year-old) Socialist leaders. This was an inadequate substitute for the kind of party machine that was needed, particularly since most of the *quadras* owed their influence to ministerial posts that they would lose in the March 1993 elections. Delors's behavior indicated that he hoped the Socialists would come to him.

Pascal was also thinking about France, having decided to run for Parliament in a constituency near his summer home in Normandy. The Socialists' imminent loss of power meant that he could no longer hope for a Parisian high place – his goal of becoming Directeur du Trésor was no longer realistic. He had to think about his career, therefore. Delors's presidency would soon end. He might "reintegrate" the French *inspection des finances* and wait patiently for the French political situation to change, but the troubles of the Socialists gave every sign of durability. He could find a niche for himself in the EC administration, perhaps as a Director General, and work for the Community, but this would be tricky because he had a large number of enemies and because it would separate him further from France. Or he could look for something in the private sector where his consummate managerial talent might be an asset. Whatever he chose, running for Parliament was a gesture toward political presence in France. He would lose, like most other Socialist candidates, and his campaign became a particular lightning rod for anti-European feelings, particularly from farmers. But by fighting the good fight he might buy a better chance in the future. Pascal's losing quest meant that he would be less able to concentrate on Commission matters for several months in early 1993, however. Jean-Pierre Jouyet substituted for him in most things, but he did not have Pascal's weight.

It was a sign of how difficult the situation had become that the formal ratification of Maastricht passed by without doing very much for Delors's morale and his strategic position. The second Danish second referendum, on May 18, 1993, succeeded by 56.8 to 43.2 percent.[76] The German Parliament then ratified in June (even if the full legal effect of ratification was postponed until the Federal Constitutional Court ruled in the fall).[77] Finally, Major managed to get the British Parliament to ratify in late July, not before having been humiliated on a Labour motion to include the Social Charter. It took a vote of confidence and Major threatening to call a new election with the Tories way down in the polls to bring Tory forces into line. The political blood lost made Major's tenure precarious.[78]

It was the new EMS crisis that made Maastricht ratification anticlimactic. The ERM never recovered after September 1992. The French franc remained a target, not because of fundamental weaknesses in the French economy, but for political reasons. The French had pursued their "strong franc" policy to root out inflationary tendencies and restructure the French economy. In many ways it had been successful, even if it contributed to a dangerous rise in French unemployment. The central purpose of the new Center-Right government elected in March 1993 was to prepare victory in the 1995 presidential elections. Carried to power by a landslide against the Socialists, the new Balladur government faced this high unemployment, made much worse by recession. It made political sense to try to stimulate the economy in a counter-cyclical way, but Balladur's initial attempts underestimated the problem. It quickly became common knowledge that Balladur would have to produce more ambitious plans because of growing pressure from his own majority and business circles, and this tempted the speculators anew. Balladur was in a difficult situation. He could lower French interest rates only to a point. Beyond this, given the Bundesbank's hard line, the franc's value would fall below its narrow-band ERM limit. This could be prevented if the Bundesbank were willing to lower its own rates, but whether it would do so was uncertain.

This was what the money markets needed. Balladur would be pushed to lower French rates and it was likely that the Bundesbank would not help out. The franc's value would then slip. Speculation would cause the franc to fall further and it was a solid bet that Balladur would be unable to raise French interest rates to counteract this, for reasons of domestic politics. Speculation against the franc would create a situation in which devaluation, or some equivalent change, would ensue.[79] Heavy betting began in June 1993. By mid-July, when the Bundesbank quite spectacularly refused anything more than a token reduction in its Lombard rate, speculators shifted into high gear, sensing that Balladur was caught. The franc's situation thus deteriorated and the ERM, notwithstanding gigantic market interventions by the French and German Central Banks, brave French talk, and Commission expressions of confidence, moved again towards crisis.[80] When on July 29 the Bundesbank again refused to lower rates substantially there was no alternative but to change the ERM. The Bank of France was rapidly running out of reserves.

The choices available to the hastily convened meeting of the EC monetary committee on July 31 were all difficult. The franc could have been devalued, but this would have been politically costly for Balladur while providing encouragement to anti-EC forces in France. The EMS could have been ended, but this would have been a huge defeat for the EC. The ERM could have been suspended for a specified period and its currencies allowed to float, but the outcome of this was unpredictable and, in addition, it would be a public humiliation for EMU plans. The German currency itself could have been removed from the ERM for a limited period. This was Delors's preferred option, since it placed responsibility for the difficulties on German unwillingness to concede on its domestic policies. The Germans were willing, but the Dutch and Belgians, whose currency was tied to the Deutschmark, insisted on following it, making the option unworkable. Finally, the narrow band within which most ERM currencies fluctuated could be widened, allowing more room for floating. This was what the monetary committee finally chose. The ERM narrow band was widened to a margin of 15 percent. This measure, announced as temporary, came as close to allowing a general currency float ("dirty floating" was the term used in financial circles) as was compatible with EMS credibility. In theory, the possibility of a 30 percent movement around the Deutschmark allowed ERM participants margin enough to stimulate economies beset by recession. This might solve the speculation problem for the time being.[81]

The EMS crisis created deep new uncertainty about the future of EMU. The line of the moment was that the EMS was not moribund, but in "suspended animation."[82] The most unpleasant scenario was that "dirty floating" would ultimately give way to complete floating, since in a deep recession member states would find it difficult to resist the quick fix of a competitive devaluation. The British had already got away with it and strong forces had gathered to promote it in France. Any spell of competitive devaluations would wreck prospects for EMU altogether. Even if this could be avoided, however, whether "dirty floating" would eventuate in a return to a "narrow" narrow band was uncertain. Without a serious narrow band it would become more difficult to move towards EMU, since monetary convergence was at the base of the EMU program. And even with an eventual return to the narrow band, EMU convergence targets would be hard to reach in the schedule set out in Maastricht. Stretching the Maastricht timing would make it more difficult for "Southern" EC members to justify tough domestic policy choices in the name of convergence, which meant that they would be less likely to make such choices. To be sure, EMU stage 2 would begin on schedule in January 1994. It was movement to stage 3 which counted, however, and it had become virtually certain that the 1997 date for moving had been made unfeasible. Without convergence as projected, January 1999, the latest date in the Maastricht text, might also be improbable.

The currency crisis thus meant that EMU would either be slowed down, as Kohl announced, or renegotiated. Either scenario modified the situation dramatically. EMU had always been premised on building in firm commitment to schedule. Without such firm commitment a whole new range of possibilities was opened. If EMU, and Maastricht, were renegotiable, then its opponents, such as the British and the Bundesbank, had new space to act. And if EMU were seen to be less than irrevocable, all kinds of movements and counter-movements in the financial sphere became possible. Whatever the optimistic announcements made in elite circles, then, the future of the central element of the Delors strategy had become profoundly uncertain.

Turmoil enveloped the Commission at a moment when all was not well in the workings of the "house" either: 1993 brought a new Commission to break in. For some time Delors had wanted to reorganize the foreign affairs side of the Commission along more functional lines. Assigning foreign affairs portfolios in new ways went along with this hope to reorganize the appropriate Commission services, whose divisions were a nightmare. Delors thus gave diplomatic matters to Hans van den Broek, the former Dutch Foreign Minister, and foreign trade matters to Leon Brittan. This was a risky operation because it put two very strong personalities into a struggle over ill-defined administrative and political territory, but possible benefits were great. Van den Broek was tough and seasoned enough to fight through complex bureaucratic problems to create the new "foreign office" Directorate General IA which was needed (and which Gunther Burghardt and a small staff, including Lodewijk Briet, were already designing).[83] Leon Brittan was a sharp negotiator and the best available talent to take on the vital last stages of the Uruguay Round talks. He was also a seasoned Commission infighter who would be loath to allow van den Broek take away one inch of his own turf. This had its advantages. Van den Broek and Brittan were strong liberals who in other circumstances might have made common cause against Delors. Dividing foreign affairs to rule them was therefore good politics.[84] But for the first months of the new Commission the confrontation was so noisy that other Commission work became painful and difficult.

The house was troubled in other ways. For one thing, people had begun to lose patience with the Delors way of doing things. The payoffs from success which had led administrators to redouble their efforts began to dissipate after Maastricht. Many of those who had credited Delors with the Commission's great successes after 1985 were concluding that the Commission's newfound problems were also the President's responsibility. At high Commission levels one sometimes even heard it said that Maastricht had been a mistake. Moreover, post-Maastricht did not bring much new by way of reorganizing Commission services beyond the division of foreign affairs and changes in the realm of industrial policy.[85] The larger reorganizational plans contained in the "screening" report were unimplemented. Delors's presidency would leave the Commission apparatus largely unreconstructed. Finally, the Delors team's penchant for appointing reliable, often French, administrative leaders from outside while the cabinet did most of the operational definition of policies and strategic coordination had begun to produce resentment at the middle levels of the services. Creating a cadre of "sure" people at the top of hierarchies angered internal aspirants to such positions who might otherwise have experienced career advancements. Delorist presidentialism suffered in consequence. As the external environment grew stormier, the atmosphere inside the Commission also worsened. External adversity and internal discontent were combining to create an aura of *fin de règne*.

From White Paper to White Paper

It would have been to underestimate Jacques Delors, particularly in such a context, not to expect one last powerful sprint. As the strategic cycle of Delors's presidency approached conclusion in 1993 the economic situation overshadowed everything else. By 1993, 17 million people were out of work across the EC and without new action the figure could well exceed 20 million by the end of the century. Such a trend could unravel European societies. Recession meant growing budget deficits and financial problems for social programs, prompting renewed elite agitation against European welfare states. There was also a chorus of argument that labor market rigidity made EC wage levels sticky and prevented the creation of new low-wage employment. Discussion took place against a background of major labor shedding. Firms compressed employment in response to uncertain economic circumstances. In Germany, big engineering firms with a long tradition of high-wage jobs and cooperative relationships with strong unions announced tens of thousands of dismissals. Many German combines admitted to changes of strategy involving "delocalizing" parts of their operations to cheaper labor areas.[86] Some began to take much more adversarial positions towards the unions. The solidity of the German model had been one of Europe's great hopes.

Another basic decision point was at hand, as in the mid-1980s. Different schools of thought competed for influence, with profound implications for the European Union (EU) which officially came into being after the ratification of Maastricht in November 1993. The first, argued most forcefully by the British but widely shared in elite quarters, was reinvigorated neo-liberalism. The time had come to end European exceptionalism in social policy which, neo-liberals alleged, stood in the way of flexibility in wage levels and labor mobility. The neo-liberals aimed at the liquidation of the "European model of society" in favor of one that would compete on labor costs, with market-driven wage lowering. Cutting back on social programs to "make individuals more responsible" was also on their agenda. That serious efforts at wage lowering would depress consumption and enhance investment difficulties seemed to escape the neo-liberals, as did the risk of social disorder in allowing large groups to fall into poverty. In addition, neo-liberalism dismissed virtually everything that the Delors strategy advocated, except the Single Market, and advocated turning European Union into a wider unregulated free-trade zone.[87]

The second position, a mirror image of the first and with growing popular support (on both Right and Left), was national populism. EU member states should pull back from internationalization to restore national policy autonomy. Then they should stimulate their national economies and float their welfare states. Accentuated national pride, or simple nationalism, would provide political sustenance for this. National populism would almost certainly make economic matters worse. It was also a direct threat to the future of European Union. Its worst danger was xenophobia. Not accidentally, many of the same people advocated this type of economic strategy and agitated against immigrants.

A third position, most often heard on the social democratic Left, urged massive work-sharing programs. Its different formulations usually advocated national policies promoting substantial reductions in the length of the working week. Often this position came with the advocacy of smaller changes in labor market regulation, particularly in minimum wage legislation, which would also promote the employment of lower-cost labor. The centralizing thrust of these well-meaning suggestions implied the introduction of greater rigidity into European labor markets, however. Moreover, there was a thorny issue of reducing wages commensurate with the reduction in working hours. Doing so was absolutely essential lest work-sharing make European competitive situations worse, but it was doubtful that any EU society had the institutions and outlooks needed to negotiate such massive income redistribution.

The debate struck at the very core of the Delorist mission, whose whole purpose had been to regenerate European economic vibrancy, reconsecrate Europe's mixed economy, and rejuvenate humane arrangements of social solidarity among different groups. The neo-liberals, who believed in a harsh, almost Malthusian, utilitarianism, wanted to end this European model of society and Delorist European Union along with it. The national populists advocated reactionary and fallacious economic reasoning that would wreak havoc in the international economy and cause deeper material distress at home. National populism could also destroy European Union altogether, and it bore the type of dangerous political currents which Community Europe had been founded to marginalize. The work-sharing plan touched sympathetic Delorist chords, but work-sharing legislated from the center, as many of its advocates desired, would increase rigidity at a moment when more decentralized flexibility was what was needed.

After the Edinburgh European Council in December 1992 the Commission President began his breakaway. The 1985 White Paper *Completing the Single Market* had been the launching pad for Delors's success. The 1993 White Paper *Growth, Competitiveness, Employment* would point European Union to a post-Delors future. Delors chose the Copenhagen European Council in June 1993 for his first move. By force of intellect and surprise Delors convinced the heads of state and government that business as usual was not enough, and that a White Paper outlining a new medium-term development strategy was needed. Once approval came at Copenhagen Delors knew that he could count on an active and sympathetic Belgian presidency to facilitate the job and allow the Commission to design a program whose logic would point forward well beyond the life of the Commission under Delors.[88]

The paper, which involved a difficult mobilization of the entire Commission, began and ended with the issue of unemployment. "There is no miracle cure," it announced. None of the solutions currently on offer – protectionism, a "dash for economic freedom" through government spending, reducing working hours and job-sharing at national level, a drastic cut in wages – would work. The roots of the problem lay much deeper. The European economy's potential growth rate had been shrinking over decades, unemployment rising over trade cycles, investment declining, and the EC's competitive position worsening in employment, exports, innovation, and product development. The Single Market had been helpful, but not enough, in struggling against such deep tendencies. The rest of the world, confronted with the same challenges of globalization and competitiveness as the EC, had also been changing. Europe had to take new "ways forward into the twenty-first century" or decline, and employment policy was the matter around which the new map should be drawn. Europe should begin with a job-creation target of 15 million new jobs by the year 2000 through "an economy that is healthy, open, decentralized and based on solidarity." Government budget deficits should be reduced to overcome recession, public spending should be restructured to promote sound investment, stable monetary policies pursued, global interdependence intelligently recognized, and space granted to local initiatives.

New competitiveness would flow from astute industrial policy redefined as "creating as favorable an environment as possible for company competitiveness" in the advanced technology areas where the future lay. Maximizing the Single Market was an important place to start, and the EC and member state governments should cooperate to make European regulation simple and consistent. They should also provide stimuli for flexible small and medium-sized industries and accelerate the establishment of the "trans-European networks" mandated by Maastricht, borrowing extensively in new ways to do so.[89] These networks in transportation, telecommunications, and energy would rapidly cut transaction costs and push Europe further towards an "information society." Including the CEECs would help integrate Eastern Europe and stimulate new growth. "Encouraging intercompany cooperation will gradually become a basic principle and not just one 'aspect' of Community" research and development policy, targeted on new information technologies, and bio- and "ecotechnologies." Europe should move as rapidly as possible towards advanced informational and environmentally clean market niches.

Redefined social solidarities were essential. The key phrase was that "the new model of European society calls for less passive and more active solidarity." A negotiated, decentralized, and rapidly evolving "sort of European social pact" was proposed, in which "new gains in productivity would essentially be applied to forward-looking investments and to the creation of jobs." Wage-earners would be asked to accept annual raises pegged at 1 percent below productivity gains in the interests of job-creating investments. Solidarity across generations and regions, and against poverty and exclusion were also fundamental. Most important, however, was flexibilizing "national employment systems." This meant a number of things, beginning with a basic Delorist commitment to lifelong education and training. Labor markets, both outside and inside firms, should also be flexibilized. Much more extensive active labor market policies should encourage mobility and the circulation of information. The document proposed decentralization of policy inside "employment areas."[90] The cost of unskilled and semi-skilled labor should be reduced by lightening the burden of social insurance expenses in the wage bill (the paper suggested that some of the tax revenues needed to compensate for this might come from the carbon dioxide tax). Unemployment policy also needed a full overhaul to prevent long-term unemployment by creating incentives to re-enter the labor market.

Subsidiarity dictated that the bulk of action be taken by member states. Cooperation and coordination were the key, to be begun by Council of Ministers' reflections on the different specific chapters of the program. On Community level priorities were the Single Market, helping small and medium-sized enterprises, pursuing social dialogue (in part to kindle needed new outlooks of "active social solidarity"), working on the trans-European networks, and "preparing forthwith and laying the foundations for the information society."

No one who read the White Paper could fail to be impressed, in particular when the Commission's effort was contrasted with other programmatic contenders on the field. Moreover, no one familiar with Europe's recent history could overlook that its vertabrae were trademark ideas of Jacques Delors. Pursuing the Single Market was central. EMU and its guidelines were at the core of the paper's macroeconomic policy recommendations. "Horizontal framework" industrial policy, a difficult creation of the Maastricht period, was the heart of suggestions about competitiveness, backed by solid policy legacies from the Single European Act and Maastricht (Community research and development framework programs and "trans-European network" programs). Promoting intercompany coop-eration was what had been experimented in the electronics episode in 1991 and then followed in other Commission industrial policy efforts. Shifting to "active social solidarity" was a more precise definition of the Delorist belief that basic social decisions were best negotiated among social partners. The White Paper's emphasis on "social dialogue" tapped another Delorist policy legacy. The White Paper agreed with liberals about the need to deregulate labor markets and make the welfare state less rigid, but within a broader context designed to prevent social divisions from themselves rigidifying.

After the White Paper there remained one last piece to be put into place, the Uruguay Round. Here another Delorist bet paid off. Sir Leon Brittan proved to be a first-rate choice for GATT negotiator. His burgeoning desire to be successor to Delors as Commission president made him doubly atten-tive to the concerns of the French. Sir Leon found a worthy ally in the Balladur government, which itself had a difficult domestic political hand to play, given long-standing commitments on agriculture. Delors himself played a significant role. The key was separating a final deal on agriculture from other differences. The Uruguay Round deadline was met on Decem-ber 15, 1993, when Sir Leon and Mickey Kantor agreed to disagree on audiovisual materials, financial services, and subsidies for shipping and aircraft. Against all odds and in the midst of a severe internal Community crisis, the Delors "after 1992" agenda had been completed. Maastricht had been negotiated and ratified, the second Delors package passed, CAP reform worked, the Uruguay Round completed, the EEA and stage 2 of EMU begun. The new White Paper could endow Europe with a well-drawn map.

The White Paper was Jacques Delors's last big gamble, or perhaps, as a British journalist aptly labeled it, "something of a last will and testament."[91] What its consequences might turn out to be were anyone's guess. There was quite a bit of power behind its recommendations, however, since, in many ways, they were structured around ongoing mandated programs and ideas to which member states had committed themselves. The effort was clearly to free the Europe from the mud in which it had become mired, give it a burst of new momentum, and sketch out a new map for its further progress. It might work.

Conclusions: The Delors Strategy at the End of the Day

The end of Jacques Delors's decade as President of the European Commission coincided with the downward cycle of his strategy. Economic reconfiguration that began with dismantling protected national markets and creating a united regional market space was nearly completed. Beyond this, to Delors there was no point to the endeavor unless Europe's societal distinctiveness could be perpetuated. Here there was a solid new *acquis communautaire* in the area of regional redistribution (social and economic cohesion). And there were a good many new "evolutive" commitments on the books of European Union (EU), most far away from permanent definition. Whether Maastricht's Common and Foreign Security Policy (CFSP) would amount to more than warmed-over European Political Cooperation (EPC) was uncertain. What social Europe would amount to was ill-defined. Whether "co-decision" for the European Parliament would help to shrink EU's democratic deficit was difficult to foresee. Economic and Monetary Union (EMU), perhaps the most important matter to Delors, was threatened by monetary and economic problems. Lesser matters like European citizenship, "third-pillar" issues(immigration policy, common policing) and industrial policy were unfocused. Yet another uncertainty was the meaning of enlargement to the EFTA countries which EU accepted and whose populations then accepted EU (for the fate of referenda on EC membership in the Nordic countries was itself uncertain).

The successors to the Commission under Delors would have an opportunity to reconsider these issues because Maastricht had scheduled a review conference for 1996. Whether at that point, however, the populations of a good many EU member states would be any more likely to want "more Europe" than they had during the Maastricht ratification period was doubtful. Solid opposition from certain member states also made it doubtful if anything resembling the Delorist dynamics of the later 1980s could be regenerated so quickly. Moreover, Europe's underlying economic problems, declining competitiveness, and rising unemployment would persist even if there were recovery from the recession of 1992–3 and the 1993 White Paper were taken to heart. Finally, EU's "back yard" in the Balkans, the former Soviet Union, and even some of the CEECs would almost certainly continue to flower with noxious weeds.

As Delors prepared to hand over to his successor there were thick clouds over the top of the mountains and a danger that they might obscure the path forward. Delors had nonetheless done a great deal, in a difficult post-Maastricht setting, to ensure that general directions to the future had been set. The second Delors package consolidated EU's financial positions until the end of the century and solidified important parts of the *acquis communautaire*. The CAP reform made possible an end to many of the absurdities in European agriculture without sacrificing EU's farm competitiveness and rural distinctiveness. Against all odds the Uruguay Round had been successfully concluded, promising more open international trading arrangements constraining even giants like the Americans and Japanese. The EFTA countries were well on their way into the EU "village," whether as new EU members or as participants in the European Economic Area (EEA), and solid lines had been cast eastward to the Central and Eastern European countries (CEECs). Finally, the 1993 White Paper, full of creative ideas, could help make a big difference in reconfiguring the European economy.

Strategies and Their Problems

The distant origins of the Delors strategy could be found in France's agonizing policy reappraisal in the early 1980s. At its heart was a re-evaluation of France's place in a newly threatening international economic setting. It was no longer possible for a medium-sized society like France to go it alone in economic policy terms, as it had tried after 1981. Mitterrand and his team, including Delors, decided to transfer goals of economic competitiveness and international political prestige from the domestic arena to the EC. In doing this France had solid comparative advantages in political coherence, derived from its eminently steerable presidential regime, superior administrative capacities and foreign policy, and military distance from Atlanticist orthodoxies. Hopes for success flowed also from the situations of other major EC member states. The Germans, given their history, would be in no position to translate superior economic power into political leadership, but needed a more dynamic European economy. The British were in too much conflict about the EC to use their own resources to be leaders. The course thus seemed open for the French and their new energy opened up the necessary interstate political conditions for renewed European activity.

When he assumed the duties of Commission President in 1985, Jacques Delors, an architectural associate in designing this new Europe option, had reflected a great deal about Europe. French desires for new European activism and German willingness to cooperate made a renewal of European integration possible, but Delors also understood that such things, in themselves, were not enough to make it happen. Leadership from the Commission was an essential ingredient. The institutional and constitutional flexibility of the European Commission meant that in the right circumstances and the right hands the Commission could be turned towards new policy activism and creativity. There were thus two elements to European renewal: a favorable diplomatic context and a Commission capable of setting new agendas.

Setting goals

Delors labored mightily, for a long time with extraordinary success, to get the Commission to perform and to create propitious interstate conditions. The political opportunity structure that he faced was open, if constrained. Initiatives had to encourage and cement favorable interstate coalitions and have real economic payoffs. The initial task was constructing a launching pad that central member states would either favor or have considerable difficulty in refusing. French and German economic and political strategies had converged, reinvigorating a Franco-German couple prepared to cooperate, within limits, in new European construction. Italian enthusiasm could usually be counted on. Most of the small states were strongly Europeanist. Bringing in the British was the last major part of the puzzle, made easier after long-standing budgetary issues had been cut down to manageable size by Mitterrand and Kohl just prior to Delors's arrival. The problem then became largely a function of finding proposals that played enough to British neo-liberalism to lower the British guard against the further pooling of sovereignty down the line.

The "1992" concept – the White Paper and the Single European Act, whose successes were sealed by the passage of the first Delors package – fit the bill perfectly. It was skillfully designed to draw upon discussions which the Community had already had and to appeal to commitments which member states had already made. The Delors strategy carefully sought to mobilize discursively from within the Community's traditional political and legal vocabulary, from the center of the Community's existing trade-market mandate. The program also played carefully to "return to the market" ideologies then at their height of contagion. Finally, it was managed delicately to minimize member state fears of future spillover. Creating new integrationist momentum out of the "1992" launching point was nonetheless Delors's central goal.

Delors's secret was to use the results of the Single Market launch to create new opportunities for wider-ranging programmatic initiatives. The image of "Russian dolls" describes a strategy that sought to reinvest the political returns of success into new, broader rounds of change. The hope was that successful new European activism would shift the location of member state problem-solving more to Community level and create an irresistible logic of Europeanization. There was a great deal of the "Monnet method' in the Delors strategy, therefore. A premium was placed on locating new programs which promised linkages to more far-reaching areas, pulling "on the thread which would untangle some knots and, step by step, the rest would fall into place."[1] Member states would be carried forward in their commitments to European integration by the unintended consequences of decisions made to resolve specific problems.

Delorism was a hybrid version of the Monnet method, however. Not only did it seek to use policy linkages strategically, it also promoted public dramatization of what was at stake. At critical junctures Delors emphasized the high political importance of direct confrontation with central problems, even when, again in Monnet's words, they did "not exist on their own but are the product of circumstances." The Commission President thus combined the St Simonian qualities of a Monnet-style "engineer of spillover" and those of a statesman. The mixture inevitably introduced complexity into Delors's tenure. Monnet, the *grand commis*, understood that engineering spillover was best carried on with great discretion, minimizing anything which might alert actors to unforeseen medium-term implications of what they were presently doing. "Putting people up against their responsibilities," as Delors, the Jansenist politician, was wont to do, was far from Monnetist discretion. To Delors, people had also to understand the broader historical contexts and meanings of their choices. Delors, the statesman, was a teacher. Fundamental political choices demanded the resources of commitment that only full understanding could elicit.

For a few miraculous years after 1985 the strategy worked very well. Expanding the Community, which had often led to difficulties, worked in the cases of Spain and Portugal to create better prospects for new coalition building. Regional redistribution initiatives in the first Delors package, a central breakthrough, could be presented in solid economic terms as internal North–South transfers necessary for the prosperous North to benefit from a more open EC market. Institutionally the notion of intra-Community solidarity had political importance far beyond its economic significance, as an entering wedge for state-building. Henceforth, every new market-connected proposal led the "South" to argue forcefully for new gestures of solidarity. Even convinced anti-federalist Northerners then faced a difficult trade-off between further market openings and enlarged interstate solidarity with federalist implications.

In this context, as long as the Franco-German couple remained solidly behind new initiatives and was willing to take the lead in paying for them (a task which the French graciously left largely to the Germans), it was possible for the Commission to propose new policy packages that, if properly designed to take into account plausible member state coalitions, would stand a good chance of acquiring enough support to place reluctant member states in a difficult position to exercise determined opposition. One of the more notable victims of Delorist strategy, Baroness Thatcher, put this well in her recollections of the 1986 London European Council:[2]

> I had witnessed a profound shift in how European policy was conducted – and therefore in the kind of Europe that was taking shape. A Franco-German bloc with its own agenda had reemerged to set the direction of the Community. The European Commission, which had always had a yen for centralized power, was now led by a tough, talented European federalist, whose philosophy justified centralism.

The post-1985 recovery of European economies was the final dimension of the Commission's favorable opportunity structure. Renewed economic optimism made it easier for everyone to contemplate change and brought with it important pressure group influence in favor of Community action, particularly from business. To be sure, this recovery was partly a function of the business cycle. It was also a function of improved economic confidence tied to renewed EC energies, and this was what counted for the EC.

The claim is not that Delors and the Commissions over which he presided were *the* independent variables. The European Community, like any modern socio political entity, cannot be reduced to such simplistic causal terms. The Commission was one actor among many, but an essential one. The European system after 1985 was a knot of complex processes. The Commission played a central animating, agenda-setting, and political role, however. Without its far-sighted analyses of Europe's environments, its skillful designs, and shrewd politics much less would have happened, perhaps very little at all. Delors's strategy took this into account. As other actors entertained policy options proposed by the Commission and these options succeeded, the Commission would reap rewards in terms of increased credibility and clout that could then be reinvested in further new options.

There was an important hook in the strategy from the outset. The Single Market program and its adjuncts were designed to bring the Community to a point where it might begin shifting towards "state building." Delors believed that market liberation would imply new programs to generate the regulation and public goods that the new market would need to function properly. In addition, as this happened the balance of regulatory functioning and power should begin shifting from member states towards the EC. Maastricht was meant to promote the decisive shifts between market and state building and from member states towards Europe.

There were important "in-house" dimensions to this. Unless Commission resources could be mobilized to produce proposals, argument, and political momentum for the strategy few results would be possible. Manufacturing such things inside the Berlaymont involved "presidentializing" the college, lining up commissioners and the administration behind Delors's priorities. Delors himself was the key to such presidentialization, through his intellectual and political skills, his ability to "work" the European Council and his role as international statesman. The rest of the job was assigned to Pascal Lamy and the Delors cabinet. The first moment, from the arrival of Delors in 1985 through the first Delors package, was particularly perilous. Delors, Lamy, and the team pushed and prodded a somewhat demoralized house to new heights of production, quality, and energy, in large part by force of their own greater energy and determination. Successful use of the internal Commission opportunity structures, as well as external processes, was part of the Delors strategy.

Three contradictions

There were three fundamental contradictions in Delors's vision. The first was a function of the strategy's sequential unfolding from market to state building. Market building, "1992," was to be a launching pad for state building. The Delors strategy's gamble was that a combination of evidence and argument about the functional need for new "Euroregulation" plus persuasive political mobilization in favor of "organizing" the new Single Market would be enough to move strongly into state building, working from the success of "1992." This was a high-stake bet, however, and odds against complete success were great. Plans other than Delors's were on the field. A number of member states, not only the British, had little patience for European state building and would try to keep new European integration confined within the Community's traditional trade-market mandate. Even among the member states who wanted European state building there were important disagreements over its extent and the forms which it should take. The Germans, many smaller EC members and the Delors team were federalists. But the all-important French, strong advocates for an "organized space," were avid confederalists. Finally, to the degree to which state building touched upon foreign policy and defense areas it touched another set of divisive issues, among them NATO and ties to the US. All this meant that market building stood a greater chance of succeeding than state building. In the worst case this could leave Europe economically liberalized but under-regulated, Delors's least preferred outcome.

The second contradiction lurked in what was traditionally referred to as the Community's "democratic deficit." The "Monnet method" was consciously elitist. For everyone to benefit, European construction had to proceed in the shadows of democratic accountability as ordinarily understood. After 1985 Delors had no choice but to work within a European institutional system reflecting this philosophy. There was an appointed Commission empowered with sweeping powers of policy proposition, there were secretive and opaque Councils of Ministers, and there was a powerful Court. Then there was an impotent talking-shop of a Parliament. Connections between each of these institutions and any mass European political culture were tenuous. Moreover, they were all knit into a system whose operations were perplexingly complicated and largely unfathomable to non-specialists.

Delors was a genuine democrat, nourished in the parliamentarist, civil libertarian French Catholic Left. He fully understood the necessity and utility of presenting his case to groups outside the Community's immediate system and systematically sought opportunities to communicate with as many publics as possible. The persistence of issues of democratic deficit created a fundamental problem, however. Regenerating European integration and working major institutional changes to promote substantially greater EC democracy were practically contradictory. Delors did virtually everything he could to democratize without alienating critical member state support for his policy course, but his margin for maneuver was narrow.

How fundamental issues of democratic deficit might have been addressed was itself quite unclear. Little consensus existed about how to do so and profound issues of political philosophy remained open. Should the legitimacy of Community Europe be built on a transnational European political culture focused upon the European Parliament? Or should it follow from a full 'Europeanization" of national parliamentary lives and political cultures? Neither option had been pursued far enough to understand its implications. There was virtually no trans-Community political culture and, with few exceptions, the Europeanization of national parliamentary lives and political cultures had barely begun. Moreover, in the absence of anything resembling a genuine European mass political life many, if not most, member state regimes routinely played exculpatory political games with the Community, using the EC as a scapegoat for difficult national decisions, particularly in the economic realm. This was one of the reasons periods of economic difficulty tended to coincide with periods of Communithy/Union downturn. These exculpatory practices, in turn, opened the road to ambitious politicians seeking a theme to break into the limelight by invoking nationalism against the "Brussels bureaucrats."

The danger was not abstract. Success at the level of Delors's ambitions meant that new EC policies would impact seriously on ordinary people. The more this was true, the more likely it became that ordinary people would demand an accounting. Delors and the Commission could hope that the weight of new Community activities would be largely benign and that this accounting would lead both to an enhancement of the Community's reputation and a deepening of trans-European political culture. But it was in the nature of things that many of the EC's new programs would work their benign effects, even if things turned out well, over the medium term. The Delors strategy might bring substantial disruption in the short run, particularly in the realm of employment. When member state publics came to confront such matters it would be difficult to avoid a Community crisis.

The third contradiction was inherent in the strategy's purpose of pyramiding one advance into another as rapidly as feasible. It seems strange in retrospect, but the Delors strategy had few provisions for handling the quite likely eventuality of the cessation of forward movement, for consolidating and administering the Community's new successes. Given EC history the Commission had to keep going as fast as possible because once it stopped it would become very hard to get started again. But by going as fast and as far as it could into unknown territory the Commission almost guaranteed that it would get into trouble. Delors's own outlook and character compounded this danger. The Commission President, an indefatigable militant reformist, was convinced that Europe had only a very few years to work very large changes and that these changes had to be built one upon the other. Delors was a political realist whose strategies were carefully calibrated to move things forward in the light of what was possible. But it was axiomatic that neither he nor the Commission would be in anything like complete control of the Community's agenda. When powerful member states decided to add to or impose upon the Delorist program there was little the Commission President could do to stop them. There was a risk of programmatic overload, therefore, of putting more things on the table than the Community's various systems could handle.

Three contingencies

Even at the moment of its greatest successes the Delors strategy's momentum was contingent on a favorable array of three contextual variables. The first was member state receptivity to European-level solutions to problems. Resort to European, as opposed to national, problem-solving had to make sense in the abstract and be congruent with domestic political vectors. The Commission's first triumphs were largely initially cost free for ordinary Europeans. They followed more from their role as signals to elite actors rather than their actual impact, which would only follow their implementation. The initial moments when the Commission and its allies reinvested returns from Single Market successes into new programs – the high "Russian dolls" period – were thus bound to be relatively easy going compared to what came later. Once the policies began to bite EC politics would become more complicated and difficult. Given predictable lag in actual impact of the early programs, any initially negative effect on ordinary EC citizens, which even the Cecchini Report predicted, might well occur at just that moment when Delors and allies were making their "turning point" moves.

This important matter of political timing was correlated with political circumstances in key member states. The mid-1980s, when the Delors strategy began its successful ascent, was a moment when the most important EC governments were in the hands of powerful leaders at the peaks of careers: François Mitterrand, Helmut Kohl, Margaret Thatcher, and Felipe Gonzales had all become legends, the Christian Democrats remained in firm control of Italy, and figures like Lubbers, Schluter, Soares, and

Papandreou had solid positions in smaller states. It was in the nature of things that such circumstances would not last forever. What might happen to the Delors strategy if governments in the most important EC member states like Germany, France, the UK, and Italy were weakened by domestic political problems? In retrospect it is clear that the domestic factors structuring the political opportunities for Delors and the Commission immediately after 1985 were unusually encouraging. Because of this the longer the Delors strategy was pursued the more difficult it would become to pursue further. This is tremendously important in the light of Delors's strategic logics. Delors sought to pyramid resources gained from the success of the easiest programs to promote a move from market building to state building. Later, when the great turning point towards state building occurred (Maastricht?), it was quite possible that the impact of earlier policies on ordinary Europeans and the declining support that besets all long-sitting political elites in democracies would combine to lessen member state willingness to sustain it.

The international changes that occurred after 1989 were the second major contextual contingency. German unification, the pro-market revolutions of Central and Eastern Europe, and the disaggregation of ex-communist federal states were huge, unpredictable events. Changing American behaviors in consequence were important as well. The US was unsure of itself in a new setting in which the end of the division of Europe rendered the military basis of US political power in Europe much less persuasive. It was not surprising that great new uncertainty created unsure footing for Delors, the Commission, and other key actors. Even if it was not alone, however, the Commission responded overconfidently in anticipating the rapid success of benign Eastern European transitions and the effectiveness of marketization. And if it was politically essential and morally courageous for Delors to support rapid German unification he thereby bought into the dangerous consequences of the ways in which unification was worked. It is clear that the primary motivations of the Commission President were to use the international changes to enhance the foreign political stature and role of the Community. It is also clear that Delors and the Commission were under strong pressure from both the French and Germans to do what they did.

It is quite wrong to assert, as many writers to do, that these changes were *the* causes of Delors's difficulties in the early 1990s. They were significant mainly as part of a cluster of causes that disrupted and added great new complexity to a Delorist strategy already stretched to the limit. Even before the world around it changed the Community had already assigned itself a staggering number of difficult tasks. Putting Eastern Europe and the divisive idea of a Community foreign and defense policy on the table was tempting fate. The Commission general program for 1991, the critical year, had 11 general priorities. As Jacques Delors knew full well, this was too many. The agenda was too long, complicated, and varied. The risk of the overload interfering with clear discussion and provoking conflict was great.

The third, and undoubtedly most important, contingency was economic. Initial Delorist successes coincided with an upturn in the business cycle in the later 1980s, the first such to occur after the "Eurosclerosis" period beginning 1979. The contrast was great between earlier recession and confusion and renewed growth coming simultaneously with the enunciation of the "1992" program. Undoubtedly the renewal of European integration helped stimulate the return of economic optimism. Conversely, the upturn in economic activity provided a major boost for the Delors strategy. It was easy to be misled by what happened, however, and to conclude that the Community's new initiatives has solved Europe's economic problems and brought a return to steady growth and prosperity.

When the business cycle later turned down, however, Europe and the Delors strategy would both inevitably be hurt. The British recession, which began earlier than others, may thus have provided one additional reason for British reticence about Europe. The continent was spared the downturn suffered by the US, Canada, and the UK in 1991, in part because of demand from Germany connected with unification. When things on the continent finally broke in 1992, the EC faced the worst recession in decades. GDP growth rates dropped towards negative levels in 1993, unemployment shot up, and optimism evaporated. Despite extravagant claims, the vaunted Single Market program had neither prevented a deep economic shock nor attenuated Europe's long-term steady loss of employment. Worse still, the anti-inflationary economic policy concerns which had taken over most Community member states in the 1980s, and which the EC itself had propagated into the future through EMU's convergence criteria, excluded serious counter-cyclical action either by national governments or the Community as a whole. Learned commentary in the 1993 White Paper *Growth, Competitiveness, Employment* that the "1992" boomlet had prevented the deep tendencies of Europe's economic situation from worsening was comforting, but its message that such deep tendencies persisted was harsh medicine. Ordinary Europeans were quite aware that the multiple promises made by their leaders, national and European, had not been kept. That Jacques Delors had underestimated the problems less than many others was no more comfort on economics than it had been on post-1989 international changes.

It was a commonplace that European integration could thrive only in moments of economic optimism and growth. When the economy went bad in a democracy domestic politics became volatile as people sought to protect themselves. In Community Europe, in large part because of the "democratic deficit," the leverage which these people perceived themselves to possess was national. National turning in on itself in crisis was natural, therefore, and this was what made bad economic moments equally bad for European integration. The crisis of the early 1990s was even worse, however. It was a moment of truth for elites and ordinary citizens which underlined that the good times of the postwar boom were gone never to return. To the degree to which the new Europe had been marketed, and understood, as a vehicle to make the good times return, it was bound to suffer.

Contradictions and Contingencies

Maastricht was meant to be the culminating point of the Delors strategy, when quantitative change towards uniting Europe became qualitative. Its aftermath was then meant to put all the different pieces of new policy into place. Instead, what happened was a knotting of the contradictions in Delors's strategy. The result, rather than *the* Delorist turning point, was a much more challenging strategic puzzle for the Commission President.

At Maastricht EMU was a success and important promises were made towards greater commitment to transnational solidarity. But on foreign and defense policy, which the Commission had already decided would have to be confederal in essence, there were vague commitments at best. Moreover, the explosion of crisis in Yugoslavia was already demonstrating how far member states actually were from the collaboration which even these vague commitments implied. On democratization the consequences fell far short of the problems to be solved. On substantive matters of extending and Communitarizing EC competencies conclusions were thin. And on matters of Europe's institutional structures, where the Delors strategy avidly promoted federal solutions, confederalism moved ahead.

For Delors and his team the disappointing Maastricht results were a signal that more difficult times had come. "The member states aren't as interested in Europe as they were" was a common lament, but there remained a great deal to work with. Finishing the Single Market program for January 1993, the second Delors package, CAP reform, the Uruguay Round, and enlargement were all in the pipeline, in addition to the changes towards EMU and other "evolutive" innovations programmed at Maastricht. The Maastricht ratification season confirmed the worst, however. Changing member state preferences to the detriment of the Community, the consequences of post-1989 international changes and, above all, a nosedive in the European economy, had come together to end whatever "Euroeuphoria" persisted. Delors had to regroup, take a lower profile, and refrain from further complicating the Community's agenda. However cold member states' feet seemed to have become, commitments had been made and important matters remained on the table whose implementation ought to make possible new forward momentum, even if more modest than anticipated.

This more modest strategic posture was itself disrupted by the Maastricht ratification season, the first forum for popular expression of disquiet about the "1992" program. The Single Market precipitated a wave of industrial restructuring, particularly in larger firms. Moreover, "1992" had not brought the new explosion of job creation which its advocates, not least

Jacques Delors and the Commission, had promised. Unemployment continued to rise, and what everyone had regarded as a return of relative prosperity was collapsing. There had also been an enormous amount of talk from Brussels about social Europe, but few results had followed it. The Single Market hurt the less well off disproportionately and they knew it. Commission arguments that the new Community was designed to save a special "European model of society" thus elicited a deeply skeptical response. The ratification season then became a showcase for Europe's democratic deficiencies. Where electorates were asked about Maastricht, whether by referendum or opinion polling, they often responded by denouncing earlier EC policies about which they had not been seriously consulted. Maastricht ratification also presented an ideal opportunity for nationalist forces to advance their causes. In many EC member states such forces, sometimes extremist, had already made substantial progress around immigration issues. "Brussels bureaucrats" joined immigrants as scapegoats.

The inability of the EC – and Maastricht – to deliver on its promises in foreign policy was constantly underlined by the horrors of Bosnia, following the earlier horrors of Croatia. The Community had been quite unable to act in its own back yard and limit the suffering. When its mediation gave way to joint EC–UN activities, they were hardly more effective. It may well have been that by 1992 nothing short of a massive external military intervention – involving the commitment of several hundreds of thousands of troops – would have been enough to make a significant difference. Perhaps the EC's course of peacekeeping, humanitarian aid, economic sanctions, indefatigable efforts to keep the parties talking, and occasional threats of something more military were the best that could be done. In any event, the EC looked feckless and divided.

As democratic deficit issues and foreign policy failures impacted on weakened member state governments, their room for maneuver narrowed. The Danish case was the most significant, underlined by the June 1992 "no." A tired, scandal-threatened government was unable to manage the referendum campaign properly, and the results were disastrous. The British case was similar. The results of John Major's shift of European strategy away from Thatcherite isolation increased his vulnerability to anti-European elements in his own party and raised the salience of anti-Europeanism in the British debate. In France, François Mitterrand's administration, floundering in a sea of unpopular policies and mistakes, was profoundly wounded by the Maastricht referendum. Helmut Kohl's troubles paying for unification severely weakened his hold. Political problems emerged in the larger member states where controversy over Maastricht was less important. The Gonzales era in Spain had entered a danger zone of scandals and economic problems while the Italians had begun the downward spiral which would lead to regime-threatening corruption scandals.

In this context, for Delors and the Commission in 1992 assuming a lower profile and quietly carrying out the planned sequels to Maastricht became immeasurably more difficult. Progress was slowly made, however, even if Commission-baiting and Delors-attacking made it more and more painful. The quick translation, in 1992, of the Community's political problems – the discontent of the Maastricht ratification season – into deeper economic challenges made even this revised strategic posture a tough ride. The consequences of rounds of speculation against the ERM were dramatic.

As this sequence of events proceeded the capacities of the Commission led by Delors for agenda-setting shrivelled to near zero. Everyone, including the Commission, was henceforth on a roller coaster ride whose ultimate destination was unclear. For Delors it was no longer possible to lie low, allow already programmed post-Maastricht programs to work their way through the system, and keep some semblance of forward momentum going. Henceforth it was a question of whether or not forward progress after 1985 might actually be reversed. The upward cycle of EC renewal had slowed to near standstill. Whether sucessors would have difficulty or even be obliged to backpedal remained to be seen. Delors, his team, and his Commission no longer would play much more than a small role in determining the outcomes, whatever they were. In this context Delors's last breakaways, the White Paper on competitiveness and employment and the completion of the Uruguay Round, were impressive indeed.

Despite its accomplishments, Delors's decade fell short of the President's own hopes. Delors's heroic efforts, and virtues, were partly undone by tragic contradictions deeply embedded in the EC's setting and therefore unavoidable. Their persistence underlined deeper flaws that future European movement would have to confront. It had made sense after 1985 to get the Community up and running by focusing upon programs and policies. Democratic deficit issues were not overlooked, but Delorist institutional reforms could not resolve then. The Commission President could hope that the success of new EC policies might create transnational enthusiasm. A reinvigorated European Community experienced positively by ordinary people was the best initial response to democratic deficit problems since in time it would create its own democratic political culture. The dark side of this scenario was that if the EC's new policies fell short the Community's institutional shortcomings as a democratic system could become an obstacle to further forward movement. The lack of European-wide political culture and clear, effective European-level democratic institutions would then work strongly against the Community. Indignation about the lack of real democratic consultation would supplement anger about policy results. In this context, governments would face domestic pressure to pull back from commitments to "more Europe."

This was what happened. The Maastricht ratification debate provided remarkable evidence about the lack of popular European political culture. Internationalist elites and the better educated, who were, to be sure, also better situated economically, were eager for Europeanization while lecturing the less educated and less well off in condescending terms about the need to accept policies that hurt. That the debate occurred at a moment when many EC national governments had run out of steam politically was significant. A split between popular opinion and political elites had spread across the continent, in the first instance because elite policy recipes had brought little but discomfort and disorientation since the 1970s. Post-1985 mobilization around EC programs could easily be assimilated to this same pattern of elite exhortation that did little to answer comfort popular concerns.

Next came the timing contradiction. Market building through "1992" was essential in liberalizing Europe's economic space to bring it up to global speed. It had to come first after 1985. Important in itself, it was also a vehicle to allow Delors and his allies to acquire the resources to shift to more state building. Europe's newly liberalized economic space should also be an "organized" one, and not simply a market. Strategic staging of these two moments, the first well within the EC's traditional mandate area and the second broadening it substantially, presented a challenge. Member states and elite economic interests could be counted upon to reach consensus on new market-building programs. But it was predictable that important member states, the UK and others, would oppose European-level state building, while elite economic interests were likely to be lukewarm about it as well unless the Commission and its allies could provide strong new incentives to support their proposals. State building would be even more complicated because those member states in favor of it were divided among themselves about whether it should be federalist or confederalist.

The path from "1992" to state building would have been narrow in the best of circumstances. The consequences of falling short, however, could be large. Market building was an essentially liberal activity. If market building succeeded but state building faltered, Community Europe could end up an even less "organized space" than it had been prior to the Delors presidency, more a liberal free-trade zone than the socio-political community with regulatory integrity that Delors desired. The contradiction in this strategic staging was that there was a much greater likelihood that the first, market-building, stages of the Delors strategy would work out than the second, state-building, plans.

This, in fact, was close to what happened. Delors's greatest ambition, to use the new dynamics of European integration to shore up and re-consecrate the European model of society was thus frustrated in important ways. Indeed, by the end of Delors's tenure the model was under greater pressure than it had been in 1985. Ironically, market building had been a greater political than economic success. It did not launch the European economy into the frontiers of international competitiveness. Had market building succeeded better economically, it might have been possible to resist the huge new demands for labor market and social policy deregulation that emerged in the recession of 1992–3. That such resistance was not feasible was clear from Delors's bittersweet last major act, the White Paper on employment and competitiveness of December 1993. The problem was even greater than this, however. The relative failure of state building, particularly in the social dimension area, made it plausible for popular forces, particularly those of labor, to denounce the entire Delorist strategy as pro-capitalist. Delors, after all, had done everything possible to "bring capital on board" and one cost of this, it seemed, was to leave labor and other popular groups behind. The connections between this strategic timing matter and the ways in which the democratic deficit had exploded in the aftermath of Maastricht were obvious. The result was far from what Delors had desired. Still, here, as in other areas, all had not been lost.

Jacques Delors and the coming of post-modern European politics

The postwar European capitalist order was a triumph of the modern Left temperament. National systems either achieved, or aspired to, a virtuous situation where innovative private oligopolies engaged in mass producing consumer durable goods for "deepening" domestic markets thrived with the assistance of an interventionist state armed with Keynesian instruments. All this made possible a "win-win" situation for a fleeting moment. High wages gave a broad spectrum of citizens access to rising incomes and changing lifestyles. Economic growth fed tax revenues and allowed the state to steer the economy and finance social programs. Economic margins for maneuver were sufficiently large to allow social groups to protect themselves from the harshness of the market through associational strength, often consecrated by law. Where the system reached its clearest definitions, as in Scandinavia or, in decentralized forms, in Germany beginning in the 1960s, powerful producer groups bargained with one another and the state about basic economic decisions to keep the system in balance. The orders that resulted varied in their actual partisan complexions. Some were more Christian Democratic than social democratic (with important differences in outcomes because of this), and some more or less liberal. The general logic was nonetheless infectious. The only discordant notes came from "extremes." Orthodox liberals on the Right rejected the ways in which states, producer groups, and social programs infringed upon the free play of market forces. *Communisant* forces on the Left rejected an order that made capitalism acceptable to broad numbers.

Rampant economic globalization in the wake of 1970s oil and economic policy shocks cast gigantic shadows over this happy moment. It quickly became impossible to pursue nation-state-based models of Keynesian/neo-corporatist accumulation. Mrs Thatcher's neo-liberal offensive in the UK undercut the foundations of British social democratic power and policies. After 1981 the French failed dramatically to build what had already begun to come apart elsewhere. The Swedish model, long vaunted for conciliating egalitarianism and export-led growth, collapsed in the later 1980s. *Modell Deutschland*, regarded as the ultimate way of translating high wages and social protection into internationally successful "diversifed quality production," has more recently begun to suffer its own agony – large German firms have been shedding thousands of jobs since 1992. In the 1990s more generally, European employment levels have stagnated, unemployment, much of it longterm, has risen, and growth stagnated.

In such circumstances the modern Left has lost its bearings. Its dominant social democratic component, as redefined in the extraordinary postwar boom setting, lives in a completely new world where its recipes no longer work, its ideas are discredited, and its mobilizational power is in decline. The welfarist-corporatist components of Christian Democracy are only slightly less threatened. For their part anti-capitalist Left radicalism and communism have been marginalized by economic change and the collapse of communism. Strong neo-liberalism, proposing a return to the disciplines of market harshness, a retreat from state intervention, and the deconstruction of social protection, has moved into the mainstream.

The political choices remaining after the extraordinary collapse of the Left offer few options to Europeans desiring security and prosperity. Elites invoke the constraints of globalization to push forward their painful remedies. Neo-liberals propose abrupt dismantling of the postwar order to "free the market" and allow the ebb and flow of open international trade to shape outcomes. "New" social democracy, *à la* Rocard and Gonzalez, and its moderate Christian Democratic counterpart, offer slower dismantling with less willingness to surrender national instruments to the global marketplace. The first proposal, which European electorates have by and large rejected, involves movement to market individualism and leveling down distinctive European forms of social solidarity. The second proposal brandishes technocratic and humanitarian reformist language about competitiveness to cover gentler movement in the same directions. To different degrees both camps agree that European nation states are less and less able to insulate themselves from international market flows.

The costs to ordinary people of these multiple dynamics have already been great. It is hardly surprising, if deplorable, to find some tempted by the dangerous sirens of national populism and its partner, anti-immigrant xenophobia. Those who argued that the end of the Cold War meant the "end of history" were quite wrong. Europe is on the cusp of change from a comfortable older world to something quite new. The moment may be more perilous than we have yet realized.

France, where Jacques Delors matured, was an exception to many postwar trends. It never came close to the social democratic model prevalent in Northern Europe. Its Left, competitively and destructively divided between socialists and communists, rejected the model and, partly for this reason, never had the opportunity to try another. Christian Democracy emerged powerfully into postwar politics from the Resistance but was quickly marginalized, pushed strongly Rightwards and fragmented by Fourth Republic France's political structures. Finally, France's Right was never particularly liberal, preferring protectionism, imperial comfort, and statism. That France was brought into the world of the later twentieth century at all was more the work of interventionist state elites than either Left or Right.

Jacques Delors, a maverick Left Catholic, was politically marginal in this politically marginal country. The presidentialist Left–Right polarization created by the Fifth Republic meant that he and others like him eventually found their way into the French Socialist Party. This represented little fundamental change of philosophy for Delors, however, who could continue to be himself in a party deliberately structured by François Mitterrand to gather in the wide variety of Left families that French history had sedimented. Oddly enough, this political marginality, plus Delors's exceptional talent and tenacity, were probably what made him so important to recent European events. In any event, Jacques Delors became a leader of international significance exactly when Europe transcended the Social Democrat/Christian Democratic models that many had hoped would provide a definitive solution to the problems of market societies.

The Delors strategy for Europe may be the most elaborate proposal for a new left-of-center vision we have yet seen. Its fundamental mark is the Europeanism that it advocates in response to the dramatic devaluation of national policy tools by globalization. The heart of Delorism is the defensive belief that what is genuinely distinctive in modern European society can be saved only by creative new action at European regional level. Secondly, Delorism, unlike nostalgic, strongly corporatistic social democracy, recognizes the need for genuine economic liberalization. The *sine qua non* of confronting globalization is a large and dynamic European market, open to the world. Delorism's third fundamental principle is that this market must be "organized." It needs regulation and public goods, unified economic and monetary policies, regional redistribution, innovative industrial and educational programs, and a coherent European international political position to create maximum prospects for economic success and preserve Europe's social uniqueness. Only if Europe can stay at the frontiers of international scientific, technological, and human capital achievements will it survive and thrive. Such achievements do not automatically flow from an unorganized, neo-liberal market order. Finally, a liberalized but organized market society is the way to reconsecrate Europe's unique systems of social solidarity, the "European model of society." On these issues Delorism's Left Catholicism parts company with social democracy. Solidarities are to be negotiated among social partners, but not by giant lumbering organizations. Bargained exchanges between groups with differing interests, reached in constant "social dialogue," have to take place in the decentralized way appropriate to the new economic situation. The "passive solidarities" of the postwar boom period have to give way to "active" ones, rigid bargains to "rolling" ones. Public help, of a newly flexible type (seen in Delorist policies like the Structural Funds, social dialogue, the trans-European networks, and the active labor market outlooks proposed in the 1993 White Paper), is needed to nourish this new mosaic of social cooperation.

The merits of this vision will be decided by history. What has been extraordinary is how far Jacques Delors has progressed towards its implementation. At this point it may well be the major alternative to an unappetizing and harsh liberalism. At the root of this has been Delors himself, operating in mainly the realm of ideas and conviction, using his great gifts for stimulating and mobilizing the coalitions needed to forge and then transcend existing consensus. In part he has been able to do this because he has occupied a situation on the overlapping boundaries between social democracy and Christian Democracy, continental Europe's center of political gravity. Despite their differences, leaders of each of these political traditions have become increasingly aware that without new solutions the legacies of generations are in danger. Such awareness is connected with, but does not completely explain, the willingness of key member states to contemplate new action at European level. One has to add further the hard-nosed material and political changes which led to the re-emergence in the 1980s of Europe as a plausible arena for the pursuit of the national interests of key EC players. Delors's closeness to the center of French power and his affinity for German ideas about Europe have been central. Finally, Delors's positioning on ideological and interstate grounds would not have been enough without great skills at mobilizing the Commission itself, for the Commission has always been his organizational base. Here there was another felicitous coincidence. The Commission was originally built to French administrative specifications, largely by Emile Noël, its long-term General Secretary. This French model, with which Delors and his able Commission team were intimately familiar, could thus be remoralized and mobilized quickly to generate the proposals needed to set the agendas that would optimize ideological and interstate conditions. Finally, Delors possessed an acute sense of the urgency of the historical moment, an "active pessimism" (the words are Pascal Lamy's) that flowed from a deep recognition that a century and a half of optimistic European modernization had come to an end. This led him to conclude that neither socioeconomic Maginot Lines nor hyperliberalism could save Europe. In the face of massive change, if Europe wanted to survive it had to build a new proactive defensive system. The classic urgent Delorist query of Europe – would it be willing to change to survive? – came from this active pessimism.

It is too early to pass final judgment on the Delorist vision. Many things might be said, positively and negatively, but the effects of Delors's presidency of the Commission stretch into an unpredictable future. The Delors moment is now over, however. For Europe to move forward in a post-Delors era at least two fundamental changes need to occur. The first, incipient in the Delorist scheme, involves wrenching revision of the way European politics are done. The second, following from the dramatic reconfiguration of the world around European Union, involves a basic reconceptualization of Europe itself.

There have been huge obstacles to success, as we have seen, but perhaps the most important has been the absence of mobilized democratic public commitment. In François Lamoureux's reflected words, "the most important lesson that I learned from recent debate is that a united Europe cannot come into being unless it is understood as a commonwealth of its peoples, reflected upon and built by citizens themselves." The older, always flawed, functionalist method of betting that political Europe would be induced indirectly by promoting economic integration has reached an impasse. In the absence of a democratic citizenry convinced through debate, primarily at national level, of the utility of European solutions to its problems, it will be virtually impossible to carry through the reformist and state-building dimensions of the Delorist vision. And without the relocation of some public goods to transnational level Europe may well finish as the free-trade zone that Delorism had set out to pre-empt.

The reasons should be evident. Electorates and organizations like unions have learned over decades, and in particular through the workings of postwar European national orders, to calculate and invest their resources nationally. Business interests are likely to oppose European-level reformism while at least some member states are likely to oppose European state building, as the British example in the early 1990s demonstrates. Without popular support the European-level policy and social model proposals at the heart of the Delorist vision have thus run quickly up against their limits. Such popular support is unavailable without a change in the ways in which democratic publics understand Europe.

The example of social Europe is here most telling, even though others could be found. The Commission under Delors, using the range of incentives at its disposal (financing, legitimacy, access to Commission inner circles) tried seriously to convince organized labor to invest new resources in European-level operations. Success has been limited, however, in part because unions, prototypical national associations, have stuck to their national ways of seeking influence. In the absence of national-level democratic debate and discussion about Europe's "social dimension" the limited powers of the Commission have not been enough to bring about a major change in such union outlooks. As a direct result employers have had an easy time stonewalling the kinds of change that Delors desired to promote. Firms, faced with the cold winds of the international market, are naturally averse to accepting new European-level constraints. Without significant forces to counter this aversion, firms will get their way. The longer-term logic of this situation, other things being equal, leads toward a Europe with few "social" achievements and progressive deregulation at national level that will undermine further the power of labor.

The difficulty exemplified by the knotty problem of the social dimension is not simply the disproportionately great power of capital over political decisions, although this is certainly important. As much at issue is the fact that labor and other such organizations, in whose "interests" it might be to establish European-level bargaining and social policy, have themselves not devised effective ways to introduce European dimensions into their strategic outlooks. They do not perceive Europe as a viable arena to pursue their goals, and this is only partly their fault. The universe of democratic discourse within which they operate has minimized discussion of European options and not only because popular associations, political parties, and parliaments have yet to learn the importance of Europe. European integration has historically been conceptualized as a matter of "foreign relations," and in the area of foreign relations governments and executive agencies are granted freedom from most democratic scrutiny. This institutional arrangement has had its virtues: without it there might well not be a European Union to discuss. But the events of the early 1990s have demonstrated clearly that it imparts a dangerous bias to European developments.

One major question for the future of the Delorist vision of a viable European model of society, indeed for Europe more generally, thus concerns how much genuine national democratic mobilization and debate around European issues will emerge from the crises of the post-Maastricht period. There are good reasons to worry. Governments and bureaucracies are not eager to see executive privilege become democratic domestic politics. Economic interests, primarily those of capital, are loath to relinquish political games (privileged entrée to government, choice among markets, national and European points of access for exercising influence) from which they gain advantage. Finally, the social and economic payoffs of Europe have recently been unpromising for the very groups that would need to change their perspectives on the utility of European solutions. Thus even if greater national democratic debate about Europe did emerge it could be fraught by serious reservations about the Europe that has come to exist. Still, whether and what kind of new democratic debate will occur about European options are all open, but essential, questions. It is not the least of the accomplishments of the Delors era to have put them on the agenda.

It is as necessary to change the nature of the Europe being built as well as the tools to build it. The Monnet vision was of a federation of EC member states with a substantial component of supranationality modelled on the nation state, a United States of Europe. In its earlier moments the Commission under Delors's presidency operated with this in mind. It is increasingly clear that the aftermath of 1989 makes the vision obsolete. "Europe" is no longer Western Europe, even if Western Europe and European Union are its center. Upwards of 40 nations of varying sizes and levels of development live presently in a Europe that is no longer divided by walls of Cold War. Conceiving European Union as *the* ultimate regulatory system in such a complex region would be illusory, even though it is destined to grow. Henceforth the major task of European Union, beyond continuing to strengthen itself, will be to promote interdependencies to make the larger region cohere and evolve peacefully. This will inevitably mean a Europe of "variable geometries," differing associations and affiliations among different nations according to needs. Sometimes these associations and affiliations will come into being through functional policy ties to European Union (trading arrangements, security and defense dealings, inclusion in trans-European networks, representation on different EU bodies, development and other forms of aid). Sometimes they will occur in structures brokered by, but not directly tied to, EU. Sometimes they will happen through deals between EU and other European organizations, NATO and the CSCE for example. On top of this, as recent EMU events have hinted, variable geometry inside the EU itself is not out of the question.

Organizing *this* new Europe, adapting different existing European institutions (EU itself, to be sure, but NATO, WEU, CSCE, and others) to its dimensions, are tomorrow's tasks, beginning with the 1996 review of Maastricht, and they will not be easy. Tomorrow's tasks are the results of today's good works, however. Without the Delorist campaign to "deepen" Europe, the "widening" still to come would have been immeasurably more difficult, if not impossible. This must be considered another fundamental accomplishment of the Delors era.

Notes

Introduction

The epigraph from Jean Monnet's *Mémoires* (Paris: Fayard, 1976, pp. 420–1) is my translation.

1 I am not, in the first instance, advancing an argument about "bureaucratic politics." The true Brussels bureaucracy, that little band of several thousand talented EC civil servants, produced clever ideas, wrote papers and engaged in interservice competition and collusion almost as energetically during the fallow years prior to 1985 as afterwards. The difference between EC stasis and dynamism cannot be attributed to some change in their activities, in other words. It did begin, however, in January 1985, when 17 new commissioners and, most importantly, a new Commission president, took up residence on the 13th floor of the Berlaymont, the EC's Brussels head office. The "bureaucrats" took their lead from their bosses, the commissioners, who designed the strategies which allowed the Commission to take a new lead.

2 The concept of political opportunity structure has to this point been used mainly to discuss the systemic variables within national state polities which have facilitated, channelled, and limited the effects of social protest movements erupting from outside "mainstream" mechanisms of representation like parties, interest groups and electoral processes. The most interesting use of political opportunity structure as an analytical tool is found in Sidney Tarrow's work on Italy's 1965–75 "cycle of protest," *Democracy and Disorder, Protest and Politics in Italy* (Oxford: Clarendon Press, 1989); Tarrow has also presented an elegant reading of the literature which led him to his theoretical conclusions in *Struggling to Reform* (Ithaca: Cornell UP/Western Societies Program, 1991). The

term may have been first introduced in Peter Eisinger, "The conditions of protest behavior in American cities," *American Political Science Review*, 67 (1973). Herbert Kitschelt has also made extensive and fruitful use of the concept in discussing the ways in which environmental movements in different countries do or do not transform themselves into partisan organizations: see *The Logics of Party Formation: Structure and Strategy of Belgian and West German Ecology Parties* (Ithaca: Cornell UP, 1989). See also Hanspeter Kriesi, "The political opportunity structure of new social movements: its impact on their mobilization," working paper of the Wissenschaftszentrum Berlin, 1991.

3 Here I am paraphrasing Kriesi, ibid., p. 2.

4 Tarrow's *Democracy and Disorder* is the most detailed exposition of the "cycles of protest" perspective.

5 There is a large literature, mainly from sociology, about resource mobilization. For a selection of important "founding" documents see Mayer N. Zald and John D. McCarthy, et al., *Social Movements in an Organizational Society* (New Brunswick, N.J.: Transaction, 1987), especially Zald and Ash, Zald and Berger, Zald and McCarthy. See also Frances Fox-Piven and Richard Cloward, *Poor People's Movements: Why They Succeed, How They Fail* (New York: Vintage, 1979).

6 An interesting sign of the European times – Marxism being rather still in the water – is that there is no particularly noteworthy Marxist argument about the renaissance of European integration to which to point. The French Communist Party which, along with the Portuguese party, is the last bastion of hard-nosed fundamentalism, has by and large lost its capacities to make serious arguments. For one exception see Philippe Herzog, *Europe 92: construire autrement et autre chose* (Paris: Messidor, 1989). Bernard Cassen, the Europe editor of *Le Monde Diplomatique*, is another skillful practitioner of this position. See his articles on Maastricht during 1992. Alain Lipietz has written a polemical "regulation school" variant on Marxist visions in *Berlin, Bagdad, Rio* (Paris: La Découverte, 1992). Better discussions are in P. Armstrong, A. Glyn and J. Harrison, *Capitalism Since 1945* (Oxford: OUP, 1991) and S. Marglin and J. Schor (eds), *The Golden Age of Capitalism* (Oxford: OUP, 1990).

7 Thus far such arguments usually amount to a ritual incantation that the European Business Round Table, a group of large business leaders around Philips, Volvo, and a few other conglomerates, was the architect. The "source" is often a book by the then CEO of Philips, Wisse Dekker, on Europe *Europe-1990* (Eindhoven: Philips, 1985). See also John Zysman and Wayne Sandholtz, "1992: recasting the European bargain," *World Politics*, 1 (1989).

8 Peter Gourevitch's excellent *Politics in Hard Times* (Ithaca: Cornell UP, 1986) makes this general argument as well as it can be made. Power resources analyses have often been associated with efforts to understand Scandinavian welfare states. See, for example, Walter Korpi, *The Working Class in Welfare Capitalism* (London: Routledge, Kegan Paul, 1978) and *The Democratic Class Struggle* (London: Routledge and Kegan Paul, 1983); Gosta Esping-Anderson *The Three Worlds of Welfare Capitalism* (Princeton: Princeton UP, 1990).

9 For extensive use of this concept, as well as a strong power resources analysis, see the influential textbook on European politics, edited by Mark Kesselman and Joel Krieger *European Politics in Transition*, 2nd edn (Lexington, Mass.: D. C. Heath, 1992). I also used these concepts in the comparative studies on European trade union responses to economic crisis in the 1970s, see Peter Lange, George Ross and Maurizio Vannicelli, *Unions, Crisis and Change: French and Italian Trade Unions in the Political Economy, 1945–1980* (London: Allen and Unwin, 1982) and Peter Gourevitch, Andrew Martin, George Ross et al., *Unions and Economic Crisis: Britain, West Germany and Sweden* (London: Allen and Unwin, 1984).

10 This is the central argument of Wolfgang Streeck and Philippe Schmitter in their important article "From national corporatism to transnational pluralism: organized interests in the Single European Market," *Politics and Society*, 19 (1991), no. 2, June.

11 Fritz Scharpf makes a powerful argument to the effect that the nature of policies made postwar social democratic coalitions impossible past a certain point in the 1970s, for example, rather than the reverse (the decline of coalitions making the policies unworkable). See Fritz W. Scharpf, *Crisis and Choice in European Social Democracy* (Ithaca: Cornell UP, 1991).

12 David Cameron, among others, stresses the continuity of general EC policy themes in order to relativize the importance of what happened after 1985, in "The 1992 initiative: causes and consequences," in *Europolitics*, ed. Alberta Sbragia (Washington: Brookings, 1992). It is true that reports on completing the Single Market, EMU, beefing up European Political Cooperation (EPC) towards a common foreign policy, and Social Europe were all filed away in the EC's collective closet ready for reconsideration in more propitious circumstances. The French shift opened the closet door. Strenuous efforts by Mitterrand himself to resolve the most important issues blocking EC progress at the Fontainebleau European Council – entry conditions for Spain and Portugal, the "British check," the budgetary impasse – were eminently successful. Mitterrand held no fewer than 30 bilateral meetings with the nine other EC heads of state during the 1984 French presidency. See Pierre Favier and Michel Roland-Martin, *La décennie Mitterrand*, Vol. 2 (Paris: Fayard, 1991). By way of caution, however, it is worth repeating the words of the authoritative work on the European Council that the Fontainebleau package was "a remedial exercise aimed at relieving . . . symptoms . . . rather than a preventive one to eradicate . . . root causes" – Bulmer and Wessels, *The European Council* (Basingstoke: Macmillan, 1987), p. 74.

13 This is the argument of "The European Community and 1992" by Stanley Hoffmann, in *Foreign Affairs*, Fall 1989. See also Andrew Moravscik, "Negotiating the Single European Act," *The New European Community: Decision-Making and Institutional Change*, eds in Robert O. Keohane and Stanley Hoffmann (Boulder: Westview, 1991), and, from the point of view of rational actor theorizing in comparative politics, see Geoffrey Garrett, "International cooperation and institutional choice: the European Community's internal market, *International Organization*, Spring 1992.

14 Andrew Moravscik is the most skilled recent proponent of this perspective. See his *National Preference Formation and Interstate Bargaining in the European Community, 1955–1986* (unpublished doctoral dissertation, Harvard University, 1992); "Negotiating . . ." in Keohane and Hoffmann, ibid., and "A liberal intergovernmentalist approach to the EC," *Journal of Common Market Studies,* 31 (1993), no. 4, December. See also James Caporaso, "And it still moves! State interests and social forces in the European Community," in *Governance Without Government: Order and Change in World Politics,* eds James N. Rosenau and Ernst-Otto Czempiel (Cambridge: Cambridge UP, 1992).

15 Robert Keohane's *After Hegemony* (Princeton: Princeton UP, 1984) might serve as an elegant model for this "story."

16 G7 is an acronym for the annual summit of the governments of the seven wealthiest big OECD nations.

17 The work of Ernst Haas is central. See *The Uniting of Europe: Political, Economic and Social Forces* (Stanford: Stanford UP, 1958) and *Beyond the Nation State: Functionalism and International Organization* (Stanford: Stanford UP, 1964). See also Leon Lindberg and Stuart Scheingold, *Europe's Would-Be Polity* (Princeton: Princeton UP, 1970) and the edited volume by the same authors, *Regional Integration: Theory and Research* (Cambridge: Harvard UP, 1971).

18 See, for example, Jeppe Tranholm-Mikkelsen, "Neo-functionalism: obstinate or obsolete? A reappraisal in the light of the new dynamism of the EC," *Millennium, Journal of International Studies,* 20 (1991), 1; David Mutimer, "1992 and the political integration of Europe: neofunctionalism reconsidered," *Revue d'intégration Européenne/Journal of European Integration,* XIII (1989), 1; and Philippe Schmitter, "Reflections on Europe's would-be polity," paper for the Ninth Conference of Europeanists, Council for European Studies, Chicago, March 1992.

19 On the importance of this see Sophie Meunier-Atsahalia, "Harmonization and mutual recognition in the EC after 1985," unpublished paper for the American Political Science Association Annual Meetings, 1993. More broadly, see Anne-Marie Burley and Walter Mattli, "Europe before the court," *International Organization,* Winter 1993.

20 The phrase, often uttered in academic conferences on the EC, is Wolfgang Streeck's.

Chapter 1   Prologue: Europe Comes Alive

1 There are three useful biographies of Jacques Delors: Gabriel Milési's *Jacques Delors* (Paris: Pierre Belfond, 1985), Alain Rollat's *Delors* (Paris: Flammarion, 1993), and Charles Grant, *The House That Delors Built* (London: Nicholas Brearly, 1994). All are useful for Delors's French career, with Rollat's supplying useful citations from Delors's writings, and Grant much the best on the EC years. Milési stops at the point of Delors's appointment to the European Commission in 1984 and Rollat's might as well, given the thinness of his

analysis. Another biography by Bernard Maris, *Jacques Delors, artiste ou martyr* (Paris: Albin Michel, 1992) has recently appeared, but is virtually worthless. For a sampling of Delors's own writings see Jacques Delors, *Changer* (Paris: Stock, 1975); *En sortir ou pas*, with Philippe Alexandre (Paris: Grasset, 1985); and *La France par l'Europe* (Paris: Clisthène-Grasset, 1988), translated as *Our Europe* (London: Verso, 1991).

2 "Sciences Po" – the Institut d'Études Politiques, is a preparatory intellectual environment for the École Nationale d'Administration (ENA) and other elite destinations. ENA – which produces *énarques* – is a national training school for French high administrators, founded immediately after World War II. Between ENA and the prestigious École Polytechnique the bulk of the French public and private sector elites are trained and socialized. See Irène Bellier, *l'ENA* (Paris: Seuil, 1993).

3 Jansenism, after the seventeenth–century Dutch theologian Cornelius Jansen, was a reform tendency in Catholicism, ultimately condemned by the Pope. Jansen's target, in his multi-volume discussions of the teachings of St Augustine, was Jesuit doctrine. Jansenism was eventually repressed in France, but not before leaving strong legacies.

4 For the best introduction to this school of thought see Michel Winock, *Histoire de la revue "Esprit"* (Paris: Seuil, 1975). See also John Hellman, *Emmanuel Mounier and the Catholic Left, 1930–1950* (Toronto: University of Toronto Press, 1981).

5 Hervé Hamon and Patrick Rotman's *La deuxième gauche* (Paris: Ramsay, 1982) tells this important story very well. For the broader context of French unionism see George Ross, "The perils of politics," in Peter Lange, George Ross and Maurizio Vannicelli, *Unions, Crisis and Change: French and Italian Trade Unions in the Political Economy, 1945–1980* (London: Allen and Unwin, 1982). See also Robert Wattebled, *Stratégies catholiques en monde ouvrier dans la France d'après-guerre* (Paris: Éditions ouvrières, 1990).

6 Clubs flourished as a way of intervening in Left politics at a moment when unreformed communists were unapproachable, the socialists were in precipitous decline, and the Parti Socialiste Unifié (PSU) was multiplying its internal divisions. See Jeanine Mossuz-Lavau, *Les clubs et la politique* (Paris: Armand Colin, 1970).

7 Income growth would be programmed over several years, alongside industrial growth and investment targets, following discussions among the "social partners" which the planners would facilitate. Then specific contracts could be annually negotiated in each branch of the public sector to distribute an annual pay envelope derived from the general plan. Delors had first sketched these ideas while working with the CFTC. He had an unusual chance to introduce them publicly when he played an important role in the resolution of the spring 1962 miners' strike, the first really important industrial conflict in the Gaullist Fifth Republic. Delors's preface to a reprinting of Pierre Massé's classic book on French planning, *Le plan ou l'anti-hasard* (Paris: Hermann, 1991) is worth reading in this respect.

8 For a time Delors, the self-professed autodidact, taught economics at the

University of Paris-Dauphine, with immense success.

9 His entry into the *Parti Socialiste (PS)* in 1974 involved a minor degradation rite. His local section, dominated by the Socialists' left-most faction, the CERES, submitted him to interrogation about the sincerity of his socialist commitments and kept him waiting before deciding to admit him, despite, or rather because of, his national fame. For some time thereafter he was watched suspiciously.

10 Along with a second devaluation, the first of which occurred in November 1981, plus severe budgetary squeezes Delors de-indexed wages from inflation levels, an essential first step towards bringing France's inflation rate down to manageable levels.

11 Mitterrand, torn between the Delors line of austerity within the EMS or a "go it alone" nationalist line which would have pulled France at least temporarily out of the ERM in order to cushion threats to domestic living standards, chose the Delors line. Delors was thus a central figure in the French Left's great policy turn.

12 Delors also came very close to being appointed prime minister in autumn 1982 and in March 1983.

13 The founding fathers, Jean Monnet and Robert Schuman, were explicitly functionalist in their political approaches. See Ernest Haas's classic work *The Uniting of Europe* (London: Stevens, 1958) for an exposition of functionalism as a theory of integration which, in its naive optimism, also demonstrates the weaknesses of the theory. See also H. Brugmans, *Prophètes et fondateurs de l'Europe* (Bruges: Collège de l'Europe, 1974).

14 The French acquired needed resources – coal in particular – strategic comfort about German intentions and considerable political clout. The Germans, following Konrad Adenauer's strategy for reconstituting German sovereignty, won needed postwar credibility plus prospects for enhanced trade and economic growth. Of specific importance to Adenauer was reacquiring German sovereignty over the Saar region. ECSC was a beginning to this. See Jean Monnet, *Les États-Unis d'Europe ont commencé: la Communauté Européenne du charbon et de l'acier* (Paris: Laffont, 1955), also J. R. Gillingham, *Coal, Steel and the Rebirth of Europe, 1945–1955* (Cambridge: Cambridge UP, 1991).

15 The Labour government, whose lead the Tories followed after 1951, opted for a catastrophic course of imperial rather than a European postwar development strategy. Alan Milward provides a magisterial review of this in *The Reconstruction of Western Europe 1945–1951* (London: Methuen, 1984). See also Miriam Camps, *Britain and the European Community 1955–1963* (Oxford: OUP, 1964).

16 Chapter 4 of Christian Pineau's recently published memoirs, with Christiane Raimbaud, *Le grand pari* (Paris: Fayard, 1991) provides a good description of the EDC battles in France. See also Robert Marjolin, *Le travail d'une vie* (Paris: Robert Laffont, 1976); Robert Schuman, *Pour l'Europe* (Paris: Nagel, 1963). In English, see Edward Fursdon, *The European Defence Community: A History* (London: Macmillan, 1980).

17 The acronym for the European Community has changed over time. The fa-

vored usages for the first two decades were EEC and Common Market. Since then, and particularly in the recent period, EC and Community have been the terms of choice. To simplify, we will use these last two throughout, until 1993 when the official name changed to European Union (EU).

18 At French insistence, largely on Jean Monnet's urgings, they also negotiated Euratom, a European Atomic Energy Authority, at the same time. It never amounted to much. Thus, including the ECSC there would henceforth be three European Communities, in legal terms.

19 Perhaps the best policy history of the Community is Loukas Tsoukalis, *The New European Economy: The Politics and Economics of Integration* (Oxford: OUP, 1991). For lucid accounts of policy-making see Helen Wallace, William Wallace and Carole Webb, *Policy-Making in the European Community* (Chichester: Wiley, 1983) and Stephen George, *Politics and Policy in the European Community* (Oxford: Clarendon, 1985). For an accessible, useful history in French, see Charles Zorgbibe, *Histoire de la construction européenne* (Paris: PUF, 1993). See also Joel Boudan and Max Gounelle, *Les grandes dates de l'Europe communautaire* (Paris: Larousse, 1989).

20 Commissioners, when they are sworn in, pledge to abandon narrow national identifications in the interests of the greater Europe. Their practical abilities to do so, as well as their abilities more generally, have always varied greatly.

21 When agricultural matters were at issue, for example, it was composed of agriculture ministers, for financial matters, finance ministers, etc. The "General Affairs Council," which tended to larger and more "transversal" matters, was composed of ministers of foreign affairs.

22 The Brussels-based Economic and Social Committee, an official assembly composed of interest group representatives, researched and reported on important issues, but had even less power than the European Parliament.

23 The Brussels bureaucracy, translators subtracted, is smaller than that of a large municipal government. It is tentacularly connected to member state governments and interest groups.

24 *Engrenage* is a French term. Literally, it would mean "getting caught up in the gears." In political terms it means, roughly, an "action trap" in which agents, once set on a specific course of action, find themselves obliged to take a set of further and much broader actions that point them in a direction in which they did not necessarily intend initially to go.

25 For a full review of General de Gaulle's European visions and actions one has to go to Charles de Gaulle, *Mémoires d'espoir*, Vol. II, *L'Effort* (Paris: Plon, 1971); *Discours et messages*, Vol. IV (Paris: Plon, 1970); *Lettres et carnets*, Vol. IX (Paris: Plon 1986). Jean Lacouture's wonderful biography of the General *De Gaulle*, Vol. 3 *Le souverain*, Part II (Paris: Seuil, 1986) is the most useful secondary overview. Alain Prate's *Quelle Europe?* (Paris: Julliard, 1991) gives a spirited defense of de Gaulle's federalism in part 4. See Edmond Jouve, *Le Général de Gaulle et la construction de l'Europe*, 2 vols, (Paris: LGDJ, 1967). Chapter 4 of Zorgbibe, *Histoire de la construction européenne*, "La conception gaullienne de 'l'Union d'Etats' ", contains a good discussion plus, in appendix, the first version of the Fouchet Plan, the Gaullist regime's proposal for

EC institutions.

26 De Gaulle had earlier blocked Great Britain's first membership application (in 1962), on the grounds that Britain was insufficiently European. See Camps, *Britain and the European Community*. The Luxembourg compromise (January 1966) is reprinted in Zorgbibe, ibid., pp. 86–8.

27 See Andrea Boltho (ed.), *The European Economy* (Oxford: OUP, 1982).

28 For the disagreements of economists about this see Tsoukalis, *The New European Economy*, pp. 21–30.

29 The effects of the GATT's Kennedy Round made this less significant than the Rome Treaty's authors anticipated.

30 The Norwegians negotiated entry as well, but the treaty of accession was rejected by a national referendum.

31 The failure of the EC to develop a common approach to energy in the earlier period undoubtedly made a difference.

32 This was the term which de Gaulle claimed to have actually used, even though everyone always cited it as the *Europe des patries*.

33 EMS was also a "two-speed" affair, including only some EC members (not Britain, of course). On EMS see Peter Ludlow, *The Making of the European Monetary System* (London: Butterworths, 1982); Loukas Tsoukalis, *The Politics and Economics of European Monetary Integration* (London: Allen and Unwin, 1977); Roy Jenkins, *European Diary* (London: Collins, 1989) and Valéry Giscard d'Estaing's *Le pouvoir et la vie*, 1 (Paris: Compagnie 12, 1988) provide practitioners' points of view.

34 On the European Council see Simon Bulmer and Wolfgang Wessels, *The European Council* (Basingstoke: Macmillan, 1987).

35 The issue was real. Three-quarters of the EC budget was used to finance the CAP which, in turn, maintained agricultural prices and subsidized exports on the international market in order to subsidize farmers. Since British agriculture was small and what there was was very efficient, British contributions to the CAP went overwhelmingly to French, German, and Italian farmers.

36 Margaret Thatcher's *The Downing Street Years* (New York: Harper Collins, 1993) contains several trenchant discussions of the "British Check" issue. See chapter XVIII in particular.

37 Interestingly enough, the two most important EC actions from this period were both associated with the Belgian Viscount Davignon, European Commissioner for Industrial Policy. Beginning in the later 1970s Davignon, using ECSC emergency powers which flowed from a declaration of "manifest crisis," promoted a draconian restructuring of the European steel industry which, if it cost tens of thousands of jobs, probably saved the industry. See Yves Mény and Vincent Wright (eds), *The Politics of Steel: Western Europe and the Steel Industry in the Crisis Years (1979–1984)* (Berlin: de Gruyter, 1987). Then in the early 1980s Davignon fostered the Esprit program for technological research and development in electronics – the official program, after a small trial period, beginning in 1984. Esprit was particularly important because it promoted Europe-wide cooperation, seeking to create high-tech success on a European plane in an industrial area where national champions had theretofore been the rule. On

Esprit and other such matters, see Wayne Sandholtz, *High-Tech Europe: The Politics of International Cooperation* (Berkeley: University of California Press, 1992).

38 Many of the policy ideas that we now greet as a gale of creativity originated in these accomplishment-fallow years, including completing the internal market, Economic and Monetary Union (EMU), regional development funds, and social Europe. Few of these schemes came much closer to policy than press releases, however.

39 There are two each from the five largest member states and one each from the smaller ones.

40 At least theoretically it also organizes the interservice consultation needed for the production of complicated policies whose scope overlaps several DGs. In recent practice, however, the president's staff has done the bulk of such consultation, as we will see.

41 The real power in the Commission thus devolved upon three or four figures like Etienne Davignon, François-Xavier Ortoli, and Lorenzo Natali, who saw to it that their pet projects made progress. Davignon's successful sponsoring of DG XIII and the Esprit research program is a good example of this. The glue of the Commission's operations was not the Commission president, but the Secretary General, Emile Noël, who had run the "house" from the beginning.

42 The first real success was the adoption in February of the Esprit program. On the budget problem see Thatcher, *Downing Street Years*, pp. 537–41.

43 The British were net budget contributors because British agriculture received much less from the CAP than other countries.

44 Jacques Attali reports that Mitterrand first spoke with Kohl about nominating Delors on May 28, 1984, and once again on June 26. See Attali, *Verbatim* (Paris: Fayard, 1993), pp. 641–2 and 658–61. Both moments were prior to the end of the Mauroy government in July.

45 Given the nature of the French presidency such weaknesses had not been central because the Élysée did foreign policy on its own.

46 First of all there were the more evident credentials. Delors knew Europe and its logics from his Europarliamentary and ministerial days. Indeed, no Left French politician except Mitterrand himself could make a greater claim to contributions towards unblocking the EC's gridlock in the early 1980s. Moreover, there were few who could rightfully claim to have played a larger role in "turning around" the French Left's policies to more greater realism centering upon the reconstruction of the international positions of French firms and the French treasury. Delors also knew "the capitals" very well.

47 A number of Delors's major speeches have been reprinted in his *Le nouveau concert européen* (Paris: Odile Jacob, 1992), including this first speech to the European Parliament.

48 New harmonization of social rules to prevent "social dumping" would be necessary and, Delors also queried, "when will we have the first European-level collective agreement?" Economic convergence among the EC's different national economies would be needed, implying new mechanisms to redistribute

resources from North to South. The CAP had to be reformed. The EMS had to be reinforced – in the direction of a single currency. Finally, European institutions had to be changed to transcend the Luxembourg compromise, which held the EC hostage to "you get this, I get that" patterns of interstate dealing.

49 The Treaty itself speaks of completing the internal market after the "first stage," and the European Council had started announcing the need to do so in 1982. David Cameron provides a useful overview of the evolution of the single market notion in his chapter of Sbragia (ed.), *Europolitics*, p. 31.

50 Delors describes this in his preface to Paolo Cecchini, *The European Challenge* (Aldershot: Wildwood House, 1988). The best succinct summary of the network of reports and actions leading up to 1985, during the Community's period of crisis, can be found in Jean de Ruyt, *L'Acte unique européen*, 2nd edn (Brussels: Éditions de l'Université Libre de Bruxelles, 1989), Chapters 2 and 3. For the key "pre-Delors" proposals see the Genscher–Colombo initiative of 1981, in *Europa Archiv*, no. 2, 1982; the 1989 Stuttgart European Council's "Solemn Declaration on European Union" (reprinted as Annex 3 in de Ruyt), the European Parliament draft treaty on European Union of 1984, a product of Altiero Spinalli's hard work (see François Capotorti et al., *Le Traité d'Union européenne, commentaire du projet adopté par le Parlement européen le 14 février 1984* (Brussels: Éditions de l'Université de Bruxelles, 1985) and the Dooge Committee report on institutional questions submitted in 1985 (Annex 4 in de Ruyt).

51 For the text, see EC Commission, *Completing the Internal Market. White Paper from the Commission to the European Council* (Luxembourg: EC, 1985). As far as we have been able to reproduce the White Paper story the idea itself came from Jacques Delors, perhaps from his experience as Chair of the European Parliament Monetary and Finance Committee in 1980. The Delorist provenance of the idea is confirmed by Delors's first speech to the Parliament in January 1985. Jean-Louis Lacroix, the leader of the Commission's miniscule planning staff (labelled the "Lacroix group" at the time and composed of three or four people) was the source of the 1992 timing. The idea was then sent out to the appropriate Commission DGs for initial work (DGs III and XV, Internal Market plus Finance and Company Law, and the Legal Services). In later January the first draft project came back, "typically DG III," essentially about market harmonization. In February there was hard discussion about adding the harmonization of indirect taxation. The Delors cabinet itself was divided about this, with François Lamoureux advocating it and Jerome Vignon strongly opposed. Delors sided with Lamoureux and harmonizing indirect taxation was included. Delors then started to argue that the project was "too deregulatory" and advocated the inclusion of language about cooperation among firms and company law and some vague social wordage. The final product, with all of these things included, was then packaged by Cockfield, who himself wrote the introductory text practically overnight. The policy development problem encountered in these few months, one which caused considerable discussion, was getting the different DGs together to cooperate. This task was the Delors

cabinet's real baptism under fire.

52 For the French "1992" was partly a way to offload blame for a number of difficult decisions on to "Europe" in order to pursue the deflationary restructuring line that Delors had played such a role in setting earlier. It also could give the Mitterrand regime a new strategic bedrock – European integration – to replace the Left Social Democracy which had earlier held together France's cantankerous Left coalition. Finally, given German reluctance, and to a degree, lack of capacity for, dominating the EC politically, the French might take the lead and gain some power thereby, in particular to pursue Mitterrand's neo-Gaullist foreign policy purposes on a European stage.

53 The British could then calculate that if they played their later cards correctly, "1992" might lead to the neo-liberal free-trade-zone Europe which they really wanted.

54 Parallel events, like the final clarification of the British Check situation at the Brussels European Council in March, helped the British mood as well.

55 The Dooge Committee wanted to make treaty changes to alter Council decision rules to qualified majority voting after the European Parliament had, by simple majority, approved Commission decisions, while also giving the Commission increased powers of implementation. It proposed tying these changes to the impending round of ratifications of the enlargement of the Community to include Spain and Portugal. For the substance of Milan see the *Bulletin of the EC*, June 1985, pp. 13–18.

56 Even though interstate negotiations about one thing or another had been a constant in EC history, almost always they had been undertaken when interstate consensus existed and there was no need for legal formalities. There had been only one previous official IGC under the Rome Treaty, in fact, convened in 1964 to discuss the relatively uncontroversial matter of merging the ECSC, Euratom, and the EC.

57 The British had been lobbying strongly against any treaty renegotiation, and had circulated a memorandum to this effect during the preparation of the Milan European Council. See Thatcher, *Downing Street Years*, pp. 548–51.

58 See *EC Bulletin*, July–August 1985, pp. 7–11.

59 Internal market, economic and social cohesion, technological research and development, environment, cultural, and monetary questions.

60 The term is used by de Ruyt in his account of the Conference, based upon a close reading of the negotiating papers: de Ruyt, *Acte européen*, p. 70.

61 For the Luxembourg European Council see *EC Bulletin*, no. 11, 1985, pp. 7–21; no. 12, pp. 7–15.

62 See, in particular, Emile Noël, "The European Community today: what kind of future?," in *Government and Opposition* 22(2), Winter 1987. Also EC *Bulletin* October 1985, pp. 7–9.

63 The Single European Act is *single* because there is only one text to modify all of the EC Treaties, not because of the Single Market.

64 Under the decision-making rules of "qualified majority" the four largest EC members – Germany, France, Italy, and the UK – have ten votes apiece, Spain has eight, Belgium, the Netherlands, Greece, and Portugal three, and Luxem-

bourg two. The qualified majority needed to carry a decision is 54 of the 76 possible votes. This system makes it impossible for the big EC members to unite and carry issues over the wishes of smaller states while allowing a coalition of two large and one small member to block proposals.

65 In a qualified majority area the Parliament could propose amendments. The Commission would then have to approve these amendments – creating dense new areas of contact between Commission and Parliament. If the Commission did approve, the Council could then only change the legislation by unanimity.

66 It would be foolish to claim that the Commission played the central role in the actual processes of mutual interstate maneuvering which decided final results at the Luxembourg European Council. But the Commission, and particularly Delors, who with Lorenzo Natali and Carlo Ripa di Meana were the Commission's representatives at the talks, was totally aware of the issue linkage and package building implications of the ways in which it had structured and promoted the Single Market program.

67 "Special chefs" is the term used, despite its "Franglais" origins, by Anglophones inside the Commission to refer to the policy preparation meetings prior to the discussion of policy proposals by the weekly *Chefs de Cabinet* meetings.

68 Researchers have yet to produce a good mapping of this resource mobilization, but we suspect, and we are not alone, that scholars who find strong business interest in "1992" put the cart before the horse. Business enthusiasm for the Single Market seems to have been rather more a product of the policy program than one of its primary causes and it may well be that much initial business support, including its organizational expression, may have been drummed up by the Commission.

69 The real "Cecchini Report," after Paolo Cecchini, who coordinated the work, was published by the Commission in multiple volumes beginning in 1988. Numerous abridgments and partial presentations were also published around this date. See, for example, *European Economy*, 35, March 1988, "The economics of 1992: an assessment of the potential economic effects of completing the internal market of the European Community" (Luxembourg: EC); Jacques Delors et al., *1992 le défi* (Paris: Flammarion, 1988).

70 See Michael Emerson, *What Model for Europe?* (Cambridge: MIT Press, 1988) for a contemporary discussion of this.

71 This was a matter of proposing a program to make good on the "social and economic cohesion" clauses in the Single European Act which would combine some serious commitment to preventing the Single Market from penalizing the EC's less developed members and "paying off" new members Spain and Portugal. Commissioner Gregory Varfis wrote the document.

72 Agriculture Commissioner Frans Andriessen was responsible for the initial document.

73 The original document, "Com. 100" in its first form, was subsequently published as *Réussir l'Acte Unique Européen: une nouvelle frontière pour l'Europe*, in Supplement 1/87 to the *EC Bulletin*.

74 In the old system the EC received revenues from the CAP and customs revenues plus a percentage of VAT tax receipts – nominally 1.4% but in fact 1.25% because the British rebate was financed out of VAT resources. The new system included these resources plus a percentage of national GNP.

75 The package also included automatic stabilizers in yet another (and as it turned out, largely ineffective) way to control production.

76 There had been considerable discussion, with little actual change, about reforming the ERDF in the early 1980s. The Commission put forth a strong proposal for change in 1981 and the Council finally passed a very watered-down reform in 1984. Marc Smyrl notes that the most important thing about it was that, "by accepting the Commission's revised proposal, the European Council put itself formally on record as being in favor of the increasing integration of national development schemes with Community-wide regional policy, as well as of the eventual movement from projects to integrated programs." This citation is from Mark Smyrl's excellent unpublished paper "Reform of European Community Structural Funds," Harvard Center for European Studies, 1991, p. 16. In other words, the 1984 reform would provide Delors with the legitimacy to move more strongly in 1987.

77 Greece, which had joined in the early 1980s, and Ireland, the other two poor EC members, had already been arguing that the Single Market threatened them.

78 These principles included principles of "partnership" among the Commission, member states, and regions involved; of EC "complementarity" to real, existing local programs; and "additionality" – no more local budget relieving. The whole involved dealing with regional governments. .Problems arose in cases where there were no such things, as in Greece. The Greeks were obliged to create them in consequence.

79 Before the effects of doubling had been folded in, and for the FEDER alone, contributions amounted to 4.49% of total investment in Portugal, 4.22% for Greece, 3.23% for Ireland, and 1.16% for Spain. Delors took to comparing the program with the Marshall Plan. For a general description see *Vademecum sur la réforme des fonds structurels* (Luxembourg: EC, 1989) and for detail see the *Rapport annuel sur la mise en oeuvre de la réforme des fonds structurels* (for 1989 Luxembourg: CEE, 1991; for 1990 Com(91) 400, December 4, 1991). See also EC Commission, *Les régions dans les années 1990* (Luxembourg: CEE, 1991); Yves Doutriaux, *La politique régionale de la CEE* (Paris: Presses Universitaires de France, 1991).

80 *EC Bulletin*, Supplement 1/87, citation from p. 7. Excerpts from the speech are also reproduced in Delors, *Concert*, pp. 50–60.

81 The passage of the directive of liberating capital flow was the other preparatory move for EMU, beyond the Delors package.

82 The first broaching of EMU had come in consequence of the famous Hague Summit of 1969, convened to discuss the Community's next steps in the light of the successful completion of its "first stage," the creation of a customs union and the CAP. In a context marked by signs that the Bretton Woods arrangements were coming apart, the EC thus prepared the Werner Report of 1970,

which presented a plan for creating EMU. In March 1971 member states announced "their political will to establish an economic and monetary union." Initial steps, including establishing the monetary "snake" in 1972, followed, but momentum, together with the Werner Report and the snake, were swallowed up later when these same member states, in dispersed order, sought national trajectories out of disturbing new economic circumstances. The EMS, with its ERM to promote a zone of monetary stability, was established in 1979 to salvage something. But full EMU had found its way back into the closet. The Commission, Delors, and the European Council started to pull it out at the Milan Summit in June 1985 with the Single European Act's somewhat incidental, but quite significant, commitment to "enhance the Community's monetary capacity with a view to economic and monetary union." It was this commitment to renew an earlier commitment not honored which Delors used as the foundation stone for his 1988 proposal.

83 British Prime Minister Thatcher announced that the British did not favor important dimensions of the proposed EMU, the single currency in particular. But she was willing to allow discussion to go further.

84 The phrase, in French, was that the Social Charter "*aurait un caractère obligatoire.*" The speech is reproduced in Delors, *Concert,* pp. 71–80.

85 See the Beretta Report, CES 1069/87, November 19, 1987 for the Economic and Social Committee's initial contributions. Its conclusions are also reproduced in Venturini, *Un espace social européen à l'horizon 1992* (Luxembourg: EC, 1988) as Annex 6.1. The ESC submitted a new opinion in February 1989, see CES 270/89. The European Parliament then discussed this, see JOCE, C 96, April 17, 1989. There are interesting adridged statements of different institutional positions in *Social Europe,* 1/90, Martine Buron for the European Parliament and François Staedelin for the ESC. Buron's comment notes the shift in emphasis away from citizen towards worker in the Charter, which brought in its wake the disappearance of an earlier clause concerning the right of a mimimum income for all.

86 This was later published as Patrick Venturini, *Un espace social* .

87 The results of an EC interadministrative discussion, presided over by Commissioner Manuel Marin, to produce a coherent program were published in a special edition of *Social Europe,* "The social dimension of the internal market," in 1988.

88 The list of 30 items covered rights to freedom of movement, employment and remuneration, improvement of living and working conditions, freedom of association and collective bargaining, vocational training, equal treatment for men and women (including measures to enable men and women to reconcile occupational and family obligations), information, consultation and participation for workers, health and safety at the workplace, protection of children and adolescents, and the rights of the elderly and the disabled. Every worker was to have a right to adequate social security and those without subsistence because of inability to participate in the labor market should have sufficient resources, but "according to arrangements applying in each country."

89 In the words of the adopted Charter, "The European Council invites the Commission to submit as soon as possible initiatives which fall within its powers, as provided for in the Treaties, with a view to the adoption of legal instruments for the effective implementation, as and when the internal market is completed, of those rights which come within the Community's area of competence."

90 See Com(89) 568, Brussels, November 29, 1989 for the full text. A table of the proposed initiatives is presented in *Social Europe*, 1/90, pp. 52–76.

91 Eliane Vogel-Polsky in E. Vogel-Polsky and J. Vogel, *L'Europe sociale, 1993: illusion, alibi ou réalité* (Brussels: Éditions de l'Université Libre de Bruxelles, 1991) carefully enumerates the changes between the Commission's proposed draft and the somewhat weakened document approved later by the Council: see pp. 165–75.

92 The "social partners" reached "opinions" on macroeconomic policies (a paper in November 1986 full of pious generalities about investment and job creation), on "new technologies" (March 6, 1987) and on "the strategy of cooperation for growth and employment" (November 1987). By then, however, conversation had petered out. The two opinions are reproduced in Annex 4 of Venturini, *Un espace social.*

93 On the employers' side, the UNICE Secretary General, Zygmunt Tyszkiewicz, could not have been clearer about lack of interest in real negotiating; see "European social policy – striking the right balance," *European Affairs*, Winter 1989. On the union side the problem was more that ETUC was a resource-poor and largely ineffectual organization. Moreover, since the ETUC was an organization of national union confederations, and since in two very important cases (the German DGB and the British TUC) these confederations themselves had no statutory purchase on negotiations, there could be no question of the ETUC itself negotiating.

94 See Janine Goetschy, "Le dialogue social européen de Val Duchesse," in *Travail et Emploi*, 1/91 for the antecedents of post-1985 "social dialogue."

95 Nonetheless an agreement on training in the public sector between ETUC and CEEP was actually reached and signed later, in September 1990.

96 See Goetschy in *Travail et Emploi*, p. 17. The Commission's projects for a European Company Law are also worth mentioning in the context of "social dialogue." This Law had a long history – the idea first appeared in 1970 and eventually was encoded in the ill-fated Vredeling Directive of 1980, which proposed coupling incorporation at European level with obligatory workers' participation in the firm. The Vredeling proposal died in the Council. The Commission's 1989 proposals also made some form of workers' participation obligatory for European incorporation, but specified that participation might take three possible forms: employee representation on company boards (with both German and Dutch variants possible), representation through separate works' councils (the French model), and a collectively bargained form which should include information rights (for the British). The new proposal ran into serious resistance as well.

97 Delors, *Concert*, p. 73.

98 The reader will find an excellent, detailed overview of the Community's foreign relations in Part III of Peter Ludlow and Anna Morphy (eds), *The Annual Review of European Community Affairs 1990* (London: Brassey's, for the Centre for European Policy Studies, 1991).

99 Delors's speech is reproduced in *EC Bulletin*, Supplement 1, 1989.

100 Delors's speech to College of Europe, Bruges, October 1989, reprinted in Jacques Delors, *Impératif et urgence de l'Europe communautaire* (Paris: Bureau de Représentation en France de la Commission des Communautés Européennes, 1990).

101 Over the years the EFTA countries had made trade-cooperation agreements bilaterally with the EC. Thus free trade in industrial goods had been agreed. EFTA also adopted the EC's Single Administrative Document (SAD) for international border controls and participated in European standard-setting organisms. In fact, EFTA had become closely dependent upon trade with the EC economically to the point where by the late 1980s the point of staying outside the EC had been lost. Among other things, large corporations based in EFTA countries were relocating inside the Community in ways which threatened the EFTA economies themselves.

102 This "piece" was to be limited. EFTA wanted to keep agriculture outside.

103 By obliging EFTA to negotiate with the EC as a single unit and thereby accepting supranationality in principle, rather than allowing EFTA member states to negotiate bilaterally as had been the case in the past, the EC was intent on socializing EFTA members towards eventual membership. EFTA would also have to accept the entire *acquis communautaire* – 10,000 pages of the EC's accumulated rules, regulations, and laws. EFTA members would thus get more or less full access to the Single Market, but without political control over future EC decisions. See Finn Laursen, "The Community's policy towards EFTA: regime formation in the European economic space," *Journal of Common Market Studies*, June 1990; Helen Wallace and Wolfgang Wessels, "Towards a new partnership: the EC and EFTA in the wider Western Europe," EFTA *Occasional Paper 28* (Geneva, 1989).

104 The story of how the EC acquired this new responsibility is not completely known, even though it may well concern one of the more important turning points of the post-Cold War era in international politics. Axel Krause, in *Inside the New Europe* (New York: Harper Collins, 1991) tells part of it (pp. 292ff.). Somehow, in the spring of 1989, after having long played down the importance of the Single Market program and railing occasionally against the dangers of "fortress Europe," the US changed position on the EC. Bush announced this in a graduation speech at Boston University in May. Delors was then invited to Washington with full honors in June, in part to establish regularized EC–US consultations. Insiders claim that it was Delors's own powers of persuasion about Eastern Europe over lunch with Bush which led the Americans to consider giving the Community the important new foreign policy role of coordinating aid to Poland, Hungary, and Czechoslovakia. Almost certainly underlying this was American realization that the US no longer had the economic resources to assume such roles itself. It was at the 1989 G7 Summit

in Paris when the decision was actually taken. Here it is certain that skillful politicking on the part of Delors, his staff, and Helmut Kohl hammered out the new position, with Brian Mulroney of Canada making the actual proposition.

105 The EC accounted for fully 45% of the $30 billion plus – of which Germany contributed about 60% with France and Italy, far behind, as the next most important European donors. The US, by comparison, gave 6.7% and Japan slightly less. The aid was of varying kinds: credits, grants, investment guarantees, debt relief, and currency stabilization plans, to be distributed subject to five conditions – adherence to the rule of law, respect for human rights, introduction of multiparty systems, free and fair elections, and progress towards the development of market-oriented economies. The IMF and the World Bank, the so-called Bretton Woods Institutions, gave about $9 billion in various forms, on top of the $31 billion from G-24. Debt forgiveness from the Paris club has to be added to the total. See Jeanne Kirk Laux, "Reform, reintegration and regional security: the role of Western assistance in overcoming insecurity in Central and Eastern Europe," Working Paper 37, Canadian Institute for Peace and Security, October 1991.

106 The European Bank for Reconstruction and Development (EBRD), of which the EC itself had 3% of the stock, with Community member states holding over 40%, has to this point done very little. Apparently it has had great difficulty working out what its place might be. As a "merchant bank" to facilitate private investment it has run up against the decided reluctance of private investors to move into unstable Eastern Europe. As a "technical assister" it has hesitated to step on the toes of powerful donors to its own capital, the EC in the first instance.

107 German unification was in the forefront of Delors's mind in early September 1989, during his visit to Harvard to dedicate the Minda de Gunzburg Center for European studies.

108 The 24th *Annual Report* (1990) of the EC reviews this (Luxembourg: EC, 1991). See also Christian Tomuschat, "A united Germany within the European Community," *Common Market Law Review*, 27 (1990). See EC Commission, *The Impact of German Unification on the European Community* (Luxembourg, 1990).

109 See Gerd Langguth, "Germany, the EC and the architecture of Europe," *Aussenpolitik*, Spring 1991.

110 The gratitude of Jacques Delors for Kohl's critical 1988 support in the difficult passage of the *paquet Delors* was undoubtedly an important favor, in turn, in predisposing him towards the position he took on East Germany in 1989. Close and regular contacts existed throughout this period between Delors's own staff, Pascal Lamy, and Gunther Bughardt in particular, and the Chancellor's advisors. Commission Vice-President Martin Bangemann, former German Economics Minister, was also important, particularly in putting together the Commission's specific programs for integrating the former East Germany into the EC.

111 Ludlow and Murphy provide an excellent detailed overview of the EC's com-

plex, if limited, foreign relations, in Part II of *The Annual Review of European Community Affairs.*

112 If the 12 Foreign Ministers could reach consensus there might be a common European position, otherwise member states pursued their own goals. On EPC see A. Pipjers et al., *European Political Cooperation in the 1980s, a Common Foreign Policy for Western Europe* (Dordrecht: Martinus Nijhoff, 1988); Martin Holland (ed.), *The Future of European Political Cooperation* (London: Macmillan, 1991).

113 See Hubert Vedrine and Jean Musitelli, "Les changements des années 1989–1990 et l'Europe de la prochaine décennie," *Politique Étrangère*, Winter 1991.

Chapter 2   Inside the Berlaymont

1 The lunch was usually served buffet-style. The only time the menu changed was in early springtime when two things coincided. The first was one of the President's occasional visits to the lunch and the second was that the Commission's cook was in line for promotion. Those seeking the independent variable opted, after some thought, for the second.

2 Over the months, it turned out, international affairs more generally were the topic of choice.

3 I learned this in a completely serendipitous way. Being worldly enough to know the rarity of Monte-Christo cigars, and after waiting for a decent moment after Pascal lit up, I had been tempted to take the second cigar. I stopped myself and Jean-Luc eventually took it. Later, in discussion with Jean-Luc, I happened to mention that I had not understood the etiquette of the cigar ritual and had had difficulty restraining my desires. Jean-Luc looked horrified and announced, "Thank God you didn't take it. It took me three years to get a cigar. I don't know what would have happened, what Pascal would have done, if you had taken my cigar. It would have perhaps taken me three years to get another one." The implication, of course, was that Pascal controlled everything, down to the consumption of tobacco.

4 The entire Commission moved its proceedings, including its Wednesday meeting, to Strasbourg for the week of parliamentary plenary sessions. This transhumance, lived by everyone as a huge interruption, was also a very big expense. Everything needed for the meeting had to be trucked to it in large metal boxes.

5 They composed "notes to the file" which summarized general tendencies, wrote succinct memos to Pascal and Delors and redrafted the documents in their areas which had percolated up from different sources, in particular the services.

6 Christine Verger, Delors's advisor for parliamentary affairs and for his *domaine réservé* in French life was the only woman. She was later joined by Geneviève Pons, who replaced Lodewijk Briet in competition policy and the environment. Verger, along with several other cabinet members whose activities I duly inves-

tigated and recorded, was an important source of wisdom and information for me, as were Fabrice Fries and Pierre Nicolas. Parts of this text concerning them were edited out for its final version in order not to overwhelm readers with a complicated cast and huge detail.

7 Cabinets tend to reflect the nationality of their commissioners, and most often also contain at least one member from another member state, if only because diluting mononational teams gives each commissioner the right to have an additional cabinet member.

8 The École Nationale d'Administration (hence *énarques*) in Paris is a *"grande école"* where young people in their very early 20s are trained to become top civil servants. The school was founded after World War II and had acquired a formidable, and quite justified, international reputation for producing first-rate, polyvalent and hyper-ambitious administrators. In the French Fifth Republic after 1958 *énarques* had branched out to assume prominent positions in government and the private sector. At my arrival there were only three *énarques* in the cabinet, including Pascal, Jean-Luc Demarty, who handled agriculture, and Fabrice Fries, who came at the same moment I did.

9 François had been in the CERES faction of the French Socialist Party. The Center for Socialist Education and Study had been the left-most grouping of the PS in the period of the 1970s when the PS was moving towards power.

10 Since then Delors has produced an edited collection of these speeches which will save the interested reader most of the week which it took me: see *Le nouveau concert européen* (Paris: Odile Jacob, 1992).

11 Joly described his daily routines methodically. "First of all, there are programs which are up and running, 'mature subjects,' which I have to monitor. Here you have to use your judgment about how much attention to pay." Most pressing was the second type of problem, developing new proposals. Joly was expected to be on top of everything happening in his area, to make sure that what happened was what the President wanted. For this he had to know exactly what the President wanted and, in a more strategic sense, why he wanted it, where it fitted. "Here I have to work most closely with Pascal and the President to make sure that they know exactly what's coming." For this sort of thing it was essential to be able to reach deeply into the policy pipeline, through networks and using presidential power in order to make sure the right kinds of things were being produced. Notes and dossiers had to be constantly written, read, and passed upwards for Pascal's consideration. Sometimes policy proposals had to be sent back to their authors, even stopped altogether. Sometimes Joly might take the policy development task in hand himself, usually on the level of conceptual development but sometimes even down to the actual writing. All of this involved constant meetings. Finally, there had to be space to nurse new projects, things which would break in the future.

12 The Confédération Française Démocratique du Travail – the CFDT.

13 In 1991 this had become Jerome Vignon's operation, the *cellule de prospective*. When Patrick had been in it it had been called the Groupe Lacroix, after its founder.

14 It may have been true that MacSharry was not a great conceptualizer. He was, however, a tough and shrewd negotiator, and, in circumstances when reform was not a high priority, this was what was most important in an agriculture commissioner.

15 The agency was the CIASI – the Comité Interministériel pour l'Aménagement des Structures Industrielles.

16 Pascal also kept his contacts in the Socialist Party alive, serving on various party committees.

17 "Team 92" was a speakers' bureau sponsored by the Washington, D.C. delegation of the EC.

18 Staffs, sometimes very large ones, were close by, and well armed with all sorts of "gamed" solutions to anticipated problems. But they could be accessed only by notes passed in and out of the negotiating room by the one staff liaison person allowed to second the two official delegates, who were thus mainly on their own. I discuss how all of this worked at Maastricht later in detail.

19 Cabinet members are usually chosen for their proven skills, but there is an inevitable amount of cronyism and national preference. The most important explanation for cabinet variations beyond personnel choice is the relationship between commissioners and their cabinets. Some commissioners may use their cabinets to superlative ends. Others are not skilled users of cabinets at all. Commissioner–service dimensions vary as well. Some commissioners interact with and shape the products of their services with great skill. Others may become the "tools" of these services such that the task of political guidance of policy production lapses altogether. Still others may have little or no effective contact with services, leaving this task to their cabinets. There are directors general today who rarely saw their commissioners – one spoke of "once a month," for example.

20 One small illustration of this will help. I sent the preliminary manuscript for this book to Pascal by two-day courier on Monday, December 13, 1993, just after the Brussels European Council which had considered the White Paper on competitiveness and growth (whose preparation had been a long, hugely draining and difficult task coordinated by Pascal). Pascal must have received the text on Thursday of that week. He read it that weekend and faxed me a set of extraordinarily useful, sometimes sharp, comments on Monday December 20, 1993.

21 François Lamoureux notes in his own response to my preliminary manuscript (faxed one day after Pascal's) that "there is a whole history to write on the theme of the telephone and European decision-making." The theme is "the continuity of public service, another reconfiguring of the French system (remember the 'performances' of the telephone exchanges at Matignon and the Élysée) imported to Brussels which led us to be seen as *bêtes curieuses* by other cabinets who were much more able to live life than we were."

22 Pascal was particularly proud of the reforms which he had introduced in the creation of the Commission's annual program. Traditionally this had been done from the "bottom up," with the "services" asked to present their priorities by a certain date after which these priorities were negotiated out to become a

program. This effectively placed the Commission at the mercy of an annual opening of the filing cabinets. Pascal had insisted on changing to a top-down approach. The Commission – in fact usually Pascal, the President's cabinet and their administrative networks and, above all, Delors – would first decide generally what its priorities for the coming year would be, and then the services would go to work. This proactive approach had the great virtue of being more permeable to Delors's strategic concerns.

23 This gatekeeper work has a behind-the-scenes dimension as well. When Pascal saw undesirable work flowing upwards, beyond inciting cabinet members to deploy their efforts to modify or stop it, he could himself intervene directly with other cabinets and the services.

24 Delors had recruited some of these high officials from within the Commission, but he had not hesitated to go outside when he felt it useful. In the closed circles of ambitious Commission insiders this was not well received, since every outsider at the top meant one less insider. In an administration where there were large numbers of potential chiefs, lots of intrigue, and very few top posts, the method was not great for morale and provided his enemies with another weapon against him.

25 Pascal also assiduously "sold his product" by receiving and contacting representatives of important private interest groups and the press. It was often much easier for Pascal rather than Delors to deal with important business leaders, for example, since the press did not follow him around the way they did his boss.

26 Cabinet members, particularly the younger ones, did eat lunch together in the "minus one" level of the Berlaymont, where the food was good, copious, and cheap. Their conversations over lunch were rarely about business, however. Much civil servant lore was exchanged, and there was constant complaining about Brussels (which was "boring" for exiled and would-be Parisians) and the usual small talk about films and books. Pascal ran, of course, while François and Jean-Charles somehow found time to play tennis occasionally. There were a couple of quite posh "Eurocratic" social clubs in Brussels where people went to eat and socialize, but I never heard anyone in the Delors cabinet talk of visiting them. Pascal sometimes went to important social occasions, usually for Commission-political purposes. But one sensed that this was not his style.

27 This is discussed in more detail in chapter 5.

28 This was an interesting remark not only on the face of it but also because the German in question completely overlooked the fact that there were two genuinely German cabinets in the building, Bangemann's and Budget Commissioner Peter Schmidhuber's.

29 Delors himself, when I first approached him about his staff, looked stern and said "the most important thing is that they have to *implicate* themselves."

30 François Lamoureux, who himself served as number two in Edith Cresson's prime ministerial cabinet, noted that even the "cigar ceremony and the agenda ceremony during the cabinet lunch" were Parisian institutions. For further evidence of the Frenchness of the model see *Le Figaro*'s recent series on the

Balladur cabinet "La vie quotidienne à Matignon aujourd'hui," December 17 and 18, 1993. Pascal himself claimed to have combined the model of a French prime ministerial cabinet, with which he was intimately familiar, and elements of the Élysée staff.

31 More generally, as a standard reference work on French cabinets notes, "*un cabinet, c'est* une équipe *autour d'*un patron." Guy Thuillier, *Les cabinets ministériels* (Paris: Que sais-je?, 1991), p. 19.

32 One has only to run down the list of cabinet members – omitting Pascal Lamy and François Lamoureux – and their portfolio attributions to see this. If we classify Delorist strategy in 1991–2 into three key rubrics, "organized space" (meaning the various dimensions of "Euroregulation"), international affairs and institutional issues, every cabinet member had a stake in at least one of these.

Cabinet member	*Strategic dossier*
Leygues	Organized space: industrial policy, cohesion
	Institutional: personnel
Dixon	Institutional/organized space: EMU
	International: USSR and Eastern Europe
Zepter	International: GATT, EFTA negotiations
Demarty	Organized space: CAP reform
Briet/Pons	Organized space: European economic coherence and EC competition law; environment
Verger	Institutional: relations with PE
Venturini	Organized space: social, HDTV, culture.
Nicolas	International/institutional: presidential organization

33 Among an international group of high civil servants this meant full awareness of France's particular – *colbertiste?* – tradition of public service.

34 Like all complex organizations, the European Commission was filled with conspiratorial rumors about the occult workings of networks, the bulk of which being either untrue or tremendously exaggerated. It was nonetheless the case that there were mobilizable networks of many kinds. There were national networks, for example, including a powerful French one, there were political networks, including a socialist one, and there were more informal networks of friends and contacts developed during careers in the Commission's services.

Chapter 3 "After 1992" Begins

1 TV sets were *de rigueur* for watching news. Delors's was occasionally used for other purposes, as I discovered a few weeks later. Delors was away in Washington when in mid-evening I found one of Pascal's secretaries sitting on Delors's couch watching a soccer match. She did not look like a happy sports fan. It turned out that Pascal had assigned her to watch the game because Delors liked to call in from wherever he was to check the scores of any game in which he was

particularly interested.

2 Tommaso Padoa-Schioppa, who was a very close advisor to Delors throughout the EMU period, was a major advocate of these negative arguments. See his edited book *Efficiency, Stability and Equity* (Oxford: OUP, 1987)

3 The Werner Report foresaw the "total and irreversible convertibility of currencies, the elimination of margins of fluctuation in exchange rates, the irrevocable fixing of parity rates and the complete liberation of movements of capital." All of this was to be achieved in three stages. See "Report to the Council and the Commission on the Realization by Stages of Economic and Monetary Union in the Community," *Bulletin of the EC*, Supplement 3, 1970.

4 An excellent source for this earlier moment is Loukas Tsoukalis, *The Politics and Economics of European Monetary Integration* (London: Allen and Unwin, 1977).

5 See Peter Ludlow, *The Making of the European Monetary System* (London: Butterworths, 1982). Alain Prate, who was involved in the creation of EMS, has a blow-by-blow description in *Quelle Europe?* (Paris: Julliard, 1991), chapter X.

6 Which the British opposed. See Margaret Thatcher, *The Downing Street Years* (New York: Harper Collins, 1993), p. 555.

7 In anticipation he had assigned monetary affairs to himself when he divided up Commission portfolios in 1984. This meant that only one other commissioner, Henning Christophersen, in charge of financial matters, would get close to the EMU loop.

8 Delors was a veteran member of this very small clique of European financial policy operators, introduced while French Minister of Finances. From 1984 he had been a regular at governors' meetings in Basel. The economists included Niels Thygesen and Alexandre Lamfalussy. Lamfalussy would later become the first director of EMU's stage 2 "institution."

9 A sample of the papers which they discussed, as well as the Delors Report itself, is contained in Committee for the Study of Economic and Monetary Union, *Report on Economic and Monetary Union in the European Community* (Luxembourg: EC, 1989)

10 She claims that the Delors Report "confirmed our worst fears." Not only was the EMU plan objectionable in narrow terms, "there was also plenty of material in the treaty about regional and social policy – costly Delorsian socialism on a continental scale." *Downing Street Years*, p. 708. Thatcher was under very great internal pressure at this point to join ERM.

11 Among the things which upset Delors was the fact that his report was not explicitly endorsed as the way forward, the irreversability of movement after stage 1 was not confirmed and the timing of the proposed IGC was left somewhat up in the air.

12 For Thatcher's recollections, see *Downing Street Years*, pp. 750–2.

13 The Committee was chaired by Elisabeth Guigou, then on Mitterrand's staff, later to become his Minister for European Affairs.

14 For a succinct summary of the Commission's case, see *European Economy*, 44

(1990), "Executive summary," pp. 9–14. The entire issue, entitled "One market, one money: an evaluation of the potential benefits and costs of forming an economic and monetary union," contains detailed arguments for EMU. See also *European Economy*, "The economics of EMU," special issue, 1990.

15 Rome I was called to prepare a CSCE summit and talk about relations with the Soviet Union.

16 This was especially true after Kohl had forced it into a currency reform around unification which it opposed. Here we follow Loukas Tsoukalis's argument in Chapter 7 of *The New European Economy: The Politics and Economics of Integration* (Oxford: OUP, 1991). Other member states were arrayed between the French–Commission positions and the Germans. The Italians were the warmest advocates – EMU would provide weak Italian governments with an exogenous source for the economic discipline which they were unable to produce domestically. The Dutch, important financial players, were closer to the Germans.

17 See EC Commission, *Draft treaty amending the treaty establishing the European Community with a view to achieving Economic and Monetary Union* (Sec(90) 2500), Brussels, December 10, 1990.

18 Luxembourg had presided over the Single European Act negotiations and had a strong belief in its diplomatic capacities (despite its miniscule size) to bring member states together for new and important initiatives.

19 One of the great mysteries in the IGCs, in general, was the role played by the Secretariat-General of the Council, which did the work of actually organizing the meetings – preparing and circulating papers and minutes. François Lamoureux, whose job was also to monitor and cajole the Secretariat, had a tendency to demonize it.

20 They proposed, instead, a "hard ecu" which would be managed by an extension of the existing intergovernmental EMS system called a "European Monetary Fund." For a full proposal see *Europe Documents*, 1682, January 10, 1991.

21 For the text see *Europe Documents* 1688, February 1, 1991

22 See CONF-UEM 1608/91, letter from Pierre Bérégovoy and Roland Dumas to Jean-Claude Juncker, January 26, 1991.

23 Summary drawn from Sec(91) 222, Brussels January 31, Minutes of Second Ministerial EMU Meeting of January 28.

24 The moment was ripe for Major to open a campaign of seduction towards Kohl. The Gulf War granted the British new resources from their early and energetic involvement on the US side. The Germans had lost resources because of their own non-involvement.

25 In private Delors was unsure of Major. Joly urged him to think more about the implications of changed British tactics, which he did, very carefully.

26 The final matter on the table was the creation of a "mechanism of financial assistance" to shore up specific economies which suffered unforeseeable external shocks (military issues, market instabilities, etc.). There was disagreement here as well, despite strong Commission pleas in favor of such a mechanism. There were strong statements by Giovanni Ravasio of the Commission (Direc-

tor General of DG II) to COREPER and, more importantly, Delors to the ministers, defending the technical-economic and political reasons for such a mechanism, advanced as another manifestation of social and economic cohesion.

27 See Sec(91) 418, EC Commission, Brussels, February 26, 1991, Minutes of the 3rd Ministerial, February 25.

28 What follows is culled from my personal notes on the speech.

29 ECOFIN had had its first "multilateral surveillance" session on the same day as the second EMU ministerial meeting at the end of January, and the fact that a number of EC economies were way out of line was evident. ECOFIN had in fact issued a gentle warning to the Germans about the size of their projected budget deficit.

30 This was after a very difficult dinner with Major in London.

31 The Delors speech is reproduced in the *Bulletin of the EC*, Supplement 1, 1989.

32 In the meantime the Belgian government had submitted an influential memorandum on co-decision and common foreign policy on March 20, 1990.

33 See the conclusions of the two Dublin European Councils in *Dossier: The European Council* (Luxembourg: Group of the European People's Party of the European Parliament, 1991).

34 The Parliament prepared its second "Martin Report" setting out its desires during the summer of 1990. In addition there was a special report by Giscard d'Estaing on subsidiarity and one by Maurice Duverger on relationships with national parliaments preparatory to the "Assises" (a conference of EC parliaments) in Rome in October. The Council prepared hastily over the fall. See Annex III to COREPER document CONF-UEM 1701/90, a summary of the first Intergovernmental Conference on Political Union Ministers Meeting.

35 There was a great deal of "pre-conference" discussion to which the Parliament contributed resolutions and reports. Kohl and Mitterrand also sent another message to the European Council in early December which stressed that the IGC should move in a federalizing direction on several matters, that the European Council should be made stronger, that WEU be brought into common foreign and security policy, and that national and regional parliaments should be more closely involved. The Dutch formally objected to the proposals about the European Council.

36 For the Commission opinion see EC Commission, *Political Union* (Luxembourg: EC, 1990).

37 The *Premières Contributions de la Commission à la Conférence Intergouvernementale "Union Politique"* (Sec(91) 500) (Brussels: Commission, 1991), a compendium of all of the Commission papers, was published on March 30, indicating how far behind events the Commission had fallen.

38 This process was not atypical. Claus-Dieter Ehlermann and others made it quite clear that the Single European Act had in fact been put together by a group of about the same size – four or five at its heart, and including only ten or so at its largest.

39 All of this made François's days rather hectic. The first week that I tracked his schedule François, besides meeting with this informal steering group more

than once, was thrashing out Commission papers on European Citizenship – "I got mad, all they talked about were rights, never duties" – met for the tenth time on a project for a common foreign and security policy, hammered out a proposal for "hierarchy of norms" in the treaty to distinguish between laws and lesser pieces of legislation in order to clarify the European Parliament's areas of "co-decision," met with a working group (for four hours on Saturday) on the "social chapter," and talked widely about institutional matters more generally. He also sat in on the Commission meeting on the "energy" text, which he had written, reporting with delight that Sir Leon Brittan, not François's favorite commissioner, had been beaten 10–2. Finally, after trying very hard to get DG III, Perissich's shop, to produce ideas about "trans-European networks," he had threatened them, "either you do it right now or we'll do it for you." François had done all of this while presiding over a special chefs meeting to harmonize Single Market standards for motorcycles, helping Pascal prepare the *Chefs de Cabinet* meeting, receiving lobbyists from the French tobacco monopoly concerned about changes in indirect taxation, and helping Jerome Vignon draft a preface – in Delors's name – to a book about the Community. He had also seen a few journalists – "I've got to sell my products, haven't I?" – and supervised Lodowijk Briet's ever less pleasant joustings with Brittan on mergers and acquisitions policies. On top of this he had to deal with COREPER about the negotiations, touching bases with Delors as often as needed. In this typical week he had also somehow found time to go to the movies and absorb enough to have a lively discussion with me about the film and play tennis on Sunday.

40 Some Commission insiders, invariably drawn from the large group who had a history of complicated interactions with François's fabled temperament, were eager to tell me that all of this was François's fault. If it seemed evident that François did have many too many things to do, the causes of Commission slowness went much deeper than this, however.

41 An index of this was that during the critical first half year roughly three-quarters of the conversations at cabinet lunches were about international matters.

42 Andriessen and Matutes "shared" DG I, while Marin's activities were in DG VIII, which was one of the Commission's less effective services.

43 In the Delors cabinet foreign policy specialists had come and gone more rapidly than anyone else, on an average once a year since 1987. Berhard Zepter, the current one, was a skilled German diplomat with wide experience and contacts. He had to track a highly divided Commission operation riven by rivalries and coordinate with at least three "bosses" of his own – Burghardt at EPC, Pascal Lamy, and Delors himself. Bernie was a devotee of rock climbing who claimed that climbing up perpendicular Alpine walls trained his nervous system for the job.

44 For specific details as finally formulated in the Commission's paper to the IGC see *Premières Contributions*, pp. 11–59.

45 It was a joint Mitterrand–Kohl declaration in April 1990 which first proposed convening the IGC on political union. Then on December 6, 1990 another

Kohl–Mitterrand letter enjoined the impending IGC towards intergovernmental rather than supranational approaches to decision-making in any CFSP. For
a good setting of this discussion see Frédéric Bozo, "French security policy and
the new European Order," in *Security and Strategy in the New Europe*, ed. Colin
McInnes, (London: Routledge, 1992). See also the essays in Patrick McCarthy
ed., *France–Germany 1983–1993* (London: Macmillan, 1993), especially those
by McCarthy and Roger Morgan.

46 The UK had gone marching off with the US in classic "special relationship"
style. The French had joined the march, in Mitterrand's words, to be present at
the table after the conflict ended. The French had done this, however,
only after independent maneuvering which had angered the British and
the Americans. The Germans had been quiet, hiding behind their Constitution, until shamed into providing some cash. The Italians and Spanish had
made token contributions, while smaller EC member states were divided between hawks like the Dutch and the Portuguese and doves like the Belgians,
who had difficulty generating the energy to sell the British a few artillery
shells.

47 The questionnaire – UP 9 dated January 25 – can be found as Annex 2 in
Sec(91) 261, the minutes to the fourth COREPER meeting.

48 The Dumas – Genscher paper can be found in EC Commission, Sec(91) 259,
February 6, 1991.

49 Dutch Foreign Minister van den Broek gave an important interview to *Le
Monde* (February 8, 1991) during this period which outlined the WEU-
"bridge" position clearly as well as expressing considerable reticence about
binding foreign policy commitments. The British also foresaw an added possible benefit. Perhaps the French could be drawn back into NATO inner circles
if pro-NATO EC members took a careful, conciliatory negotiating stand on
WEU.

50 Excerpts from the speech can be found in *Agence Europe*, no. 5429, February
11–12.

51 Here Taft reminded his listeners of the contents of the Baker speech in Berlin
in December 1989, which pointed in these directions.

52 This defeat caused considerable consternation. Delors was furious at
MacSharry and gave Pascal instructions to tell the cabinet to "cut off communications" with the MacSharry cabinet in retaliation (an order that was eventually forgotten). When Pascal announced this to us over lunch, with his usual
slightly ironic overtones, François, sitting next to me, mumbled that "this is
going to cause Joly some problems." Joly Dixon was married to a member of the
MacSharry cabinet!

53 The Rome II European Council had put together a list, called the ASOLO list,
in December 1990, including industrial and technological cooperation in
armaments, technology transfer and arms exports to third countries, nuclear
non-proliferation, arms control, peace-keeping with the UN, participation in
humanitarian aid interventions, questions relative to the CSCE, relations with
the USSR, and transatlantic relations.

54 Interview with Delors, *Wall Street Journal*, March 7, 1991.

55 London *Daily Telegraph*, March 7, 1991.

56 The *Daily Telegraph*, which had completely lost any self-control on matters European, reminded its readers that "the Beelzebub of Brussels" was making his first speech in the UK since "his incendiary speech to the TUC in 1988 . . . Delors wants to create European institutions, like airports in some Latin American jungle, long before the people are ready to use them."

57 This was a symbolic act, since ratifying a new treaty was exclusively a member state concern.

58 For a superb review see Shirley Williams, "Sovereignty and accountability in the European Community," in *The New European Community: Decision-Making and Institutional Change*, eds Robert O. Keohane and Stanley Hoffman (Boulder: Westview, 1991).

59 In large part this was because the governments understood full well that commissioners, if they swore an oath not to act as representatives of their native lands, were, in fact, in Brussels in part to defend the interests of their country when they were threatened.

60 There was also a problem about the number of commissioners. Each big member state had two, the small ones only one. Distributing the work to 17 commissioners made for too much fragmentation of responsibilities and clearly hurt the effectiveness of the Commission. There was talk at the beginning of the IGC about reducing the number of commissioners to 12, or, alternatively, of appointing 12 full and five "junior" commissioners – Delors's preference – but it did not get far. Member states all wanted as much as they already had. Moreover, with the likelihood of enlargement in the near future, the issue would then have to be faced. Why face it twice?

61 See the discussions and documents attached to the Fourth and Eighth Permanent Representative sessions, Sec(91) 261 and Sec(91) 491 respectively. The group worked from a presidency document UP/26/91.

62 One consequence of this was that François's proposal suggested that the Council's existing ability to issue regulations should be abolished. For the specific language see *Premières Contributions*, pp. 61–3.

63 In his internal note to Delors François commented that this was the French administration's thesis that the Council should legislate by regulation.

64 This was the very difficult meeting when Delors and MacSharry had their homeric disagreement about agricultural prices.

65 See Article 149, paragraph 2 of the Rome Treaty modified by the Single European Act.

66 A brief review of these matters can be find in the IGC working paper UP/13/91 of February 1, 1992.

67 Parliament proposed two readings of Commission propositions, and in each the Parliament could propose amendments. If these amendments failed to produce full agreement on a text by Council and Parliament, there would be final resort to a Concertation Committee, in which the Commission would also participate. Either this Committee would adopt the text or the matter would drop. Any text which it did adopt, however, would then go back to Council and Parliament. If both approved, the text would pass. If either or both did not

approve, the text would fail and the procedure would end. The basic criteria of co-decision were satisfied, since both Council and Parliament would act as EC co-legislators and, most important, the Parliament would acquire the right to stop texts with which it did not agree. Cf. Annex II of UP/13/91 of February 1, 1991.

68 The whole thing would take a maximum of 15 months, statutorily, in order to prevent procedural complexity from jamming the legislative pipeline. It also invoked various types of Council majorities – unanimity, qualified, simple – for various stages. After first reading, failure of the Council to agree to a Commission text amended by Parliament would lead directly to conciliation – in which Council, Commission, and Parliament together undertook to produce a new text. The second reading would be of this new text with the Commission retaining the right to re-examine its proposal. If Parliament rejected the text, the procedure was finished. If it agreed, amended, or was silent, the text would go back to the Council. The Council then might accept or reject the text, or remain silent about it for a statutory period, which would lead to adoption. But if the Council amended it, it went back to Parliament, which then either rejected it or accepted it.

69 See *Premières Contributions*, pp. 60–75.

70 Passage of the co-decision paper through the Commission, beyond the issue of hierarchy of norms, had been relatively uneventful, despite the fact that François et al. had presented the commissioners with what was practically a polished product in early February. In special chefs the Bangemann cabinet had made a number of useful suggestions about timing and simplifying the second-reading procedure. Bangemann, undoubtedly following the German position, had also tried to remove an important part of the Commission's second-reading role, and had been followed by the Andriessen cabinet, which proposed a watered-down amendment to the same effect, but François had argued them down.

71 See Conf-UP 1723/91 of February 13. The Germans proposed that Parliament could ask the Commission to "examine the possibility of presenting a proposition." If the Commission rejected this, or didn't act for six months, Parliament could present its own proposition.

72 In the process he had stopped efforts in the areas of tourism, youth, the protection of animals, and civil defense and protection.

73 On the environment the Commission's proposal sought to improve on the Single European Act clause in the direction of qualified majority, improve the Commission's powers of execution and get greater environmental consideration into other Community policies. Here Delors had a strong sense that advanced environmental policy practices could very well turn into a comparative advantage internationally for the Community.

74 They were helped by Jean-Marc Ouazan, a former cabinet member and Delors loyalist, who continued to handle "social affairs" consulting with the Commission.

75 This would have made it more difficult to pass legislation than simple qualified majority.

76 13th meeting of Permanent Representatives, April 11.
77 On "competencies," Delors announced that there wasn't much to report except forthcoming Commission papers – particularly on the social dimension, with which the Parliament was very engaged – because little progress had been made.
78 It wasn't hard to read the message: "If you press too hard on this, you might not get co-decision the way you want it."

Chapter 4   Organizing European Space

1 Both Poncet and Chaban Delmas were key French members of the "European Movement," a linear descendant of Jean Monnet's original Europe Committee.
2 The speech is reproduced in Delors, *Le nouveau concert européen* (Paris: Odile Jacob, 1992), pp. 81–97.
3 For beginning readers, the EC itself produces a good introduction, see Europe Documentation, *A Common Agricultural Policy for the 1990s* (Luxembourg: EC, 1989). For further reading, see François Duchène et al., *New Limits on European Agriculture* (London: Croom Helm, 1985); Alan Winters, *The Economic Consequences of Agricultural Support* (Paris: OECD, 1987); Dimitrios Demkas et al., "The effects of the Common Agricultural Policy of the European Community," *Journal of Common Market Studies*, 2 (1988).
4 The key document here is the 1985 Commission Green Paper, *Perspectives for the Common Agricultural Policy* (Brussels: EC, 1985).
5 These 1988 measures included a system of budget stabilizers, including a set-aside program, plus the doubling of the Structural Funds, including the EAGGF, the rural development fund.
6 For a good detailed discussion see Anna Murphy, *The European Community and the International Trading System*, 2 vols (Brussels: CEPS Papers 43 and 48, 1990). See also Rene Schwock *US–EC Relations in the Post-Cold War Era* (Boulder: Westview Press, 1991), Chapters 9–10.
7 François Lamoureux, who had little patience for the "carrot counters" and for agriculture in general, was also in the loop. "The *paquet Delors* gave us four years of peace . . . without hearing about agriculture. Now we're at it again." Agricultural problems were quite likely to recede very soon. Agricultural populations were aging and leaving the land. In time the ability of farmers to "hold up" politicians would be attenuated.
8 Demarty intimated that the MacSharry cabinet was not as helpful as it might be. MacSharry himself had ambitions for a triumphant return to Irish politics in ways that may have colored his choices.
9 What happened was that oilseed imports grew, largely from North America, as grain subsitutes for animal feeds because grains were included in CAP protection while oilseeds were not. The Community's oilseeds mechanisms, in which quasi-protectionist price support operations were triggered when EC oilseed prices fell to a certain point, then worked to stimulate excessive EC oilseed production, which was then dumped on the international market, wreaking

havoc with the price levels that American farmers would otherwise have received. This was what led to the GATT dispute on oilseeds with the US, which raged during 1991–2.

10 The acute problem of protected grain markets and unprotected grain substitute markets (the case for oilseeds) would also be solved, since EC grains would recapture the EC market share that had been lost and things like the oilseed dispute would have no further reason to exist.

11 Jean-Luc went into greater detail about the large choices for a deficiency payment system. Supports should be based on acreage rather than production levels to cut back on intensification. Supports should not be regionalized, because of the political complexities which this might engender. Aid should be "modulated" in favor of small and medium-sized farms, both to control outputs and to limit budgetary outlays. Some small international protection should be maintained, along with a set of market intervention controls. Long discussions would be necessary about the range of products which should be included.

12 Jacques Delors on "Rural Development and the Common Agricultural policy," given to the European Conference on Rural Society, Brussels, Economic and Social Committee. November 6, 1990.

13 One interesting detail about the entire plan was that there developed an agreed taboo to refrain from acknowledging that CAP reform was in any way connected to the Uruguay Round.

14 The reflections paper is *Communication of the Commission to the Council: The Development and Future of the CAP*, Com(91) 100 dated February 1, 1991 at Brussels.

15 Ripa voting against and Andriessen abstaining (on the grounds that the document would pose problems for the Uruguay Round negotiations, presumably because it was not liberal enough).

16 See *Communication of the Commission to the Council and to the European Parliament: The Development and Future of the Common Agricultural Policy*, Com(91) 258, Brussels, July 11, 1991.

17 As Jean-Charles put it, "when we're really strapped it often works to call a meeting, say, late Friday afternoon . . . then as things get along towards the moment when most people normally go home or out to eat dinner, we start to gain our advantage. When their attention begins to wander, they daydream about the drink they'd like to have or the people they'd like to see, we then turn up the heat. The longer we keep at it, the more likely we are to win. By midnight we're a length ahead of them."

18 *La Politique Industrielle dans un Environnement Ouvert et Concurrentiel: Lignes directrices pour une approche communautaire* (Com(90) 556), EC Commission, Brussels, October 30, 1990.

19 For an accessible popularization of the Commission line, see Martin Bangemann, *Les clés de la politique industrielle en Europe* (Paris: editions d'Organisation, 1992)

20 The trends in question had been largely drawn from Michael Porter's theories which were all the rage in DG III. For the key text see Michael Porter,

The Competitiveness of Nations (New York: Free Press, 1990). There were skeptics, however. One DG IV informant of mine remarked caustically that Porter and DG III argued in a circular way, "you are competitive because you are competitive."

21 The paper claimed, among other things, that the sector suffered from a lack of financial resources, partly because of insufficient risk-taking by banks.

22 This was not surprising from a DG which was a technocratic "machine to produce research programs." DG XIII's life had begun under Etienne Davignon as a task force hived off from DG III in the early 1980s to mine the EC research and development territory established by the new Esprit program. DG XIII's programs almost always had snappy acronyms like Esprit, Drive, Aim, Cost, Fast, Jessi. The Community's own publicity booklet *Research and Technological Development Policy* (Luxemburg: EC, 1988) is the most accessible introduction to EC research activities.

23 DG XIII was particularly sensitive about this after a *Financial Times* article intimated that important Commission insiders felt that the electronics crisis raised "serious questions about the value and purpose of EC [research] programs," that big electronics companies "have become unhealthily dependent on EC subsidies and trade protection," and that "EC technological support has been spread too thinly across too many projects." Finally, "blame is increasingly placed on DG XIII . . . critics accuse it of being more interested in empire building and forging cosy links with industry than in devising effective technology policies." The *FT* article focused largely on Esprit, DG XIII's bread-and-butter research program. It noted that "although Esprit has improved technical information flows between companies, it has produced little commercially useful technology." See Guy de Jonquieres, "EC aid has failed to make electronics groups competitive," and "Giving direction to the single market," *Financial Times*, October 22, 1990.

24 Part of the passion which motivated DG IV's response came from the fact that Sir Leon Brittan had not been invited to the meetings of commissioners concerned with electronics convened by Delors (which included Pandolfi and Bangemann), a slight which was corrected beginning in January.

25 Brittan gave an important speech on industrial policy to the College of Europe on January 29 which publicly expressed the internal line which he had taken in inter-Commission meetings on electronics.

26 DG IV's "industrial database," constituted out of newspaper clippings, was mainly about antitrust and merger matters and had little real information about industrial economic structures.

27 More than once she intoned that "Europe wouldn't suffer much from the collapse" of any one of the big electronics firms.

28 One official was blunt: "Check out Lamy's friends, his classmates at ENA, see what Elisabeth Guigou is up to" – Guigou was Mitterrand's Minister for European Affairs.

29 Colette Flesch, from Luxembourg, was the new Director General of the incessantly belittled DG X, for Information, while Renée van Hoof-Haferkamp was the head of Commission Conference and Interpretation Services, also

a director general's position, The latter was quite powerful, having served personally as highest level translator from the days of Jean Monnet onwards.

30 Perissich had been one of the most important appointments in Delors's attempts to "take the house in hand" by moving new and trusted people into top administrative posts. Ehlermann had been the head of Legal Services, one of the key inside figures in the Single European Act and, more recently, in preparing the papers for the IGCs and, for a while, been Delors's *porte parole*, a position which put him into daily close contact with the President. Delors did not let people as close to him functionally as Ehlermann had been without ascertaining their complete loyalty and this, in turn, demanded intense devotion and effort on the part of those so engaged. Since Ehlermann had also been an important Delors–Lamy appointment one could presume that he had been placed in DG IV, a central agency in the 1992 and after-1992 plans, so that the President would at least have an inside track to discussion of competition policy, on occasion to moderate the strong liberalism of his commissioner, Sir Leon Brittan.

31 He denounced their pointless "agitation" on the Gulf War. "We needed a President to say '*merde*, that's enough' to the Commission. I didn't have the courage to go and tell my colleagues to stop screwing things up ['*ils n'ont pas cessé de m'emmerder*'] . . . I'm not Jean Monnet, I fear."

32 The real puzzle was finding ways to coordinate public and private actions in the present which would create a positive "strategic game" in electronics. In the meantime, existing market imperfections could be invoked to justify more energetic and proactive public action than simply "taking" what the market gave. See chapter 6, "Industrial Policy and Models of Society," in Alexis Jacquemin, *The New Industrial Organization* (Cambridge, Mass.: MIT Press, 1992).

33 The very next week there was a seminar sponsored by the *cellule de prospective* reporting out research by the Boston Consulting Group on prospects – unbelievably expensive and risky – for entry into the DRAM game.

34 See Eric le Boucher, *Le Monde* April 4 and 5, 1991.

35 An interview with Alain Gomez, CEO of Thomson, in *Le Monde*, April 22, 1991, implied as much. Gomez came out and clearly demanded that the EC allow the electronics industry five years of trade protection from the Japanese. To Gomez, a European option was the best way out for the firms, but in its absence – which he clearly anticipated – "there remains what they call 'industrial policy' . . ."

36 Some time was spent, over very good food, one presumes, explaining to the firms that the EC had to work within the constraints of GATT and its own competition policy.

37 Here it was necessary to enlighten the companies that EC money would not be used to take over losses, but for new investment, and that this could only be done in certain zones, given the operations of the Structural Funds after 1988.

38 Much of this is hinted in Guy de Jonquieres's excellent *Financial Times* piece on April 29, 1991. Also involved were subsidies for research into liquid crystals.

39 The underlying logic here had been that jointly arrived at by DG XIII and the *cellule de prospective.*

40 The Council published a resolution on November 18 on electronics, See *Agence Europe*, November 22, 1991.

41 The Japanese had proposed that their MUSE system be adopted as an international norm at a global conference in Dubrovnik in May 1986.

42 Eureka was a broad European collaborative research program begun in 1985. Eureka project 95 developed an HDTV system (1,250 lines on the screen, 50 images per second).

43 MAC stood for Multiplexed Analogue Components. For the EC's first discussion of this see 86/529/EEC.

44 Directive of 3 November, 1986, 86/529/EEC, OJ L311/28.

45 The Japanese MUSE system was judged to be technically inferior while the Americans were, at that point, absent from the game.

46 Indeed, the first of these sets went on the market – at exhorbitant prices – in February 1991. Plans, underwritten by the EC, had been made to broadcast the 1992 Olympics, as well as programs at the Seville Universal Exposition, in full HDMAC to whet public appetites.

47 The group included Pandolfi, who was in charge, Brittan, Bangemann and Jean Dondelinger, and Delors.

48 Roughly speaking, the interests aligned in the following way: equipment manufacturers (Thomson, Philips, Nokia, Bosch) favored a new standard; private broadcasters (Sky (Murdoch), TF1, the German private broadcast group VPRT, and Berlusconi) were against; the public broadcasters (French and German bound favorably by their governments, RAI) favorable; satellite operators – among the majors only the Astra operators against.

49 DG X was worried about broadcasters, DG XIII was obssessed with technology, DG III concerned about regulation, and DG IV on alert against constraints on the market.

50 Patrick noted, prior to the February 20 Commission meeting, that the "elaboration of the report . . . uncovered strong divergences among the services, due in part to the imperialist style of DG XIII."

51 The paper itself noted that "European firms represent the only competitive alternative to the global pre-eminence of foreign producers, notable from South-East Asia. This situation is, however, fragile. If HD-MAC products cannot be commercialized or it their introduction is held up significantly beyond 1992, the entire European strategy in favor of HD-MAC will be compromised."

52 Jean-François Lacan, "La stratégie européenne pour la télévision haute définition devrait être réorientée." *Le Monde*, February 12, 1991.

53 Of the five choices in the DG XIII document Pascal argued strongly against the first – going directly to digital and abandoning MAC – and the second: going directly from PAL to HDMAC without the transition stage of D2 MAC. Approach 3, D2 MAC to HDMAC via a directive on standards, included six different options. From these Pascal argued for a choice between obligatory MAC except for already operating services which would have a grace period and a simulcast formula. He further argued that both went in the direction of

what Delors wanted. On the margins of his meeting agenda, among his more technical and political scribbling, was the phrase which Patrick had used earlier: "at this stage a clear message is needed."

54 Nick Costello, the young British expert on telecommunications in the Pandolfi cabinet, one day handed me a note from his computer printer which spoke more elegantly than any technical talk. In *Max Weber on Law in Economy and Society*, the great German sociologist announced that "Within those territories where it had lasting effects the French Revolution destroyed . . . every type of voluntary association which could not be expressly licensed for narrowly defined special ends, as well as all associational autonomy in general . . . The trend was reversed, however, by the economic needs of capitalism." So much for Delorist *dirigisme*!

55 The minutes of this meeting, which were circulated inside the Commission and to participants, demonstrate clearly the tone of the proceedings. The head of each branch association simply made a detailed statement of position. As this happened, the wide range of disagreement became clear.

56 On the eve of this meeting Jean-François Lacan unloaded another very sharp and critical article in *Le Monde*, March 26, 1991.

57 The MOU was meant to tie the different parties legally into a consortium to promote the diffusion of 16 × 9 television. The Directive's job would be to impose a standard.

58 Arguments about the inadequacies and, sometimes, incompetence, of various commissioners were a favorite in-cabinet line to account for unfavorable outcomes. Often it was true. In this case there were reasons to entertain a different hypothesis, however. Pandolfi was under huge pressure from inside the Commission: there were good reasons to suspect that DG XIII, his own service, was completely on the Delors-standard side. He thus mistrusted his own director general, Michel Carpentier. Keeping his cabinet in the dark was a method of making sure that presidential pressure could be controlled, since it frustrated the "horizontal" intelligence-gathering which was the basis of the Delors cabinet's game. By wandering off on his own, Pandolfi, who was also under huge pressure from the industry, could maximize his room to maneuver.

59 A "framework" draft for negotiations dated May 6 had a list of generally agreed principles concerning HDTV and the desirability of a European norm, including D2 MAC, and agreement for a consortium to "promote 16 × 9 D2 MAC" services which bound broadcasters, manufacturers, satellite operators, and cable operators to a schedule for introducing 16 × 9 programming. The Commission, finally, was to come up with an unspecified amount of money to support the consortium, plus privileged acess to the MEDIA program for HDTV production.

60 It had been difficult even to get to this point, said Patrick, since Pandolfi in his diplomatic dealings with different industry interests "seems to change his mind after each one he talks to." As this happened the substance of the planned Directive was watered down to the point where Patrick thought that the manufacturers would reject it.

61 Further talk produced little more except anxiety that unless legislation were produced soon it would be too late to prevent a regulatory "gap" between the expiration of the 1986 Directive and the implementation of the new one.

62 See "Communication de M. Dondelinger . . . relative à l'encouragement de la production audiovisuelle dans le contexte de la stratégie de Télévision à haute Définition," Brussels, European Commission, no date. The Parliament, strongly supportive, tried to soften the Directive a bit, particularly the time line for its introduction, but the *rapporteur* noted that "one thing has complicated our task, the lack of progress towards the MOU. A vicious circle has developed . . . certain actors don't want to sign [the MOU] and the adoption of the directive is conditioned by the lack of the MOU."

63 The Council adopted the Parliament's time line proposals after the Commission had refused most of them while also removing the obligation for simulcast after January 1995, replacing it with financial incentives.

64 See *Agence Europe* 5622, December 4 for the Commission's response to the Parliament; *Agence Europe* 5633 and 5634, December 19 and 20 reviews the Council deliberations.

65 *Agence Europe*, 5743, June 4, 1992, describes the plan. The Council, which deliberated on the plan in spring 1992, was divided about the amount of money involved and reached no clear resolution.

66 *Financial Times,* June 5, 1992.

67 The Rome Treaty rules on competition are in Articles 85 to 94. For a brief exposé see EC, *EEC Competition Policy in the Single Market* (Luxembourg: EC, 1989). The merger control regulation of December 21, 1989 (EEC 4064/89) is reproduced in Peter Montagnon (ed.), *European Competition Policy* (London: Royal Institute for International Affairs/Frances Pinter, 1990), Appendix II. See also Heinrich Holzer, "Merger control," chapter 2 in the same volume.

68 The Commission publishes an annual report on competition policy which gives a good idea of the range of its activities. The most recent ones, beginning with the 19th report, for 1989, the year of passage for the merger regulation, are those that count for us.

69 Already in 1990 there had been a major deal between Renault and the Commission to reduce by half a reimbursement of state aids decided in 1988: 20th Competition Policy Report, Draft, p. 242. Air France had also been obliged to reconfigure parts of its takeover of UTA. ibid., pp. 133ff. On the table was also a "state aids" case against the French PMU (the pari-mutual betting network, a sacred national institution) in which the intervention of Prime Minister Rocard had been felt. The massive aid which the French government had proposed for Bull in the context of the EC's industrial policy discussions added another enormously contentious item.

70 Almost everyone showed up, including the secretaries, except Jean-Charles, François, and Delors himself. Excellent Dutch gin was the central attraction. Pascal appeared briefly, but said little. When I asked Lodewijk and Joly about the infrequency of such events they both noted that Pascal disapproved of them. Joly then recounted a story about the most recent such event, a cocktail party given by the Brittan staff. The Delors team had met to plan their

collective strategy for this occasion – nothing that the Delors cabinet did was unreflected, apparently: "the Brittans had invited the secretaries . . . we had to figure out how to respond . . . finally we told them not to come . . . the Brittans laughed at us." They were still laughing, according to my British informants.

71 Pons had come from Paris in 1989 to the Commission's Legal Services. Prior to her assumption of Lodewijk's position, François had spent several weeks having her circulate around EC departments, especially DG IV. She was the wife of Jean-François Pons of DG II.

72 As Geneviève broke her way into the competition policy routine she quickly found herself quite as overworked as Lodewijk had been – one day she described having been in the office past midnight on Saturday pouring over state aid dossiers and they "turned out the lights, I had to find my way out using my cigarette lighter" – but handled it with grace. Both Pons and Lodewijk before her were also in charge of environment policy, and neither had enough time to give the matter justice. This was a particular problem because the Environment Comissioner, Carlo Ripa di Meana, was among those who refused to play the college game and went off on his own. Pons also regretted the time constraints because of a deep interest in environmental issues.

73 For the legislation see Supplement 2/90 of the *EC Bulletin*.

74 François knew competition policy inside out. And his political background implied that he had few liberal doubts about voluntaristic industrial policies. This fact was reinforced by his Commission background: He had been one of Viscount Davignon's key aides in putting together the Davignon plans to restructure European iron and steel a decade back. He also shared with Delors a burning passion for developing European-level competitiveness.

75 Alcatel-Alsthom-CGE, the mother company of Alcatel, was a giant in electricity as well as the prime contractor for the French TGV trains.

76 See the Commission's press release, IP(91)303, April 12, 1991. For greater detail, see the ruling – Affaire no. IV/MO42: Alcatel/Telettra.

77 The other European players were Varta/Bosch (together 23%), Tudor (14%), and Hawker (6%). The top three world players were US and the fourth Australian.

78 Article 2, paragraph 2, EEC 4064/89.

79 This was consistent with his simultaneous movement against the German merger of Varta and Bosch in car batteries.

80 A great deal was made of the need for battery companies to grow larger in order to support the research and development needed to develop electric cars.

81 See Commission press release IP(91)415.

82 Boeing had purchased de Havilland Canada a few years before from the Canadian government, with the idea that synergies might exist which would allow it to move into a new market segment, but had subsequently decided that conditions were not favorable

83 The Canadians were not concerned per se with antitrust issues, but rather with

Aérospatiale-Alenia's intentions about future investment and production at de Havilland's Toronto plant. Would the Europeans push forward to expand the de Havilland product line, or would they replace it by the ATR line and turn the Toronto operations towards subcontracting for the European planes? How much money were the Europeans prepared to invest? How much employment would be maintained? The Canadians, and Ontario in particular, were undergoing a very serious recession and were profoundly worried, for industrial policy reasons, about de Havilland. The conservative Canadian federal government and the social democratic provincial government were also at loggerheads about how to deal with the situation. In this setting the ATR consortium was playing hard ball to get as much Canadian help for the takeover as possible, while giving as few promises in exchange as it could get away with. See Jeanne Laux, "The Tories and industrial policy," *Canadian Forum*, March–April 1992.

Chapter 5   Reading the Non-Papers

1 NATO's very quick proposal to establish a European-manned rapid deployment force, which would be under British command and which might conceivably be "double-hatted" with WEU, was a shrewd play to these concerns.
2 The Americans were caught in something of a time bind, however, because international changes had moved so fast that NATO was without a new strategy, such that the Alliance was itself busily engaged in retooling while the EC itself discussed such matters. It was no accident, therefore, that Secretary of State Baker had despatched his loyal assistant Robert Zoellick to give a major speech about the "New Atlanticism" to the Atlantic-Brücke in later April.
3 The EBRD had great difficulty deciding what its place might be. As a "merchant bank" to facilitate private investment it ran up against the decided reluctance of private investors to move into unstable Eastern Europe. As a "technical assister" it hesitated to step on the toes of powerful donors to its own capital, the EC in the first instance. Finally, Jacques Attali's verbal and financial extravagance – both evident in the Bank's opening, was frowned upon by many key professionals.
4 For a particularly useful, if strongly critical, evaluation of Western responsibilities, see Peter Gowan, "East Central Europe: forced decollectivization or development," *World Policy Journal*, Winter 1992.
5 Moreover, things had been further complicated by the rapid collapse of COMECON trade patterns and the disintegration of the Soviet Union. Earlier the CEECs had been able to trade to their east, however unsatisfactory the arrangements. Henceforth this possibility was limited. Generating substitute exports to the West has proved very difficult.
6 The USSR was promised 500 million ecus in food and humanitarian aid in later 1990, which was held up until difficulties with the Balkans were resolved. Then, as the Soviet Union dissolved it became very difficult to know how to deliver

what had been promised. Later, a further 1,250 million ecus were loaned to the new Commonwealth states.

7 In this context, increasingly insistent requests for more money from the CEECs, especially when accompanied by acerbic criticisms of the ways in which PHARE operated, made Brussels officials ever more irritable. Furthermore, moving the G-24 operation beyond its initial stage of emergency aid into "closer to the market" areas of technical assistance, training, and efforts to find targets and sources of investment proved very complicated.

8 Morgan Stanley estimated that, other things being equal, the 7 million unemployed in the CEECs in 1991 could well become 19.2 million in 1992 and 25 million by 1995: Morgan Stanley International, *Eurostrategy* 14, London, January 9, 1992, cited in Bernard Cassen, "Un plan Marshall pour les pays de l'Est?" in *Le Monde Diplomatique*, February 1992. Cassen estimated that the CEECs could well need upwards of $100 billion annually to overcome their difficulties – compared to the roughly $40 billion over several years actually pledged.

9 The negotiating directives were adopted in December 1990 involving the development of political dialogue, economic cooperation, harmonization of legislation, cultural cooperation, and some reference in preambles about prospects for later joining the EC. Poland, Hungary, and Czechoslovakia were the countries in question.

10 On agriculture the EC's proposals were rejected outright. On textiles the EC proposed tying the opening of the market to the Uruguay Round over ten years. The CEECs rejected this.

11 In the early autumn 1991, at a critical point in the political "marination" of the CAP reform, violent protests by French farmers against the small amounts of Eastern European meat which had slipped into the Community demonstrated what might happen.

12 See *Europe Documents* no. 1646/47 (September 7, 1990) for the *Cadre Général des accords d'association (accords européens) entre la CEE et les pays d'Europe Central et Orientale, défini par la Commission Européenne.*

13 In Delors's words, "others are talking in terms of immediate Community membership . . . as if the [CEECs] . . . were ready, economically and politically, to embrace pluralist democracy and operate a market economy; as if this scenario raised no financial or institutional problems. Perhaps I should remind them that Spain and Portugal spent seven years preparing." Speech to European Parliament, *Bulletin of the European Commission*, Supplement 1/90.

14 Spain and Portugal had both applied for membership very soon after the collapse of their dictatorships and, even if it took several years to reach agreement, the prospect of membership had been economically and politically very important to each. It had not escaped the CEECs' notice that when Spain and Portugal had applied the actual disparity between their economic circumstances and those of the more advanced Community members was hardly smaller than those between the CEECs and EC members.

15 Andriessen argued that the principles of "derogation" from Community obliga-

tions had been useful in the past and should be considered again. In particular, "a member state's need to catch up economically does not prevent it from accepting binding commitments in the field of security or defense." For a concise exposition of this see Frans Andriessen, "The integration of Europe: it's now or never," *European Affairs*, December 1991.

16 See Finn Laursen, "The Community's policy towards EFTA: regime formation in the European economic space," *Journal of Common Market Studies*, June, 1990; Helen Wallace and Wolfgang Wessels, "Towards a new partnership: the EC and EFTA in the wider Western Europe," EFTA *Occasional Paper 28* (Geneva, 1989).

17 EFTA member states were not allowed to negotiate bilaterally and would also be required to deal *en bloc* later with the EC in the administration of the new EEA.

18 EFTA was understandably reluctant to give the EC the two-pillar, "take it or leave it" decision structures that the EC proposed, advocating instead full fledged meetings of 19 member states.

19 EFTA agriculture was even more highly subsidized and protected than the EC's.

20 This was one of the most difficult issues. The Community wanted a deal in which access to the Single Market gave EC fishermen access to EFTA fishing resources in exchange. Iceland, following its post-Cod War policies, refused to allow anyone into its territorial waters and was willing to forgo EEA altogether to maintain this position. The Spanish and Portuguese wanted new fishing rights to come out of EFTA shares, particularly those of Norway.

21 The Austrians and the Swiss were both adamant about not allowing full and free transportation through their Alpine passes, on environmental grounds.

22 The application finally came in winter 1992.

23 Much later *The Economist* published an intelligent paper on these things: "Why Brussels Sprouts," December 26, 1992–January 8 1993.

24 See Conf-UP/91, *Non-Paper, projet d'articles de traité, en vue de mise en place d'une union politique* (Brussels, April 17, 1991).

25 For a sharp journalistic account of these dynamics, see *The Economist*, April 2, 1992. The Delors team did not find everything about the non-paper bad. If Luxembourg had "bracketed" extensions of qualified majority voting for later discussion, it had accepted many of the Commission's suggestions about new and redefined competencies. "Competence" clauses on education and consumer rights had been added, for example.

26 The non-paper's proposals on co-decision were based on an earlier proposal by Genscher and De Michelis and were probably the highest common denominator obtainable, given French and British opposition to much change.

27 A number of such areas were already broached, including EC activities in the CSCE, disarmament, issues surrounding nuclear non-proliferation, and security issues with economic pertinence such as technology transfer in armaments areas and arms exports.

28 The WEU Treaty would run out in 1998, necessitating either renegotiation or

termination.

29 The final, June, version of the non-paper included a long list of changed provisions for old EC "competencies" on research and development and the environment plus new ones on energy, "trans-European networks" in transportation, telecommunications and energy infrastructures, public health, education, training and youth, culture and cultural patrimony, consumer protection, cooperation and development, and industrial policy. Ultimate consecration of most or all of these areas could, in the logic of the EC, take on considerable future importance, even though their wording was conservative and, for the most part, decision rules – qualified majority or unanimity – were bracketed. See Annex VI to Sec(91) 1189, dated June 10, 1991, Minutes of 21st COREPER meeting on Political Union, May 31, 1991. Annex VIII of the same document presented an extremely interesting polling of member states about the expansion of qualified majority voting in general which did not cover the new "competence" areas. All member states, except the UK, were willing to extend qualified majority voting in the social area. The British, not surprisingly, systematically refused to contemplate any new qualified majority voting.

30 *Financial Times*, April 8, 1991.

31 François expressed considerable unhappiness with Joly Dixon, Jean-François Pons, Giovanni Ravasio, and David Williamson – the EMU team – who were, he thought, ready for a low-cost deal on EMU which, in particular, leveled any Community pretensions for economic policy setting. This would turn EMU into what François called a "budgetary" arrangement. He added that Williamson was prepared to concede on social policy. François also announced, revealingly, that Delors had stopped both sets of concession, but François had been the direct instrument. When Delors was asked what had happened, he announced to those concerned that "François did it."

32 The Germans had wanted to allow certain opt-out possibilities for harmonization which Noël had accepted and there had also been waffling on the cooperation procedure. Delors wanted to stop him, but feared the disruption that this might cause. François recollected Delors then saying, "if you do, I'll disavow it." François had been barely 35 years old at the time, Noël was his boss and, more important, had virtually run the Commission for many years. He then recalled the many other occasions, including the Delors package, when many in the Commission entourage had wilted in the heat of difficult bargaining. He and Delors had been the major barriers to important concessions, he claimed, which would have amounted to "1992 on the cheap."

33 Minutes of Fifth Ministerial Meeting on Political Union (May 13–14, 1991) Sec(91) 962, pp. 3–4.

34 Perhaps the highlight of this was a lunch gathering around Delors in Brussels of the "Action Committee for Europe" on May 28. The lunch was chaired by Jacques Chaban Delmas, and attending were Alfred Dregger (president of the CDU/CSU group in the Bundestag), a representative of the leadership of the SPD, Etienne Davignon, Peter Sutherland, Gaston Thorn, Max Kohnstamm, and others. The communiqué which they produced was strongly federalist and

they each went out to lobby where they could in this direction.

35 See minutes of the 20th Permanent Representatives discussion (May 28, 1991), Sec(91) 1106, Annex 1. The Commission also proposed amendments to the CFSP provisions in the same message.

36 The Portuguese and Irish remained open, Denmark lukewarm, the French hesitant, and the British opposed.

37 See Conf-UP 1826/91, June 14, 1991.

38 He then criticized the Luxembourg proposals for being built on a conception of two different entities – CFSP and EC – rather than on a unified Community. He concluded that the role of the Commission should be reinforced in the process in order to endow it with greater coherence. Minutes of the Fourth Ministerial meeting of the IGC on Political Union (April 15, 1991), Sec(91) 749, pp. 1–5.

39 This was something of a concession, in fact, since the US had earlier been strongly opposed even the limited autonomy for WEU that the Luxembourg non-paper proposed. See minutes of the 16th meeting of COREPER on Political Union, Sec(91) 927, May 13, Annex IX.

40 See, in particular, the discussion with van den Broek in the *Wall Street Journal Europe* on April 26, with its theme that Western security was indivisible. The US had to be kept in Europe, in large part to prevent smaller countries like the Netherlands from being dominated by the bigger European powers. The French were signaled out, partly because "its presidential system . . . allows it to impose its will on EC states run by fragile coalitions" like the Dutch.

41 Americans had been in Europe in pursuit of their own interests, the French noted. With the end of the Cold War American interests would prove much less intense, hence the need for the Europeans to reconstruct their own defense. Mitterrand was simultaneously preparing his "European Confederation" conclave for Prague in June. The event would turn into a fiasco.

42 Kohl visited Washington in the third week of May, where he was the object of assiduous attention.

43 See *Le Monde*'s account of the ministers' meeting, June 6, 1991.

44 See Sec(91) 1106/2, Annex to Minutes of 20th Meeting of Permanent Representatives on Political Union (June 6, 1991).

45 The Germans had even proposed giving the Parliament the right of legislative initiative. The Commission was adamantly opposed.

46 See Sec(91) 749, Minutes of Fourth Ministerial Meeting on Political Union (April 15, 1991), pp. 5–7.

47 Delors, from European Parliament debate on political union, April 17, 1991.

48 The entire idea of distinguishing between "laws" – which implied certain institutional processes – and other Community legislative instruments strongly divided the member states throughout the first stages of negotiation. By mid-June, when the personal representatives reviewed the Luxembourg use of the term in its new text, the Spanish, Irish, Dutch, and British all opposed the idea of "law." The Danish were also opposed, but to their minds the real issue was not "law" but the actual extent of co-decision which it would imply, since co-decision would occur on matters of law. See Minutes of the 23rd Meeting of

Personal Representatives on Political Union, June 13, 1991, Sec(91) 1295, pp. 2–3.

49 Minutes of Sixth Ministerial Meeting on Political Union, June 17, 1991, Sec(91) 1351, pp. 5–8.

50 The 15th and 17th Personal Representives Meetings both discussed the social clauses, covering and recovering the same ground in each case. See Sec(91) 864 of April 24, just after the Luxembourg non-paper, and Sec(91) 957 of May 6, 1991.

51 See Sec(91) 864, Annex IX.

52 Patrick Venturini and Carlo Savoini of DG V were the main sources of support. Savoini was something of a financial godfather for ETUC and the sectoral European Industry Committees.

53 The Spanish paper is reproduced in Annex XIX of Sec(91) 631, dated April 2, including minutes of the 12th COREPER meeting of March 25–26, 1991.

54 The paper pointed to Article 2 of the Rome Treaty, the Werner and MacDougall Reports (1970 and 1977), the 1987 Padoa-Schioppa report and, finally, the Delors Report of 1989.

55 Annex IV in Sec(91) 962, dated May 15, 1991, minutes of the Fifth Ministerial Meeting on Political Union (May 13–14, 1991).

56 Good examples were discussions of the role of the EC Monetary Committee in EMU, the bulk of which was entrusted to the Monetary Committee itself, and consideration of proposed statutes for the new central banking system, worked up by the Central Bank governors. On the first see Sec(91) 636, dated April 5, 1991, Minutes of the seventh COREPER meeting on EMU (April 2, 1991). On the statutes of the Central Banking System see Sec(91) 963, dated May 13, 1991, Minutes of the 10th COREPER meeting on EMU, May 10, 1991.

57 See Sec(91) 1218, dated June 11, 1991, Minutes of the Sixth Ministerial EMU Meeting (June 10, 1991).

58 She added further that the Delors–Pascal shared propensity to neglect ritual "coordination" and refrain from "stroking" the troops was demoralizing. Delors had an unfortunate habit of calling Commission meetings during summer vacations, for example, and neglected holiday celebrations.

59 This resonated with remarks I had heard from cabinet members themselves. Jean-Charles, whose whole life depended upon rapid cooperation from the services, even queried over lunch one day whether other cabinet members had noticed that "there is more and more bad work rising up through the system these days."

60 In part Millan assumed an overdetermined role. His portfolio involved advocacy for the EC South, so he was always demanding more resources and always calling attention to the limits which insufficient resources caused.

61 A good example of this was his proposal for a separate Environmental Fund (LIFE) which made good sense but which was prepared and publicly announced largely outside usual Commission operations. Ripa drove Lodewijk Briet and his successor in the Delors cabinet, Geneviève Pons, to distraction by such techniques, even though both were fundamentally sympathetic to Ripa's genuine commitment to environmentalist causes.

62 DG XXII coordinated the Structural Funds – necessitated, in theory, because the major Structural Funds were scattered through DG VI (agriculture), DG V (social), and DG XVI (regional policy). DG XXIII was to do the same for "Enterprise Policy." Each of these had about 50 people. The two task forces had been tacked on to the Commission organigram as new tasks had appeared, in the interests of flexibility, but at the cost of influence.

63 Many in targeted areas were thereby also granted time to organize resistance.

Chapter 6 Turning Point – Onward or Downward?

The epigraph appears in Delors, *Le nouveau concert européen* (Paris: Odile Jacob, 1992), p. 270 (drawn from an interview in the French magazine *Belvedère*, October 15, 1991).

1 See *Agence Europe*, no. 5524, June 30, 1991, for the presidency conclusions of the European Council.

2 This was largely to weaken the Spanish position that cohesion had to be brought into the treaty negotiations themselves. The Delors speech is reproduced in Annex 1 of Sec(91) 2052, Minutes of the 31st Permanent Representatives Meeting, October 17–18, dated October 22, 1991. He presented a measured defense of what had been done since the first Delors package, while recognizing the problems which existed in addition to granting that Spain – for whom the exercise was primarily designed – was in a particularly difficult situation. Spain, he noted, "given the size of its population and because of the fact that all of its regions are not underdeveloped . . . benefits less than the other countries from the structures in place both in terms of revenues and expenditures . . ." Delors had all kinds of proposals for what to change – increasing the Structural Funds, the institution of an environmental fund to help less developed areas conform to the Community's environmental policies, CAP reform, hints at a more progressive system of EC funding which would tie contributions to prosperity, and a range of programs to compensate and cushion less-developed regions against EMU convergence and possible short-term shocks. In fact, little progress was made. The Spanish sensed that the IGCs were their moment to move.

3 This was, of course, a classic case of a powerful member state seeking to offload responsibility for a set of very difficult domestic policy issues on to the Community. But it might move in the directions of minimizing the content of the "third pillar" and Community "state building" for which Delors and the Commission had hoped. Pascal Lamy was pleased. "Kohl really saved us a lot of time there," he noted, implying that had the Commission brought forth such proposals the process would have been lengthy and difficult. See *Agence Europe*, 5523, June 29, 1991, p. 5.

4 Indeed, the Yugoslavian situation had taken up most of the first day of the summit, pre-empting agenda time which might otherwise have been devoted to the IGCs. See *Agence Europe*, 5523, June 29, 1991, p. 3.

5 The Slovenians had desperately tried to get Delors's attention in March, but Delors had refused to receive them.

6 See *Agence Europe*, June 29, 1991, 5523, p. 8 for the text.

7 The French military was configured for East–West conflict plus police operations in existing or former colonies. Any Yugoslav operation would have involved extended conventional warfare commitment with large numbers of troops on the ground. The French were not ready for this.

8 Henry Wynaents, the former Dutch Ambassador to Yugoslavia, was the head of the initial EC mediating group and wrote a revealing book about his experiences, *L'Engrenage* (Paris: Denoel, 1992).

9 At Brioni the Community persuaded Slovenia and Croatia to defer implementing their declarations of independence and secured permission to send 50 monitors to oversee the cease-fire in Slovenia.

10 The Dutch and UK wanted to delay the conference because of the scale of the fighting. The French and Germans wanted to call it right away before things got worse. See Trevor Salmon, "Cracks in European unity? Testing times for European political cooperations: the Gulf and Yugoslavia, 1990–1992," *International Affairs*, April 1992.

11 Despite a typically triumphalist Luxembourg announcement on June 18 that a deal had been done – which the Norwegians later denounced – disagreements about fish, Alpine transit, and the cohesion fund persisted. See *Agence Europe*, 5551, August 23, 1991.

12 They were trade in agricultural goods (where the CEECs unhappily produced commodities in abundance which were virtually the same as those which the EC produced in mountains), textiles (which the Portuguese were very worried about), and labor movement. In part the talks were troubled because the CEECs knew full well that the Commission would propose a change in its bargaining mandate in September. See *Agence Europe*, 5562, September 7, 1991, p. 7.

13 This meant, of course, that the neutral Austrians (and the other neutrals in the wings) would be obliged to accept a CFSP which would include some ties to WEU.

14 Delors had a propensity for calling Commission meetings in August, usually to respond to crises, which often happened in August – perhaps another sign of the menaces to the European model of society. This was resented in the house.

15 Pascal had done double duty in July. As Delors's "sherpa" for the G7, he had to do the final preparation for the London summit, which involved more intense weekend meetings on top of those that had preceded the European Council. The G7 was important to Delors and the Community, first of all because of the British presidency, which would be a test of John Major's intentions and capacities.

16 The EC Audit Court would two years later have strong words of criticism about the ways in which aid to the former USSR was distributed.

17 See Delors's remarks at Luxembourg in *Agence Europe*, 5522, Friday June 28, 1991, p. 7.

18 The document was circulated by the Commission on September 24 as Sec(91) 1778.

19 Not surprisingly, on defense, the Dutch were more Atlanticist than the Luxembourg non-paper had been, affirming the complementarity between NATO and WEU in unambiguous ways.

20 *Agence Europe* provides a detailed reading of all these changes, in nos 5566 (September 13, 1991), pp. 3–8; 5574 (September 25, 1991), pp. 3–4; and 5575 (September 26, 1991), pp. 3–4.

21 Sec(91) 1829, Minutes of the 26th Meeting of Permanent Representatives, September 26, 1991.

22 The Dutch had ineptly united otherwise disagreeing member states to make "Black Monday" inevitable. Dutch federalism united an "anti-federalist" camp including the usual members – the UK, Denmark, and Portugal. Strongly integrationist member states concluded from this that the Luxembourg non-paper was the best deal possible in the circumstances and calculated that they would gain from sinking the Dutch non-paper in order to oblige others to accept some version of Luxembourg's initial conclusions. The British, the most important anti-integrationists, would thus find themselves under stronger pressure to make concessions. For an excellent account of this coalition juggling see David Buchan, "EC sails towards safe harbour," *Financial Times*, October 2, 1991. See also *Agence Europe*, no. 5577, September 28, 1991, p. 3.

23 The Commission, on the basis of a report from McKinsey, the consultants, estimated that the Japanese would quickly take nearly 30% of the European market, other things being equal. See Martin Bangemann, *Les clés de la politique industrielle en Europe* (Paris: Éditions d'Organisation, 1992), pp. 117–18; "Impact of Japan's EC auto deal," *Financial Times*, September 26, 1991.

24 The famous MIT study of car production was devastating in its assessment of European efficiency. See James Womack, Daniel Jones and Daniel Roos, *The Machine That Changed the World* (New York: Macmillan, 1990).

25 Nissan, Honda, and Toyota had built major assembly plants in the UK, while Honda had bought a major stake in Rover, the major remaining British manufacturer.

26 Lamoureux, as we have mentioned, was a veteran of the Davignon steel years, had a strong Delorist "European organized space" view on industrial policy and, finally, was in constant touch with the French government and French carmakers.

27 The "agreement" was, in fact, a series of different documents and bargains. The fullest exposition of the deal was published by the French Parliament. See *Agence Europe*, no. 5647, January 16, 1992.

28 The French parliamentary report indicated that Andriessen had made a "conclusive oral statement" to the Japanese on this subject, and that, in the event transplants exceeded their projected numbers, the Japanese would cut back on direct imports.

29 Calvet clearly wanted the EC to establish something like the existing French situation of high protective barriers against the Japanese. Failing this, he

argued for strong French nationalism. For those wanting a compact compendium of all the most negative French feelings about Maastricht and the EC see "Maastricht, le théâtre de l'ambigu," by Jacques Calvet, CEO of Peugeot, in *Le Monde*, April 9, 1992, p. 2.

30 In the elegant phraseology of *Agence Europe*, this text was "prepared in close cooperation with bodies representing the motor vehicle industry, given that most of the efforts to be made will be the responsibility of the firms" – no. 5720, April 30, 1992.

31 See Com(92) 166 final, *The European Motor Vehicle Industry: Situation, Isues at Stake, and Proposals for Action* (Brussels, May 8, 1992).

32 See ibid., pp. 13ff. The new training proposals assumed the new Article 123 of Maastricht. The program, something of a gift to the companies, was to occur without insisting upon any "social" trade-offs from the companies. This upset DG V, Mme Papandreou, and the ETUC. Moreover, since it represented a major new expenditure from the European Social Fund which would occur largely outside regional policy guidelines, it also upset DG XVI and Bruce Millan.

33 Ibid., p. 10. Research and development was to be focused upon "technological priority projects geared towards developing key technologies and achieving a better return on R&D investment in terms of industrial competitiveness." Projects would be generated "bottom up" from firms, in ways which would encourage inter-firm cooperation. The market orientation of research and development was one of the goals of the internal market DG III and high-tech DG XIII, but anathema to Brittan and competition policy DG IV.

34 Sec(91) 629, *La promotion de l'environnement compétitif pour les activités industrielles basées sur la biotechnologie dans la communauté* (April 16, 1991).

35 Com(91) 335, *Nouveaux défits aux industries maritimes*, Brussels, September 6, 1991.

36 This is Bangemann's general point in *Les clés*, Part 2, chapter 1.

37 For a concise and "official" statement of the general outlook, see Alexis Jacquemin and Jean-François Marchipont, "The new Community industrial policy," *Revue d'Économie Politique*, 102(1), January–February 1992. Jacquemin was the leading economist of the *cellule de prospective* and Marchipont the head of DG III's industrial policy unit.

38 Jouyet, a young French Catholic Leftist who was president of one of Delors's French "clubs," had also been brought on board as a potential successor to Pascal Lamy, who, rumor had it at the time, was one of two competitors to become Directeur du Trésor in France.

39 The breakdown was into groups of 20 and below, 20–39, 40–59, and 60-plus. ATR–de Havilland would control 50% of the world and 67% of the EC market for 20–70-seat planes.

40 DG III presented data that showed how much market share would change if the parameters of market share were altered. If operational aircraft no longer sold new were included ATR–de Havilland's share went down considerably, as it did when the market included 19-seat planes and/or regional jet aircraft.

41 He even threatened to resign from the Commission if the ruling was not accepted.

42 This kind of local implantation had become a common strategy in aircraft production. The actual intentions of ATR remained mysterious even to Brittan, however. His cabinet eventually concluded that ATR itself was divided about the desirability of the deal. It was under pressure from its own employees on the jobs issue. Moreover, de Havilland was a troubled plant, anachronistically organized – it was almost completely integrated and made most of what went into its planes – and suffered from labor rigidities.

43 Petite had been key to the Cockfield cabinet after 1985, an important person in the Scrivener cabinet (following the indirect taxation dossier) and then, briefly, in – of all places – the Merger Task Force of DG IV.

44 There was also a backlash against Brittan *inside* the Commission, led by Bangemann, who wanted to remove Brittan's exclusive powers in competition policy and share them out to the other commissioners and services directly implicated. Nothing came of this.

45 De Havilland was bailed out by the Canadian and Ontario governments and then practically given away (for roughly $100 million) to Bombardier, a Quebec conglomerate that made a specialty of accepting industrial gifts from various governments.

46 See Sec(91) 1326, *Communication to the Commission from Sir Leon Brittan, July 2, 1991, Subject: Improving transparency in the financial relationship between public authorities and public companies.* The communication itself, destined to member states, is in Sec(91) 1321.

47 Delors and the cabinet judged both the Brittan and the Cardoso schemes to be "extremist," in the words of Jean-Luc Demarty, in charge of the Cardoso dossier. They hoped to see deregulation very slowly phased in over a long, staged, period. Eventually Brittan's strong proposal was beaten back, and a softened version of the Cardoso proposal was accepted. The documents are published in *Agence Europe*, nos 1756 and 1757, January 28 and 29, 1992.

48 See *Agence Europe*, nos 5582 and 5583 (text of the Anglo-Italian document entitled *Declaration on European Security and Defense*), October 5 and 7, 1991.

49 For the full texts see *Agence Europe*/Documents 1735 (Anglo-Italian) and 1738 (Franco-German), October 17, 1991.

50 See "The Alliance's new strategic concept," *NATO Review*, December, 1991. Also the Rome Declaration on Peace and Cooperation, *Agence Europe*/Document 1744, November 13, 1991.

51 Here it was a matter of qualified majority voting and in what circumstances, or unanimity.

52 The Dutch proposed including research framework programs, multi-annual environmental programs, the missions of the Structural Funds, blueprints for trans-European networks, and the principles and program in the development area.

53 The Parliament made its unhappiness clear in the monthly "interinstitutional conferences" but little further budging was to be expected. See, for example,

the minutes from the October 1, interinstitutional conference (Sec(91) 1924) and, more pointedly, those from the November meeting (Sec(91) 2123), when most of the dies were already cast.

54 See the Minutes of the Ninth Ministerial Meeting on Political Union, Sec(91) 2093, October 28, 1991 (dated November 4, 1991).

55 One of the more interesting changes of the fall followed the introduction by the Germans of a text on harmonizing and Communitarizing asylum laws. See Sec(91) 1960, Minutes of 28th and 29th COREPER on Political Union, October 10–11, 1991, Annex 2, dated October 15. This came as a complement to another German proposal to create a "Europol" police coordination agency. The full list of proposals for new competencies from member states and Commission included trans-European networks, transport safety, public health, development policy, education, culture, energy, industrial policy, tourism, civil protection, youth and animal protection. See Richard Corbett, "The Intergovernmental Conference on Political Union," *Journal of Common Market Studies*, XXX(3) (September 1992), pp. 287–8.

56 See Sec(91) 2084, Minutes of 32nd and 33rd COREPER Meeting on Political Union, October 24–25, 1991 (dated November 4).

57 Then he listed eight problems where big issues were left to resolve (including whether or not to have a 1996 revision clause, what basic structures, the CFSP, judicial and home affairs, co-decision, competencies, economic and social cohesion).

58 On the matter of competencies, the easiest, Delors thought, it was a matter of deciding whether Maastricht was to produce a major Rome-style treaty, or a less ambitious Single-Act document. Beyond this, he posed the classic Delorist question of whether the EC was primarily a market or something greater – particularly in the area of industrial policy.

59 Sec(91) 2093. Delors's speech, the first exposition of the fruits of Jean-Charles Leygues's second Delors package efforts, is reprinted in Sec(91) 2158, November 11, 1991.

60 It is impossible to know, within certain narrow limits, how effective Delors's and the Commission's efforts in the last stages actually were. Frans Andriessen, reporting to the Commission after the November ministerial "conclave" at Noordwijk which boiled down most of the debate on questions to be passed to Maastricht, announced that, at least on Commission competencies, the "result was better than could have been hoped for" on matters like the right to withdraw legislation, space for Commission initiative on foreign policy and immigration, and the general interinsitutional equilibrium.

61 By trying to calm down the Spanish Delors was currying favor with the northeners in addition to guarding against one of the more important threats to a Maastricht deal. At the same time, however, by proposing to deal with cohesion through his second package he was preparing the ground for the package's success *after* Maastricht, and thus strengthening the Commission's position in the "after 1992" moment that would then open.

62 The circuitous course of the Commission's Directive on maternity leave in the fall of 1991 was exemplary. Over time the amount of income to be guaranteed

in maternity leave was whittled down to a bare minimum while its nature was transformed into "sick pay."

63 In an expanded Article 118 the Community could "sustain and complete" the action of member states, under qualified majority in the Council, in the area of health and safety (as in the Single European Act) plus working conditions, information and consultation of workers, equality between men and women regarding the labor market and treatment at work, the integration of people excluded from the labor market (training). In addition, action on a unanimous basis was proposed on social security and social protection, the "representation and collective defense of interests of workers and employers, including cogestion" (excluding wages, trade union rights, the rights to strike and lock-out). See Sec(91) 2160, Tenth Ministerial, Annex 2.

64 The joint letter and treaty proposals from ETUC General Secretary Emilio Gabaglio, UNICE's Zygmunt Tyskiewicz, and Mr Ellerkmann, General Secretary of CEEP, the public sector employers' association, are included in Annex IV of the Minutes of the 37th COREPER Meeting on Political Union, November 7, 1991 (dated November 8).

65 The text is reproduced in Sec(91) 2146, dated November 11, 1991.

66 The matter of decision rules on joint actions remained very sticky. Those who opposed common action (the UK, Denmark, and Portugal) insisted instead upon unwieldy rules which would make timely decision-making very difficult.

67 *Agence Europe*, no. 5509 of November 15, 1991 gives a good review of the Noordwijk discussions. Delors's major contribution was to suggest that the competency discussion could be made easier with a shorter and more meaningful list by pruning the existing shopping list of unimplementable and vague commitments.

68 See Sec(91) 2322, Commission declaration about the two IGCs dated November 27, 1991. The document was republished as *Les enjeux de Maastricht* by the EC French Delegation (Paris: EC, 1991), p. 10.

69 *Enjeux*, ibid., pp. 15–18.

70 Much of the rest of the Commission's paper was designed to translate the treaty discussion into simple language, commend the Dutch for introducing the "Committee of Regions" as an analogue to ECOSOC (the consultative Economic and Social Committee), and to urge simplifying the list of competencies and allowing more qualified majority voting.

71 For this non-paper see Annex 1 to Sec(91) 1381/2, Minutes of the 13th COREPER Meeting on EMU of July 2, 1991, dated July 8, 1991.

72 See ibid., Annex 2, for the Dutch agenda and timetable.

73 See Sec(91) 1441, Minutes of 14th COREPER EMU Meeting on July 9, 1991, dated July 11, 1991.

74 See Sec(91) 1381/2 for this discussion.

75 See Annex 1 of the Minutes of the 14th COREPER Meeting on EMU, September 3, 1991, dated September 4.

76 At this point in 1991 American Express judged that only three current EC members would meet the convergence criteria – Luxembourg, France, and Denmark – with Germany itself excluded. Among potential EFTA members of the EC by the time a decision to move to stage 3 would be in order, only

Austria and Norway would fit. See *Agence Europe*, 5573, September 23–24, 1991, p. 15.

77 The Dutch non-paper can be found in Annex 1 of Sec(91) 1910, Minutes of the 18th EMU Meeting of COREPER, October 1, 1991 (dated October 10, 1991).

78 President Baron of the Parliament also pushed strongly for a definitive date for transition to stage 3, a stronger EMI in stage 2 and, above all, the introduction of much more substantial mechanisms for democratic scrutiny of the EMU processes and institutions.

79 Dixon, "A message from Mr Jacques Delors," to the first international conference on the statistical aspects of financial instrument denominated in ecu, Luxembourg, *Eurostat* Doc. 60E, September 24, 1991.

80 This point is made in M. J. Artis, "The Maastricht road to Monetary Union," *Journal of Common Market Studies*, XXX(3) (September 1992), p. 305.

81 In the matter of monitoring the Commission had to fight to protect its monopoly to propose. In that of enforcing the issue was whether, and to what extent, to block member state efforts to monetize deficits. See Sec(91) 2056, Minutes of the 19th COREPER Meeting on EMU, October 22, 1991 (dated October 25, 1991).

82 When in late October Delors cited to the Parliament the absence of discussion of social matters in EMU – and that, in consequence, the IGC had "focused too much on the budget and currency" – he was making this point. That it fell on deaf ears was painful, but eventually there would be a showdown on social policy, and the themes had to be raised wherever and whenever appropriate. See *Agence Europe*, 5596, October 25, 1991, p. 9 for excerpts from Delors's speech.

83 See Sec(91) 2060, dated October 30, 1991. Dutch Finance Minister Wim Kok's accompanying letter is in Annex 1 of Sec(91) 2143, Minutes of the 20th COREPER Meeting on EMU, November 4–5, 1991 (dated November 11, 1991).

84 The Dutch also tried to settle the matter of how to strengthen the ecu, proposing to fix the currency composition of the ecu basket at the start of stage 2. The Germans led the charge against this and the proposal was ultimately defeated. The Germans were unhappy as well about proposals to endow EMI with its own capital, which made it "too supranational," and this became another final Maastricht issue. The Dutch paper left open important dimensions of the excessive-deficit procedure for Maastricht, in particular the actual quantitative criteria, along with the specific definition of clauses for financial assistance to member states in exceptional circumstances. See Sec(91) 2143.

85 Once again Delors gave a magisterial exposé on his package plans to the November ministerials while Commissioner Christophersen did similarly to the November interinstitutional conference. See Delors in Sec(91) 2193, Minutes of the Ninth EMU Ministerial, November 11–12, 1991 (dated November 14, 1991) and Sec(91) 2181/2 on November 29, 1991, which reproduces Christophersen's speech to the November 12 interinstitutional conference on

EMU.

86 See Sec(91) 2428, Minutes of the 11th (and last) Ministerial Meeting of the EMU IGC, December 2–3, 1991 (dated December 4, 1991).

87 Since Mitterrand himself was the agent, through Roland Dumas, for making the proposal, and given Mitterrand's secretiveness, it is not easy to know where it came from originally. François Lamoureux, well ensconced on the second floor of Matignon next door to "Edith," may have had some small degree of paternity, however. According to his version, the "irreversibility" suggestion came from him at a special interministerial meeting on November 28 – the only such meeting called by a French prime minister since the beginning of the IGCs. In any event, Delors had sent François to Paris in have him in a position to do such things.

88 The Germans were not simply pushing the brakes to the floor, although it is true that they were also doing this. The French proposal had apparently been drawn up in some haste and the 1999 clause, as presented, would allow member states which had not fulfilled convergence conditions to participate in the final vote – something which, in the minutes, is underlined that the French "had not foreseen."

89 The British and Danes rejected this approach. The problems over whether the EMI in stage 2 would be "supranational" – symbolized by the presence of officers who were not Central Bank governors and the existence of genuine EMI capital reserves – was also largely resolved by allowing a token president and "resources" for the EMI which would be voluntarily "put at the disposition" of EMI by national banks with some posssibility for EMI to manage these reserves.

90 The French wanted to bind the Commission to an obligation of transmitting directly to the Council the demands of any member state about EMU. The Commission managed to limit this to a short list of matters.

91 For the Commission's fuller views, see the French Delegation's *Les enjeux de Maastricht*, pp. 47–67.

92 This was pretty much the original ASOLO list from the Rome II European Council of December 1990.

93 WEU would be governed politically by the "union," while it would look towards NATO in operational realms.

94 Policies on asylum, the rules concerning external border crossings and their control, immigration policies, drugs, international fraud, cooperation in civil matters, cooperation in penal matters, customs cooperation, police cooperation on terrorism, drug trafficking and other major international crime concerns.

95 The "Protocole sur la Politique Sociale" and the "Accord" spelling out the engagement are on pp. 196–201 of the official Traité sur l'Union Européenne (Luxembourg: CEE, 1992).

96 Patrick Venturini, monitoring Maastricht by telephone calls to Pascal's secretary, Claire, was pleased by the social protocol. He had been afraid up to the very last minute that either the British would force agreement on a completely watered-down social section or that some form of generalizable "opting out"

would be devised. The "deal by 11" meant at last that some of Patrick's legislation might pass and, quite as important, that the "negotiate or we'll legislate" provisions might energize social dialogue.

Chapter 7   Last Sprint Towards European Union

The speech in the first epigraph (to the European Parliament on February 2, 1992) is published in full in *Bulletin of the European Communities*, Supplement 1/92 (EC: Luxembourg, 1992). For the third epigraph see Commission of the European Communities, *Growth, Competitiveness, Employment: The Challenges and Ways Forward into the 21st Century* (White Paper, December 1993), *Bulletin of the European Communities*, Supplement 6/93 (EC: Luxembourg, 1993), p. 10.

1 The Delors staff documentalists had been told that "the Breydel" was neither strong nor large enough to handle all the records which the Delors presidency had accumulated over the years. Moving meant that they had to "downsize" the files. The dark corridors of the Berlaymont were thus piled high with dossiers and documents which would end up in the trash – a scholar's nightmare!

2 "Edith's" government in Paris could never overcome its bad start and it was ended by its most fervent advocate, President Mitterrand, in spring 1992. François Lamoureux eventually returned to Brussels, working for a time in Legal Services before eventually becoming a director in DG III for Industrial Policy, in autumn 1993. Putting François in such a pivotal position was a smart appointment. He, perhaps more than anyone else who might have gotten the job, believed in the need to "organize" Europe's industrial space.

3 Hugo Paemen, for example, an original para-cabinet member, was now chief Uruguay Round negotiator. Nicolas Van der Pas, one of Zepter's predecessors, was central in the EEA dealings with EFTA countries, Claus-Dieter Ehlermann, former Delors press secretary, had become head of DG IV, Michel Jacquot, former agricultural operative in the cabinet, head of the EAGGF, etc. Gunther Burghardt and Lodewijk Briet, among others, were already hard at work upstairs in the Breydel devising schemes and structures for the CFSP. There was increasingly another source of recruitment to the core of Delors's and Pascal's skeleton of reliable people: external appointments – often French.

4 The Social Protocol meant new reflection on legislation "at 11." Which of the outstanding Directives would be best to reintroduce to test the "social partners,' " desire to negotiate? Patrick and Delors were already leaning towards the proposal for "information and consultation" which was part of the Social Charter. The process was carried out in 1993–4.

5 Since the entire program could not be completed in time, Delors wanted to make certain that at least the most symbolic policies were in place so that "1992" really did involve a Europe "without [most] borders."

6 The Commission had abruptly held up several important British civil engineering projects because of British slowness in completing environmental impact

reviews.

7 Ripa had done end runs on the college to announce new policy initiatives before they had gone through the usual processes, among other things. The Ripa problem would soon be partly resolved, however. After Italian elections di Meana went off to become a minister in the Italian government.

8 Jean-Charles, on top of personnel matters, noted that "60% of DG XI people are external appointments, off the usual Community career line, and they are overwhelmingly Green activists." Pascal added that, from his experience, the Environmental Council of Ministers itself was a "Green club."

9 There is an interesting sidelight to this. Fabrice, *énarque* and *normalien*, had come from the French Cour des Comptes to serve primarily as Delors's principal speech-writer. But Pascal had a routine to induct, train, and test newcomers from outside which involved rapid *tours de piste* around the Commission and, as with Fabrice, through the cabinet's own history. Trying to piece together how the first Delors package had been put together was no easy task. There was a slim paper trail, but not much more. Fabrice's paper turned out to be a first-rate piece of research on Commission policy development, and passed Pascal's first test with flying colors. Pascal had also called a rare cabinet afternoon seminar meeting in February 1991 to think through the issues of the second package.

10 Leygues had taken on the job of outlining the second Delors package in the middle of the electronics imbroglio and the "screening" exercise. Jean-Charles thus had to set his alarm for 2 a.m., work for two hours, then go back to sleep at 4 a.m. before getting up to drive his daughters to school after breakfast.

11 The Spanish would later insist upon a near doubling of the Structural Funds – after the initial doubling in the first Delors package – reforms in their working, plus a "cohesion fund" to go to Southern member states (the Structural Funds going to regions) to compensate for the disproportionate financial impact of environmental policies, trans-European network expenses and, above all, EMU convergence programs, on poorer countries.

12 This new category of expenses had already become substantial in *ad hoc* ways, in fact – expenditures outside the Community had doubled after 1988 largely because of demands for aid from ex-Communist countries and former Soviet republics.

13 EC Commission, *From the Single Act to Maastricht and Beyond: The Means to Match Our Ambitions*, Com(92) 2000 final (Brussels: EC Commission, 1992), also published in *Agence Europe* documents, 1762/63, February 19, 1992.

14 See also *The Community's Finances between Now and 1997*, Com(92) 2001 (Brussels: EC Commission, 1992). Michael Shackleton's "The Delors II budgetary package," in *The European Community 1992, Annual Review of Activities*, ed. Neill Nugent (Oxford: Blackwell/*Journal of Common Market Studies*, 1993) is indispensable. Table 1 provides a good breakdown of the proposed figures.

15 For the final Commission proposals on reform see Com(91) final (Brussels: EC Commission, 1991). The Commission published a readable summary of what

was at stake in the CAP reforms as *Agriculture in Europe, Development, Constraints and Perspectives* (Luxembourg: EC, 1992).

16 A penultimate Portuguese presidency paper concentrated on three central problems – how big a reduction in grain prices was sustainable, how much compensation should go to farmers (replacing price supports) and whether it would be temporary or permanent, and milk quotas.

17 The US had just announced retaliatory measures against the EC on soybeans, following condemnation of EC practices by a GATT panel. See *Agence Europe*, 5722, May 4, 1992,

18 The raspberry regulation involved special measures for raspberries intended for processing. The UK insisted upon it to help out Scottish growers.

19 For a review of the complicated adjustment deals which were necessary, see *Agence Europe*, 5735, May 22, 1992. The citation is from the *Financial Times*, May 22, 1992.

20 For a summary and references to the legislative texts, see European Commission, *XXVIth General Report on the Activities of the European Communities, 1992* (Brussels/Luxembourg: EC, 1993), pp. 168–70. For the Council agreement see Council of the EC, General Secretariat, Press Release 6539/92, 1579th Council Meeting – Agriculture, May 18–21 (Brussels: Council of the EC). See also Alan Swinbank, "CAP reform, 1992," *Journal of Common Market Studies*, 31(3) (September 1993).

21 The Commission asserted that more than half the EC's farmers were aged over 55, a fact which led to a reconfiguration of the early retirement package already in practice. Since the vast majority of these farmers have no heirs as practitioners of agriculture, some of the political strength of agriculture was bound to decline in any event.

22 Italy's presence on this list was unusual, prompted by discovery that Italy might soon become a "net contributor" to the EC. This was not true, according to Michael Franklin's modelling, presented in *The EC Budget* (London: Royal Institute of International Affairs, 1992). Franklin's calculations, summarized in *The Economist*, December 12, 1992, showed the four net contributors in 1992, with Germany, approximately triple in per capita net contribution at 140, next Britain at 52, France at 26, and the Netherlands at 7. Italy was fifth in 1992, slightly beneficiary, but likely to fall into the other column as a result of the second Delors package.

23 Lionel Barber, *Financial Times*, September 14, 1992.

24 The areas of particular concern were foreign policy, culture, and education. One of the great ironies was that a principal leader in the anti-Maastricht struggle and one of the petitioners to the Karlsruhe Court was Manfred Brunner, a Bavarian Free Democrat who had resigned from his position as *chef* of Martin Bangemann's cabinet to take up the anti-Maastricht crusade.

25 For the Bundesbank's first major post-Maastricht pronouncement see *Agence Europe*, 1764, March 2, 1992.

26 These included the single currency and the "European citizenship" proposal to allow foreign EC citizens to vote in local elections.

27 François Mitterrand's speech introducing the process is reproduced in *Le Monde*, April 14, 1992.

28 A good example of this was the contribution of Peugeot-Citroën CEO Jacques Calvet in *Le Monde*, April 9, 1992.

29 Perhaps the best anti-Maastricht document from this period is Marie-France Garaud and Philippe Séguin, *De l'Europe* (Paris: Le Pré aux Clercs, 1992). For an excellent, thoughtful reflection on the debate see also Laurent Cohen-Tanugi, *L'Europe en danger* (Paris: Fayard, 1992).

30 For background on the Danish case see the papers in Morten Kelstrup (ed.), *European Integration and Denmark's Participation* (Copenhagen: Copenhagen Political Studies, 1992). See also Jens-Henrik Haahr, "European integration and the Left in Britain and Denmark," *Journal of Common Market Studies*, March 1992.

31 The Irish protocol to Maastricht (no. 17) stated simply that the new treaty should not be construed to prevent the application of Article 40.3.3 of the Irish Constitution.

32 For an excellent review of the Yugoslav imbroglio in 1991 see Eric Remacle, *La politique étrangère européenne: de Maastricht à la Yougoslavie* (Brussels: GRIP, 1992).

33 Respect for a set of human rights instruments, respect for frontiers, respect for minority rights, respect of Yugoslav international engagements in international affairs (disarmament, nuclear non-proliferation, regional stability, etc.).

34 In private Jacques Delors could barely contain his fury and despair about this, not simply because of such political damage, but because it was not in his nature to stand aside and countenance the massive settling of historical scores which was underway in Yugoslavia.

35 See Hans J. Nielsen, "The Danish voters and the referendum in June 1992 on the Maastricht Agreement," in Kelstrup, *European Integration and Denmark's Participation*.

36 For a sampling of the variety of Danish "no" views see Hanne Norup Carlsen, Ross Jackson and Niels I. Meyer (eds), *When No Means Yes: Danish Visions of a Different Europe* (London: Adamantine Press, 1993).

37 The Danes had supported membership in 1972 by 63–37% and ratified the Single European Act in 1986 by but 56–44%. See Toivo Miljan, *The Reluctant Europeans* (London: Hurst, 1977).

38 Female "nos" could have been for both programmatic and employment reasons. Denmark had developed a classic Scandinavian welfare state whose staffing was strongly feminized. Anxiety about the welfare state flowed from budgetary threats which the Danish government had already made as much as worries about the fiscal effects of intra-EC transfer payments implied by "social and economic cohesion."

39 Ayres and Geyer dichotomize the yes–no split as (a) rich and well educated vs poor and poorly educated; (b) bourgeois (party) voter vs voters from left and right oppositional groups; (c) non-environmentalists vs. environmentalists; and (d) active and interested vs apathetic and parochial: Jeffrey Ayres and Robert Geyer, "Defying conventional wisdom: political opposition to integration in Denmark and Canada," unpublished paper for the 1993 Meeting of the American Political Science Association.

40 Delors had been talking more generally about institutional implications of enlargement in the context of preparing the Lisbon summit and many in the press, particularly in the UK, inaccurately attributed the Andriessen leak to Delors.

41 The hard-line opposition was on the far Left – the Left Socialist Party – which argued that the EC was not sufficiently social democratic and the far Right, the Progress Party, which argued that it was not sufficiently neo-liberal.

42 The non-EC venue of this meeting may seem strange. Most of the participants were at a NATO meeting in Oslo, hence the hasty convocation of the others to Oslo.

43 François's reflections can be found in François Lamoureux, "Subsidiarité: mode d'emploi," unpublished paper for a conference of the Mouvement Européen in Paris on February 6, 1993 "Démocratie et subsidiarité dans l'Union Européenne." As an illustration of the kind of detailed meddling which Community action should avoid he cites a wonderful example drawn from a November 1991 Directive on pork production (no. 91/630) "Pigsties should be built in order to allow each pig to lie down, rest and get up again without difficulty, to have its own place to rest, and to see other pigs."

44 The paper, which began to circulate in the autumn in preparation for the Birmingham European Council, was called the "Proposal for an interinstitutional agreement on the principles of subsidiarity," Sec(92) 1990, final version dated October 27, 1992, summarized in *Agence Europe*, 5833, October 10, 1992.

45 The Luxembourg and the Greek parliaments would both ratify Maastricht in July.

46 *The Economist*, June 20, 1992, has a good review of the British position.

47 These things had often played a role in past relationships between France and Europe. beginning in the EDC, continuing in the negotiations around the Rome Treaty, and reaching their climax in the high Gaullist years of the early 1960s when De Gaulle tapped deep French feelings in blocking British entrance to the Community, insisting upon the Plan Fouchet, proceeding to the "empty chair" episode, and crafting the Luxembourg compromise.

48 Jacques Julliard, *Le Nouvel Observateur*, September 16, 1992.

49 Results and analysis can be found in *Le Monde*, September 22, 1992.

50 The French were the major EC oilseed producers. For a good general overview of the Uruguay Round from a French vantage point see "Multilatéralisme: le GATT en crise," in *Ramses 93* (Paris: IFRI, 1993).

51 US tactics were designed to panic business interests into pressuring the EC to concede more on agriculture in general while the mobilization of American farm lobbies was very visible. The Americans wanted subsidized oilseed exports cut by 50%. Outstanding issues in agriculture at this time, beyond oilseeds, included the volume of subsidized EC exports – the US demanded that it be reduced by 24% with the Commission willing to go only to 14% (the French refused even this and were willing to talk of reductions only in financial terms, not in terms of trade volume). The Americans invoked an earlier draft Uruguay Round "final act" in support of their position. There were persistent differences on whether the CAP's new deficiency payments were subsidies, but

here there was some flexibility. There was firm disagreement about how much protection the EC would be allowed to have on non-grain products in exchange for the dramatic reductions in subsidized grain exports. Finally, the EC wanted the Americans to sign a "peace clause" in which they would renounce future confrontations on issues which the Uruguay Round settled. See *Agence Europe*, 5835, October 14, 1992 and *The Economist*, October 24, 1992.

52 Mitterrand threatened to boycott the Birmingham European Council in October if a Uruguay Round deal involving more EC concessions were on the table.

53 Delors was within his rights in doing so, since he was one of the four commissioners officially charged with conducting the GATT dealings. MacSharry's version of what happened was published in the *Irish Times* December 15, 1993.

54 Earlier, at his press conference after the Birmingham European Council, Delors had used one of his inimitable "family" metaphors to urge that the "adolescent" EC demonstrate its maturity by saying "no to its big brother." On the Chicago situation see *Agence Europe*, 5853, November 7, 1992; *Financial Times*, November 7, 1992 and *The Economist*, November 14, 1992, p. 52.

55 Both sides were to cut export subsidies by one third and refrain from further challenges to subsidy arrangements for a period of six years. The Community agreed to reduce farm subsidies by 20%. The EC was allowed to exclude acreage subsidies from the calculation. The text of the press release about the Blair House agreement is in *Europe Documents*, no. 1811, November 26, 1992.

56 It also provided a dangerous precedent for the Center-Right government which was certain to run France after the 1993 elections and pandered to anti-EC sentiments in France.

57 Even Helmut Kohl allowed himself to attack the Commission in the fall of 1992, claiming that it was "too powerful, constantly expanding and exterminating national identities," cited in the *Financial Times*, September 25, 1992. EC civil servants had began to resent the new difficulties into which their leaders had plunged them as well. See Jean de la Guérivière, "Les mal-aimés de Bruxelles," in *Le Monde*, October 13, 1992. Jean de la Guérivière is the author of an excellent brief introduction to the world of the Eurocrats, *Voyage à l'intérieur de l'Eurocratie* (Paris: Le Monde Éditions, 1992). One of the immediate responses of the Commission was to think about improving its public relations work, a response which usually went along with castigation of DG X, whose job it was to handle Commission public relations. This led to the commissioning of a consultant's report from a French advertising expert which was naively shown off to the public in early 1993 and laughed into rapid obscurity. The consultant recommended selling the Commission with techniques worthy of soap or sports shoes. Delors, in the meantime, had developed some more creative thoughts on communications and transparency, including assigning a commissioner the direct task of dealing with member state parliaments on European issues (former Portuguese Foreign Minister de Pinheiro was actually given this task in the third Commission under Delors, in early 1993). See "Brussels tries to plug an information gap," *Financial Times*, October 26, 1992.

58 David Marsh's recent *The Bundesbank: The Bank That Rules Europe* (London: Heinemann, 1992) provides a shrewd overview of the "Buba's" position. See also John Goodman, *Monetary Sovereignty: The Politics of Central Banking in Western Europe* (Ithaca: Cornell UP, 1992).

59 The most exhaustive review of the ERM events of 1992–3 is in David Cameron's "British exit, German voice, French loyalty: defection, domination and cooperation in the 1992–93 ERM crisis," delivered at the 1993 Meetings of the American Political Science Association.

60 There may have existed a serious imbalance between the funds in trade and the capacities of Central Banks to constrain outcomes. A currency trader was quoted about Black Wednesday in the *Financial Times*, September 16, 1992, as saying "the central banks were buying sterling and the rest of the world was selling. It was not context." From Cameron, ibid., p. 9.

61 The ERM had not been realigned since 1987, in fact. Ruud Lubbers, the Dutch Prime Minister, later announced that the failure to arrange a realignment was "a black page in the book of 1992."

62 At the Bath Council the British and others put strong pressure on the Germans to lower rates but the Germans refused. In the following days the Bundesbank asked the German government to work for a realignment. This message was never fully conveyed to the others, largely an error of omission by the French Treasury Director, Trichet, who was also secretary of the EC Monetary Committee. As a result, with the pound coming under heavy pressure and the lira being devalued, the Bundesbank lowered its rates only slightly, not enough to stop the movement. When Schlesinger, Bundesbank President, remarked to a German business paper that a large realignment was needed, a huge new rush on the pound occurred. The best recapitulation of these events is in the *Financial Times*, December 11, 1992.

63 In consequence Delors had done little to discourage the fatal and premature transformation of the EMS into a system of quasi-fixed exchange rates.

64 Cameron, "British exit, German voice, French loyalty," pp. 31–8, presents a detailed review of this Franco-German struggle.

65 A hastily called European Council at Birmingham in October did little to confront outstanding issues, however, except to set the agenda for the all-important Edinburgh summit in December. A discussion on subsidiarity produced little new clarity, with conclusions put off to Edinburgh in December. In the meantime the Commission would continue to work at a declaration about "subsidiarity" to reassure the public that the Community really did want to become "closer to its citizens." Much of the discussion on subsidiarity was based on preliminary papers from the Commission, the Council's Legal Services reflecting on the implications of Maastricht's Article 3B, and a COREPER report for the Council Legal Services: see *Agence Europe*, 5832, October 9, 1992; for the COREPER document see *Agence Europe*, 5833, October 10, 1992. The German memorandum is summarized in *Agence Europe*, 5834, October 12–13, 1992. The rest of the Birmingham agenda-preparing involved Foreign Ministers trying to find a way to help the Danes to hold another referendum on Maastricht, finance ministers looking more carefully at economic problems,

reviews of the second Delors package proposals, and further reflection on enlarging the Community.

66 The document, "Denmark at the heart of Europe," was submitted on October 30. It made clear that the Danes wanted to opt out of stage 3 of EMU (the single currency), and any common defense policy, desired further clarification about European citizenship and its relationship to Danish citizenship, justice and internal affairs cooperation in "Pillar 3," and wanted the Community to make some kind of gesture about transparency and subsidiarity. Subsequently Delors and others had made it crystal clear that any scenario which would involve renegotiation of Maastricht was not allowable.

67 Such matters would pass either by a five-sixths majority in its Parliament or by a combination of simple parliamentary majority and referendum.

68 The text can be found in part B of the presidency conclusions of Edinburgh as reproduced in *Agence Europe*, 5878, December 13, 1993. Richard Corbett's "Governance and institutional developments," in *The European Community 1992*, ed. Neill Nugent, p. 35, provides a dense summary of the European Council's "decision" on Denmark (a highly irregular ruling, in fact, for which the EC treaties made no provision).

69 For the "British list" see *Agence Europe*, 5873, December 7–8, 1992. Beyond social legislation, the British suggested a number of environmental regulations as targets for their anti-Commission diatribe.

70 This was particularly directed to the Commission in its proposition force role. It was enjoined to hold maximal pre-legislative consultations, and carry out careful justification of new proposals in terms of subsidiarity and self-monitoring in executive behaviors.

71 The pre-Edinburgh deal was that enlargement talks could begin only after Maastricht ratification.

72 See *Agence Europe*, 5867, November 28, 1992. Shackleton, in Neill Nugent (ed.), *The European Community 1992*, in Table 1, p. 13, compares the Commission's original proposal with the British counterattack and the final result.

73 For the text see Council of the EC, *European Council in Edinburgh 11–12 December, 1992: Conclusions of the Presidency.*

74 The Schengen countries were well on the way to achieving the program, but a number of important details of the computer and police system needed to track people once internal border controls were removed were not yet in place. The three non-Schengen EC members (the UK, Ireland, and Denmark) were outside these matters.

75 See *Agence Europe*, 5878, December 13, 1992, Appendix 4 to Part A of Presidency Conclusions.

76 The Schluter government had fallen in the meantime, leading to a changed coalition in which the Social Democrats assumed leadership. This gave the socialists a much greater stake in the outcome and they pulled out all the stops, as did the virtual totality of the Danish political class, trade union leadership, and business elites. In this context the persistent strength of the "nos," again led by intellectuals (Drude Dahlerup, a sociologist, was the most prominent figure) and "ex-68ers" and supported by less well-off strata in the population,

was significant.

77 It took months before the issues were resolved. The central issues posed involved "basic human rights" in the German Basic Law, which plaintiffs claimed would be violated by the implementation of Maastricht. The rights in question involved the possibility of loss of sovereignty in a number of areas, particularly EMU, without proper consultation. More generally the appeals were premised on the failure of Maastricht to include sufficient remedies for the Community's democratic deficit while simultaneously proposing major shifts of sovereignty in the monetary area, echoing the positions of the Kohl government all along. Ironically one of the leaders in bringing cases to the Karlsruhe Court – there were several – was Manfred Brunner, who had been Martin Bangemann's *Chef de Cabinet* in Brussels. See Peter Norman, "Maastricht casts its shadow across Germany," *Financial Times*, June 28, 1993.

78 See the *Financial Times*, July 24–25, 1993, for extensive commentary on the vote.

79 See *The Economist*, July 17, 1993, for a good review of the developing situation.

80 For a good review of the setting see the *Financial Times*, July 24–25, 1993 and *The Economist*, July 31, 1993.

81 The Franco-German couple felt the strains of the moment very deeply. The usually discreet Edouard Balladur blamed the Germans publicly. The Germans did not appreciate this any more than the words the British had spoken in September 1992. The Franco-German relationship had lived through crises before, however. Balladur was very careful in the immediate aftermath not to lower French interest rates abruptly, indicating both to the Germans and, quite as important, to impatient elements in French business and his own majority, that his government remained committed to a strong franc policy. Helmut Kohl, while admitting publicly that the situation would slow down the EMU timetable for "a year or so," a statement which infuriated Delors, was quick to announce that nothing fundamental had really changed in his government's commitment to Maastricht and European Union.

82 The words are Lionel Barber's, from the *Financial Times*, August 3, 1993.

83 Burghardt and his small staff also quite quickly began putting together a set of modest proposals for initial CFSP "joint actions."

84 Doing so also made it possible to give the competition policy portfolio to Karel Van Miert, a socialist whose pro-Delors performance had been one of the few success stories of the second Commission under Delors.

85 A number of dispersed industrial policy matters were moved to DG III, where François Lamoureux took charge of them. DG V was also "taken in hand" with the coming of the new Social Affairs Commissioner Padraig Flynn, but the results were uncertain.

86 The major automobile firms, in serious financial problems, led the way. Mercedes changed its corporate strategy altogether, locating an assembly plant for the first time in North America, while Volkswagen went on a four-day week to begin long overdue restructuring.

87 Major's statement, which infuriated Delors, appeared in *The Economist*, September 25, 1993, pp. 27–9.

88 Member state submissions are reproduced in detail, and mainly in their original languages, in Part C of the White Paper, published in a separate volume of the *Bulletin of the EC*, Supplement 6/93.

89 The sums proposed were quite large and were very carefully scrutinized by ECOFIN. Much of the money over the first years had already been budgeted in the second Delors package. See the *Financial Times*, December 13, 1993.

90 Work-sharing, where firms were able to promote it "from below" (the document cited Volkswagen) was fine.

91 Lionel Barber, in the *Financial Times*, November 24, 1993.

Conclusions: The Delors Strategy at the End of the Day

1 Jean Monnet, *Mémoires* (Paris: Fayard, 1976), pp. 420–1.

2 Thatcher then goes on, revealingly, to note that "the Foreign Office was almost imperceptibily moving to compromise with these new European friends." *The Downing Street Years* (New York: HarperCollins, 1993), pp. 558–9.

Bibliography

Andriessen, Frans, "The integration of Europe: it's now or never," *European Affairs*, December 1991.

Armstrong, P., Glyn, A. and Harrison, J., *Capitalism Since 1945* (Oxford: Oxford University Press, 1991).

Artis, M. J., "The Maastricht road to Monetary Union," *Journal of Common Market Studies*, XXX(3) (September 1992).

Attali, Jacques, *Verbatim* (Paris: Fayard, 1993).

Bangemann, Martin, *Les clés de la politique industrielle en Europe* (Paris: Éditions d'Organisation, 1992).

Bellier, Irène, *l'ENA* (Paris: Seuil, 1993).

Boltho, Andrea (ed.), *The European Economy* (Oxford: Oxford University Press, 1982).

Boudan, Joel and Gounelle, Max, *Les grandes dates de l'Europe communautaire* (Paris: Larousse, 1989).

Brugmans, H., *Prophètes et fondateurs de l'Europe* (Bruges: Collège de l'Europe, 1974).

Bulmer, Simon and Wessels, Wolfgang, The *European Council* (Basingstoke: Macmillan, 1987).

Burley, Anne-Marie and Mattli, Walter, "Europe before the court," *International Organization*, Winter 1993.

Cameron, David, "The 1992 initiative: causes and consequences," in *Europolitics*, ed. Alberta Sbragia (Washington: Brookings, 1992).

—— "British exit, German voice, French loyalty, defection, domination and cooperation in the 1992–93 ERM crisis," unpublished paper for the American Political Science Association annual meeting, 1993.

Camps, Miriam, *Britain and the European Community 1955–1963* (Oxford: Oxford University Press, 1964).

Caporaso, James, "And it still moves! State interests and social forces in the European Community," in *Governance Without Government: Order and Change in World Politics*, eds James N. Rosenau and Ernst-Otto Czempiel (Cambridge: Cambridge University Press, 1992).

Capotorti, François et al., Le *Traité d'Union européenne, Commentaire du projet adopté par le Parlement européen le 14 février 1984 (Brussels:* Éditions de l'Université de Bruxelles, 1985).

Cecchini, Paolo, The *European Challenge* (Aldershot: Wildwood House, 1988).

Cohen-Tanugi, Laurent, *L'Europe en danger* (Paris: Fayard, 1992).

Committee for the Study of Economic and Monetary Union, *Report on Economic and Monetary Union in the European Community* (Luxembourg: EC, 1989).

Corbett, Richard, "The Intergovernmental Conference on Political Union," *Journal of Common Market Sutdies*, XXX(3) (September 1992).

de Gaulle, Charles, *Discours et messages*, Vol. IV (Paris: Plon, 1970).

—— *Mémoires d'espoir,* Vol. II, *L'Effort* (Paris: Plon, 1971).

—— *Lettres et carnets*, Vol. IX (Paris: Plon, 1986).

Dekker, Wisse, Philips, *Europe-1990* (Eindhoven: Philips, 1985).

Delors, Jacques, *Changer* (Paris: Stock, 1975).

—— *En sortir ou pas*, with Philippe Alexandre (Paris: Grasset, 1985).

—— *Impératif et urgence de l'Europe communautaire* (Paris: Bureau de Représentation en France de la Commission des Communautés Européennes, 1990).

—— *La France par l'Europe* (Paris: Clisthène-Grasset, 1988), translated as *Our Europe* (London: Verso, 1991).

—— *Le nouveau concert européen* (Paris: Odile Jacob, 1992).

Delors, Jacques et al., *1992 le défi* (Paris: Flammarion, 1988).

Demkas, Dimitrios et al., "The effects of the Common Agricultural Policy of the European Community," *Journal of Common Market Studies*, 2 (1988).

de Ruyt, Jean, *L'Acte unique européen*, 2nd edn (Brussels: Éditions de l'Université Libre de Bruxelles, 1989).

Dossier: The European Council (Luxembourg: Group of the European People's Party of the European Parliament, 1991).

Doutriaux, Yves, *La politique régionale de la CEE* (Paris: Presses Universitaires de France, 1991).

Duchêne, François et al., *New Limits on European Agriculture* (London: Croom Helm, 1985).

EC Commission, *Perspectives for the Common Agricultural Policy* (Brussels: EC, 1985).

—— *Completing the Internal Market. White Paper from the Commission to the European Council* (Luxembourg: EC, 1985).

—— *A Common Agricultural Policy for the 1990s* (Luxembourg: EC, 1989).

—— *EEC Competition Policy in the Single Market* (Luxembourg: EC, 1989).

—— *Vademecum sur la réforme des fonds structurels* (Luxembourg: EC, 1989).

—— *Draft treaty amending the treaty establishing the European Community with a view to achieving Economic and Monetary Union* (Sec(90) 2500), Brussels, December 10, 1990.

—— *La Politique Industrielle dans un Environnement Ouvert et Concurrentiel: Lignes directrices pour une approche communautaire* (Com(90) 556).

—— *Political Union* (Luxembourg: EC, 1990).

—— *The Impact of German Unification on the European Community* (Luxembourg, 1990).

—— *Communication of the Commission to the Council and to the European Parliament: The Development and Future of the Common Agricultural Policy* (Com(91) 258), Brussels, July 11, 1991.

EC Commission, *Communication of the Commission to the Council: The Development and Future of the CAP* (Com(91)100), February 1, 1991.

—— *La promotion de l'environnement compétitif pour les activités industrielles basées sur la biotechnologie dans la communauté* (Sec(91) 629), April 16, 1991.

—— *Les régions dans les années 1990* (Luxembourg: CEE, 1991).

—— *Nouveaux défis aux industries maritimes* (Com(91) 335), Brussels, September 6, 1991.

—— *Premières Contributions de la Commission à la Conférence Intergouvernementale "Union Politique"* (Sec(91) 500) (Brussels: Commission, 1991).

—— *Rapport annuel sur la mise en oeuvre de la réforme des fonds structurels* (1989 Luxembourg: CEE, 1991; 1990 Com(91) 400, December 4, 1991).

—— *Rapport final sur le choix des normes devant mener à l'introduction de la télévision à haute définition en Europe* (Sec(91) 315).

—— Sec(91) 418, EC Commission, Brussels, 26 February 1991.

—— *From the Single Act to Maastricht and Beyond: The Means to Match Our Ambitions* (Com(92) 2000 final) (Brussels: EC Commission, 1992), in *Agence Europe*.

—— *The Community's Finances between Now and 1997* (Com(92) 2001) (EC: Brussels, 1992).

—— *The European Motor Vehicle Industry: Situation, Isues at Stake, and Proposals for Action* (Com(92) 166 final,) Brussels, May 8, 1992.

—— *XXVIth General Report on the Activities of the European Communities, 1992* (Brussels/Luxembourg: EC, 1993).

EC Council Secretariat, CONF-UEM 1701/90.

—— CONF-UEM 1608/91.

—— Conf-UP/91 *Non-Paper, projet d'articles de traité, en vue de mise en place d'une union politique* (Brussels, 17 April, 1991).

—— Annex 1 to Sec(91) 1381/2, Minutes of the 13th COREPER meeting, July 2, 1991.

—— Sec(91) 1441, Minutes of 14th COREPER EMU meeting on July 9, 1991, dated July 11, 1991.

—— Sec(91) 1910, Minutes of the 18th EMU meeting of COREPER, October 1, 1991.

—— Sec(91) 2056, Minutes of the 19th COREPER meeting on EMU, October 22, 1991.

—— Sec(91) 2060, dated October 30, 1991.

—— Sec(91) 2084, Minutes of 32nd and 33rd COREPER meeting on Political Union, October 24–5, 1991.

—— Sec(91) 2428, Minutes of the eleventh Ministerial meeting of the EMU IGC, December 2–3, 1991.

—— Sec(91) 1381/2.

—— "Press Release 6539/92" 1579th Council Meeting – Agriculture, 18–21 May, 1992.

EC French Delegation, *Les enjeux de Maastricht* (Paris: EC, 1991).

Eisinger, Peter, "The conditions of protest behavior in American cities," *American Political Science Review*, 67 (1973).

Emerson, Michael, *What Model for Europe?* (Cambridge, Mass.: MIT Press, 1988).

Esping-Anderson, Gosta, *The Three Worlds of Welfare Capitalism* (Princeton: Princeton University Press, 1990).

Europe Documents no. 1646/47 (September 7, 1990) for the *Cadre Général des accords d'association (accords européens) entre la CEE et les pays d'Europe Centrale et Orientale, défini par la Commission Européenne.*

—— no. 1682, January 10, 1991.

—— no. 1688, February 1, 1991.

European Economy, 44 (1990).

—— "The economics of EMU, special issue", 1990.

Favier, Pierre and Roland-Martin, Michel, *La décennie Mitterrand*, Vol. 2 (Paris: Fayard, 1991).

Fox-Piven, Frances and Cloward, Richard, *Poor People's Movements: Why They Succeed, How They Fail* (New York: Vintage, 1979).

Fursdon, Edward, *The European Defence Community: A History* (London: Macmillan, 1980).

Garaud, Marie-France and Seguin, Philippe, *De l'Europe* (Paris: Le Pré aux Clercs, 1992).

Garrett, Geoffrey, "International cooperation and institutional choice: the European Community's internal market," *International Organization*, Spring 1992.

George, Stephen, *Politics and Policy in the European Community* (Oxford: Clarendon, 1985).

Gillingham, J. R., *Coal, Steel and the Rebirth of Europe, 1945–1955* (Cambridge: Cambridge University Press, 1991).

Giscard d'Estaing, Valéry, *Le pouvoir et la vie*, 1 (Paris: Compagnie 12, 1988).

Goetschy, Janine, "Le dialogue social européen de Val Duchesse," *Travail et Emploi*, 1 (1991).

Goodman, John, *Monetary Sovereignty: The Politics of Central Banking in Western Europe* (Ithaca: Cornell University Press, 1992).

Gourevitch, Peter, *Politics in Hard Times* (Ithaca: Cornell University Press, 1986).

Gourevitch, Peter, Martin, Andrew, Ross, George et al., *Unions and Economic Crisis: Britain, West Germany and Sweden* (London: Allen and Unwin, 1984).

Gowan, Peter, "East Central Europe: forced decollectivization or development," *World Policy Journal*, Winter 1992.

Grant, Charles, *The House That Delors Built* (London: Nicolas Brearley, 1994).

Haahr, Jens-Henrik, "European integration and the Left in Britain and Denmark," *Journal of Common Market Studies*, March 1992.

Haas, Ernest, *The Uniting of Europe: Political, Economic and Social Forces* (Stanford: Stanford University Press, 1958).

—— *Beyond the Nation State: Functionalism and International Organization* (Stanford: Stanford University Press, 1964).

Hamon, Hervé and Rotman, Patrick, *La deuxième gauche* (Paris: Ramsay, 1982).

Hellman, John, *Emmanuel Mounier and the Catholic Left, 1930–1950* (Toronto: University of Toronto Press, 1981).

Herzog, Philippe, *Europe 92: construire autrement et autre chose* (Paris: Messidor, 1989).

Jacquemin, Alexis, "Industrial policy and models of society," in Alexis Jacquemin, *The New Industrial Organization* (Cambridge, Mass.: MIT Press, 1992).

Jacquemin, Alexis and Marchipont, Jean-François "The new Community industrial policy," *Revue d'Économie Politique*, 102(1), January–February 1992.

Jenkins, Roy, *European Diary* (London: Collins, 1989).

Jouve, Edmond, *Le Général de Gaulle et la construction de l'Europe*, 2 vols (Paris: LGDJ, 1967).

Kelstrup, Morten (ed.), *European Integration and Denmark's Participation* (Copenhagen: Copenhagen Political Studies, 1992).

Keohane, Robert, *After Hegemony* (Princeton: Princeton University Press, 1984).

Kesselman, Mark and Krieger, Joel, *European Politics In Transition*, 2nd edn (Lexington, Mass.: D. C. Heath, 1992).

Kitschelt, Herbert, *The Logics of Party Formation: Structure and Strategy of Belgian and West German Ecology Parties* (Ithaca: Cornell University Press, 1989).

Korpi, Walter, *The Working Class in Welfare Capitalism* (London: Routledge, Kegan Paul, 1978).

—— *The Democratic Class Struggle* (London: Routledge and Kegan Paul, 1983).

Krause, Axel, *Inside the New Europe* (New York: Harper Collins, 1991).

Kriesi, Hanspeter, "The political opportunity structure of new social movements: its impact on their mobilization," working paper of the Wissenschaftszentrum Berlin, 1991.

Lacouture, Jean, *De Gaulle*, Vol. 3, *Le souverain*, Part II (Paris: Seuil, 1986).

Lange, Peter, Ross, George and Vannicelli, Maurizio, *Unions, Crisis and Change: French and Italian Trade Unions in the Political Economy, 1945–1980* (London: Allen and Unwin, 1982).

Langguth, Gerd, "Germany, the EC and the architecture of Europe," *Aussenpolitik*, Spring 1991.

Laursen, Finn, "The Community's policy towards EFTA: regime formation in the European economic space," *Journal of Common Market Studies*, June 1990.

Laux, Jeanne, "The Tories and industrial policy,"*Canadian Forum*, March–April 1992.

Lindberg, Leon and Scheingold, Stuart, *Europe's Would-Be Polity* (Princeton: Princeton University Press, 1970).

—— *Regional Integration: Theory and Research* (Cambridge: Harvard University Press, 1971).

Lipietz, Alain, *Berlin, Bagdad, Rio* (Paris: La Découverte, 1992).

Ludlow, Peter, The *Making of the European Monetary System* (London: Butterworths, 1982).

Ludlow, Peter and Murphy, Anna (eds), *The Annual Review of European Community Affairs 1990* (London: Brassey's, for the Centre for European Policy Studies, 1991).

Marglin S. and Schor, J. (eds), *The Golden Age of Capitalism* (Oxford: Oxford University Press, 1990).

Maris, Bernard, *Jacques Delors, artiste ou martyr* (Paris: Albin Michel, 1992).

Marjolin, Robert, *Le travail d'une vie* (Paris: Robert Laffont, 1976).

Marsh, David, *The Bundesbank: The Bank That Rules Europe* (London: Heinemann, 1992).

Martin Holland (ed.), *The Future of European Political Cooperation* (London: Macmillan, 1991).

Massé, Pierre, *Le plan ou l'anti-hasard* (Paris: Hermann, 1991).

McCarthy, Patrick (ed.), *France–Germany 1983–1993* (London: Macmillan, 1993).

Mény, Yves and Wright, Vincent (eds), *The Politics of Steel: Western Europe and the Steel Industry in the Crisis Years (1979–1984)* (Berlin: de Gruyter, 1987).

Meunier-Atsahalia, Sophie, "Harmonization and mutual recognition in the EC after 1985," unpublished paper for the American Political Science Association Annual Meetings, 1993.

Milési, Gabriel, *Jacques Delors* (Paris: Pierre Belfond, 1985).

Miljan, Toivo, *The Reluctant Europeans* (London: Hurst, 1977).

Milward, Alan, *The Reconstruction of Western Europe 1945–1951* (London: Methuen, 1984).

Monnet, Jean, *Les États-Unis d'Europe ont commencé: La Communauté Européenne du charbon et de l'acier* (Paris: Laffont, 1955).

—— *Mémoires* (Paris: Fayard, 1976).

Montagnon, Peter (ed.), *European Competition Policy* (London: Royal Institute for International Affairs/Frances Pinter, 1990).

Moravscik, Andrew, *National Preference Formation and Interstate Bargaining in the European Community, 1955–1986* (unpublished doctoral dissertation, Harvard University, 1972).

—— "Negotiating the Single European Act," in *The New European Community: Decision-Making and Institutional Change*, eds Robert O. Keohane and Stanley Hoffmann (Boulder: Westview, 1991).

—— "A liberal intergovernmentalist approach to the EC," *Journal of Common Market Studies*, XXXI(4) (December 1993).

Mossuz-Lavau, Jeanine, *Les clubs et la politique* (Paris: Armand Colin, 1970).

Murphy, Anna, *The European Community and the International Trading System*, 2 vols (Brussels: CEPS Papers 43 and 48, 1990).

Mutimer, David, "1992 and the political integration of Europe: neofunctionalism reconsidered," *Revue d'intégration Européenne/Journal of European Integration*, XIII(1) (1989).

Nielsen, Hans J., "The Danish voters and the referendum in June 1992 on the Maastricht Agreement," in Kelstrup (ed.), op. cit.

Noël, Emile, "The European Community today: what kind of future," in *Government and Opposition*, 22 (2), Winter 1987.

Norup Carlsen, Hanne, Jackson, Ross and Meyer, Niels I. (eds), *When No Means Yes: Danish Visions of a Different Europe* (London: Adamantine Press, 1993).

Padoa-Schioppa, Tommaso, *Efficiency, Stability and Equity* (Oxford: Oxford University Press, 1987).

Pipjers A. et al., *European Political Cooperation in the 1980s, a Common Foreign Policy for Western Europe* (Dordrecht: Martinus Nijhoff, 1988).

Porter, Michael, *The Competitiveness of Nations* (New York: Free Press, 1990).

Prate, Alain, *Quelle Europe?* (Paris: Julliard, 1991).

Raimbaud, Christiane, *Le grand pari* (Paris: Fayard, 1991).

Remacle, Eric, *La politique étrangère européenne: de Maastricht à la Yougoslavie (Brussels:* GRIP, 1992).

Rollat, Alain, *Delors* (Paris: Flammarion, 1993).

Ross, George "The perils of politics," in Lange, Ross and Vannicelli, op. cit.

Sandholtz, Wayne, *High-Tech Europe: The Politics of International Cooperation* (Berkeley: University of California Press, 1992).

Scharpf, Fritz W., *Crisis and Choice in European Social Democracy* (Ithaca: Cornell University Press, 1991).

Schmitter, Philippe, "Reflections on Europe's would-be polity," paper for the Ninth Conference of Europeanists, Council for European Studies, Chicago, March 1992.

Schuman, Robert, *Pour l'Europe* (Paris: Nagel, 1963).

Schwock, Rene, *US–EC Relations in the Post-Cold War Era* (Boulder: Westview Press, 1991), Chapters 9–10.

Shackleton, Michael, "The Delors II budgetary package," in *The European Community 1992, Annual Review of Activities*, ed. Neill Nugent (Oxford: Blackwell/*Journal of Common Market Studies*, 1993).

Swinbank, Alan, "CAP Reform, 1992," *Journal of Common Market Studies*, XXXI(3) (September 1993).

Tarrow, Sidney, *Democracy and Disorder, Protest and Politics in Italy* (Oxford: Clarendon Press, 1989).

—— *Struggling to Reform* (Ithaca: Cornell UP/Western Societies Program, 1991).

Thatcher, Margaret, *The Downing Street Years* (New York: HarperCollins, 1993).

Thuillier, Guy, *Les cabinets ministériels* (Paris: Que sais-je?, 1991).

Tomuschat, Christian, "A united Germany within the European Community," *Common Market Law Review*, 27 (1990).

Tranholm-Mikkelsen, Jeppe, "Neo-functionalism: obstinate or obsolete? A reappraisal in the light of the new dynamism of the EC," *Millennium, Journal of International Studies*, 20(1) (1991).

Tsoukalis, Loukas, *The Politics and Economics of European Monetary Integration* (London: Allen and Unwin, 1977).

—— *The New European Economy: The Politics and Economics of Integration* (Oxford: Oxford University Press, 1991).

Tyskiewicz, Zygmunt, "European social policy – striking the right balance," *European Affairs*, Winter 1989.

Vedrine, Hubert and Musitelli, Jean, "Les changements des années 1989–1990 et l'Europe de la prochaine décennie," *Politique Étrangère*, Winter 1991.

Venturini, Patrick, *Un espace social européen à l'horizon 1992* (Luxembourg: EC, 1988).

Vogel-Polsky, E. and Vogel, J., *L'Europe sociale, 1993: illusion, alibi ou réalité* (Brussels: Éditions de l'Université Libre de Bruxelles, 1991).

Wallace, Helen, Wallace, William and Webb, Carole, *Policy-Making in the European Community* (Chichester: Wiley, 1983).

Wallace, Helen and Wessels, Wolfgang, "Towards a new partnership: the EC and EFTA in the wider Western Europe," EFTA *Occasional Paper 28* (Geneva, 1989).

Wattebled, Robert, *Stratégies catholiques en monde ouvrier dans la France d'après-guerre* (Paris: Éditions ouvrières, 1990).

Williams, Shirley, "Sovereignty and accountability in the European Community," in *The New European Community: Decision-Making and Institutional Change*, eds Robert O. Keohane and Stanley Hoffman (Boulder: Westview, 1991).

Winock, Michel, *Histoire de la revue "Esprit"* (Paris: Seuil, 1975).

Winters, Alan, *The Economic Consequences of Agricultural Support* (Paris: OECD, 1987).

Womack, James, Jones, Daniel and Roos, Daniel, *The Machine That Changed the World* (New York: Macmillan, 1990).

Wynaents, Henry, *L'Engrenage* (Paris: Denoel, 1992).

Zald, Mayer N. and McCarthy, John D. et al., *Social Movements in an Organizational Society* (New Brunswick, N.J.: Transaction, 1987).

Zorgbibe, Charles, *Histoire de la construction européenne* (Paris: PUF, 1993).

Zysman, John and Sandholtz, Wayne, "1992: recasting the European bargain," *World Politics*, 1 (1989).

Index